Lecture Notes in Computer Science 2693

Edited by G. Goos, J. Hartmanis, and J. van Leeuwen

Springer
Berlin
Heidelberg
New York
Hong Kong
London
Milan
Paris
Tokyo

Alejandra Cechich   Mario Piattini
Antonio Vallecillo (Eds.)

Component-Based Software Quality

Methods and Techniques

Springer

Series Editors

Gerhard Goos, Karlsruhe University, Germany
Juris Hartmanis, Cornell University, NY, USA
Jan van Leeuwen, Utrecht University, The Netherlands

Volume Editors

Alejandra Cechich
Universidad Nacional del Comahue
Departamento de Ciencias de la Computación
Buenos Aires 1400, 8300 Neuquén, Argentina
E-mail: acechich@uncoma.edu.ar

Mario Piattini
Universidad de Castilla-La Mancha
Grupo Alarcos, Escuela Superior de Informática
Paseo de la Universidad, 4, 13071 Ciudad Real, Spain
E-mail: Mario.Piattini@uclm.es

Antonio Vallecillo
Universidad de Málaga
Departamento de Lenguajes y Ciencias de la Computación
Campus de Teatinos, 29071 Málaga, Spain
E-mail: av@lcc.uma.es

Cataloging-in-Publication Data applied for

Bibliographic information published by Die Deutsche Bibliothek
Die Deutsche Bibliothek lists this publication in the Deutsche Nationalbibliografie;
detailed bibliographic data is available in the Internet at <http://dnb.ddb.de>.

CR Subject Classification (1998): D.2, K.6

ISSN 0302-9743
ISBN 3-540-40503-8 Springer-Verlag Berlin Heidelberg New York

Springer-Verlag Berlin Heidelberg New York
a member of BertelsmannSpringer Science+Business Media GmbH

http://www.springer.de

© Springer-Verlag Berlin Heidelberg 2003
Printed in Germany

Typesetting: Camera-ready by author, data conversion by Olgun Computergrafik
Printed on acid-free paper   SPIN: 10927953   06/3142   5 4 3 2 1 0

Preface

As Component-Based Software Development (CBSD) starts to be effectively used, some software vendors have started to successfully sell and license commercial off-the-shelf (COTS) components. CBSD advocates the use of prefabricated pieces, perhaps developed at different times, by different people, and possibly with different uses in mind. The goal, once again, is the reduction of development times, costs, and efforts, while improving the flexibility, reliability, and maintainability of the final application due to the (re)use of software components already developed, tested and validated.

So far, most of the efforts from the Software Engineering community have concentrated on the functional aspects of CBSD, but leaving aside the (difficult) treatment of the quality issues and extra-functional properties of both components and component-based systems. However, this kind of property deserves special attention, since such properties may have even more importance than the other technical issues when building any commercial or industrial application.

The particular nature of COTS components (black-box binary entities developed by third parties, and independently deployable in unforeseen contexts) require that specific quality mechanisms are put in place for their effective integration in the development life-cycle of software applications. First, components need to be properly documented and offer measurement mechanisms in order to be assessed and evaluated for selection. Second, both the quality and some of the extra-functional properties of the final system heavily depend on the individual properties of its constituent components, and therefore some traceability between the quality attributes at these two levels is required. Finally, the use of third-party COTS components may also introduce risks, such as potentially harmful side-effects for the system, or quality degradation of the final product. COTS component testing and certification may offer partial solutions to these problems.

Our knowledge about several research and industrial initiatives trying to address some of the quality issues involved in CBSD motivated us to edit the present volume. In order to gather as many initiatives as possible, a "Call for Chapters" was issued in June 2002, requesting novel works and experiences related to software component quality, both at the individual component and composed system levels. As stated in the Call for Chapters, the main objective of the book was to provide an overview of the state-of-the-art in Component-Based Software Quality (CBSQ), discuss the main techniques and methods currently used in industry and academia, and analyze the most critical aspects related to CBSQ, such as component assessment, selection, quality evaluation and monitoring, testing, etc.

As a response to this public call, 21 chapter proposals were received from the most relevant research groups in this emerging discipline. After a thorough peer-review process, 16 proposals were finally accepted, those included in this volume.

A first chapter written by the editors serves as an introduction to the topics covered by this book, and aims at describing the best practices in software components assessment. The goal of this introductory chapter is to highlight the specific nature of COTS and of COTS-components-based systems, introduce the basic concepts and common vocabulary used in the different approaches and practices, and identify the main problems that challenge CBSQ. This chapter also provides a basis for discussing the different approaches presented in this book.

The other chapters are organized into five parts, corresponding to the five main dimensions of quality assessment and CBSQ: COTS selection, testing and certification, quality models, formal approaches to quality assessment, and component-based systems quality management.

Four chapters comprise the first dimension, COTS selection. First, C. Alves discusses the new challenges that arise during the requirements engineering process for COTS-based systems. She presents an overview of a COTS selection process specially designed to help with the decision-making process. Then, H. Leung et al. present a domain-based COTS-product selection method, which uses domain models for capturing relevant features to be considered for analysis. The chapter by D. Kunda discusses the STACE framework, which recommends decomposition of high-level requirements into a hierarchy of social and technical criteria comprising functionality characteristics, technology factors, product quality characteristics, and social and economical factors. Finally, to address the issue of COTS selection tools, N. Maiden et al. describe the SCARLET Process Advisor, a Web-enabled workflow software tool that may guide software engineers to select software components and COTS packages.

The second dimension covers testing and certification. The chapter by A. Vincenzi et al. introduces the basic concepts of software testing, focusing on the state-of-the-art and state-of-the-practice in the context of CBSD. Then, J. Morris et al. discuss the implications of standardized testing on certification, presenting an XML-based test specification format and a system for executing these specifications. Finally, C. Atkinson, H. Gross, and F. Barbier outline the principles behind built-in contract testing that derive from built-in test (BIT), and describe how built-in testing can be naturally integrated into component-based development.

The third dimension focuses on software component quality models. First, R. Simão et al. try to identify and organize the most relevant quality characteristics of software components based on the ISO/IEC 9126 standard. The proposed quality model has been empirically validated through field research, and the results are analyzed by using a fuzzy model for software quality evaluation. Second, C. Atkinson, C. Bunse, and J. Würst present a model-driven approach for component-based development, introducing some strategies for deriving quality-related information from UML models, and then illustrating how the measurement of UML structural properties can help drive the quality assurance activities of CBSD. To address particular quality model cases, the chapter by P. Botella et al. proposes the adoption of quality models as a means for structuring the description of the capabilities of ERP systems. The ISO/IEC 9126-1 quality standard is chosen as a framework, and a methodology for tailoring it to this specific domain is described. Finally, as another particular case, J. Bosch introduces a first attempt to classify software product-line maturity levels. Based on the conceptual framework presented in his chapter, he shows how an organization can identify the different levels of intra-organizational reuse that can be accomplished, and how to embark on improvement initiatives at each level.

The fourth part deals with formal approaches to CBSQ. In the first place, the chapter by H.Y. Kim et al. presents a framework for assessing component properties (such as completeness and consistency of requirement specifications) using Z and statecharts. The chapter also presents an approach for verifying properties such as reliability, using two different stochastic models. Then, R. Reussner et al. introduce a method based on RADL (Rich Architecture Definition Language) as another approach for determining the reliability of component-based software architectures. The method uses the notion of parameterized contracts to analyze the effects of component interactions on the final system's reliability. Contracts involve finite state machines that allow software architectures to define how a component's reliability will react to a given deployment environment. Finally, the chapter by R. Díaz et al. discusses some efficiency issues of iterative and incremental life-cycles, which involve balancing requirements. In order to improve the consistency-checking process, they propose reusing formal verification information – previously obtained by model-checking algorithms – to reduce the amount of verifications required.

The last dimension is concerned with CBSD management. First, L. Rose introduces risk management by presenting those risks that are specific to the development and maintenance of COTS-based systems. The chapter discusses some risk mitigation techniques that can be applied to ensure successful deployment and operation of this kind of system. And, then, the chapter by S. Sedigh-Ali et al. presents a framework that aims at reducing risks by using software metrics to accurately quantify factors contributing to the overall quality of a component-based system. The framework helps guide quality and risk management by identifying and eliminating the sources of risk. Tradeoffs between cost and quality in a component-based system are also discussed, as well as analytical techniques and formal models for taking into account both cost and quality during decision-making processes.

Every chapter presents a set of issues and problems commonly encountered when researching and conducting CBSD. In all of them, the authors share their vision about the importance of quality assessment, and how quality has a strong effect on system development and deployment. We hope that the insights and experiences described in this book can provide the reader with new research directions and valuable guidelines for conducting CBSD.

We want to express our gratitude to all individuals and parties who helped us produce this volume. In the first place, we want to thank Springer-Verlag for believing in our project and for giving us the opportunity to publish this book. Special thanks to Ralf Gerstner, LNCS editor, for his kindliness, assistance, and continuous support. Many thanks to all those experts who submitted chapters, whether finally selected or not, and particularly to the contributing authors. Our gratitude also goes to the reviewers who helped in choosing and improving the selected chapters.

Finally, we want to acknowledge the public and private organizations that have helped fund this work, which has been developed under research projects and grants CICYT TIC2002-04309-C02-02, CICYT TIC 2000-1673-C06-06 (DOLMEN/MEDEO), and UNComa 04/E048, and the CYTED project RITOS2 (Red Iberoamericana de Tecnologías del Software para la década del 2000).

February 2003   Alejandra Cechich
                                                        Mario Piattini
                                                      Antonio Vallecillo

Table of Contents

Part IV   Formal Approaches to Quality Assessment

Part V   CBSD Management

Assessing Component-Based Systems

Alejandra Cechich[1], Mario Piattini[2], and Antonio Vallecillo[3]

[1] Departamento de Ciencias de la Computación
Universidad Nacional del Comahue, Argentina
acechich@uncoma.edu.ar
[2] Grupo Alarcos, Escuela Superior de Informática
Universidad de Castilla-La Mancha, Spain
Mario.Piattini@uclm.es
[3] Departamento de Lenguajes y Ciencias de la Computación
Universidad de Málaga, Spain
av@lcc.uma.es

Abstract. The last decade marked the first real attempt to turn software development into engineering through the concepts of Component-Based Software Development (CBSD) and Commercial Off-The-Shelf (COTS) components. The idea is to create high-quality parts and join them together to form a functioning system. The problem is that the combination of such parts does not necessarily result in a high-quality system. It is clear that CBSD affects software quality in several ways, ranging from introducing new methods for selecting COTS components, to defining a wide scope of testing principles and measurements. Today, software quality staff must rethink the way software is assessed, including all life-cycle phases—from requirements to evolution. Based on cumulated research efforts, the goal of this chapter is to introduce the best practices of current Component-Based Software Assessment (CBSA). We will develop and describe in detail the concepts involved in CBSA and its constituent elements, providing a basis for discussing the different approaches presented later in this book.

1 Introduction

The use of Commercial Off-The-Shelf (COTS) products as elements of larger systems is becoming increasingly commonplace. Component-Based Software Development (CBSD) is focused on assembling previously existing components (COTS or other non-developmental items) into larger software systems, and migrating existing applications towards component-based systems.

CBSD changes the focus of software engineering from one of traditional system specification and construction, to one requiring simultaneous consideration of the system's context and characteristics (such as user requirements, development costs and schedule, operating environments, etc.), the available products in the software marketplace, and viable architectures and designs. Furthermore, other engineering activities such as evaluation and acquisition processes, as well as contracting and licensing strategies, should be incorporated into the software development life-cycle.

A. Cechich et al. (Eds.): Component-Based Software Quality, LNCS 2693, pp. 1–20, 2003.

The acceptance of CBSD carries along several challenges to the techniques and tools that have to provide support for it. Some of them are known problems, such as dealing with COTS production and integration, reducing complexity while improving reliability, and creating interaction models and supporting middleware. However, other challenges are new: the definition of metrics and quality attributes to measure software components and compositions, the definition of COTS selection processes, risk analysis, costs and effort estimation, etc. These are precisely the issues addressed by Component-Based Software Quality (CBSQ), which is emerging as a cornerstone discipline for a successful CBSD.

Within the last years, software researchers and practitioners have recognized the importance of quality in CBSD, and have started working on how quality has to be established, measured, and ensured both at the individual component level and at the system level, which constitute the two flips sides of the CBSQ coin. In the first case, the problems being addressed range from the precise definition, measurement, analysis, and evolution of COTS components, to the definition of tools, methods and processes for software component development [39, 40, 52, 53]. At the system level, software researchers and practitioners have started developing procedures, techniques and models for measuring and ensuring component-based systems quality [60].

During its relatively brief history, the field of CBSQ has experienced significant progress. However, CBSQ has not yet advanced to the point where there are standard measurement methods for any of the issues mentioned above, and few enterprises properly measure COTS component quality, if measured at all. Some efforts have started to define software metrics to guide quality and risk management in component-based systems, by identifying and quantifying various factors contributing to the overall quality of the system [9, 60, 61].

Based on cumulated research efforts, the goal of this chapter is to introduce the best practices of current CBSQ, in particular those that focus on Component-Based Software Assessment (CBSA). The objective is to provide an overview of the core elements of CBSA, and of its main issues.

The structure of this chapter is as follows. After this introduction, Section 2 introduces some of the issues that currently challenge CBSQ. Then, Section 3 deals with the core elements of CBSA at the individual component level, while Section 4 focuses on assessing component-based systems. Finally, Section 5 draws some conclusions.

2   CBSQ Issues

One can argue that ensuring the quality of component-based systems is much more difficult than is the case with manufactured goods. The problem is that the raw material—the software components—may well be of uncertain quality and their uses and behavior may be only partially known, hindering the effectiveness of possible quality assessment processes.

There are many potential problems that may affect the assessment of the quality properties of components and of component-based systems. One way of categorizing these problems is as follows:

- Issues related to components when considered as individual parts, that simply provide and require services (through their provided and required interfaces).
- Issues related to component interactions, which may have an explicit context dependencies about the operating systems or middleware platforms required, performance and other quality of service (QoS) requirements, or on other components [33].
- Issues related to component compositions (the combination of two or more software component yielding a new component).
- Other issues related to acquisition risks, such as vendor maturity level and trust, economic viability, legal issues, product evolution support, etc.

Let us discuss them more in detail. The first factor concerns uncertainty as to what constitutes the quality of a component when considered as an individual resource, i.e., a building block for constructing software systems. Unlike hardware components, for which there are catalogues and data-sheet available for describing their functional and extra-functional characteristics (to enable their proper re-use), the situation is not so bright when it comes to software components. First, there is no general consensus on the quality characteristics that need to be considered. Different authors (such as McCall [47] or Boehm [10]) and different organizations (such as ISO or IEEE) propose different (separate) classifications, but there is no clear agreement on which to use. The next issue is the lack of information about quality attributes provided by software vendors. The Web portals of the main COTS vendors show this fact—visit for instance Componentsource (`www.componentsource.com`) or Flashline (`www.flashline.com`).

In addition, there is an almost complete absence of any kind of metrics that could help measuring components' quality attributes objectively. Even worse, the international standards in charge of defining and dealing with the quality aspects of software products (e.g. ISO 9126 and ISO 14598) are currently under revision. The SquaRE project [3] has been created specifically to make them converge, trying to eliminate the gaps, conflicts, and ambiguities that they currently present. Furthermore, existing international standards provide very general quality models and guidelines, very difficult to apply in specific domains such as CBSD and COTS components.

The solution to the problem is not as obvious as counting with an agreed set of quality features that the component should exhibit, together with a set of associated metrics. External factors, such as users' requirements on the global system, architectural constraints, or context dependencies, may also have a strong influence on the component quality when assessed as a potential part of a larger system. This is why components may be completely satisfactory on most of their own attributes or features, but inadequate from a compositional viewpoint. Therefore, certain key quality features of a composition are also required.

The problems with the quality features of the composition rely both on the quality features of the individual components, the way they are interconnected, and on the quality features of the interaction media or middleware used. Thus, too many factors need to be considered, and in most cases the data may come from unreliable, external sources. Even if both the components and the middle-ware deliver the level of quality advertised by their vendors, what happens if higher levels of quality are required, or when the evolution of the system impose new levels of quality over time? Should the composer attempt to work together with the component or middleware vendors to improve the components' quality?

Another problem is due to the fact of re-using components. In CBSD, re-using not only means "using more than once", but also "using in different contexts", in order to achieve all the promised advantages of CBSD [34]. For example, most people would agree that using the components' clearly defined and documented interfaces is enough to accomplish error-free compositions. But this is only true if components remain confined to the domain of origin, and are never re-used across platforms or in other contexts. However, if the components are made available across platforms, then something needs to be done to resolve the inconsistencies and mismatches that happen at all levels: syntactically, semantically, and quality-wise.

The problem of ensuring component and component composition quality is exacerbated by the intrinsic nature of COTS components. The disadvantages associated with COTS-based design include the absence of source code and the lack of access to the software engineering artefacts originally used in the design of the components. Furthermore, whether you have built your system using COTS components from many vendors, or a single vendor has provided you with an integrated solution, many of the risks associated with system management and operation are not under your direct control [44].

Managing conflicting quality requirements is another issue specially interesting in the case of component-based systems. It is necessary to have an awareness of what could lead to inadequate component quality. "Fitness for use" implies that the appropriate level of system quality is dependent on the context. Determining the required quality is difficult when different users have different (even conflicting) needs. One might be tempted to state that the user requiring the highest component quality should determine the overall level of quality of the composed system. But in this way we may be over-imposing quality requirements to the system and to its individual components, which may be rarely required in most situations (e.g. in case of requirements imposed by occasional users, which do not represent the average system users). Thus, it is always necessary to properly balance conflicting requirements.

Finally, an important issue related to CBSA is about trust. Since we are going to incorporate to our system one part which has been developed elsewhere, our fears concerning quality could be reduced if we knew, for example, how the component was developed and who developed it. Furthermore, such a component would engender more confidence if someone other than the vendor or developer could certify, for example, that state-of-the-practice development and testing processes had been properly applied, that the code has no embedded malicious behavior [65].

As we can see, there are many issues related to establishing and assessing the quality of component-based systems. Most of them are general problems of quality assessment, common to all software systems, and known for years. But some of them are new problems, caused by the introduction of COTS components and CBSD. However, CBSD and COTS components not only have introduced new problems. They have greatly helped software development technology get mature enough to overcome many of the technical issues involved, putting us now in a position from where to start effectively tackling many of the quality aspects of software development. In this sense, CBSD offers an interesting technology from where many of the quality questions and problems can be formulated, and properly addressed.

3   Assessing COTS Components

In this Section we will discuss some of the main methods and techniques for the assessment of COTS components. In particular, we will cover COTS components evaluation, certification, and testing.

3.1   COTS Components Evaluation

Typically, the evaluation of COTS components consists of two phases: (1) COTS searching and screening, and (2) COTS analysis.

COTS component *search* is a process (i.e., a set of activities) that attempts to identify and find all potential candidate components that satisfy a set of given requirements, so they can be re-used and integrated into the application. The search is generally driven by a set of guidelines and selection criteria previously defined. Some methods propose a separate process for defining the selection criteria to be used, while others dynamically build a synergy of requirements, goals, and criteria [2, 13, 31, 37, 40, 42, 46, 52, 53, 54].

For example, the OTSO (Off-The-Shelf Option) method [39, 40] gradually defines the evaluation criteria as the selection process progresses, essentially decomposing the requirements for the COTS software into a hierarchical criteria set. Each branch in this hierarchy ends in an evaluation attribute: a well-defined measurement or a piece of information that will be determined during evaluation. This hierarchical decomposition principle has been derived from both Basili's GQM [5, 6] and the Analytic Hierarchy Process [59].

In the CAP (COTS Acquisition Process) proposal [52, 53], the first step is the identification of the criteria used for evaluating candidate alternatives. Requirements are translated into a taxonomy of evaluation criteria (called "Tailor & Weight Taxonomy"), and prioritized (or weighted) according to the Analytic Hierarchy Process, which also takes into account the stakeholders' interests.

COTS *screening* aims at deciding which alternatives should be selected for a more detailed evaluation. Decisions are driven by a variety of factors—foremost are several design constraints that help define the range of components. Some methods include *qualifying thresholds* for screening, i.e., defining and documenting the criteria and rationale for selecting alternatives. Some other methods estimate how much effort will be needed to actually apply all evaluation criteria to all COTS component candidates during the screening phase.

The results of the evaluation of the COTS alternatives is then used for making a decision. A COTS *analysis* phase starts, in general, from a set of ranked COTS software alternatives where the top-ranked alternative is measured against a set of final make-or-buy decision criteria, using for instance a *weighted scoring method*, which assigns weights to each criteria. However, measuring all applicable criteria for all COTS software alternatives can be expensive since: (i) there may be too many COTS software alternatives; (ii) the set of evaluation criteria could be quite large; and (iii) some of the criteria might be very difficult or expensive to measure (e.g., reliability).

The effectiveness of a COTS evaluation method depends on the expressiveness of the criteria selected for evaluation. A trade-off between the effectiveness of the evaluation criteria and the cost, time, and resource allocation of the criteria must be reached.

In COTS selection, both phases—search and screening, and COTS analysis—are based on statements about the requirements that need to be much more flexible than traditional ones, i.e. the specified requirements should not be so strict that either exclude all available COTS, or require large product modification in order to satisfy them. *Requirements Elicitation* is an activity by which a variety of stakeholders work together to discover, and increasingly define, requirements. Creative thinking is used by requirement elicitation teams to re-structure models, conceptualize, and solve problems. Some COTS evaluation proposals include processes to acquire and validate customer requirements [14, 42, 46], while others build a selection process based on iteratively defining and validating requirements [2, 43]. For instance, the proposal by Alves and Finkelstein [2], identifies first a set of high-level goals using traditional elicitation techniques, such as use-cases, which are then used for identifying possible COTS candidates in the marketplace. Then, new goals can be identified from these components, and the process starts again. The proposal by Franch *et al.* [14] uses a two-level selection process: the global level is responsible of combining the selection requirements from different areas in an organization, while the local level is responsible of carrying out the individual selection processes.

However, selecting COTS is not all about confronting component's services against technical and extra-functional requirements. As we mentioned earlier, there is also the issue of trust. Then, some selection methods also include a supplier selection process. The idea is to establish a supplier selection criteria, evaluate potential suppliers, rank them according to the agreed criteria, and select the best-fit supplier(s) [42, 44, 46, 71]. For instance, the V_RATE method [44] defines a taxonomy of vendor risk assessment, which produces a vendor-risk profile tied to real-world performance histories. This profile can be used to assess the risk associated with the use of a product in a particular environment, and to identify areas for additional risk-mitigation activities.

Finally, selection cannot be based on *exact* criteria in real applications. Usually, users' requirements are expressed in vague terms, such as "acceptable" performance, "small" size, or "high" adaptability. Measuring COTS components' quality attributes against such vague requirements is difficult. The QUESTA approach [31] addresses this issue by defining some mapping functions, that allow the assignments of values to such vague requirements.

3.2   Component Certification

Certification is the "procedure by which a third-party gives written assurance that a product, process, or service conforms to specified requirements" [17]. Current certification practices are basically process oriented, and usually require early life-cycle processes stressing the software product.

The particular nature of COTS components and component-based systems also present some challenges to traditional certification. Software certification must determine whether the software delivers all the functionality that is expected to deliver, and ensures that it does not exhibit any undesirable behavior. Ideally, the desirable behavior corresponds to specified requirements, although having to deal with missing requirements is unavoidable [70]. Therefore, certifying a software product, such as a component, is highly dependent on the quality of its requirements specification as well as on the quality of its documentation.

Documentation is one of the key issues in CBSD, specially at the component level. The black-box nature of components forces documentation to contain all details needed to understand the functionality provided by the component, describe how to deploy and install it, and how it should be connected to the rest of the components in the system. Furthermore, documentation should also describe the component's context dependencies and architectural constraints. Certification strongly relies on the component documentation, since it provides the "contract" with the requirements that the component behavior should conform to.

Another important problem related to component certification has to do with the application context. In practice, it is very difficult to certify that a component will behave in a correct manner *independently* from the context in which it will operate. However, certifying that a component works as expected within a given context or application can be more easily accomplished, since it is a matter of testing it in that particular environment.

Applying software testing techniques and conforming to standards on quality of components appear to be the most recommended approaches for certification. As a guidance, the ISO WD-12199-V4 standard [37] is directly applicable to COTS. It establishes: (1) requirements for COTS software products; (2) requirements for tests (including recommendations for the documentation of the tests); and (3) instructions on how to test a COTS against quality requirements (instructions for testing, in particular for third party testing).

Thus, in the context of CBSD, testing becomes the cornerstone process for certification.

3.3   Component Testing

Software component testing techniques focus on the expected behavior of the component, trying to ensure that its exhibited behavior is correct [8]. Black-box testing does not require any knowledge of the internals of the part being tested, and therefore is very appropriate for testing COTS components, whose source code is not available. Strategies for black-box testing include test cases generation by equivalence classes, error guessing and random tests. These three techniques rely only on some notion of the input space and expected functionality of the component being tested [8, 30, 50].

Component-based black-box testing techniques are also based on interface probing [41, 51]. A developer designs a set of test cases, executes a component on these test cases, and analyzes the outputs produced. There are a number of black-box methods for evaluating a component: manual evaluation, evaluation with a test suite, and automated interface probing. They will depend on how much the process can be automated, and the sort (and amount) of information available about the component. One of the major disadvantages of interface probing is that, frequently, a large number of test cases have to be created and analyzed. In addition, developers may frequently miss major component limitations and incorrectly assume certain component functionality. This may lead to incorrect use of the component when it is integrated with the final software system [51].

A different approach can be followed by automatically creating a system model from these individual requirements, and then automatically generating the test cases corresponding to them. In other words, from the requirements, a system model is automatically created with requirement information mapped to the model. This information can then be used to generate different tests [68].

Reflection and component metadata can also be effectively used for component testing. First, reflection enables a program to access its internal structure and behavior, providing a mechanism for interrogating and manipulating both. For instance, Sullivan has used reflection to load a class into a testing tool, extracting information about some its methods, and calling them with the appropriate parameters [55, 67]. Moreover, since the execution of methods in a class can create and use instances of other different classes, the approach is also helpful to test the integration of classes. Component metadata available in most existing component models can also be used to provide generic usage information about a component, which can be used for testing [15, 32].

CBSD also introduces some additional challenges to testing: components must fit into the new environment when they are re-used, often requiring real-time detection, diagnosis, and handling of software faults.

The BIT (Built-in Tests) technology developed within the Component+ European project [27] proposes embedding self-test functionality into software components, producing self-testable components that can help detect dynamic faults during run-time. This is a significant advance for improving software reliability and fault-tolerant capabilities in CBSD [36, 74]. There are some variations for building BIT-based COTS, such as including the complete test suite inside the components [75], or just embedding a minimal set of information, such as assertions, inside the components, which can be used at a later stage to define more complex tests [48]. In both cases there are some issues to consider. First, including complex tests means consuming space, which can be wasted if only a few number of tests are actually used. But if just a few information is included, or a small number of tests is embedded, additional external software need to be used to complement the provided tests, or to construct the tests from the component specifications. Current approaches try to show how built-in tests might be integrated by using flexible architectures, without requiring additional software, and hence minimizing the time spent on testing (see, e.g., [36]).

Finally, testing individual components is not enough for guaranteing the correctness of the final system. The way in which components are connected and interact introduce new properties to the system. Therefore, defining "good" stand-alone component tests may not be enough. Developing a foundation for testing component-based software is also a complicated issue, even though formal models of test adequacy for component-based software are being developed [58].

4   Assessment of Component-Based Systems

The assembly of an application based on third-party developed components does not necessarily assure a defect-free system, even if its constituent components haven been individually tested and certified. Furthermore, a component-based system needs to be tested on several aspects such as strategic risk analysis; risk-based process definition (for software components); risk-based design of component software (including initialization, fail-safe and fault-tolerant concepts, and built-in tests); risk-based component software analysis and design testing; software testing, including failure-mode and stress testing; documentation review; and assessment of hardware requirements [23].

In this Section we will concentrate on those quality issues than trespass the individual COTS components frontiers, and that arise only when the components are combined to form a functioning system.

4.1   COTS Integration and Software Architecture

In CBSD, most of the application developer's effort is spent integrating components, which provide their services through well-defined interfaces. It is extremely important that component services are provided through a standard, published interface to ensure interoperability [33].

Component architectures divide software components into requiring and providing services: some software components provide services, which are used by other components. The system's *Software Architecture* connects participating components, regulating component interactions and enforcing interaction rules. Software architectures and component technologies can be considered as complementary, and there is ample scope for their conceptual integration [73].

Some of the quality properties at the system level must be also enforced by the system's software architecture, which have to use the components' individual quality properties to deliver the required level of system quality. In addition, interaction patterns (usually encapsulated into *connectors* in the architecture) have also an strong effect on the global system quality, and their quality properties should also be incorporated into the quality assessment of the final system.

Another important issue when integrating components to build a functioning system deals with the mismatches that may occur when putting together pieces developed by different parties, usually unaware of each other. In this sense, Basili *et al.* [77] present a general classification of possible kinds of mismatches between COTS products and software systems, which includes architectural, functional, non-functional, and other issues. Incompatibilities are essentially failures of the components' interactions, so the authors claim that finding and classifying these interactions may help finding and classifying the incompatibilities.

Three aspects of inter-component interactions and incompatibilities can be considered: the kind of interacting components, the interoperability level required (syntactic, protocol, or semantic), and the number of components participating in the interaction. Different incompatibilities have different solutions, and the classes of problems are specific to the particular development phases. As another example, the work by Egyed *et al.* [28] combines architectural modelling with component-based development, showing how their mismatch-detection capabilities complement each other. The software architecture provides a high-level description of the components and their expected interactions. Architectural mismatches can be caused by inconsistencies between two or more constraints of different architectural parts being composed.

As important as determining architectural mismatches is calculating the integration effort. Decisions on component-based systems investments are strongly influenced by technological diversity: current technology is diverse and brings with it thousands of choices on components, with their opportunities and risks. Firms that avoid single technologies, and implement a diverse set of technologies and/or applications tend to focus their investments on innovative infrastructure, which might be the basis for new component-based system. Determining the effort required to integrate components into that infrastructure is essential to make a decision on migrating to CBSD. However, estimation is not straightforward. BASIS [4], for example, combines several factors in order to estimate the effort required to integrate each potential component into an existing architecture—architectural mismatches, complexity of the identified mismatch, and mismatch resolution. The final estimate describes the complexity of integrating a COTS component and is called the *difficulty of integration* factor. We should note that the BASIS approach also includes techniques for evaluating the vendor viability and the COTS component itself, determining a relative recommendation index for each product based on all factors.

Measuring complexity of the component's interactions also implies analyzing interfaces and messages. Some proposals in this direction propose to measure the complexity of the interactions—and their potential changes—by using metrics derived from information theory. For instance, the L-metric [18, 64] offers a static quantitative measure of the entropy caused by how the components interact as the system performs.

Finally, architectures used to build composite applications provide a design perspective for addressing interaction problems. Although little attention is paid to the evolvability of these architectures, it may also be necessary to estimate the effect on evolution in a system design in order to improve its robustness [24].

4.2   Cost Estimation

All CBSD projects require a cost estimation before the actual development activities can proceed. Most cost estimates for object-based systems are based on rules of thumb involving some size measure, like adapted lines of code, number of function points added/updated, or more recently, functional density [1, 26]. Using rules such as the system functional density, the percentage of the overall system functionality delivered per COTS component can also be determined, considering that the number of COTS components in a system should also be kept under a manageable threshold. However, in practical terms, rules such as functional density imply that (1) there must be a way of comparing one system design to another in terms of their functionality; (2) there must a way to split functionality delivered by COTS from that delivered from scratch; and (3) there must be a way to clearly identify different COTS functionalities.

Cost is not independent but a function of the enterprise itself, its particular software development process, the chosen solution, and the management and availability of the resources during the development project. The cost of updating and/or replacing components is highly situational, and depends on the organization's specific internal and external factors. Cost estimation should include the cost of project management, direct labor, and identification of affected software, affected data, and alternative solutions, testing and implementation. The accuracy of most cost estimates should improve during a project as the knowledge of the problem and the resources required for its solution increases. Some cost models are iterative, indicating change and re-evaluation throughout the solution stages. The most extended model on COTS integration cost—the COCOTS model [10, 22]—follows the general form of the COCOMO models, but with an alternative set of cost drivers addressing the problem of actually predicting the cost of performing a COTS integration task. Five groups of factors appear to influence COTS integration cost as indicated by the relatively large set of drivers: product and vendor maturity (including support services); customization and installation facilities; usability; portability; and previous product experience. In addition, COCOMO II model drivers such as architecture/risk resolution, development flexibility, team cohesion, database size, required reusability, etc., can be added to produce an integral COTS cost model. The goal is to provide the infrastructure for an easy integration of multiple COTS components. However, a cost model cannot easily put aside each of the problems encountered when integrating multiple COTS. In the migration to a component-based system, we would like to exercise the policy *Don't throw anything away, use and re-use as much as you can*. However, integrating existing software and COTS components as a whole is not a trivial task and may cause too many adaptation conflicts.

The cost model should provide mechanisms for dealing with the more common and more challenging integration problems, such as the following.

- Problems that happen when two or more components provide the same services with different representations.
- Problems that happen when a component has to be modelled by integrating parts of functionality from different components (or from other sources).

- Problems that happen when the resulting architecture does not cover the desired application requirements.
- Problems that happen when two or more integrated components with different implementations fail to interoperate.

While these problems might represent mainly one-time costs, the management-phase costs of CBSD recur throughout the system life-cycle, including during maintenance.

One of the most important problems of the maintenance process is the estimation and prediction of the related efforts. The different maintenance activities may present several related aspects: re-use, understanding, deletion of existing parts, development of new parts, re-documentation, etc. These aspects are relevant to all classes of systems, including object-oriented and component-based systems [29]. However, one of the most important distinguishing factors in CBSD is the separation of the interface and the implementation. The interface is usually realized by one or more components. Larger components may have more complex interfaces and represent more opportunity to be affected by change. Thus, components and component-based systems by nature are a source of changes stressed by potentially incompatible versions of components, which may compete with themselves.

When adapting a component-based system to changing requirements, invariant conditions are usually specified via constraint languages or specifically defined mechanisms. For instance, the context-based constraint (CoCon) mechanism [43] specifies one requirement for a group of indirectly associated components that share a context, which refers the state, situation or environment of each component. The mechanism requires that monitoring points (interception points between components) be determined for each invocation path. However, the main problem of this approach is precisely how to determine the context's property values of the components involved in this path.

In general, component technologies also impose some design constraints on software component suppliers and composers. These constraints are expressed as a component model that specifies required component interfaces and other development rules [33]. The focus of actual compositional rules is on syntactic aspects of composition, as well as on environmental and behavioral ones. For example, Ralf Reussner *et al.* [56] deal with the prediction of properties of compositions based on the properties of their basic components. Parameterized contracts that depend on the environment are defined, allowing timing behavior (and hence reliability) be analyzed by including timing behavior of the environmental services used by the component.

Reasoning abut behavioral composition is also as important as detecting interaction mismatches. The *Predictable Assembly from Certifiable Components* (PACC) [63] is an initiative at the Carnegie Mellon University–Software Engineering Institute (CMU-SEI) that tries to provide support for predicting behavioral properties of assemblies before the components are actually developed or purchased. *Prediction-Enabled Component Technology* (PECT) is a technology that supports composing systems from pre-compiled components in such a way that the quality of the system can be predicted before acquiring/building its constituents [35]. PECT makes analytic assumptions explicitly ensuring that a component technology satisfies the assumptions through a demonstration of "theoretical validity". It also ensures that predictions based on an analysis technology are repeatable through a demonstration of "empirical validity". Current research efforts focus on prediction of assembly properties such as latency and reliability.

Documentation is also another key to the success of the CBSD. In case of component-based systems, documentation should contain all the information about the system's structure and internal interconnections. For instance, *Ensembles* [72] is a conceptual language which enriches the system documentation by making explicit the links between component properties and component interactions. Ensembles also support graduated and incremental selection of technologies, products, and components.

In general, the composer does not need to understand all aspects of a component-based system, but should be able to identify its constituent components, and be able to search for components that may provide the functionality required by the architecture. In addition, it has been suggested that component documentation should be extensible, allowing the composer to insert details about component adaptations directly onto a system document library or annotating components. For example, annotations can be used to perform dependence analysis over these descriptions [66]. In addition, the system documentation should be closely tied to the composing tools, so the selected and tailored components are easily translated into reusable component libraries [16].

4.3   CBSD Risk Analysis

Software development is a quickly changing, knowledge-intensive business involving many people working in different phases and activities. Activities in software engineering are diverse, and the proportion of component-based systems is steadily growing. Organizations have problems identifying the content, location, and use of diverse components. Component composition requires access to tangible and intangible assets. Tangible assets, which correspond to documented, explicit information about the component, can vary from different vendors although usually include services, target platforms, information about vendors, and knowledge for adaptation. Intangible assets, which correspond to tacit and undocumented explicit information, consist of skills, experience, and knowledge of an organization's people.

Although the Risk Management Paradigm [76] continues to be useful as an overall guide to risk analysis, the majority of risk management studies deal with normative techniques for managing risk. Software risks may come from different dimensions: (1) environmental contingencies such as organizational environment, technologies, and individual characteristics; and (2) risk management practices such as methods, resources, and period of use [7, 57].

A few studies have classified software risk items, including CBSD risk analysis. These studies consider CBSD risks along several dimensions, providing some empirically-founded insights of typical cases and their variations. For example, the BASIS technique [4] focuses on reducing risks in CBSD by means of several integrated processes. One of them, the Component Evaluation Process [54], tries to reduce the risk of selecting inappropriate COTS components. Another process aims at reducing the risk of downstream integration problems through early assessment of the compatibility between a chosen COTS product and an existing system. Finally, a third process tries to reduce risks throughout the development life-cycle by defining built-in checkpoints and recommending measurement techniques. A vendor analysis is carried out along with these three processes.

Software project managers need to make a series of decisions at the beginning of and during projects. Because software development is such a complex and diverse process, predictive models should guide decision making for future projects. This requires having a metrics program in place, collecting project data with a well-defined goal in a metrics repository, and then analyzing and processing data to generate models. It has also been shown how metrics can guide risk and quality management, helping reduce risks encountered during planning and execution of CBSD [60, 61]. Risks can include performance issues, reliability, adaptability, and return on investment. Metrics in this case are used to quantify the concept of quality, aiming at investigating the tradeoffs between cost and quality, and using the information gained to guide quality management. The primary considerations are cost, time to market, and product quality.

4.4   Software Product Lines

In this last Section we will discuss the quality assessment issues of one of the most promising approaches for developing component-based systems, specially in some well-defined application domains: *software product lines* [11, 21, 69].

A software product line is a "set of software-intensive systems sharing a common, managed set of features that satisfy the specific needs of a particular market or mission and that are developed from a common set of core assets in a prescribed way" [21]. So, within the product line, it is necessary to determine what products are needed, how to develop those products, how to manage the evolution of them, and how to re-use them. The idea is to achieve high levels of intra-organizational re-use. Products become "components" in a product line approach, where product-line architectures are the basis for software component re-use.

Software product lines not only help developing software applications, but also help dealing with some quality issues in a controlled way. Of course, dealing with quality assessment and risk management in product lines involves a whole world of new methods and techniques—from requirement analysis to testing. However, the common nature of SPL facilitates the treatment of some of their quality issues.

For example, Chastek *et al.* [20] specify requirements for a product line using a model whose primary goal is to identify and analyze opportunities for re-use within requirements. The model has two main characteristics: (1) it specifies the functionality and quality attributes of the products in the product line;

and (2) its structure shows decisions about commonalities across the product line. The work products are based on object modelling, use-case modelling, and feature-modelling techniques. They form the basis of a systematic method for capturing and modelling the product line requirements, where five types of analysis are introduced: commonality and variability analysis, model consistency analysis, feature interaction analysis, model quality analysis, and requirements priority analysis.

As another example of mastering quality in software product lines, the framework published in [21] describes the essential practice areas for software engineering, technical management, and organizational management. A *practice area* is a body of work or a collection of activities that an organization must master to successfully carry out the essential work of a product line. The software engineering practice areas include those practices needed to apply the appropriate technology to create and evolve both core assets and products. The framework seems to have some similarities when compared to CMMI models [38, 62], where the major organizing element is the *process area*. Here, a process area is a group of related activities that are performed collectively to achieve a set of goals. Hence, the wide acceptance of the "capability models" has turned research into developing maturity models for product lines [12], which aims at providing guidelines for dealing with intra-organizational re-use.

On the other hand, testing in product lines environments involves testing assets as well as products. But a software product line organization must maintain a number of complex relationships. There are relationships between the group that develops the core assets and those who develop products, between the general product line architecture and specific product architectures, between versions of these architectures and versions of products. As a general rule, McGregor proposes structuring the relationships among test artifacts to mirror the structure of the relationships among production artifacts, so a more efficient test implementation can be produced [49]. In this case, the test architect carries the responsibility for achieving the quality properties defined in the test plan. The architect defines the structure of the test software and defines the basic test assets. This test software architecture can then be specialized to the specific environment, quality properties, and constraints of a given product.

Finally, the use of metrics has proven to be helpful in assessing particular situations to guide architectural decisions. For product line architectures (PLA), the work reported by Dincel *et al.* [25] focuses on PLA-level metrics for system evolution. In particular, they provide an incremental set of metrics that allows an architect to make informed decisions about the usage levels of architectural components, the cohesiveness of the components, and the validity of product family architectures. However, the experience with these metrics is limited, requiring further validation.

5   Conclusions

There are many benefits derived from CBSD, which has become one of the key technologies for the effective construction of large, complex software systems in timely and affordable manners. However, the adoption of component-based development carries along many changes that touch beliefs and ideas considered to be core to most organizations. These adjustments, and the approaches taken to resolve contention, can often be the difference between succeeding and failing in CBSD undertaking.

So far, most of the efforts from the Software Engineering community have focused on the technical and technological issues of CBSD. But once the situation starts to be stable at these levels, and component-based software commences to be effectively used in commercial applications and industrial environments, the focus is changing towards the quality aspects of CBSD.

In this chapter we have tried to provide an overview of the core concepts of component-based software quality (CBSQ), and the main issues related to component-based software assessment (CBSA). From here, the chapters in this book present some of the current initiatives for dealing with CBSQ issues, from COTS assessment to product lines maturity levels. However, much work still remain to be done in this emerging area in order to effectively address the many difficult challenges ahead.

Acknowledgments

This work is partially supported by research projects and grants CICYT TIC2002-04309-C02-02, CICYT TIC 2000-1673-C06-06 (DOLMEN/MEDEO), UNComa 04/E048, and by CYTED project RITOS2 (Red Iberoamericana de Tecnologías del Software para la década del 2000).

References

1. C. Abts. COTS-Based Systems (CBS) Functional density – A Heuristic for Better CBS Design. In *Proc. of the First International Conference on COTS-Based Software Systems*, Springer-Verlag, pp. 1–9, 2002.
2. C. Alves and A. Finkelstein. Challenges in COTS Decision-Making: A Goal-Driven Requirements Engineering Perspective. In *Proc. of the 14th International Conference on Software Engineering and Knowledge Engineering, SEKE'02*, 2002.
3. M. Azuma. SquaRE, the next generation of the ISO/IEC 9126 and 14598 international standards series on software product quality. In *ESCOM (European Software Control and Metrics conference)*, April 2001.
   http://www.escom.co.uk/conference2001/papers/azuma.pdf
4. K. Ballurio, B. Scalzo, and L. Rose. Risk Reduction in COTS Software Selection with BASIS. In *Proc. of the First International Conference on COTS-Based Software Systems*, Springer-Verlag, pp. 31–43, 2002.
5. V. Basili. Software Modeling and Measurement: The Goal/Question/Metric Paradigm. Tech. Report CS-TR-2956, University of Maryland, 1992.
6. V. Basili and H. Rombach. Tailoring the Software Process to Project Goals and Environments. In *Proc. of ICSE'87*, IEEE CS Press, pp. 345–357, 1987.
7. V. R. Basili and B. Boehm. COTS-based systems top 10 list. *IEEE Software*, 34(5):91–93, 2001.

8. B. Beizer. *Black-Box Testing. Techniques for Functional Testing of Software and Systems.* John Wiley & Sons, 1995.

9. M.F. Bertoa and A. Vallecillo. Quality Attributes for COTS Components. In *Proc. of ECOOP 2002 QAOOSE Workshop,* June 2002.

10. B. Boehm, C. Abts, and E. Bailey. COCOTS Software Integration Cost Model: an Overview. In *Proc. of the California Software Symposium,* 1998.

11. J. Bosch. *Design and Use of Software Architectures: Adopting and Evolving a Product Line Approach.* Addison-Wesley, 2000.

12. J. Bosch. Maturity and Evolution in Software Product Lines: Approaches, Artefacts and Organization. In *Proc. of the Second Software Product Line Conference,* pp. 257–271, 2002.

13. P. Bose. Scenario-Driven Analysis of Component-Based Software Architecture Models. In *Proc. of the First Working IFIP Conference on Software Architecture,* 1999.

14. X. Burgués, C. Estay, X. Franch, J.A. Pastor, and C Quer. Combined Selection of COTS Components. In *Proc. of the First International Conference on COTS-Based Software Systems,* Springer-Verlag, pp. 54–64, 2002.

15. A. Cechich and M. Polo. Black-box Evaluation of COTS Components using Aspects and Metadata. In *Proc. of the 4th International Conference on Product Focused Software Process Improvement,* Springer-Verlag, pp. 494–508, 2002.

16. A. Cechich and M. Prieto. Comparing Visual Component Composition Environments. In *Proc. of the XXII International Conference of the Chilean Computer Science Society,* IEEE Computer Society Press, 2002.

17. Brussels CEN. EN 45020:1993 General Terms and Definitions Concerning Standardization and re-lated activities, 1993.

18. N. Chapin. Entropy-Metric For Systems With COTS Software. In *Proc. of the 8th IEEE Symposium on Software Metrics,* IEEE Computer Society Press, 2002.

19. M. Charpentier. Reasoning about Composition: A Predicate Transformer Approach. In *Proc. of Specification and Verification of Component-Based Systems Workshop, OOPSLA 2001,* pp. 42–49, 2001.

20. G. Chastek, P. Donohoe, K. Kang, and S. Thiel. Product Line Analysis: A Practical Introduction. Tech. Report CMU/SEI-2001-TR-001, Carnegie Mellon, Software Engineering Institute, 2001.

21. P. Clemens and L. Northrop. *Software Product Lines - Practices and Patterns.* Addison-Wesley, 2001.

22. COCOTS. COnstructive COTS Model. http://sunset.usc.edu/research/COCOTS/, 2001.

23. W. T. Council. Third-Party Testing and the Quality of Software Components. *IEEE Software,* 16(4):55–57, 1999.

24. L. Davis and R. Gamble. Identifying Evolvability for Integration. In *Proc. of the First International Conference on COTS-Based Software Systems,* Springer-Verlag, pp. 65–75, 2002.

25. E. Dincel, N. Medvidovic, and A. van der Hoek. Measuring Product Line Architectures. In *Proc. of the International Workshop on Product Family Engineering (PFE-4),* 2001.

26. J. Dolado. A Validation of the Component-Based Method for Software Size Estimation. *IEEE Transactions on Software Engineering,* 26(10):1006–1021, 2000.

27. EC. IST-1999-20162, Component+. www.component-plus.org, 2002.

28. A. Egyed, N. Medvidovic, and C. Gacek. Component-based perspective on software mismatch detection and resolution. *IEE Software Engineering,* 147(6):225–236, 2000.

29. F. Fioravanti and P. Nesi. Estimation and Prediction Metrics for Adaptive Maintenance Effort of Object-Oriented Systems. *IEEE Transactions on Software Engineering*, 27(12):1062–1084, 2001.

30. J. Gao, K. Gupta, S. Gupta, and S. Shim. On Building Testable Software Components. In *Proc. of the First International Conference on COTS-Based Software Systems*, Springer-Verlag, pp. 108–121, 2002.

31. W. Hansen. A Generic Process and Terminology for Evaluating COTS Software - The QESTA Process. http://www.sei.cmu.edu/staff/wjh/Qesta.html.

32. M. Harrold. Using Component Metadata to Support the Regression Testing of Component-Based Software. Tech. Report GIT-CC-01-38, College of Computing, Georgia Institute of Technology, 2001.

33. G. Heineman and W. Council. *Component-Based Software Engineering - Putting the Pieces Together*. Addison-Wesley, 2001.

34. C. Szyperski. *Component Software. Beyond Object-Oriented Programming*. Addison-Wesley, 1999.

35. S. Hissam, G. Moreno, J. Stafford, and K. Wallnau. Packaging Predictable Assembly with Prediction-Enabled Component Technology. Tech. Report CMU/SEI-2001-TR-024, Carnegie Mellon, Software Engineering Institute, 2001.

36. J. H'ornestein and H. Edler. Test Reuse in CBSE Using Built-in Tests. In *Proc. of the 9th IEEE Conference and Workshops on Engineering of Computer-Based Systems. Workshop on Component-based Software Engineering*, 2002.

37. ISO International Standard ISO/WD 121199. ISO/WD 12199 - V4.: Software Engineering - Software product evaluation - Requirements for quality of Commercial Off The Shelf software products (COTS) and in-structions for testing, 2001.

38. L. Jones and A. Soule. Software Process Improvement and Product Line Practice: CMMI and the Framework for Product Line Practice. Tech. Report CMU/SEI-2002-TN-012, Carnegie Mellon, Software Engineering Institute, 2002.

39. J. Kontio. OTSO: A Systematic Process for Reusable Software Component Selection. Tech. Report UMIACS-TR-95-63, University of Maryland, 1995.

40. J. Kontio, S. Chen, and K. Limperos. A COTS Selection Method and Experiences of its Use. In *Proc. of the 20th Annual Software Engineering Workshop, NASA Software Engineering Laboratory*, 1995.

41. B. Korel. Black-Box Understanding of COTS Components. In *Proc. of the 7th International Workshop on Program Comprehension*, IEEE Press, pp. 92–99, 1999.

42. D. Kunda and L. Brooks. Applying Social-Technical Approach for COTS Selection. In *Proc. of the 4th UKAIS Conference*, University of York, 1999.

43. A. Leicher and F. B'ubl. External Requirements Validation for Component-Based Systems. In *Proc. of CAiSE 2002*, LNCS 2348, Springer-Verlag, pp. 404–419, 2002.

44. H. F. Lipson, N. R. Mead, and A. P. Moore. Can We Ever Build Survivable Systems from COTS Components? In *Proc. of CAiSE 2002*, LNCS 2348, Springer-Verlag, pp. 216–229, 2002.

45. J. Magee, N. Dualy, S. Eisenbach, and J. Kramer. Specifying Distributed Software Architectures. In *Proc. of the 5th European Software Engineering Conference*, LNCS 989, Springer-Verlag, pp. 137–153, 1995.

46. N. Maiden, H. Kim, and C. Ncube. Rethinking Process Guidance for Selecting Software Components. In *Proc. of the First International Conference on COTS-Based Software Systems*, Springer-Verlag, pp. 151–164, 2002.

47. J. McCall, P. Richards, and G. Walters. Factors in software quality, volume III: Preliminary handbook on software quality for an acquisition manager. Tech. Report RADC-TR-77-369, vol. III, Hanscom AFB, MA 01731, 1977.

48. E. Martins, C.M. Toyota, and R.L. Yanagawa. Constructing Self-Testable Software Components. In *Proc. of the 2001 International Conference on Dependable Systems and Networks*, pp. 151–160, 2001.

49. J. McGregor. Testing a Software Product Line. Tech. Report CMU/SEI-2001-TR-022, Carnegie Mellon, Software Engineering Institute, 2001.

50. De Millo. *Software Testing and Evaluation*. Benjamin/Cumming Publishing Co, 1987.

51. C. Mueller and B. Korel. Automated Black-Box Evaluation of COTS Components with Multiple-Interfaces. In *Proc. of the 2nd International Workshop on Automated Program Analysis, Testing, and Verification, ICSE 2001*, 2001.

52. M. Ochs, D. Pfahl, G. Chrobok-Diening, and Nothhelfer-Kolb. A COTS Acquisition Process: Definition and Application Experience. Tech. Report IESE-002.00/E, Fraunhofer Institut Experimentelles Software Engineering, 2000.

53. M. Ochs, D. Pfahl, G. Chrobok-Diening, and Nothhelfer-Kolb. A Method for Efficient Measurement-based COTS Assessment and Selection - Method Description and Evaluation Results. Tech. Report IESE-055.00/E, Fraunhofer Institut Experimentelles Software Engineering, 2000.

54. S. Polen, L. Rose, and B. Phillips. Component Evaluation Process. Tech. Report SPC-98091-CMC, Software Productivity Consortium, 1999.

55. M. Polo. Automating Testing of Java Programs using Reflection. In *Proc. of the ICSE 2001 Workshop WAPATV*, IEEE Press, 2001.

56. R. Reussner and H. Schmidt. Using Parameterised Contracts to Predict Properties of Component Based Software Architectures. In *Proc. of the 9th IEEE Conference and Workshops on Engineering of Computer-Based Systems. Workshop on Component-based Software Engineering*, 2002.

57. J. Ropponen and K. Lyytinen. Components of Software Development Risk: How to Address Them? A Project Management Survey. *IEEE Transactions on Software Engineering*, 26(2):98–112, 2000.

58. R. Rosenblum. Adequate Testing of Component-Based Software. Tech. Report 97-34, Department of Information and Computer Science, University of California, Irvine, 1997.

59. T.L. Saaty. *The Analytic Hierarchy Process*. McGraw-Hill, 1990.

60. S. Sedigh-Ali, A. Ghafoor, and R. Paul. Metrics-Guided Quality Management for Component-Based Software Systems. In *Proc. of the 25th Annual International Computer Software and Applications Conference*, IEEE Computer Society Press, pp. 303–310, 2001.

61. S. Sedigh-Ali, A. Ghafoor, and R. Paul. Software Engineering Metrics for COTS-Based Systems. *IEEE Computer Magazine*, pp. 44–50, May 2001.

62. SEI. CMMI Product Suite. `http://www.sei.cmu.edu/cmmi/products`.

63. SEI. Predictable Assambly from Certifiable Components (PACC). `http://www.sei.cmu.edu/pacc/index.html`.

64. M. Shereshevsky, H. Ammari, N. Gradetsky, A. Mili, and H. Ammar. Information Theoretic Metrics for Software Architectures. In *Proc. of the 25th Annual International Computer Software and Applications Conference*, IEEE Computer Society Press, 2001.

65. M. Sparling. Lessons Learned Through Six Years of Component-Based Development. *Communications of the ACM*, 43(10):47–53, 2000.

66. J. Stafford and L. Wolf. Annotating Components to Support Component-Based Static Analyses of Software Systems . Tech. Report CU-CS-896-99, University of Colorado at Boulder, 1999.

67. G. Sullivan. Aspect-Oriented Programming using Reflection and Metaobject Protocols. *Communications of the ACM*, 44(10):95–97, 2001.
68. L. Tahat. Requirement-Based Automated Black-Box Test Generation. In *Proc. of the 25th Annual International Computer Software and Applications Conference*, IEEE Computer Society Press, pp. 489–495, 2001.
69. A. van der Hoek. Capturing Product Line Architectures. In *Proc. of the 4th International Software Architecture Workshop*, 2000.
70. J. Voas. Certifying Software for High-Assurance Environments. *IEEE Software*, 16(4):48–54, 1999.
71. K. Wallnau, S. Hissam, and R. Seacord. *Building Systems from Commercial Components*. Addison-Wesley, 2002.
72. K. Wallnau and J. Stafford. Ensembles: Abstractions for a New Class of Design Problem. In *Proc. of the 27th Euromicro Conference*, IEEE Computer Society Press, 2001.
73. K. Wallnau, J. Stafford, S. Hissam, and M. Klein. On the Relationship of Software Architecture to Software Component Technology. In *Proc. of the ECOOP 6th International Workshop on Component-Oriented Programming (WCOP6)*, 2001.
74. Y. Wang and G. King. A European COTS Architecture with Built-in Tests. In *Proc. of OOIS 2002*, LNCS 2425, Springer-Verlag, pp. 336–347, 2002.
75. Y. Wang, G. King, M. Fayad, D. Patel, I. Court, G. Staples, and M. Ross. On Built-in Test Reuse in Object-Oriented Framework Design. *ACM Journal on Computing Surveys*, 32(1), 2000.
76. R. Williams, J. Walker, and A. Dorofee. Putting Risk Management into Practice. *IEEE Software*, 14(3):75–82, 1997.
77. D. Yakimovich, J. Bieman, and V. Basili. Software architecture classification for estimating the cost of COTS integration. In *Proc. of ICSE'99*, pp. 296–302, 1999.

COTS-Based Requirements Engineering

Carina Alves

Department of Computer Science
University College London
c.alves@cs.ucl.ac.uk

Abstract. In this chapter we discuss the current trends and challenges that arise in the COTS-based requirements engineering. When acquiring COTS products, customers are put into unexpected situations over which they have no control. Therefore, requirements have to be more flexible in order to meet the products constraints. We point out the main research efforts that have been done to support the COTS-based requirements process and discuss the advantages and drawbacks of each proposal. We argue that the matching process between products' features and users requirements is a fundamental issue to be treated during the evaluation process. In this context, we propose a goal-oriented approach to identify mismatches and deal with conflicts.

1 Introduction

The prospect of reducing time and cost associated with software development has led organizations to an increasingly interest in acquiring and integrating commercial products instead of developing systems from scratch. The large availability of both generic and domain-specific COTS (Commercial-Off-The Shelf) packages is a key-driving factor that supports the development of COTS-based systems. However, in order to obtain all the potential benefits from this new development paradigm, we have to meet the challenge of selecting the "right" product. In other words, it involves the evaluation of available COTS products in the market with respect to the needs and constraints of each buyer, which means that COTS alternatives have to be assessed against the customer requirements. It is important to note that we cannot assume the existence of the best product for all situations, if a product meets the needs of organization A, it does not necessarily is suitable for organization B that has a different business process and consequently different organizational requirements. Therefore, COTS evaluation has to be specific for each particular organization. Note, however that we incite the use of previous experiences from other organizations as a guideline for similar selection processes.

COTS-based systems comprise a spectrum, ranging from COTS-solution systems at one extreme, to COTS-intensive systems at the other extreme [15]. A COTS-solution system refers to a system in which one substantial product is tailored to provide a complete solution. For example, Enterprise Resource Planning packages (ERP) provide an extensive set of fully integrated functionalities.

A. Cechich et al. (Eds.): Component-Based Software Quality, LNCS 2693, pp. 21–39, 2003.

The goal of ERP software products is to integrate all departments and functions across an organization into a single system that can serve the needs and requirements of those departments. Since ERP systems are designed to support very different organizations from various business domains, the success of an ERP installation is critically dependent on the customization process that requires organizational change through business process re-engineering.

COTS-intensive systems are far more complex; this sort of system integrates many products from different vendors that have to be tailored and integrated to provide the system functionality. Many conflicts can be originated from incompatibilities between products that are been integrated. In such situations, developers have to be prepared to adapt and change the conflicting products. Note that it is very likely that suppliers will not support the adaptation process and you have to cope with the problem of understanding how the packages operate without even having any bit of the source code. You might be thinking, "if I could see the source code, this problem could be sorted out"; certainly, the source code can be helpful. However, what are you going to do with millions of lines of code? How can you find a particular function that is causing integration problems? Why should you spend a lot of time trying to understand a piece of complex code if a new version is probably arriving on the market in the next months? While it is practically impossible to obtain a fully understanding on the products internal behavior, new methods and techniques should be able to support the uncertainty associated with the COTS evaluation process. We argue that a well-defined and systematic evaluation process is a fundamental activity of COTS-Based Development (CBD).

In any development process, requirements engineering plays an important role for the satisfaction of users since systems are developed with the goal of meeting users needs. In particular, the requirements engineering (RE) process for COTS-based systems is affected by problems that are very different from those of traditional systems. For instance, COTS products are designed to meet the needs of a marketplace instead of satisfying the requirements of a particular organization. To complicate matters, developers have limited access to product's internal design and the typical description of commercial packages is very often an incomplete and confused textual description. In fact, there is a lot of uncertainty with regard to how the COTS features and quality properties are satisfied. When selecting COTS products, customers have to evaluate products' features against her requirements. Obviously that not all desired requirements can be satisfied by available packages. In this way, we stress the importance of analyzing the matching between features and requirements as a way to identify possible conflicts and inconsistencies. Therefore, resolving such conflicts is a necessary condition for successful development of COTS-based systems.

This chapter discusses some new challenges that arise during the RE process for COTS-based systems. We present an overview of the COTS selection process, including a comparison of the main COTS selection methods proposed in the current literature. Another important aspect of selection that is treated in this chapter is the decision-making process. Following, we give a brief discussion about the traditional requirements engineering process. We believe it is important to analyst the main RE activities in order to understand the differences that arise when developing COTS-based systems. We then discuss some of these new issues and provide guidelines to support the COTS-based requirements engineering process. Finally, we propose a framework to support the conflict management process.

2   Background

The nature of COTS suggests that the model of component-based software development should be different from the conventional one. As a result, a significant shift has been observed from the development-centric towards a procurement-centric approach. In traditional development process, requirements are specified then high-level architecture design is produced followed by detailed design and implementation. While in CBD there is a simultaneous process of requirements specification, architecture design and COTS evaluation/integration. Developers have to take into account all these potentially conflicting issues and perform tradeoffs among them. This step encompasses the balancing and negotiation of requirements, environment constraints factors and package features where the final selection has to reflect the decisions made during the tradeoff analysis. Note that even if you are following a spiral development (which is very likely), first you have to define the main requirements and then start the architecture design but in CBD these activities are performed all together. As we are going to see later, requirements do not need to be acquired in very detail, as they will be constrained by the COTS design. In fact, packages features can be a way of getting a better understanding about customers goals. Apart from the differences presented in the RE process, new activities will become part of the COTS-based development process, for example adaptation and integration.

2.1   COTS Selection Methods

The selection process is a critical activity of COTS-based development when the quality and suitability of the product have to be verified with respect to organization requirements and business expectations. As mentioned earlier, this chapter will focus on the COTS selection and how the requirements process is affected. Firstly, we describe the main approaches to support the selection of COTS products including a discussion about how the requirements process is covered in each approach. The OTSO (Off-The-Shelf Option) [8] method was one of the first COTS selection methods proposed in the literature. It is a well-defined process that covers the whole selection process. The definition of hierarchical evaluation criteria is the core task of this method, which consists of the hierarchical set of functionalities, architectural constraints, and organizational characteristics. The evaluation activity identifies four different sub-processes: search criteria, definition of the baseline, detailed evaluation criteria definition, weighting of criteria. Surprisingly the method considers quality aspects (e.g. reliability, portability, etc.) as extra factors that may influence the decision but

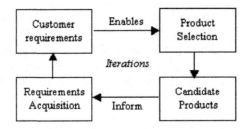

Fig. 1. Overview of PORE's iterative process

are not necessarily included in the evaluation criteria. However, we consider such characteristics fundamental criteria to assess COTS suitability, for example, if you are integrating several components into an integrated system, you should verify how well they interoperate before buying them. OTSO also support the cost estimation of each alternative using cost models, it breaks down the acquisition cost into three main classes: acquisition costs, further development costs and integration costs. Although having proved to be successful in building the evaluation criteria, this approach has limitations on how to conduct the requirements acquisition process. The method assumes that requirements already exist since it is based on a fixed and pre-defined requirements specification that will be part of the evaluation criteria. Moreover, OTSO just mentions the possibility to have non-required features but do not provide any strategy on how to deal with them. Note that such situations are very common in CBD and need to be properly examined as they can determine the success of COTS-based systems. The method relies on the use of AHP technique [13] for conducting the evaluation of products in order to support the decision-making. Although suffering from some weaknesses as those stated above, the OTSO method served as an initial step for further approaches.

Another important contribution for COTS selection is the *PORE* (*Procurement-Oriented Requirements Engineering*) [11]. The method is a template-based approach to support selection that is based on the iterative process of requirements acquisition and product evaluation (see Fig. 1). At the beginning of the process there are few requirements specified and a large number of candidate products. Using the templates several times, it is possible to refine the product list until the most suitable product is selected. In particular, the templates are derived from empirical studies about current processes and problems encountered during the selection activity. PORE integrates various techniques, methods and tools, such as: knowledge engineering techniques, multi-criteria decision making methods, and requirements acquisition techniques. It also provides guidelines for designing product evaluation test cases, which guide the evaluation team to acquire product information to select or reject products.

The method suggests the use of fit criteria to determine whether or not a solution satisfies the original requirements. According to the method, the compliance between features and requirements is a fundamental step for effective product selection. However, the compliance process is not examined in sufficient detail. For instance, it is not clear how the matching between products features and requirements is performed and how products that do not satisfy the requirements are eliminated from the candidate list.

CRE (COTS-Based Requirements Engineering) [1] is a method that emphasizes the importance of non-functional requirements as decisive criteria to evaluate alternative products. In particular, quality attributes are very difficult to be verified mainly because suppliers do not provide a complete description of quality aspects (stability, flexibility, performance, etc.). Furthermore, non-functional requirements can be often interacting, such that attempts to achieve one requirement can hurt or help the achievement of other. The method is proposes the use of the NFR Framework [4] to model non-functional requirements. CRE supports the evaluation of candidate products through the definition of systematic criteria that includes a clear description of quality attributes that potential candidates have to meet. Moreover, the method provides guidelines on how to acquire and specify non-functional requirements. CRE emphasizes that evaluating and analyzing all relevant quality features of COTS candidates takes a great amount of time, typically more than the organization has. Therefore, it is both necessary and cost-effective to select the most promising candidates for detailed evaluation. As drawback, the method does not address issues of quality testing and it is not clear how the product's quality issues are verified with regard to customers non-functional requirements. Another problem with the method is concerned to the lack of support in cases when non-functional requirements are not properly satisfied.

CARE (COTS-Aware Requirements Engineering) [5] is a goal and agent oriented requirements engineering approach that explicitly supports the use of off-the-shelf products. CARE emphasizes the importance to keep requirements flexible since they have to be constrained by the capabilities of available COTS. In this approach requirements are classified as: native (requirements acquired from customers) and foreign (requirements of the COTS components). The method considers that bridging the gap between the sets of native and foreign requirements is a critical task and that it is necessary to explore different alternatives of matching. Although the approach points out the importance of mapping system requirements and products specification, it does not provide or suggest any systematic solution to support the possible mismatching between both specifications. CARE is based on the i* notation to describe the process methodology. The process model ontology includes actors, goals, resources, dependencies and relationships. The authors developed a prototype called CARE assistant tool as a first attempt to model the interdependencies among requirements that are represented in this approach as goals.

It is interesting to note that most of the selection methods assume the existence of a predefined and fixed set of requirements (i.e. the evaluation criteria) in which the candidate products must be assessed against it. We believe that following such approaches developers take the advantage of having a well-defined and systematic process. However, it also involves the definition of strict requirements, which means that either promising candidate products have to be eliminated be-

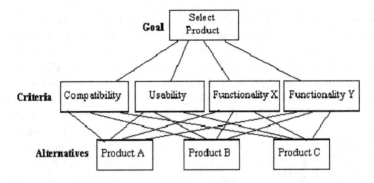

Fig. 2. Overview of decision-making process

cause they not meet the stated requirements or that large product modifications will be needed to satisfy such requirements. Moreover, many methods propose the prioritization of requirements in order to conduct the evaluation of products but do not tackle the complex matching between prioritized requirements and COTS features. We consider the matching process a critical issue where features should be mutually balanced against requirements in a very interactive way.

2.2   Multi-criteria Decision Making

It is practically impossible to conduct a comprehensive discussion about COTS evaluation without mentioning multi-criteria decision making techniques since they have been largely used in many selection methods. The basic concepts of MCDM (*Multi Criteria Decision Making*) approaches are establishing a set of criteria that products should meet, assigning scores to each criterion based on its relative importance in the decision and then ranking products based on their total scores. Fig. 2 depicts an overview of the selection decision-making. A three levels hierarchy represents: at the first level, the main goal for the decision making process; the evaluation criteria at the second level; and finally at the third level the alternative candidates. The two most used approaches are the AHP (*Analytic Hierarchy Process*) [13] and WSM (*Weighted Scoring Method*) [8]. Using the WSM technique, the overall score of each alternative is calculated using the following formula:

$$Score_a = \sum_{j=1}^{n} weight \times score_{aj}$$

where a represents an alternative, and n the number of criteria.

Weights are assigned by customers and represent the importance they give to a particular requirement to be met. The score represents the compliance of the attributes been evaluated. WSM can be confusing since the resulting scores only represent the relative ranking of alternatives and the differences in their value does not give any indication of their relative superiority. For more complex decision-making processes, a more effective technique is the AHP. This technique provides a hierarchical approach for consolidating information about alternatives using pair-wise comparisons and the overall priorities are computed using an eigenvalue technique of matrix comparison. The technique suggests that comparing criteria in pairs brings more reliable results.

WSM technique has some limitations when applied in COTS assessment, for instance: (i) this approach produces real numbers as results, so they can be misinterpreted as the real differences between the alternatives rather than the relative ranking; and (ii) difficulty in assigning weights when the number of criteria is large. AHP has many advantages over WSM, some previous experiments claim that AHP give decisions makers more confidence in their decisions. As pointed out by Ref. [14], the main limitations of these techniques for requirements prioritization are: (i) they assume that requirements are independent; and (ii) the calculation model involves a very high number of pair-wise comparisons. These techniques are also weak in supporting comparison between interdependent requirements. However, interactions between requirements are very usual, in special non-functional requirements that are well known as interacting both in conflict or synergy.

3   Traditional Requirements Engineering

The focus of this chapter is Requirements Engineering (RE) for COTS-based development. Therefore, it is worth to discuss the traditional RE process in order to identify the similarities and differences between both processes. The main goal of the RE process is discovering the users needs with regard to the new system to be developed, documenting it in a clear way, analyzing possible conflicting requirements, negotiating such requirements until an agreement has been achieved then validating the requirements taking into account consistency and completeness issues.

Before discussing RE activities in more detail, let us define what requirements engineering is about. Ref. [16] provides a clear definition: "Requirements engineering is the branch of software engineering concerned with the real world goals, functions, and constraints on software systems. It is also concerned with the relationship of these factors to precise specifications of software behavior, and to their evolution over time and across software families." In other words, requirements engineering must address the goals why the software is needed, the functionalities the software must provide and the constraints under which it must operate. This definition also suggests the RE process is a multidimensional one. The whole system has to be considered under many facets, for example, socio-economic, organizational, technical, evolutionary, and so on. Moreover, there are multiple parties involved in the process, each one having different background, skills, knowledge and concerns. Very often this diversity give rise to conflicting viewpoints. The RE process covers many intertwined activities, namely: elicitation, analysis and negotiation, documentation, validation. Fig. 3 shows the iterative process between the activities, which is known in the literature as Spiral Model [9].

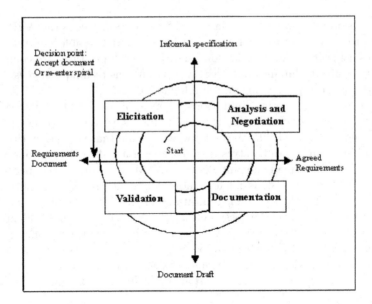

Fig. 3. Spiral model of the requirements engineering process

Elicitation. In this phase, the individuals who will be affected by the system are identified; they include customers, end-users, managers and others involved in the organizational processes. These individuals are called stakeholders. System requirements are acquired from stakeholders, generally through interviews, use of scenarios, consultation of documents, etc. It is also necessary to understand the application domain and business problem in order to gain a deep understanding about what are the real needs to be solved.

Analysis and Negotiation. Once requirements have been obtained, it is very likely that some requirements will conflict since they reflect the needs of different stakeholders that have different views and desires. In general, requirements analysis is interleaved with documentation when problems are highlighted and discussed. Negotiation is the process of discussing requirements in conflict and reaching some commitments that all stakeholders can live with.

Documentation. The agreed requirements are documented with their priorities and assumptions. The requirements document usually includes natural language descriptions and diagrams. For more complex systems, requirements can be formally specified using logic in order to have a precise description of the system to be developed.

Validation. This is the process of verifying that the requirements represent an acceptable and consistent description of the system that will be implemented. During the validation, analysts discover requirements problems, such as: ambiguities, completeness, conflicts not detected before.

Apart from the activities described above, the RE process also involves the management of requirements. In fact, requirements always evolve, as the system environment change and stakeholders needs change. Therefore managing change is an important activity in RE, it consists on the process of assessing the impact of proposed changes to requirements.

An important research topic in RE is goal-oriented requirements engineering. In fact, goals have been recognized as a leading concept in the RE process and this area has received increasing attention over the last few years. Various approaches have been proposed to specify goals in the requirements engineering literature. The NFR Framework [4] concentrates on the explicit representation and analysis of non-functional requirements. In order to carry out this task, the framework first gives the meaning of non-functional requirements as *softgoals* whose satisfaction cannot be established in a clear-cut sense. It also provides a set of abstractions for modelling non-functional requirements, supports design decisions with design rationale and evaluates the impact of decisions. Another important work in goal-oriented RE is the KAOS method [10]. This approach aims at supporting the whole process of requirements elaboration. The method consists in identifying goals and refining them into subgoals represented by a graph structure inspired by the AND/OR trees used in problem solving until the subgoals can be assigned to single agents such as humans, devices and software. In KAOS the goals can be also formally specified using temporal logic. The approach supports the identification and resolution of conflicts between goals, and the identification and resolution of exceptional agent behaviors, called obstacles that violate goals. In our approach, we use the KAOS language to specify goals. The rationale for that is because goals provide the right level of abstraction required by the development of COTS-based systems.

4   Requirements for COTS-Based Systems

In traditional system development, the requirements engineering (RE) activity basically consists of eliciting stakeholders needs, refining the acquired goals into non-conflicting requirements statements, and finally validating these requirements with stakeholders. The main goal of the requirements engineer is to ensure that the requirements specification meets stakeholders' desires and it represents a concise and clear description of the system to be developed. Broadly speaking, the specified requirements will be translated into software architecture and ultimately, implemented. Therefore, it is reasonable to assert that requirements play a controlling role in system development [15]. The RE process for COTS-based development is affected by problems that are very different from those of traditional systems. We discuss some of these challenges as follows.

4.1   Requirements Flexibility

In COTS-based development, requirements statements need to be much more flexible and less specific. Developers should specify requirements mainly as desirable needs rather than as strict constraints. For instance, suppose the following situation where a financial management system will be acquired by a bank in which end users include cashiers who are not expected to have a deep knowledge on information systems. Therefore, learnability (i.e. the facility for a user to learn how to use the system) is a critical quality attribute for the selection of this package. However, let's say that none of the evaluated products satisfies the desired learnability, some packages have a good documentation but the graphical interface is quite complicated, others have a very intuitive interface but the documentation only consists of a general user guide. When buying COTS products we have to priorities our needs in order to accept limitations of functionalities that cannot be met.

Another major difference between traditional RE and COTS-based RE is that the latter do not need to be complete. Instead, initial incomplete requirements can be progressively refined and detailed as soon as products are found. In fact, requirements elicitation loses its importance, as most of the requirements should be directly obtained from products features. High-level goals are identified using typical elicitation techniques, such as interviews and use cases. From these goals, possible COTS candidates are identified in the marketplace.

After that, new functionalities that were not initially perceived can be found in products, refined goals can be operationalized by features what means that requirements are expected to be highly influenced by products. When developing systems with the goal of maximizing the use of COTS, the specified requirements should not be so strict that either exclude the use of COTS or that require large product modification in order to satisfy them. In fact, an interesting approach is to let the available COTS features determine requirements [6]. Consequently, it is necessary to achieve the best balancing of requirements precision and flexibility. We suggest that the number of "hard" requirements should be minimized to the definition of the main functionality of the system while more "fluid" requirements should be the majority of requirements statements.

It is interesting to note that the evaluation of COTS demands some inexact matching between customers requirements and products features, for example: there may be requirements not satisfied by any available package, requirements satisfied by some joint packages, requirements partially satisfied, features not initially requested but that can be helpful, irrelevant features or even unwanted features. Moreover, there are some cases where critical requirements cannot be entirely satisfied without considerable product adaptation and other cases where these requirements must be compromised to accept products constraints. In all these situations developers have to perform an extensive negotiation process. In other words, the negotiation encompasses the balancing of conflicting interests between what is wanted and what is possible to meet.

An additional complication is that very often package specifications might have incompleteness and inconsistencies. In fact, vendors can hide some functions as a way to warrant their intellectual property, competing vendors can also describe features using different terms as a way to gain competitive advantages. Therefore, during the evaluation process it is necessary to perform a complex compliance-checking between the requirements specification and the many COTS specifications that are under evaluation.

4.2   Loss of Control

COTS products are developed based on a set of requirements that vendors believe will meet the widest number of customers. Vendors try to meet the needs of a marketplace instead of satisfying the requirements of a particular organization. In fact, COTS are designed to satisfy very general requirements. An additional complication is that vendors have full control over the product releases and upgrades. Therefore, customers are put into unexpected situations over which they have no control [3]. For example, consider you had bought a product from a supplier that introduced a new packaging strategy, which included a new function that you do not want into the COTS you had purchased. In this situation you have no choice but to update the new product or to change to another supplier and perform a new assessment process.

Vendors develop new features that differentiate from their competitors, consumers are forced to upgrade no matter if they want or not with the prospect of loosing vendor support, features that succeed in the marketplace are quickly copied by competitors, forcing a new round of innovation. COTS developers need to invent requirements based on their perceptions on what are the marketplace expectations. The sources of requirements usually include internal developers, marketing consultants, and old customers. Companies who bring innovative and creative features in their products may gain competitive advantage. However, developers should not consider too complex and unrealistic requirements that are not possible to implement with the resources available, as time to market is an important concern when developing COTS. Therefore, developers have to priorities implementing those requirements that seems to be the most important ones for the next release. According to Ref. [7], the decision regarding which sort of requirements to implement may depend on the maturity of the market domain. In stable markets, developers should focus on creative features, while in unstable and immature markets it is more important to support the main functionalities that satisfy the customer needs. On the other side, when developing systems from COTS packages that are available in the marketplace, customers are required to specify requirements based on the features provided by the packages. This in turn requires the customer to have a detailed understanding of COTS features to identify misfitting elements.

Moreover, it is also necessary to decide which parts of the package must be adapted to satisfy critical requirements as well as to adjust the organization business process. For instance, the success of an ERP (Enterprise Resource Planning) installation is critically dependent on the customization process where developing systems from ERP packages requires organizational change through business process re-engineering. Fig. 4 provides a comparison between the development of COTS products and systems that integrate COTS.

4.3   Evolving Requirements

In traditional system development, requirements always evolve as the environment in which these systems operate change; stakeholders also change their needs

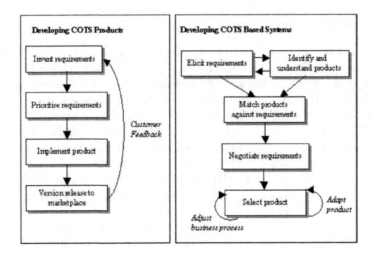

Fig. 4. Comparison between development of COTS products and COTS-based systems

as far as they get a better understanding of the system being developed. Evolution in requirements is unavoidable and must be considered as a natural part of the development process. Therefore it is not true to think that such changes are originated due to poor requirements engineering process. Broadly speaking, in traditional system development, changes in requirements might lead to instability but as soon as the changes are managed and requirements agreed, the situation is controlled. However, if we are developing COTS-based systems, requirements are likely to change more frequently than in traditional development. This situation mainly occurs because of the high volatility of COTS marketplace that launches new releases in a very short period of time.

In many cases COTS packages include more functionalities than the customer really need. Therefore, these extra capabilities impose constraints and limitations over requirements creating different circumstances for the requirements engineer that now has to deal with undesired features. Thus, this new situation leads to a continuous process of negotiation. We have to keep the decisions made during the assessment process in order to understand the reasons that forced requirements to change or why a particular product was eliminated. Capturing such rationale facilitates adaptation to ongoing changes. Competitive pressures in the marketplace force vendors to innovate and differentiate products features rather than standardize them.

5   Conflict Management for COTS-Based Systems

In the previous sections we have discussed some important aspects of COTS-based requirements engineering. As we have discussed before, it is very likely that conflicting situations arise since buyers and vendors usually have incompatible objectives. Checking whether a product meets a requirement or not is

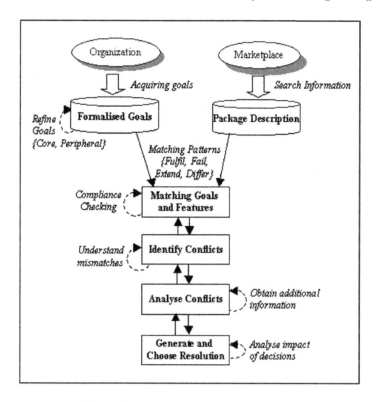

Fig. 5. Conflict management framework

often difficult due to the evolving and unclear nature of COTS packages. In our approach, the matching between goals and COTS packages consists of evaluating how refined goals can be operationalized by features. In other words, it is a kind of compliance-checking mechanism, as stakeholders have to reach an agreement that their goals are sufficiently achieved in terms of features.

Rather than eliminating conflict, we aim at proposing a course grain framework that handles conflicts in order to achieve the best balancing between COTS constraints and customers needs. Note that the proposed framework should be used as part of the selection process so that any other method described before could be used in conjunction. However, the conflict management framework extends the selection activity, as conflicts will exist even after the "best" product has been selected. Actually, many unexpected issues can arise during the adaptation and integration of the product into the organization. The following activities are part of the conflict management process. We illustrate it with a bookstore system acquisition. Fig. 5 presents an overview of the conflict management framework. It starts with the description of goals and candidate products that should be obtained from the organization and marketplace, respectively. The elements of these two specifications have to be compared in order to find similarities and divergences, i.e. how goals are met or not by the features. After

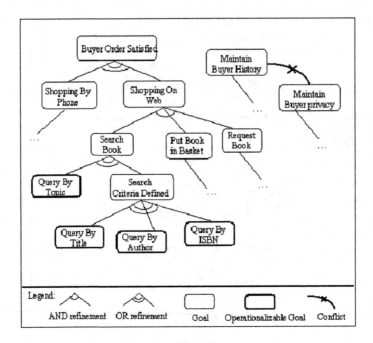

Fig. 6. Goal refinement for the bookstore system

identifying the mismatches, we can start the conflict resolution process that is iterative by nature as different parties are involved. Note, however, that finding a mismatch does not necessarily mean that a conflict exists. Further analysis is necessary to characterize real conflicts and generate resolutions.

5.1 Acquiring Goals

As we described before, the first step of any system development is specifying stakeholders requirements. We are following a goal-oriented RE approach called KAOS language [10] to specify goals. The motivation for that is because KAOS provides both a graphical specification of goals (tree decomposition) that is very suitable to represent goals in terms of features to be achieved as well as a formal language that can be used to specify critical goals. Fig. 6 illustrates part of the goal refinement for the bookstore system using AND/OR decomposition. For instance, the goal BuyerOrderSatisfied is decomposed into ShoppingByPhone and ShoppingOnWeb through an OR link. The ShoppingOnWeb has the following subgoals: SearchBook, PutBookinBasket and RequestBook.

The customer should be able to search books by topic or query criteria, such as: by title, Author or ISBN. Note that these subgoals are operationalizable goals, in other words, they don't need further refinement as they clearly represent a functionality that the system has to accomplish. In addition to goal refinements, conflicts between goals can be made explicit, for example, the goal

MaintainBuyerHistory means that the system should store relevant information of registered customers. This goal seems to conflict with MaintainBuyerPrivacy, as customers may not want to have their personal information collected. Later we will discuss some possible resolutions for this conflict.

During the refinement process it is necessary to identify goals that helps comparing candidate products. We propose two categories of goals: peripheral and core. The former are goals that help to distinguish between products (i.e. goals not supported by all products) while the latter are goals that are provided by most available products then they are not too important for the decision process. For example, the Goal Query BookByTitle is supported by both packages (example of core goal) while the Goal KeepBuyerHistory is supported only by product B (peripheral goal).

Thus, this goal can be a decisive criterion and should be investigated in order to support the decision of selecting one product instead of others. Besides the classification of goals as *core* and *peripheral*, we propose two attributes for goals description:

Desirability. The importance of a goal described in the customer specification to be satisfied by a particular feature provided by the package.

Modifiability. The capacity to restructure a goal definition when a conflict arises between a specified goal and any feature provided by the package.

In other words, desirability specifies the priority of goals; here a possible way is assigning numbers that represent the relative importance of goals as applied in some MCDM methods. Modifiability is related with the feasibility to either change a critical goal or a feature whenever a conflict arise. This attribute is considered a central aspect of the proposed framework as conflicts are handled through change and redefinition of goals.

5.2   Matching Goals and COTS Features

From the acquired goals, possible COTS candidates are identified in the marketplace. To understand a product, we must understand the functionalities the product provides, quality aspects, legal issues (i.e. licences, vendor support), organizational issues affecting the product's operation. Consequently, the evaluation process involves the consideration of technical and non-technical issues. We assume that these features were obtained from analysis of product specification, demonstration sessions and evaluation tests. At the beginning of this process, core goals are very important because they help to define the system domain. However, as soon as the main packages are identified core goals lose its importance to peripheral ones. In general, packages features are expressed in natural language, at this point we do not provide any automatic mechanism to compare these features against goals specified in KAOS. On the other hand, as a first attempt we have proposed the following matching patterns in order to formalize the matching process:

Fulfil	– feature exactly satisfies a customer goal
Fulfil	$\equiv \forall g \in \mathsf{Goal}, \exists f \in \mathsf{Feature}, \mathsf{Matching}(g,f) \Rightarrow \mathsf{FullSatisfy}(g,f)$
Differ	– product provides feature that partially satisfies a goal requested by customer
Differ	$\equiv \forall g \in \mathsf{Goal}, \exists f \in \mathsf{Feature}, \mathsf{Matching}(g,f) \Rightarrow \mathsf{DifferSatisfy}(g,f)$
Extend	– product provides an extra feature that was not requested by customer goals
Extend	$\equiv \forall g \in \mathsf{Goal}, \exists f \in \mathsf{Feature}, \mathsf{Matching}(g,f) \wedge \neg\mathsf{Requesting}(g,f)$
Fail	– product does not provide a feature that was requested by customer goal
Fail	$\equiv \forall g \in \mathsf{Goal}, \exists f \in \mathsf{Feature}, \mathsf{Matching}(g,f) \Rightarrow \neg\mathsf{Satisfy}(f,g)$

Patterns fulfil and differ are overlap relations; more specifically the former is considered a kind of full overlap between elements i.e. when a goal can be exactly mapped into the feature specification of a particular product whereas latter is called a partial overlap. On the contrary, extend and fail patterns are divergence relations; extend represents extra elements in the feature specification that are not initially requested in the goal specification and fail represents goals that cannot be met by the feature specification. Fig. 7 shows a graphical representation of each matching pattern comparing elements from the goal specification against features of a package specification. It is important to note that all candidate packages have to be evaluated (i.e. features matched) against specified goals.

5.3   Identifying Conflicting Issues

From the matching situations, we can identify potential conflicts. Note that the fulfil pattern does not originate conflicts. Therefore, we do not need to take into account these features. On the other hand, all other patterns might be a source of conflict and need to be explored. The Differ pattern can introduce conflicts as in this case the product has a feature that partially meets a particular goal. For example, product A partially meets the goal BookPriceDisplayed but instead of displaying the price when the book is found as stated in the goal specification, the product displays the price only when the buyer requests the book.

5.4   Analyzing Type of Conflict

The aim of the conflict analysis is to develop a better understanding of the conflict and obtain additional information about the involved issues. In fact, there are many assumptions and motivations involved in any conflict. Assuming that conflicts are resolved through the generation of alternatives, a risk analysis should be performed as guidance in order to reach the "best" resolution (i.e. the solution that minimize potential conflicts and maximize goals satisfaction). For a conflict to be resolved constructively, the reasons of its occurrence should be explored. This mainly includes a careful investigation of how the mismatching occurs.

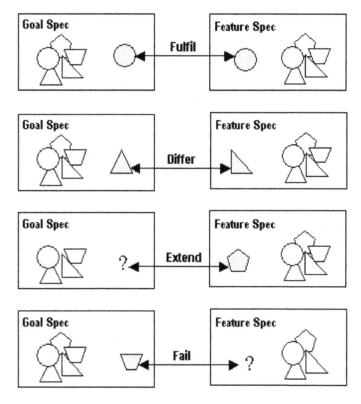

Fig. 7. Graphical representation of the matching patterns

Interestingly, identified mismatches do not necessarily leads to conflicting situations. For example, the feature DeliveryTimeDisplayed extends the requested goals, so we assume that it might cause a conflict. However, after analyzing this issue it was agreed that it could be interesting to display the delivery time after the customer has chosen the shipping facility. After a conflict has been analyzed and explored, alternative resolutions should be proposed in order to support satisfactory and consistent decisions. We believe that an effective strategy for resolution generation should be a domain-independent one. We aim at addressing this issue in future work.

5.5   Generating and Choosing Resolution Proposals

Once the resolution proposals have been identified, potential alternatives can be judged and compared. Interestingly, proposals can interact and produce a combined new proposal that also satisfies the involved issues. For example, according to Fig. 6 the goal MaintainBuyerHistory seems to conflict with Maintain-BuyerPrivacy. Some of the possible resolutions for this conflict include: notifying customers before any information is collected, collecting information only if customers agree, or do not recording any buyer history. The last alternative leads to a hard compromise between goals and should be avoided unless the goal MaintainBuyerPrivacy has very high priority. This conflict was originated within the goal specification. Consider now that all evaluated products fail with the goal MaintainBuyerHistory, here we might have two resolutions: decide if it is feasible to ask the vendor to include this function in another version (we have to discuss it with each vendor), the organization can implement it as an extra module that will be later integrated into the acquired system, or eliminate this goal if it prove to be impractical.

To determine the impact of decisions, rationale must be recorded, so that information is available if any of the conflicting issues change over time. The aim of the entire conflict resolution is to define an interactive process to explore the conflicts among goals, negotiate alternatives, identify and choose appropriate resolutions.

6   Conclusions

This chapter addresses some important issues for the successful development of COTS-based systems. We reviewed the main efforts to support the selection process, stressing its benefits and drawbacks. The use of COTS packages brings new challenges to the requirements engineering process. Although traditional RE activities are still present, extra emphasis should be given to the negotiation process. Beyond the conflicts that can arise between requirements, COTS-based RE also brings an extra source of conflicts that is the mismatching between requirements and features.

We have proposed a framework to tackle the conflicts that can arise from mismatching situations. The quality of COTS-based systems can be improved with our approach as problems with requirements satisfaction can be identified in a precise way through the use of matching patterns. However, much work remains to be done in order to develop a comprehensive treatment of conflict management for COTS-based development. As final remark, we believe that additional efforts in areas such as package certification, risk analysis, decision support, package alignment, are essential to COTS-based requirements engineering.

Acknowledgements

Special thanks to Anthony Finkelstein for his valuable comments and help with this research. This work is partially supported by CAPES grant – Brazil.

References

1. C. Alves, and J. Castro. CRE: A Systematic Method for COTS Selection. In *XV Brazilian Symposium on Software Engineering*, 2001.
2. C. Alves, and A. Finkelstein. Negotiating Requirements for COTS Selection. In *8th International Workshop on Requirements Engineering: Foundation for Software Quality*, 2002.

3. D. Carney. Requirements and COTS-Based Systems: A Thorny Question Indeed. SEI Interactive, Carnegie Mellon University, 1999.
4. L. Chung, B. Nixon, E. Yu, and J. Mylopoulos. *Non-Functional Requirements in Software Engineering.* Kluwer Academic Publisher, 2000.
5. L. Chung, and K.A. Cooper. Knowledge-Based COTS-Aware Requirements Engineering Approach. In *14th International Conference on Software Engineering and Knowledge Engineering*, 2002.
6. A. Finkelstein, G. Spanoudakis, and M. Ryan. Software Package Requirements and Procurement. In *8th International Workshop on Software Specification and Design*, 1996.
7. L. Karlsson, A. Dahlstedt, J. Dag, B. Regnell, A. Persson. Challenges in Market-Driven Requirements Engineering – an Industrial Interview Study. In em 8th International Workshop on Requirements Engineering: Foundation for Software Quality, 2002.
8. J. Kontio. A COTS Selection Method and Experiences of Its Use. In *Proceedings of the 20th Annual Software Engineering Workshop*, 1995.
9. G. Kotonia, and I. Sommerville. *Requirements Engineering: Processes and Techniques.* John Wiley & Sons, 1998.
10. A. Lamsweerde. Goal-Oriented Requirements Engineering: A Guided Tour. Invited mini-tutorial paper in *5th IEEE International Symposium on Requirements Engineering*, 2001.
11. C. Ncube, and N. A. Maiden. PORE: Procurement-Oriented Requirements Engineering Method for the Component-Based Systems Engineering Development Paradigm. In *International Workshop on Component-Based Software Engineering*, 1999.
12. B. Nuseibeh, and S. Easterbrook. Requirements Engineering: A Roadmap. In *The Future of Software Engineering.* ACM Press, 2000.
13. T. Saaty. *The Analytic Hierarchy Process.* McGraw-Hill, New York, 1990.
14. S. Sivzattian, and B. Nuseibeh. Linking the Selection of requirements to Market Value: A Portfolio-Based Approach. In *7th International Workshop on Requirements Engineering: Foundation for Software Quality*, 2001.
15. K. Wallnau, S. Hissam, and R. Seacord. *Building Systems from Commercial Components.* SEI Series in Software Engineering. Addison Wesley, 2002.
16. P. Zave. Classification of Research Efforts in Requirements Engineering. *ACM Computing Surveys*, 29(4):315-321.

Domain-Based COTS-Product
Selection Method[*]

Hareton K.N. Leung[1] and Karl R.P.H. Leung[2]

[1] Laboratory for Software Development & Management
Dept. of Computing. Hong Kong Polytechnic University, Hong Kong
cshleung@comp.polyu.edu.hk
[2] Compuware Software Testing Laboratory
Dept. of Information & Communications Technology
Hong Kong Institute of Vocational Education (Tsing Yi), Hong Kong
kleung@computer.org

Abstract. Use of commercial-off-the-shelf (COTS) products is becoming an acceptable software development method. Current methods of selecting COTS products involve using the intuition of software developers or a direct assessment of the products. The former approach is subjective, whereas the latter approach is expensive as the efficiency of the direct assessment approach is inversely proportional to the product of the number of modules in the system to be developed and the total number of modules in the candidate COTS products. With the increase in the number of available COTS components, the time spent on choosing the appropriate COTS products could easily offset the advantages of using them. A domain model is a generic model of the domain of an application system. It captures all of the features and characteristics of the domain. In this chapter, we present a new indirect selection approach, called the Domain-Based COTS-product Selection Method, which makes use of domain models. We also report a successful case study in which we applied our selection method to the development of an on-line margin-trading application.

1 Introduction

The use of commercial-off-the-shelf (COTS) products as units of large systems is becoming popular. Shrinking budgets, the rapid advancement of COTS development and the increasing demands of large systems are all driving the adoption of the COTS development approach. A COTS component is defined as an independent unit that provides a set of related functions and which is suitable for reuse [8]. COTS components are different from software components in terms of their completeness [4]. Those systems that adopt COTS development as much

---

[*] This work was partially supported by the Hong Kong Polytechnic University research grant AP205, and also by two grants from the Research Grant Council of the Hong Kong Special Administrative Region, China (Project Nos: CityU 1118/99E and HKU 7021/00E).

A. Cechich et al. (Eds.): Component-Based Software Quality, LNCS 2693, pp. 40–63, 2003.

as possible are called *COTS-Based systems (CBS)*. Compared with traditional software development, CBS development promises faster delivery with lower resource costs. The shift from custom development to CBS is not limited to new application development projects. Many maintenance projects also involve COTS products. Rather than building the whole system from scratch, a new system can be assembled and constructed by using existing, market proven and vendor supported COTS products. For example, COTS components for inventory control and accounts receivables can be purchased and integrated into an accounting system. The use of COTS products has become an economic necessity [3, 15].

Developing a CBS involves selecting the appropriate COTS products, building extensions to satisfy specific requirements, and then *gluing* the COTS products and other units together. The success of CBS development depends heavily on the ability to select the *appropriate* COTS components. An inappropriate COTS product selection strategy can lead to adverse effects. It could result in a shortlist of COTS products that can hardly fulfill the required functionality, and it might also introduce overheads in system integration and maintenance phases of a project. An effective and efficient COTS product selection process is essential to the delivery of the full potential of CBS development. If the effort required in selecting the appropriate COTS product is too high, then it may offset the time saving in using the COTS development approach.

We classify the current COTS product selection methods into three categories, namely, the *intuition* approach, the *direct assessment* approach and the *indirect assessment* approach. In the intuition approach, software developers select COTS products according to their experience and intuition. This approach is subjective, and some COTS products that are qualified candidates for an application may be omitted inadvertently.

Most of the recently proposed COTS component selection methods belong to the *direct assessment (DA)* approach, which selects COTS components directly from their source. These methods consider ALL of the descriptions of the COTS products and then try to make decisions on their suitability. For example, a recent study proposes the use of a matching process between the system requirements and the constraints imposed by the COTS products [13]. These methods all require a searching phase followed by an evaluating phase that examines both the functional and non-functional aspects of the COTS products. These approaches are more objective than the intuition-based approaches. However, the efficiency of direct assessment approach is inversely proportional to the product of the number of modules[1] in the system to be developed and the total number of modules in the candidate COTS products. The cost of selecting an appropriate COTS product can be expensive and hence, may offset the advantages of using COTS. Furthermore, we noticed that the vendor's information has not been well utilized. By making better use of the vendor's information, we can reduce the time required for selecting COTS products.

We have developed an indirect method that does not directly compare the modules of the system to be developed with the COTS product during the selec-

---

[1] The term "module" in this chapter refers to a unit of a system.

tion process. The *Domain-Based COTS-product Selection method* [11], instead of assessing all of the available COTS products, makes use of the specific domain model of the intended system to decide the suitability of the COTS product. The intention of this approach is to reduce the amount of work required for the COTS selection.

Domain modelling has been recognized as an effective tool in developing quality software. A *domain model* is a generic model of the domain in question. In other words, a domain model is the meta-model of the domain. It models a domain by capturing all the intrinsic of the domain and it also captures all the relations between these intrinsic. Hence, a domain model captures all of the properties, characteristics, functions and features of the domain. Then an application system of the domain is a refinement of the domain model. Domain models can be expressed in any appropriate software specification languages, like OMT, depending on the characteristics of the domain.

There are two basic strategies for selecting a COTS product, depending on whether an application development needs the best available COTS product:

Best-fit strategy: the selection process is aimed at identifying the best COTS product among all of the candidates.

First-fit strategy: the selection process is aimed at identifying the first COTS product that satisfies all of the requirements. If no COTS product satisfies all of the requirements, then the best product from the available COTS products is selected.

In general, the best-fit strategy will require an analysis of all of the COTS candidates, whereas the first-fit strategy may require less effort since it will stop once the first COTS candidate that meets the requirements has been identified. However, the latter strategy may not identify the best COTS product.

In Section 2 of this chapter, we provide a review of the COTS product selection methods. Section 3 presents the relationships among the domain model, COTS products and CBS. Based on the insights from these relationships, we have developed a new COTS product selection method, which is called the Domain-Based COTS-product Selection (DBCS) method. An overview of the DBCS method is given in Section 4, and detailed procedures in Section 5. In Section 6, we first analyze the efficiency of DBCS in Section 6.1. We have successfully applied the DBCS method to the development of an on-line margin-trading system for a local bank. This case study is presented in Section 6.2. In Section 7, we present our conclusions.

2   COTS Selection Methods

We first give an overview of some direct assessment methods that have been proposed for COTS product selection. They are the *Off-The-Shelf-Option* (OTSO) [7], *COTS-based Integrated System Development* (CISD) [16], *Procurement-Oriented Requirements Engineering* (PORE) [12], *COTS-based Requirements Engineering* (CRE) [1], and the *Infrastructure Incremental Development Approach* (IIDA) [6].

2.1 OTSO

Kontio proposed the *Off-The-Shelf-Option* (OTSO) selection method [8, 7]. The OTSO method assumes that the requirements of the proposed system already exist. However, in practice, the requirements cannot be defined precisely because the use of certain COTS products may require some changes to the requirements. The main principle followed by the OTSO method is that of providing explicit definitions of the tasks in the selection process, including entry and exit criteria. It also uses the Analytic Hierarchy Process as a decision-making method to analyze and summarize the evaluation results.

The inputs for OTSO include the requirements specification, design specification, project plans and organizational characteristics. The outputs are the selected COTS product, the results of the evaluation, and cost models.

The OTSO selection method comprises three phases: *searching, screening and evaluation.* Based on knowledge of the requirements specification, design specification, project plan and organizational characteristics, a set of selection criteria is set up for selecting the COTS products. The searching phase attempts to identify all potential COTS candidates that cover most of the required functionality. This phase emphasizes *breadth* rather than *depth.* The search criteria are based on the functionality and the constraints of the system.

The objective of the screening phase is to decide which COTS candidates should be selected for detailed evaluation. The screening criteria are similar to those of the searching phase. The less-qualified COTS candidates are eliminated during this stage.

In the evaluation phase, COTS candidates undergo a detailed evaluation. The evaluation criteria are defined by decomposing the requirements for the COTS products into a hierarchical set of criteria. Each branch of this hierarchy ends in an *evaluation attribute,* which is a well-defined measurement that will be determined during the evaluation. Although the set of criteria is specific to each case of COTS products selection, most of the criteria can be categorized into four groups:

- functional requirements of the COTS;
- required quality-related characteristics, such as reliability, maintainability and portability;
- business concerns, such as cost, reliability of the vendor, and future development prospects;
- issues relevant to the software architecture, such as constraints presented by an operating system, the division of functionality in the system, or the specific communication mechanisms that are used between modules.

The OTSO method uses the Analytic Hierarchy Process (AHP) to consolidate the evaluation data for decision-making purposes [14]. The AHP is based on the idea of decomposing a complex, multi-criteria decision-making problem into a hierarchy of the selection criteria. The AHP helps decision makers to structure the important components of a problem into a hierarchical structure. The AHP reduces the complex multi-criteria trade-off decisions to a series of simple pairwise comparisons and synthesizes the results. The AHP not only helps a decision-maker to arrive at the best decision, but also provides a clear rationale for making a particular choice.

A limitation of OTSO is that some of the selection criteria may not have been clearly defined.

2.2 CISD

Tran and Liu have proposed the *COTS-based Integrated System Development* (CISD) model for COTS development [16]. The CISD model is not solely for COTS product selection. It is a model that can be used to generalize the key engineering phases of selecting, evaluating and integrating COTS products for a CBS.

The inputs for the selection process are the system requirements and information about the COTS products, and the outputs include a prioritized list of the COTS products and the architecture of the system.

The CISD model consists of three distinct phases: *identification, evaluation* and *integration/enhancement*. The COTS product selection process lies within the identification and evaluation phases.

The identification phase includes all of the technical activities that are required to generate a prioritized collection of products for subsequent evaluation. It includes two sub-phases: *product classification* and *product prioritization*. In the product classification sub-phase, information on potential COTS products is collected based on the requirements of each (application) service domain. This phase is similar to the searching phase of the OTSO selection process.

In the prioritization sub-phase, candidate COTS products are screened and prioritized. Two important criteria for prioritization are interoperability and the ability to fulfill multiple requirements of the service domains. The first criterion ensures that the selected COTS candidates can be integrated readily, leading to a reduction in the overall time and effort required during system integration. The second criterion gives a higher rating to products that support multiple domains because these products can reduce the number of interconnected interfaces and architectural mismatches.

The *evaluation phase* encompasses the process of creating prototype software and temporary integration and testing of the candidate COTS products. A detailed evaluation of the COTS products is performed. Three important attributes of the COTS products are examined:

- Functionality
- Architecture and interoperability
- Performance

The *integration/enhancement* phase encompasses all of the development efforts that are required to interconnect the different selected COTS products into a single integrated system. The key advantage of the CISD model comes from its integration of the strengths of the Waterfall and Spiral models.

2.3   PORE

The *Procurement-Oriented Requirements Engineering* (PORE) method guides a software development team in acquiring customer requirements and selecting COTS products that satisfy those requirements [12]. It uses a *progressive filtering* strategy, whereby COTS products are initially selected from a set of potential candidates, and then progressively eliminated when they do not satisfy the evaluation criteria [9].

The PORE method supports an iterative process of acquiring requirements and selecting COTS products. During each of the iterations, the software development team acquires information about the customer requirements that help discriminate between the COTS product candidates. The team also undertakes multi-criteria decision-making to identify candidates that are not compliant with the requirements. Therefore, the team rejects some of the COTS candidates and then explores the remaining COTS candidates by discovering possibly new customer requirements that might discriminate more thoroughly between the remaining candidates.

The inputs of the PORE method are the attributes of the COTS products, supplier requirements, information about product branding, open standards, product certification, the development process, the supplier's CMM level [5], the product and the supplier's past record, reliability, security, and dependability. The output is the shortlist of COTS products.

PORE offers techniques such as scenarios to discover, acquire and structure the customer requirements and formulate test cases that are used to check the compliance of the COTS products with the customer requirements.

2.4   CRE

The *COTS-based Requirements Engineering* (CRE) method was developed to facilitate a systematic, repeatable and requirements-driven COTS product selection process. A key issue that is supported by this method is that of the definition and analysis of the non-functional requirements during the COTS product evaluation and selection [1].

The CRE method is goal oriented in that each phase is aimed at achieving a predefined set of goals. Each phase has a template that includes some guidelines and techniques for acquiring and modeling requirements and evaluating products.

The inputs of the CRE method include defined goals, evaluation criteria, information about the COTS candidates and test guides. The output is the selected COTS products.

This method has four iterative phases: *identification, description, evaluation* and *acceptance*. The identification phase is based on a careful analysis of influencing factors, which come from the classification proposed by Kontio [8]. There are five groups of factors that influence the selection of COTS products: *user requirements, application architecture, project objectives & restrictions, product availability* and *organizational infrastructure*.

During the description phase, the evaluation criteria are elaborated in detail with an emphasis on the non-functional requirements. This is followed by a refinement of the description of the requirements.

In the evaluation phase, the decision to select a particular COTS product is based on the estimated cost versus an analysis of the benefits. The cost model that is used is called COCOTS (Constructive COTS) [2]. In particular, the *best* COTS product is identified by continuously rejecting non-compliant candidates. COTS products that do not meet the requirements are rejected and removed from the list of candidates.

The acceptance phase is concerned with the negotiation of a legal contract with vendors of the COTS products. During this phase, the evaluation team has to resolve legal issues pertaining to the purchase of the products and their licensing.

The selection criteria of the CRE method include:

- Functional and non-functional requirements. The selected COTS products have to provide all of the required capabilities, which are necessary to meet essential customer requirements. Among these requirements, the non-functional requirements play a critical role during the assessment process.
- Time restrictions. The time available for searching and screening all of the potential COTS candidates.
- Cost rating. The cost of acquiring the COTS products. This includes expenses such as acquiring a license, the cost of support, expenses associated with adapting the product, and on-going maintenance costs.
- Vendor guarantees. This addresses the issue of the technical support that is provided by a vendor. Consideration is given to the vendor's reputation and the maturity of their organization, and the number and kinds of applications that already use the COTS product.

A disadvantage of the CRE method is that the decision-making process can be very complex, given that there are a large number of potential COTS products and many evaluative criteria.

2.5 IIDA

Fox has proposed the *Infrastructure Incremental Development Approach* (IIDA) for the development of technical infrastructure using COTS products [6]. This approach is a combination of the classical waterfall and spiral development models in order to accommodate the needs of CBS development. The process of selecting COTS products in the IIDA relies on two phases: *analysis prototype* and *design prototype*.

In the analysis-prototype phase, COTS candidates are selected from each COTS *product family*. A COTS product family is defined as a group of COTS products that perform similar functions and/or provide related services. Based on the general capabilities and basic functionalities of the COTS candidates, the qualified COTS products that fulfill the infrastructure requirement are identified in each of the COTS product families. However, the IIDA does not specify how the COTS product family is constructed or provide possible sources for that information.

The purpose of the design prototype phase is to select and evaluate the best COTS products from the earlier phase. Basic evaluation criteria include functionality and performance.

2.6   Summary of Direct Assessment Methods

Table 1 summarizes the inputs, selection procedures, selection criteria and outputs of the COTS product selection methods.

Although the five direct assessment methods (mentioned above) have some differences in their finer details, the typical steps of these methods are as follows:

1. Inspect all of the modules of each of the available COTS products to check whether they have modules that satisfy some or all of the functional requirements of the CBS being developed.
2. Check whether a COTS product also satisfies the non-functional requirements of the CBS. Non-functional requirements may include properties such as the interoperability of the modules of the COTS product with other systems.
3. Select the most appropriate COTS product that satisfies both the functional and non-functional requirements of the CBS.

The efficiency of these exhaustive direct assessment methods is inversely proportional to the product of

- the number of modules to be developed using COTS products, and
- the total number of modules in all of the available COTS products.

As more and more COTS products become available in the market, the total number of modules in all of the available COTS products will become large. Therefore, the efficiency of the direct assessment methods will decrease sharply.

3   Relationships among the Domain Model, COTS Products and CBS

The domain-based COTS-product selection method is founded on the relationships among the domain model, COTS products and CBS. In this section, we present an analysis of these relationships.

3.1   Relationships between COTS Products and a CBS

Many of the COTS products in the market are generic. The vendors of these products claim that they are applicable to systems in different application domains. A CBS development requires that we examine COTS products from multiple vendors. The selection of COTS components for an individual CBS is then a

Table 1. Comparing the direct assessment methods

	OTSO	CISD	PORE	CRE	IIDA
Input	– Requirement Specifications – Design Specifications – Project plans	– System Requirements – COTS Products	– COTS Product attributes – Supplier Requirements – Product development process	– Defined goals – Evaluation criteria – COTS Products – Test guides	– COTS from each COTS product family

Selection Procedure	– Searching
	– Screening
	– Evaluation
		– Product Identification:
		  * Classification
		  * Priorization
		– Evaluation
			– Acquires customer requirements
			– Multi-criteria decision making
			– Rejects non-compliant COTS
			– Explores other candidates for new customer reqs.
				– Identification
				– Description
				– Evaluation
				– Acceptance
					– Analysis prototype
					– Design prototype

Selection criteria	– Functional requirements – Quality characteristics – Business concerns – Relevant software architecture	– Functionality – Architecture/interoperability – Performance – Fulfil multiple requirements from the service domain	– Development process – Supplier CMM level – Product/supplier past record – Reliability – Security – Dependability	– Functional and non-functional requirements – Time restrictions – Cost rating – Vendor guaranties	– Functional requirements – Performance
Output	– Selected COTS – Evaluation results – Cost models	– Prioritized COTS products – System Architecture	– Selected COTS	– Selected COTS	– Selected COTS

Fig. 1. Many-to-many Relation between COTS and CBS

Fig. 2. Relation between a Domain Model and a CBS

many-to-many matching process (Fig. 1). The efficiency is inversely proportional to the product of the number of modules to be developed using the COTS products and the total number of modules being considered in the COTS products. If the CBS is a complex system and there are many COTS products available on the market, the system developers will have to examine many COTS products, and hence they will exert a great effort in making the selection. Consequently, this many-to-many relation may offset the advantages of using COTS development.

With the increase in the number of available COTS products and the many-to-many relation between COTS and CBS, it is difficult, without a good selection method, for system developers to examine all of the COTS products. Also, searching through a large number of available COTS products is error-prone. Ideally, the selection method should be automated to increase its efficiency and reduce errors.

3.2   Relationship between a Domain Model and a CBS

A domain model is a generic model of a domain. There may be an infinite number of systems for a domain. Hence, the relation between a domain model and an individual CBS is one-to-many. However, the relation between a domain model and an individual CBS is a simple one-to-one relation Fig. 2 [2]. This is the case because each module of the CBS should have corresponding modules in the domain model. Otherwise, the domain model is not an appropriate generic model of the domain. It is a simple relation because it is easy to identify the modules in the domain model that correspond to the CBS.

3.3   Relationship between COTS Products and a Domain Model

In general, a domain model can be supported by more than one COTS product, or the modules of a domain model can be fitted by a number of modules,

---

[2] The parallelogram represents a specific entity, which denotes a domain model and a CBS in this example. Rectangles represent a class of entities, such as multiple CBS and COTS products in Fig. 1.

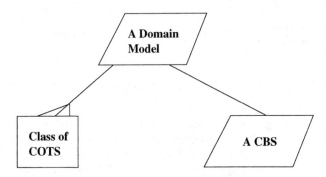

Fig. 3. Relation between Class of COTS and a Domain Model

Fig. 4. Relation between COTS, a Domain Model and a CBS

each from different COTS products. Consequently, the relation between COTS products and a domain model is many-to-one (Fig. 3).

It should be noted that the vendors of COTS products have all the information about the COTS products, including the functional and non-functional applicability of the product. Furthermore, it is a common marketing strategy that products are focused to some specific application domains instead of any domain in general. Consequently, the COTS vendors should be familiar with their target domains. Hence, it would be efficient and appropriate for the vendors to map their COTS products to the domains in which their COTS products apply. They could specify how the COTS products can be used in the applicable parts of a domain. This would not only help the software developers to select the right COTS products, but also help the vendors to market their products.

4   Domain-Based COTS-Product Selection Method

From the above analysis of the relationships between the class of COTS products, a domain model and a CBS, we notice that the relation between the class of COTS products and a domain model is a many-to-one relation and the relation between a domain model and a CBS is a one-to-one relation (Fig. 4). We can take advantages of the properties of these relations and design a new approach to select COTS products. We use the domain model as an agent between the COTS products and a CBS. The modules from the COTS products that are claimed by the vendor to be appropriate for specific modules of a domain model are first mapped to these modules by the vendors. Then, when selecting the COTS modules for a CBS, instead of selecting the COTS components directly, the corresponding modules in the domain model of a CBS are consulted first. Through the mappings between a domain model and the COTS products, the corresponding COTS modules that are (claimed to be) appropriate for the CBS module are identified. A vetting procedure is then used to select the best COTS products for the application. As the mappings between the COTS products and the domain models have been provided in terms of information on how the products can be applied to a domain, selecting an applicable COTS product can be automated based on the mappings. However, the vetting procedure cannot be fully automated because some of the functional and non-functional criteria will require human judgment.

To summarize, this method consists of two phases: set-up and selection.

1. **Set-up phase**
   When vendors rollout their COTS products, besides making the COTS products available on the market, they also need to map their COTS modules to those modules of the domains that they find are applicable. These mappings are available to the application system developers and can be accessed electronically.

2. **Selection phase**
   (a) The corresponding modules in a domain model are identified for each of the modules of the CBS in question.
   (b) The COTS modules that claim to be applicable are identified by the mappings from the domain model to the COTS modules. It should be noticed that these modules are functionally applicable to the domain models.
   (c) The non-functional properties of the identified COTS modules are assessed.
   (d) With reference to all of the assessment results, the most appropriate COTS modules are selected.

We illustrate this method with the example shown in Fig. 5. In the set-up phase, the vendor of COTS1 has identified that C11 is applicable to n1 of the domain model; the vendor of COTS2 has identified that C21 and C22 are applicable to n1 and n2, respectively; the vendor of COTS3 has identified that C31 is applicable to n2; and the vendor of COTS4 has identified that C41 and C42 are applicable to n2 and n3, respectively.

Then, when the specification of the CBS is developed, it is easy for the developers to identify that S1 corresponds to n2 and S2 corresponds to n3 of the domain model. With reference to n2 and n3, COTS modules C22, C31, C41 and C42 are identified. The next step is to validate the non-functional requirements of these four modules. One module has to be chosen from C22, C31 and C41. Since C42 is the only applicable module for S2, it will be selected if it satisfies the non-functional requirements.

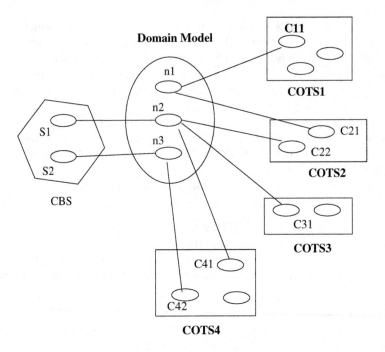

Fig. 5. An example of using the DBCS method

5   Steps of the Domain-Based COTS-Product Selection Method

In this section, we present two procedures for the domain-based COTS-product selection method. These procedures correspond to the best-fit strategy and first-fit strategy.

Before we continue our discussion, we first define some auxiliary operators. Let $elem(l)$ be a function that returns the set of unique elements from a list, l. For example, $elem([1, 1, 2]) = [1, 2]$. Let $card(S)$ be a function that returns the cardinality of a set, S. For example, $card(1, 2, 3) = 3$. Let $xtp(i, t)$ be a function that extracts the ith element from a set of tuples, which is denoted by t, and let it return the elements from the tuples in a set. If the ith element in a tuple does not exist, xtp returns an empty set. For example, $xtp(2, (a, b), (c, d, e)) = b, d$ and $xtp(3, (a, b), (c, d)) = \{\}$.

5.1   Definitions

Let there be n modules in the CBS ($n \geq 0$) and x COTS products available ($x \geq 0$). Let c_i denote an individual COTS product. Let cm_i be the set of modules of c_i. Then, (c_i, cm_i) form a tuple that captures the COTS product identifier and its set of modules. Let $L_c = [(c_1, cm_1), (c_2, cm_2), \cdots, (c_x, cm_x)]$ be the list that represents a set of x COTS products.

Let there be y COTS products among the x available COTS products that have some modules satisfying some of the functional requirements of the n CBS modules.

Let each of these y COTS products be denoted by d_i. Let dc_i be a module of d_i, and let n_i be a module of the CBS that is functionally satisfied by dc_i. Let dm_i be a set of tuples (dc_i, n_i). Then, a list, $L_d = [(d_1, dm_1), (d_2, dm_2), \cdots, (d_y, dm_y)]$, can be constructed to keep the COTS candidates together with their set of module pairs that satisfy the functional requirements of the CBS.

Since L_d is selected from L_c, $card(elem(L_c)) = x$, and $card(elem(L_d)) = y$, we have

1. $x \geq y$,
2. $xtp(1, elem(L_c)) \supseteq (xtp(1, elem(L_d)))$,
3. $\forall c_i, \exists cm_i, dm_i : (ci, cmi) \in elem(L_c) \wedge (c_i, dm_i) \in elem(L_d) \Rightarrow cm_i \supseteq xtp(1, dm_i)$.

Let the CBS have v non-functional criteria. Among the y COTS products, let there be z COTS products that satisfy the non-functional requirements of the CBS.

Let each of these z COTS products be denoted by e_i. Let ec_i be a module of e_i, which satisfies the non-functional requirements, and let n_i be a module of the CBS, which is functionally satisfied by ec_i. Let em_i be the set of tuples (ec_i, n_i).

For functional requirements, if we express the statements of the requirements in conjunction normal form, each of the requirement clauses is then either satisfied or unsatisfied. However non-functional requirements, unlike functional requirements, can have partial or various degrees of satisfaction. For example, the performance of COTS A may just meet the requirements and cost \$A, while COTS B gives a better performance than A and costs less than \$A. Then, we can say that the overall rating on the non-functional requirements for B is greater than A. This assignment of the overall rating depends on a wide variety of factors such as company policy, experience, costing and the specific CBS. Therefore, its evaluation requires human judgement and it cannot be automated. Let p_i be the overall assessment rating of the non-functional requirements of the COTS product e_i. Then, a list, $L_e = [(e_1, em_1, p_1), (e_2, em_2, p_2), \cdots, (e_z, em_z, p_z)]$, can be constructed to keep the COTS products together with their set of modules that satisfy both the functional and non-functional requirements of the CBS and their overall rating on the non-functional requirements.

Since L_e is constructed from L_d and $card(elem(L_e)) = z$, we have

1. $y \geq z$,
2. $xtp(1, elem(L_d)) \supseteq xtp(1, elem(L_e))$,
3. $\forall e_i, \exists em_i, p_i : (e_i, em_i, p_i) \in elem(L_e) \Rightarrow (e_i, em_i) \in elem(L_d)$.

Fig. 6 shows the relationship between the three types of COTS products (x COTS, y COTS and z COTS) and the CBS.

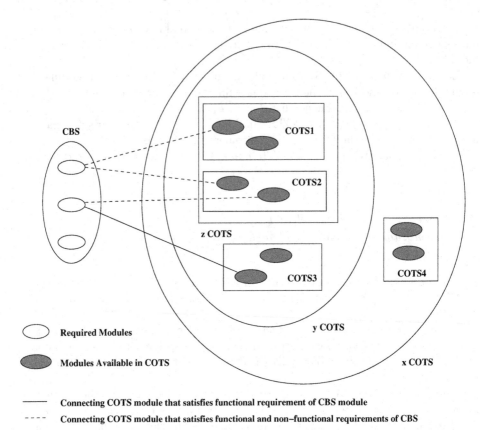

Fig. 6. CBS and related COTS

5.2   Domain-Based COTS-Product Selection
Using a Best-Fit Strategy

When selecting a COTS product using the DBCS method and the best-fit strategy, the following five steps are involved.

Step 1: *The modules that correspond to the CBS are identified from a domain model.*
The developers should be familiar with the system in question and also the corresponding domain model. Then, it is easy for the developers to build the mapping between the modules of the CBS and the corresponding domain model.

Step 2: *Identifiers of the COTS modules, which are mapped to the modules in the domain model from Step 1, are found through the mappings between the domain model and the COTS modules.*
These COTS modules are claimed (by the vendor) to functionally satisfy the modules of the domain model. Since the relation between an individual

COTS module and a specific domain model is a one-to-one mapping, the time required to search for the corresponding modules in the domain model during this step is directly proportional to the number of modules of the domain model.

If no mappings from COTS modules to a domain model are found, this means that no COTS module is applicable to that domain. Hence, the selection of COTS modules is finished with the result being no applicable COTS modules.

Step 3: *Information is collected on those COTS products that have modules selected during step 2.*

This step is used to identify the COTS products that are claimed to satisfy the functional requirements. There is no need to retrieve information about the COTS products during this step. Only the identifiers of the COTS products are required. This step is performed by consulting the mappings between the domain model and the sources of the COTS products. These mappings are provided by the vendors of the COTS products in advance, and they can be stored in computer systems or obtained through the Internet. Hence, this step is similar to retrieving information from databases.

Let the n modules in the domain model be denoted by $(n_1, n_2, \cdots, n_n)$. Let l_i denote the set of identifiers of the COTS modules that satisfy the functionality required of module n_i. Then, the list $L_n = [(n_1, l_1), (n_2, l_2), \cdots, (n_n, l_n)]$ denotes the list of modules in the domain model together with the set of identifiers of the modules of the COTS products. In the example shown in Fig. 5, there are three modules in the domain model, four COTS products available, and a total of six matching pairs of modules, so that $L_n = [(n1, c11, c21), (n2, c22, c31, c41), (n3, c42)]$. The time required to construct L_n can be seconds or minutes.

Step 4: *The COTS products are vetted against the non-functional requirements of the CBS.*

This step involves constructing $L_d' = [(d_1, dm_1), (d_2, dm_2), \cdots, (d_{y'}, dm_{y'})]$ from L_n. This includes two sub-steps: functional vetting and non-functional vetting.

- Functional vetting involves constructing the list of pairs given by $L_d'' = [(d_1, ldm_1), (d_2, ldm_2), \cdots, (d_y', ldm_y')]$ from L_n, where d_i is the ith COTS product and ldm_i is the set of identifiers of the modules of the ith COTS product that contains the functionally appropriate modules for the CBS.
- Non-functional vetting involves retrieving information about the COTS modules to form the list L_d' and checking that the non-functional requirements are met. In the example shown in Fig. 5,

$$L_d' = [\ (COTS1, (C11, n1)),$$
$$(COTS2, (C21, n1), (C22, n2)),$$
$$(COTS3, (C31, n2)),$$
$$(COTS4, (C41, n2), (C42, n3))]$$

Step 5: *The best COTS product is selected from the candidates that satisfy both functional and non-functional requirements.*

5.3 Domain-Based COTS-Product Selection Using a First-Fit Strategy

In applying the first-fit strategy, ideally, once we find a COTS product that fits all of the functional and non-functional requirements, we can stop the selection process. However, a suitable COTS product may not exist. If no COTS product satisfies all of the functional and non-functional requirements, then the one with the most modules that satisfy both the functional and the non-functional requirements is chosen.

The steps of the first-fit strategy of the DBCS method (DBCS-FF) are as follows:

0. Identify the corresponding modules of the CBS in the domain model.
1. **while** (there are unselected COTS products) **or**
                (no appropriate COTS product has been found) **{**
2.   Choose a COTS product;
3.   **if** (not all n modules in the domain model have
                mappings from this COTS product) **{**
4.   Insert the COTS product into the working list
            $L_w = [(d_1, dm_1), \cdots, (d_u, dm_u)]$;
5.   **} else {**
            Get information about the COTS products from the sources.
6.   **if** (it satisfies the non-functional requirements) **{**
                An appropriate COTS product has been found;
            }
        }
7. **} //** end while
8. **if** (no appropriate COTS product has been found) **and**
                (L_w is not empty) **{**
9.   Sort the list L_w in descending order according to $card(dm_i)$.
10.   **while** (there are COTS products in the sorted list) **and**
                (no suitable COTS product has been found) **{**
11.   Get the head of the sorted list;
12.   Retrieve information on the COTS product from the source;
13.   Check the non-functional requirements of the COTS product.
14.   **if** (it satisfies the non-functional requirements) **{**
                An appropriate COTS product has been found;
            }
15.   **} //** end while
16. **} //** end if

In using the DBCS-FF, since there are mappings between the COTS products and the domain model, all of the COTS modules that are functionally appropriate for the CBS can be obtained directly through these mappings. The DBCS-FF tries to find the first COTS product that functionally satisfies most of the modules of the CBS and also the non-functional requirements. The second half of DBCS-FF is used to handle the situation when no COTS product meets all of the functional requirements of the CBS, and the suitability of these partially matched COTS products are then accessed.

6   Discussion

Section 6.1 discusses the efficiency of DBCS while Section 6.2 substantiates the performance study by a case study of an on-line margin-trading system.

6.1   Efficiency of the DBCS Method

In this section, we make several observations on the efficiency of the DBCS method. In the set-up phase, the modules of the COTS products are first mapped to domain models by the vendors. Since the vendors have full information about the functionalities and features of the COTS products, it should be easy for them to decide how the modules are to be used in different domain modules. The mappings from the COTS modules to a domain model are reused each time a CBS from that domain is to be developed. Moreover, the mappings between the COTS modules and the domain modules help the vendors to market their products because they can demonstrate easily how their COTS products can be applied in an application domain.

Conceptually, the relation between a domain model and all of the COTS products is one-to-many. Since the mappings are developed from the COTS-product side to the domain-model side, it is still a one-to-one relation. Consequently, the complexity in developing the mapping is reduced. Furthermore, these mappings are reused in every CBS development. The mappings between the COTS products and the domain models can be managed via computing systems, and retrieving information about the COTS modules from the domain models can be done automatically. Consequently, much effort can be saved by using this approach.

In the selection phase, the first step is to identify the corresponding modules in the domain model for a CBS. This step is simple because a domain module has captured all of the features of the domain. The relation between a module of a CBS and its domain module is one-to-one. It should be easy for the developer of a CBS to identify the corresponding modules in the domain model.

Although the process of selecting the COTS products for these modules depends on the number of mappings, it is still a single and simple step because information on the COTS products can be collected through the defined mappings. Furthermore, if the mappings are well managed, after the modules of the domain models are identified, the mappings between the COTS products and the domain modules can be retrieved by automatic systems. This would be an accurate and efficient method to identify those COTS products that satisfy the functional requirements of a CBS. A weighting method based on the degree of functional fitness can then be used to help select the most suitable COTS product.

The DBCS method is an efficient method, as the one-to-many relation between a CBS and all of the COTS products is reduced to two relations, namely, a many-to-one relation between the COTS products and a domain model and a one-to-one relation between a domain model and a CBS. The latter relation is a simple relation and is handled easily. Although the former relation is complex to deal with, the vendors who possess all of the necessary information are able to easily solve this problem. We have reported the quantitative proof that the DBCS method is a more efficient method than a direct assessment method in [10].

6.2   A Case Study

We have applied the DBCS method to the development of an on-line margin-trading system and we have obtained encouraging results [11]. We have successfully developed a prototype margin-trading system for a large and leading bank in Hong Kong with the use of COTS products. The margin-trading system deals mainly with the margin trades between trading parties. It is one of the core activities in the banking and financial industry. Due to confidentiality requirements, we cannot release the functional details of this system.

In applying the DBCS method, the first requirement is the availability of a domain model for the specific application. Since an industrial-scale margin-trading domain model was not available for our research, our first step was to create such a domain model. This domain model was built by an experienced developer who had been working on a margin-trading system in a leading bank for several years. He was familiar with the business, the main activities, the detailed operations and the general architecture of a margin-trading system.

The construction of the domain model of margin-trading comprises three steps:

1. Gather domain knowledge
2. Perform domain analysis
3. Consolidate various domain models

The domain model was built using object-oriented technology and expressed in OMT (Object Modeling Technique).

In this study, we focused on the main function of the margin-trading system, namely, providing a trading environment for a dealer to perform a margin trade with various trading parties. It was decided to use COTS for two modules of the margin-trading system:

1. data security module
2. currency handling module

Fig. 7 shows the class diagram of the margin-trading system. Fig. 8 gives an example object diagram, showing a dealer starting a trading. Sample screen outputs are shown in Figures 9 and 10.

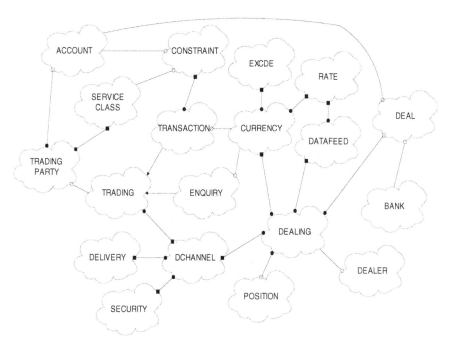

Fig. 7. Class diagram of margin-trading system

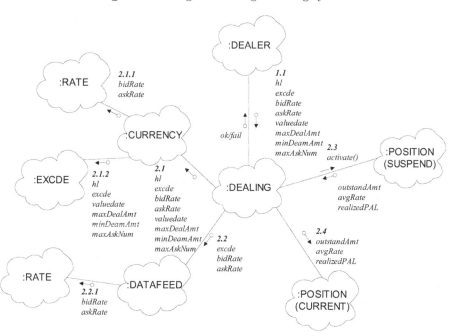

Fig. 8. Object diagram showing a dealer initializing a trading currency

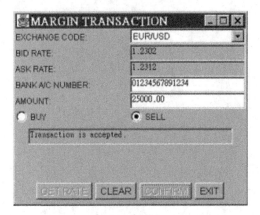

Fig. 9. Margin transaction screen at the trading site

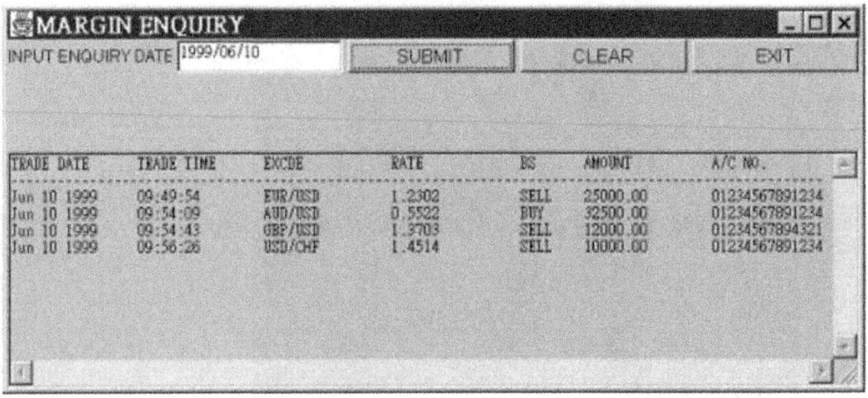

Fig. 10. Margin enquiry screen at the trading site

Before applying the DBCS to identify the best COTS available, we need to have a list of suitable COTS provided by the vendors, with the proper mapping to the domain model. As there was no such mapping available, we developed the mapping by ourselves. The non-functional criteria for the system included interoperability, performance, and ease of use.

We then mapped the modules of two COTS products to the modules of the margin-trading domain model. Afterwards, we asked the software developers to identify the COTS modules by following the steps of the DBCS method using both best-fit and first-fit strategies on the two modules.

When implementing the on-line margin-trading system in our case study, we collected data on the effort required for various activities. The data is shown in Table 2.

The values of the variables indicating the time required in various steps of our selection method are consistent with our assumptions about the expected scale of these variables.

Table 2. Values for Time Variables

Time	Scale	Effort/module
Average time for searching for a COTS product	Hours to Days	41 hours
Average time for vetting the functional appropriateness of a module of a COTS product	Hours to Days	5 hours
Average time for assessing the non-functional appropriateness of a module of a COTS product	Hours to Days	10 hours
Time required for getting information on the COTS products from the sources	Minutes	30 minutes
Average time required for identifying the modules, which are claimed to be functionally appropriate for a module of the CBS through the mappings between the COTS products and the domain model	Seconds to Minutes	30 minutes
Average time for identifying a module from a domain model	Minutes	30 minutes
Average time required for checking whether there is a mapping between a module of the COTS and the domain model	Seconds to Minutes	10 minutes

Our experience in developing the margin-trading system generated the following observations:

1. The DBCS method can reduce the complexity and improve efficiency in COTS selection. It breaks down the complicated many-to-many relationship between COTS products and system requirements into a one-to-one relation and a one-to-many relation.
2. The functional interfaces of the two COTS products used in our development did not fully match our system requirement. Software wrappers were needed to mask the mismatched interfaces. Fortunately, the effort in developing the wrappers was minimal compared to the estimated effort for developing the functionalities provided by the COTS products. We estimated that we saved two person-weeks of development time by using the two COTS products, compared to developing everything from anew.

This experiment indirectly shows that the DBCS method is better than a direct assessment method in terms of its efficiency.

Our case study also indicates that it is difficult to compare the performance of the best-fit strategy with the first-fit strategy because the performance of the latter depends on factors that cannot be fully controlled, as follows:

1. The position of the first acceptable COTS product in the sequence of COTS candidates. For example, if an acceptable COTS product happens to be the first one to be analyzed, then the first-fit strategy will succeed immediately.

2. The number of acceptable COTS products in the set of COTS candidates. If there are L acceptable COTS products in the set of N COTS candidates, then the average number of COTS products that is required to be analyzed by the first-fit strategy is L/N. The best-fit strategy will always analyze all of the N COTS products.

7 Conclusions

In this chapter, we have classified the methods for selecting COTS products into three classes: intuition, direct assessment and indirect methods. Most of the existing methods are based on selecting COTS products either by intuition or direct assessment. The former approach has the weakness of being subjective and it may omit good quality COTS candidates. The efficiency of the latter approach is inversely proportional to the product of the number of modules of the CBS in question and the total number of modules in the available COTS products. This can lead to a large selection effort that may offset the advantages of using the COTS products in the development.

We have developed a new indirect assessment method called the domain-based COTS-product selection method. We have applied the DBCS method to the development of a margin-trading system. The DBCS method reduces the complexity and improves the efficiency of COTS product selection. This is because the DBCS method takes advantage of the detailed view of the relations between the available COTS products and the CBS. Furthermore, the relations between the COTS products and the domain model are reused every time a CBS from the domain is to be developed. This helps to reduce the effort of selecting a COTS product for a CBS.

References

1. C. Alves and J. Castro. CRE: A Systematic Method for COTS Selection. In *Proc. of the XV Brazilian Symposium on Software Engineering*, Brazil, Oct. 2001.
2. C. Abts, B. Boehm and E. Bailey. COCOTS Software Integration Cost Model: an Overview. In *Proc. of the California Software Symposium*, Oct. 1998.
3. B. Boehm and C. Abts. COTS Integration: Plug and Pray. *IEEE Computer*, pages 135–138, Jan. 1999.
4. M. Broy, *et al.* What Characterizes a (Software) Component? *Software—Concepts and Tools*, 19(1):49–56, 1998.
5. Software Eng. Inst. Carnegie Mellon University. *The Capability Maturity Model: Guidelines for Improving the Software Process*. Addison-Wesley Publishing Company, Inc., Reading, Mass., 1995.
6. G. Fox, K. Lantner, and S. Marcom. A Software Development Process for COTS-based Information System Infrastructure. *Proc. of IEEE*, pages 133–142, 1997.
7. J. Kontio. A Case Study in Applying a Systematic Method for COTS Selection. In *Proc. of ICSE-18*, pages 201–209, 1996.
8. J. Kontio, S. F. Chen, and K. Limperos. A COTS Selection Method and Experiences of Its Use. In *Twentieth Annual Software Engineering Workshop*, 1995.

9. D. Kunda. Applying Social-Technical Approach for COTS Selection. In *Proc. of the 4th UKAIS Conference*, University of York, April 1999.

10. K. R. P. H. Leung and H. K. N. Leung. On the Efficiency of Domain-based COTS Selection Method. *Journal of Information and Systems Technology*, 44(12):703–715, September 2002.

11. K. R. P. H. Leung, H. K. N. Leung, and F. Suk. A COTS Selection Method Using Domain Model. Technical Report TR-20, Department of Computing, Hong Kong Polytechnic University, 1999.

12. N. Maiden and C. Ncube. COTS Software Selection: The Need to Make Tradeoffs between System Requirements, Architecture and COTS Components. In *COTS workshop*, 2000.

13. C. Rolland. Requirement Engineering for COTS-based Systems. *Information and Software Technology*, 41(14):985–990, 1999.

14. T. L. Saaty. Analytic hierarchy. In *Encyclopedia of Science & Technology*, pages 444–468. McGraw-Hill, 1997.

15. V. Tran and D. B. Lui. A Risk-Mitigating Model For The Development of Reliable and Maintainable Large-Scale Commercial-Off-The-Shelf Integrated Software Systems. In *Proc. of Annual Reliability and Maintainability Symposium*, pages 452–462, 1997.

16. V. Tran, D. B. Lui, and B. Hummel. Component-Based Systems Development: Challenges and Lessons Learned. In *Proc. of IEEE*, pages 452–462, 1997.

STACE: Social Technical Approach to COTS Software Evaluation

Douglas Kunda

Integrated Financial Management Information Systems (IBIS) Project
Ministry of Finance and National Planning, Lusaka, Zambia
dkunda@zamnet.zm

Abstract. COTS-Based Systems (CBS) development is a process of building systems from pre-fabricated Commercial-Off-The Shelf (COTS) software components. CBS success depends on successful evaluation and selection of software components to fit customer requirements. Selecting COTS software components to fit requirements is still a problem because of a number of problems including lack of a well-defined process, the "black box" nature of COTS components and the rapid changes in marketplace. This chapter reviews some existing frameworks that support COTS software selection and demonstrate that these frameworks do not adequately address the non-technical issues. The chapter then presents a social-technical approach for COTS software selection, how it deals with non-technical issues, its application in an organization and lessons learnt

1 Introduction

Modern software systems are becoming difficult and expensive to develop and organizations are turning to Commercial-Off-Shelf (COTS) software packaged solutions. COTS software package approach can potentially be used to reduce software development and maintenance costs, as well as reducing software development time by bring the system to the markets as early as possible. For example, most organizations spend too much effort defining to the lowest level of detail of the desired characteristics of the systems and how the contractor are to build the system when a COTS products already exist with nearly the same capabilities.

According to Oberndorf [27] the term "COTS" is meant to refer to things that one can buy, ready-made, from some manufacturer's virtual store shelf (e.g., through a catalogue or from a price list). It carries with it a sense of getting, at a reasonable cost, something that already does the job. The scenario of developing unique system components is replaced by the promise of fast, efficient acquisition of cheap (or at least cheaper) component implementations. Examples of COTS products include Geographic Information Systems (GIS), Graphical User Interface (GUI) builders, office automation, email and messaging systems, databases and operating systems.

A. Cechich et al. (Eds.): Component-Based Software Quality, LNCS 2693, pp. 64–84, 2003.
© Springer-Verlag Berlin Heidelberg 2003

There are two distinct ways to use COTS software. In one, a single complete working COTS software system that satisfies most of the user requirements is purchased and used as platform upon which to build a system [10]. For example a database management system can be purchased and used to build a payroll system. The second model is one which involves purchasing a number of COTS software components (usually without the source code) each satisfying some part of the requirements of the system and integrating these components into the required system [35]. The second model is important because many systems need functions in multiple orthogonal sub-domains, each of which tends to be addressed by a different COTS software package [10].

However, successful selection of COTS software to fit requirements is still problematic for a number of reasons. These include the lack of a well-defined process, the "black box" nature of COTS components, misuse of data consolidation method and rapid changes in market place. Kontio [19] points out that most organizations are under pressure to perform and therefore do not use a well-defined repeatable process. This makes planning difficult, appropriate evaluation methods and tools are not used, lessons from previous cases are not learnt and the evaluation process efficiency reduced. Another problem with COTS software selection is lack of inclusion of the "soft" issues or non-technical factors such as costs, organizational issues, vendor capability and reputation [29]. In order to address these problems a social technical framework for COTS evaluation (STACE) has been developed [20] and will be discussed in chapter.

2   Background

COTS software selection, also known as component qualification, is a process of determining "fitness for use" of previously-developed components that are being applied in a new system context [13]. Component qualification is also a process for selecting components when a marketplace of competing products exists. Qualification of a component can also extend to include qualification of the development process used to create and maintain it (for example, ensuring algorithms have been validated, and that rigorous code inspection has taken place) [7]. This is most obvious in safety-critical applications, but can also reduce some of the attraction of using pre-existing components.

There are three major strategies to COTS evaluation: progressive filtering, keystone identification and puzzle assembly [28]. Progressive filtering is a strategy whereby a component is selected from a larger set of potential components. This strategy starts with a large number of candidates set of components, progressively more discriminating evaluation mechanisms are applied in order to eliminate less "fit" components [22]. In keystone selection strategy, a keystone characteristic such as vendor or type of technology is selected first before selecting the COTS products [39]. Often, interoperability with the keystone becomes an overriding concern, effectively eliminating a large number of other products from consideration. The puzzle assembly model begins with the premise that a valid COTS solution will require fitting the various components of the system together as a puzzle and applies an evolutionary prototyping technique to build versions that are progressively closer to the final system [28].

2.1 COTS Software Evaluation Process

A number of researchers and organizations have proposed process models for evaluating COTS software (for example, [17,30]). However, most authors partition it into the following phases: requirements engineering; evaluation criteria definition, identification of candidate COTS products and assessment [8,19]. These phases are briefly discussed below (see Fig.1).

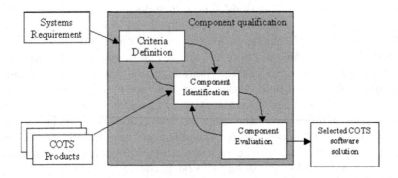

Fig. 1. COTS Software Evaluation Process

Requirements engineering covers all of the activities involved in determining requirements which will assist in establishing a basis for evaluating and selecting appropriate COTS software candidates. Tran, Liu and Hummel [35] argue that the requirements should be broken down and organized into collections of domain-specific requirements. This is important to support the early identification of candidate COTS products for evaluation as well as early identification of subsystems that cannot be supported by COTS products. In order to realize the benefits of COTS software, Vigder, Gentleman and Dean [37] suggest that a procurement process must be in place that defines requirements according to what is available in the marketplace. This is contrarily to the traditionally procurement process, which identifies strict requirements which either excludes the use of COTS components, or requires large modifications to COTS packages in order to satisfy the requirements. However, it is important that requirements are not defined so specifically that only one particular COTS product is suitable.

Defining the evaluation criteria. The criteria definition process essentially decomposes the high-level requirements for the COTS software into a hierarchical criteria set and each branch in this hierarchy ends in an evaluation attribute [19]. The criteria is specific to each COTS evaluation case but should include component functionality (what services are provided), other aspects of a component's interface, business concerns such as cost and quality aspects (e.g., reliability, portability, and usability) [8,17,35].

Identification of candidate components (alternatives). The identification of candidate components also known as alternative identification involves the search and screening for COTS candidate components that should be included for assessment in the evaluation phase [8,30]. Many authors highlight a number of techniques for identifying candidate COTS software including Internet search, market surveys, attending computer fairs and shows, invitation to tender (ITT) or request for proposals (RFP), vendor promotions and publications [19,31,35].

Assigning measure of merit to alternatives (evaluation phase). In the evaluation phase, the properties of the candidate components are identified and assessed according to the evaluation criteria [19,31]. Evaluation includes the acquisition of the products to be evaluated, developing evaluation plans, installing them, learning to use them, studying their features and assessing them against the criteria [35]. The methods and techniques for evaluation are discussed in the next section.

2.2   Methods and Techniques for Evaluation

Once the criteria are defined, the screened candidate products can be examined to observe to what extent they exhibit these or other useful attributes. The following are some of the techniques used to evaluate COTS software component:

- *Paper evaluation.* This is the process of evaluating the COTS products based on supplier data in sales brochure, technical documents, telephone conversations, web site information [22]. However, Beus-Dukic and Wellings [3] suggests that vendors claims must be viewed sceptically, therefore this technique must be used in combination other evaluation techniques.
- *Market survey.* A market survey can be made using questionnaires and interviews with vendors, trade shows, user community to compile quantitative and qualitative data about the product and vendors. Finkelstein, Spanoudakis and Ryan [12] point out that in certain circumstances, especially if the package to be bought is expensive, a request for proposal (RFP) can be issued, which enable the vendors to describe their packages in a uniform manner.
- *Experimentation.* This is a rigorous test of the product to assess its compliance with the defined criteria. The experimentation process includes the acquisition and installation of the product, design of the appropriate prototype and test plan, evaluation of product and generation of report [35]. Carney and Wallnau [8] stress the importance of conducting experimentation within the operating environment (context) in which the product will be used. Maiden and Ncube [22] recommend the use of software prototypes to assist in generating test cases for product evaluation. This especially important where the evaluator do not have prior knowledge about the candidate products or prior extensive experience generating test cases.
- *Pilot study.* A pilot study is an extended version of experimentation in which "real" data from the organization is used in the evaluation. Brown and Wallnau [6] argue that it is important to demonstrate the product or technology's feasibility with a pilot project. Sledge and Carney [34] points out that

because the potential for misinterpretation and misunderstanding when presenting or discussing a commercial product is great, hands-on evaluation of COTS products is mandatory and pilot programs are a useful way to do this.

- *Vendor analysis*. Hokey [15] points out that the vendor must be evaluated in terms of user services (installation assistance, training services and warranty) and vendor characteristics (vendor reputation and vendor stability). Checking vendor discontinuities, such as focus shifts and change of auditor, would help in this process. Haines et al. [13] and McDermid [23] argue that for safety-critical systems it is important to audit the development process that was used to develop the software including the tests carried out, conformance to standards, etc.

3 Problems with COTS Software Selection

The success of COTS-based software systems depends on successful evaluation and selection of COTS software components to fit customer requirements [22]. Successful selection of COTS software to fit requirements is still a problem because of a number of reasons. These include the following:

- *Lack of well-defined process*. Most organizations are under pressure to perform and therefore do not use a well-defined repeatable process [19]. The evaluators may not have the time or experience to plan the selection process in detail and therefore, they may not use the most appropriate methods in the selection process [19]. The resulting urgency means that evaluation decisions become pressured and a difficult decision becomes even more risky [29]. Furthermore, when the selection process is not defined, it is reinvented each time, it is performed inconsistently and learning from previous cases is difficult [19].
- *"Black box" nature of COTS components*. Lack of access to the COTS internals makes it difficult to understand COTS components and therefore evaluation is harder [37]. Sometimes even the supporting documentation for these components is incomplete or wrong. The design assumptions of the component are unknown; there is no source code when it needs debugging; and testing will be necessarily incomplete, since testing is only done for those functional capabilities that the customer care about [8].
- *Rapid changes in the market place*. The component user has little or no control over COTS product evolution [36]. Frequent releases of COTS components and rapid changes in the market place makes evaluation difficult [8]. For example, a new release of the COTS component may have a feature that is not available in the component that is currently being evaluated.
- *Misuse of data consolidation method*. A common approach to consolidating evaluation results is to use some kind of weighted sum method (WSM) [25]. However, the WSM has been criticized because assigning weights for the criteria sometimes can be inconsistent and lead to confusion about which is the most essential customer requirements [22].

However, the major problem with COTS software evaluation is that evaluators tend to focus on technical capabilities at the expense of the non-technical or "soft" factors such as the human and business issues [9,29]. Oberndorf et al. [28] highlight the usefulness defining the criteria to include such issues as vendor's time in business, responsiveness to customers and willingness to support their product. Therefore, the evaluation criteria must incorporate both technical attributes and non-technical issues such as business issues and vendor capability variables.

4   COTS Software Evaluation and Multi-attribute Decision Making

Carney and Wallnau [8] argue the COTS software selection is a form of decision making. Kontio [19], Maiden and Ncube [22] support this view and further point out that it is a Multiple Attribute Decision-Making (MADM) process. MADM refers to making preference decisions (for example evaluation, prioritization, selection) over the available alternatives that are characterized by multiple, usually conflicting attributes [41]. The goal of MADM is (a) to help the decision maker choose the best action or alternative of those studied (a choice or selection procedure), (b) to help sort out alternatives that seem "good" among a set of alternatives studied (a sorting or segmentation procedure), and/or (c) to help rank the alternatives in decreasing order of preference (an ordering or ranking procedure) [24]. According to Yoon [41], MADM share the following characteristics:

- *Alternatives*: A finite number of alternatives, from several to thousands, are screened, prioritized, selected and/ or ranked.
- *Multiple attributes*: Each problem has multiple attributes or goals or criteria. For each problem setting relevant attributes are generated, for example, to purchase a car you may have price, gas mileage, safety and warranty period.
- *Incommensurable Units*: Each attribute has different units of measurement.
- *Attribute Weights*: Almost all MADM methods require information regarding the relative importance of each attribute, which is usually supplied in an ordinal or cardinal scale.
- *Decision matrix*: A MADM problem can be concisely expressed in a matrix format, where columns indicate attributes considered in a given problem and rows list competing alternatives.

A number of MADM techniques have been applied in software selection, the most common are weighted sum or scoring method [40], analytical hierarchy method [15,19,22] and outranking method [1,25].

4.1   Weighted Sum Method

The Weighed Sum Method (WSM) or scoring method is one of the simplest and probably the most popular technique for solving multi-attribute decision problems [24]. The WSM is based on the multiple attribute utility theory with the following axiom: any decision-maker attempts unconsciously (or implicitly) to maximize some function by aggregating all the different points of view which are taken into account [38]. A score in this method is obtained by adding contributions from each alternative and since two items with different measurement units cannot be added, a common numerical scaling system such as normalization is required to permit addition among attributes values [41]. The total score for each alternative then can be computed by multiplying the comparable rating for each attribute by the importance weight assigned to the attribute and then summing these products over all the attributes.

The main advantage of the WSM is its ease of use and helping the decision-maker to structure and analyze the decision problem [24]. However, Mollaghasemi and Pet-Edwards [24] criticize the WSM arguing that this method tends to involve ad hoc procedures with little theoretical foundation to support it. This can lead to confusion about the most essential customer requirements [22] and make worst products on important attributes have the highest aggregated scores [25]. Another weakness is that it is difficult to define a set of criteria and their weights as advocated in the WSM so that they are either independent of each other or if they overlap, their weights are adjusted to compensate for overlapping areas [19]. This suggests that WSM might not be suitable for aggregating COTS software evaluation attribute data because most COTS software attributes are not independent of each other.

4.2   Outranking Method

Outranking methods are a class of multi-criteria decision-making techniques that provide an ordinal ranking (and sometimes partial ordering) of the alternatives [24]. It has been successfully applied to COTS software evaluation and selection [1,25]. Roy [32] developed the outranking approach and a family of evaluation methods collectively known as ELECTRE methods that are founded on the outranking relations. Yoon [41] points out that ELECTRE methods dichotomizes preferred alternatives and non-preferred ones by establishing outranking relationships. An outranking relationship (A outranks B) states that even though two alternatives A and B do not dominate each other, it is realistic to accept the risk of regarding A as almost surely better than B [41].

The advantage of this approach is the ability to consider both objective and subjective criteria and the least amount of information required from the decision maker [24]. Morisio and Tsoukias [25] suggest that outranking methods are appropriate when the measurement scales of criteria are of an ordinal and when it is not possible to establish trade-offs between criteria. Mollaghasemi and Pet-Edwards [24] point out that, although it can be expressed that alternative A is preferred to alternative B in the outranking method, it does not indicate by how much, for example with ELECTRE I a complete ranking of the alternatives may not be achieved. Therefore, this method is not appropriate for COTS software selection involving tenders that require explaining to the unsuccessful bidders why their bid was unsuccessful and how they were ranked.

4.3   Analytical Hierarchy Process (AHP)

AHP was developed by [33] for multiple criteria decision making and has three basic functions: (1) structuring complexity, (2) measuring on a ratio scale, and (3) synthesizing. AHP has been successfully applied in software and computer selection [42,19,22]. AHP enables decision-makers to structure a multi-criteria decision making problem into a hierarchy [41]. A hierarchy has at least three levels; the overall goal of the problem at the top, multiple criteria that define alternatives in the middle and competing alternatives at the bottom.

AHP technique is based on pair-wise comparison between the alternatives. The result of this pair-wise comparison is converted to a normalized ranking by calculating the eigenvector from the comparison matrix's largest eigenvalue. Section 1.5.3 provides a worked example of the use of AHP. The advantage of the AHP technique is that it provides a systematic approach for consolidating information about alternatives using multiple-criteria [19]. The availability of several software packages to support the AHP has made it a popular technique [24]. AHP also provides a means for measuring the consistency of the decision-maker's judgements, that is, to check the quality of the results in the comparison matrix [24,42].

AHP has been criticized regarding the rank reversal: the reversal of the preference order of alternatives when new options are introduced in the problem [11,24]. Furthermore, that the use of a 1 to 9 measurement scale is inappropriate because of the ambiguity in the meaning of the relative importance of one factor when compared to another. However, Harker and Vargas [14] argue that rank reversal occurs in AHP because ranking of alternatives depends on the alternatives considered, hence, adding or deleting alternatives can lead to changes in the final rank and this is consistent with rational behavior. Furthermore, since AHP facilitates group decision-making it would be suitable for COTS software selection process that emphasizes participation. In addition, AHP would be appropriate for aggregating COTS software evaluation attribute data comprising technical and non-technical issues because it incorporates both quantitative and qualitative data into the decision making process.

5   Social Technical Approach to COTS Software Evaluation (STACE)

A number of frameworks for evaluating and selecting COTS software components have been proposed in literature. Useful work includes Delta technology framework that help evaluate new software technology [7] and PORE, a template based method to support requirements acquisition for COTS product selection [22]. Although the Delta technology framework is useful for evaluating new technology it does not address the political and economic factors that often separate a winning technology from other contenders. The weakness of PORE method is that it is labor-intensive and vulnerable to the neglect of social issues. Another technique the OTSO [19] addresses the complexity of component selection and provides a decision framework that supports multi-variable component selection analysis but neglects the non-technical issues or "soft" factors. Other approaches, such as the Software System Evaluation Framework (SSEF) [4] focuses on assessing the software product, process and their impact on the organization but it does not provide guidance on how to define the evaluation criteria. The following presents a summary of characteristics, strengths and weaknesses of each of these frameworks.

SSEF – *Characteristics*
  - It proposes a top-down approach that identifies the important elements that a software system must include to foster high-level understanding.
  - Uses knowledge world's concepts (i.e., usage world, development world and system world).
  - Multiple viewpoints approach to evaluation (user satisfaction and economic returns).
  - Defines the elements (dimensions, factors, and categories) clearly to facilitate evaluation and reduce the evaluators' conflicting viewpoints.
  - It is organized along three dimensions corresponding to the software's producers, operators, and users.

 – *Strengths*
  - It provides a baseline for establishing metrics programs in organization [4].
  - It offers a broad system snapshot by considering a number of different perspectives (end users, developers, and operators) [7].
  - A top-down approach has the advantage of flexibility, permitting extensions by following a predefined pattern [4].

 – *Weaknesses*
  - It is not specific to COTS selection and the issues of how to define the evaluation criteria are not addressed [19].
  - It gives little detailed insight into the strengths and weaknesses of a technology in comparison with its peers [7].

OTSO – *Characteristics*
  - Provides explicit definitions of tasks in the selection process, including entry and exit criteria [19];
  - Advocates incremental, hierarchical and detailed definition of evaluation criteria;
  - Provides a model for comparing the costs and value associated with each alternative, making them comparable with each other;
  - Uses appropriate decision-making methods to analyze and summarize evaluation results.

 – *Strengths*
  - It addresses the complexity of COTS software evaluation [7].
  - The systematic repeatable process can promote learning through experience and improve the COTS selection process [19].
  - The use of the AHP provides evaluation consistency and provides structured information.

– *Weaknesses*

- AHP is only appropriate when there are few comparisons and when all criteria are independent [22]
- Neglect of non-technical issues or "soft" factors [29].

Delta – *Characteristics*

- Evaluate a new software technology by examining its features in relation to its peers and competitors
- It is a systematic approach that includes modelling and experiments.
- That technology evaluation depends on understanding technology "delta" descriptions of how a new technology's features differ from other technologies.
- Evaluates how these "delta" differences address the needs of specific usage contexts.

– *Strengths*

- It provides techniques for evaluating the product underlying technology.
- It can also facilitates individual product evaluations that concentrate on their distinguishing characteristics in relation to their technology precursors and product peers [6].

– *Weaknesses*

- It focuses on technology evaluation and neglect product and vendor evaluation
- It does not address the political and economic factors that often separate a winning technology from other contenders.

PORE – *Characteristics*

- It integrates existing requirements engineering methods and other techniques such as feature analysis and multi-criteria decision-making.
- It is template-based (templates provide guidelines for conducting evaluation).
- It advocates for a parallel and an iterative requirements acquisition and product selection/rejection.

– *Strengths*

- It provides guidance to model requirements for COTS software selection
- The parallel requirements acquisition and COTS software selection means requirements acquisition informs COTS software selection and vice versa.

– *Weaknesses*

- Use of traditional approaches make it vulnerable to neglect of social issues
- It is labor-intensive.

STACE – *Characteristics*
- It supports a systematic approach to COTS evaluation and selection
- It proposes a keystone evaluation strategy in which the underlying technology is selected before selecting the COTS products.
- It uses social-technical techniques (i.e., social-technical criteria and participation) to improve the COTS software selection process.
- It uses multi-criteria decision-making techniques (i.e. AHP) to consolidate evaluation attribute data.

– *Strengths*
- It addresses the non-technical issues through use of social-technical techniques.
- It supports evaluation of both COTS products and the underlying technology.
- It provides for reuse of lessons learnt from previous evaluation cases.
- Use of the AHP promotes consensus, transparency and consistency checking.

– *Weaknesses*
- It increases the cost of the evaluation process because of inclusion of non-technical issues and user participation.
- Some aspects of AHP having subjective bias.
- Some users/ stakeholders may not make an effective contribution.

In general what is missing in these frameworks is how to address the "soft" issues or the non-technical factors, such as costs, organizational issues, vendor capability and reputation. Therefore, STACE was developed to facilitate a systematic requirements-driven COTS software selection and address this problem using social-technical techniques. Furthermore, STACE supports the evaluation of both COTS products and the underlying technology while the other frameworks emphasize product or technology evaluation. Another advantage of STACE is that it provides for reuse of lessons learnt from previous evaluation cases by maintaining a database of evaluation results.

5.1   Objective and Principles of STACE

The STACE framework has been developed through literature survey and case studies [20]. STACE is based on a number of important principles:

– Support for a *systematic approach* to COTS evaluation and selection. Most organizations select their COTS components in an ad-hoc manner. There is a need, for example, to reuse lessons learnt from previous evaluation cases by maintaining a database of evaluation results.
– Support for *evaluation of both COTS products and the underlying technology*. Most COTS evaluation frameworks emphasize either COTS products evaluation or technology evaluation. This method proposes using keystone evaluation strategy in which the underlying technology is selected before selecting the COTS products.

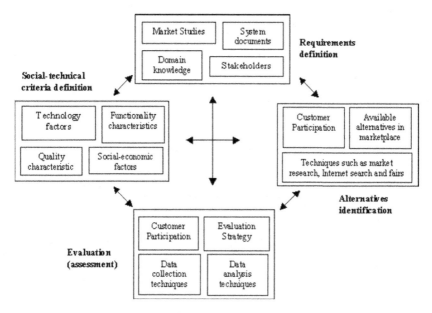

Fig. 2. STACE Framework

- Use of *social-technical techniques* to improve the COTS software selection process. This has been greatly influenced by the social-technical school and work by [26]. STACE recommends the use of a social-technical evaluation criteria and customer participation in the COTS selection process. User participation is regarded as an effective strategy as a means of improving software design outcomes and as a means of incorporating human and organizational aspects such as the design of jobs, work processes and usability [5,2].
- Use of *multi-criteria decision-making techniques* to consolidate evaluation attribute data. The STACE proposes the use of Analytic Hierarchy Process (AHP) as developed by Saaty [33] and successfully used in software selection [19,42].

5.2 STACE Method

The STACE method (see Fig. 2) comprises four interrelated processes: 1) requirements definition; 2) social-technical criteria definition; 3) alternatives identification; and 4) evaluation or assessment.

In the requirements definition process, the high-level customer and systems requirements are discovered through consultation with stakeholders, from system documents, domain knowledge and market studies. The traditional requirements engineering methods emphasize the technical issues while neglecting the equally important social issues [18]. Therefore, the STACE framework recommends the use of the social-technical approach to systems development. Customer participation is one of the strategies used in social-technical approaches to incorporate

the social issues in the development of the system. The STACE framework recommends the use of Joint Application Development (JAD) sessions and review
meetings with top management to elicit and validate requirements from stakeholders. The use of JAD or stakeholder workshops is an important strategy that
operationalizes customer participation.

In the social-technical criteria definition process, the high-level requirements
from the requirements definition phase are decomposed into a hierarchical criteria set and each branch in this hierarchy ends in an evaluation attribute [19]. The
STACE framework uses a decomposition approach that is based on social technical analysis and the AHP criteria decomposition method. The STACE framework
recommends decomposition of the high level requirements into a hierarchy of
social-technical criteria comprising functionality characteristics, technology factors, product quality characteristics, and social-economic factors. Socio-economic
factors are non-technical factors that should be included in the evaluation and
selection of COTS components such as costs, business issues, vendor performance
and reliability.

The objective of the alternatives identification process is to identify COTS
components that meet the high level requirements, so that they can be considered for a more rigorous evaluation. In the STACE framework, this phase
begins with identifying the domains relevant to the problem and understanding the types of packages available in those domains. The STACE framework
recommends a number of techniques and tools for identifying candidate COTS
products. These include networking, mailing list and user community, Internet search, market surveys, invitation to tender (ITT) or request for proposals
(RFP), vendor promotions and publications.

The evaluation or assessment phase involves contacting vendor technical support for evaluation information, reviewing vendor documentation and product
testing for quality and functionality. It also includes evaluating COTS performance, interfaces and ease of integration, comparing short-term and long-term
licensing costs against integration costs. STACE recommends the keystone selection strategy with the technology as the keystone issue. The separation of
COTS underlying technology from COTS products during evaluation allows fair
comparisons between products.

The STACE framework also recommends separating the data collection and
data analysis of the evaluation. Kontio [19] argues that the advantage of separating the data collection from analysis is to allow the use of appropriate decision
making techniques in the data analysis stage. There are a number of data collection techniques such as examining the products and vendor supplied documentation, vendor analysis, viewing demonstration and interviewing demonstrators,
executing test cases and applying the products in pilot projects. STACE proposes selecting appropriate techniques depending on resources and experience.
STACE framework recommends the use of the AHP to consolidate evaluation
data because of a number of advantages discussed in section 1.4.3.

Table 1. Social-technical criteria for GIS software selection

FUNCTIONALITY	QUALITY ATTRIBUTES
Data Capture (digitize)	Interoperability
Data Integration	Efficiency/Resource utilization
Projection and registration.	Usability
Data restructuring	**NON-TECHNICAL FACTORS**
Data and topological modelling	Vendor reputation
Information retrieval	User experience
Map overlays	Local support
Data Output	**COSTS ISSUES**
Internet support	Product cost
ODBC support	

5.3   Application of STACE Method

The STACE method was used by a public organization mandated to protect the environment and control pollution. The organization was established in 1992 with an annual budget of about $1million and employs over sixty persons, seven of which are in the IT department. The main application of IT in this organization is Geographic Information Systems (GIS). The organization was using standalone ArcInfo 4.2D and ArcView software while some of the users were trained in Idrisi. The organization installed a Local Area Network (LAN) and STACE method was used to select new GIS software in a multi-user LAN environment.

The workbook to operationalize the STACE framework was developed and used to guide the organization in evaluating and selecting COTS software. The workbook explicitly describes each stage of the STACE framework. The organization was invited to attend a workshop at which the STACE framework and workbook were presented and discussed.

STACE Process in Selecting a GIS Software. The following are the step by step description of the procedures used to evaluate and select the GIS software.

Step 1: Requirements definition. The sponsor and stakeholders from the organization were identified. It was agreed with the sponsor regarding the composition of the evaluation team and the resources required for the evaluation work. The high level user requirements were elicited from system documents, domain knowledge, and interviews with stakeholders.

Step 2: Social-technical criteria definition. The high level requirements were decomposed in social technical criteria. According to the STACE method the social-technical criteria include: 1) technology factors, 2) functionality characteristics, 3) product quality characteristics, and 4) social-economic factors. The technology criteria was not used in the hierarchy priority because technology was adopted as the keystone and therefore all the software to be selected must be compatible with the keystone in this case Windows 2000. The social-economic factors were divided into non-technical issues and cost issues because of the importance

Table 2. Relative importance of criteria

	Functionality attributes	Quality attributes	Non-technical	Costs issues	Relative importance
Functionality attributes	1	3	4	5	0.550
Quality attributes	1/3	1	2	2	0.214
Non-technical	1/4	1/2	1	2	0.142
Costs issues	1/5	1/2	1/2	1	0.094
Total					1.000

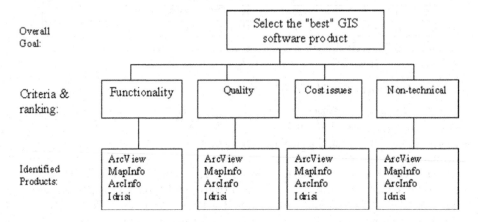

Fig. 3. Hierarchy of Criteria and GIS Products

separating cost issues from other attributes. The outcome of this process is the social-technical criteria presented in table 1.

Step 3: Using AHP to determine the relative importance of the criteria. Using pairwise comparisons, the relative importance of one criterion over another was computed. A total number of six pairwise comparisons were made to calculate the AHP's eigen vector values and these are shown in Table 2. The result in Table 2 shows that the functionality attributes is the most preferred criterion and cost issues is the least preferred criterion. Pairwise comparisons were also computed for the sub criteria to determine the relative importance of the sub criteria relative to the criteria. These are presented later in the chapter.

Step 4: Identify candidate software (vendors). The search for candidate products was conducted using the GIS user community; Internet search; vendor publications and sales promotions. The identified products were screened to reduce them to ArcView, MapInfo, ArcInfo and Idrisi (see Fig. 3). The basis of screening was the technology criteria and user experience with the products. It was required that the product must run on Windows 2000 and at least one user from within the organization must be familiar with the product.

Step 5: Evaluation and priority ranking of the candidate product. Evaluation copies of the candidate software were obtained. The evaluation involved con-

Table 3. Priority ranking of candidate product

	Relative importance	ArcView	MapInfo	ArcInfo	Idrisi
Functionality					
Data Capture	0.100	0.038	0.060	0.712	0.190
Integrate	0.100	0.222	0.057	0.681	0.040
Projection and registration.	0.100	0.109	0.042	0.666	0.182
Data restructuring	0.100	0.050	0.081	0.510	0.359
Data and topological modelling	0.100	0.050	0.081	0.510	0.359
Powerful information retrieval	0.100	0.597	0.251	0.061	0.090
Map overlays	0.100	0.034	0.063	0.684	0.219
Data Output	0.100	0.089	0.029	0.607	0.275
Internet	0.100	0.715	0.176	0.046	0.062
ODBC	0.100	0.090	0.295	0.567	0.048
Quality attributes					
Interoperability	0.540	0.169	0.451	0.261	0.119
Efficiency/Resource utilization	0.163	0.123	0.346	0.358	0.173
Usability	0.297	0.487	0.311	0.084	0.118
Non-technical factors					
Vendor reputation	0.250	0.286	0.286	0.286	0.143
User experience	0.500	0.472	0.108	0.256	0.164
Local support	0.250	0.372	0.150	0.372	0.106
Costs issues					
Product Cost	1.000	0.174	0.104	0.098	0.625

tacting vendor technical support for evaluation information, review of vendor documentation and experimenting with the product to assess its quality and functionality. It included evaluating product performance, interfaces and ease of integration, comparing short-term and long-term licensing costs. In addition data collection included interviewing actual users of the products, and examining sample outputs from projects that have used the products.

Having experimented with the software and reviewed documentation the alternatives were assessed against criteria, for example in terms of quality characteristics, pairwise comparisons are made to determine the preference of each alternative over another. The eigenvector were then calculated from these matrices and the result is shown in the Table 3. The table also provides the relative ranking of each sub criteria, for example each functionality sub criteria is of equal importance (0.100).

From table 3 above it can be concluded that regarding data capture ArcInfo is the most preferred product (preference=0.712) while ArcView is the least preferred (preference=0.038). The results also shows that ArcInfo is preferred in almost all the functionality except support for Information retrieval and support for Internet in which ArcView was preferred.

Step 6: Using AHP to synthesize the evaluation results and select the product. The priority ranking were then synthesized with the help of ExpertChoice, a

Table 4. Results of evaluation exercise

	Priority ranking of criteria	ArcView	MapInfo	ArcInfo	Idrisi
Functionality	0.550	0.274	0.110	0.480	0.136
Quality attributes	0.214	0.256	0.392	0.224	0.128
Non-technical factors	0.142	0.400	0.293	0.163	0.144
Costs issues	0.094	0.174	0.104	0.098	0.625
Overall of GIS software		**0.279**	**0.196**	**0.344**	**0.181**

software tool that supports AHP process and the results shown in Table 4. The table shows that ArcInfo is the recommended GIS software package for the organization. It can be noted from this table that although Idrisi scored highly regarding costs issues it did not emerge as the winning package because according to the organization cost issues had low ranking compared to functionality issues.

Experience in Using STACE. The organization pointed out that they found STACE framework useful because it addresses the non-technical issues and brought about decision support satisfaction. They argued that the use of AHP brought about confidence in the evaluation results and also promoted consensus in evaluation process. In addition, because the AHP provides an audit trial, it made the whole evaluation process transparent. However, the organization indicated that the AHP involved too many pairwise comparisons when the criteria increased, in their case they made over 100 pairwise comparisons for what they considered to be simple software selection process. Furthermore, they indicated that some aspects of AHP were subjective.

The organization indicated that stakeholder participation as advocated in the STACE framework is very important in COTS software evaluation and selection as it facilitates dialogue and consensus building with stakeholders. However, the organization indicated that the inclusion of stakeholder participation increases the cost of the software evaluation process.

6   Future Research

The STACE framework provides a classification of important processes (including traditional and soft factors) that support COTS software selection. The framework also allows the classification of a set of techniques and tools within each process. It highlights relationships between processes (and factors within each process) and thus facilitates the examination of relationships between factors in different processes and their impact on the success of COTS software selection process. The identification of important processes and factors supporting COTS software evaluation and selection has highlighted a number of areas that require further research. For example, future work can focus on the examination of each of the identified factor and its impact on the COTS software selection process. Further work can also investigate the relationships between the factors and the organizations, or draw conclusions about COTS component selection in different organizations.

The evaluation of the STACE framework revealed the problem of additional costs introduced by the inclusion of non-technical issues in the evaluation criteria and customer participation [21]. Furthermore, that the evaluation process takes a longer time because of additional work. A number of templates were provided to speed up the process and reduce the additional work of reinventing for evaluation criteria, each time the evaluation is done. However, the problem was not completely solved. Therefore, future work can focus on the development of a software tool to support all the processes in the STACE framework. The software tool would automate the evaluation process; suggest techniques and criteria according to the type of evaluation problem; management of past evaluation results in order to inform future evaluation cases; and support the use of a multi-criteria decision method. This would initially involve developing the prototype and then testing it in a number of organizations.

In the STACE framework, the AHP was proposed for consolidation of evaluation data because it incorporates both objective and subjective measures into decision making process. However, the AHP has a number of problems, for example that AHP has a potential for bias and subjectivity especially when dealing with non-technical issues. Furthermore, that the AHP is time consuming because of the mathematical calculations and the number of pairwise comparisons that increases as the number of alternatives and criteria increases. Therefore, further work can focus on developing a software tool that supports the AHP and addresses some of these problems. Future work can also investigate the use of other multi-criteria techniques, such as outranking.

This chapter focussed on COTS software evaluation and selection supporting the Component-based software development. However, this has implications for the other stages of the software development cycle. For example, systems built using COTS packages will require maintenance and enhancements, some prompted by vendor updates and changing customer requirements. Therefore, determining procedures or guidelines for deciding when to accept upgrades would be an interesting research area.

7   Conclusion

Component-based development is a process of building software systems by integrating multiple software that are ready "off-the-the shelf" whether from a commercial source (such as COTS) or re-used from another system. Building systems from COTS software components offers the opportunity to lower costs by sharing them with other users and has potential for reduced training and infrastructure costs. Therefore, by employing this strategy, organizations will not spend too much time on developing expensive systems, with only one customer to bear the development and maintenance costs over the life of the system.

Building of systems from COTS software depends on successful evaluation and selection of COTS software to meet customer requirements. COTS software evaluation and selection ensures that a candidate component will perform the functionality required and will exhibit the quality characteristics (e.g. performance, reliability, usability) that are required. A number of problems associated with COTS software evaluation and selection have been identified including rapid changes in market place; lack of well-defined process; "black box" nature of COTS components; and misuse of data consolidation method. COTS software evaluation and selection frameworks have been developed aimed at addressing these problems, for example the OTSO framework; Delta technology framework and PORE framework.

However, what is missing in these frameworks is the "soft" issues or the non-technical issues such as costs, organizational issues, vendor capability and reputation. Furthermore, these frameworks do not provide a means for identifying and classifying important processes and factors supporting COTS software selection for practical use. Therefore, the STACE framework was developed. The STACE framework addresses the weaknesses of the existing evaluation models by attempting to ensure that all issues (including non-technical) are structured and addressed. This is achieved by integrating social-technical criteria as well as customer participation in the COTS software evaluation process. Customer participation provides for consensus building during evaluation by allowing evaluators and stakeholders to discuss and agree on evaluation parameters. The framework also provides a structured evaluation model; thus allowing the designation of a hierarchy of selection criteria based on organizational needs. The evaluation and selection process is clearly defined, in terms of processes, techniques to be used and activities to be performed.

The STACE framework provides a classification of important processes (including traditional and soft factors) that support COTS software selection. The framework also allows the classification of a set of techniques and tools within each process. It highlights relationships between processes (and factors within each process) and thus facilitates the examination of relationships between factors in different processes and their impact on COTS-based systems success. Therefore, the framework could be used for research purposes not only in COTS software evaluation research but also in the wider software engineering research field.

References

1. Anderson E., "A heuristic for software evaluation and selection," Software Practice and Experience, Vol. 19, No. 8, pp. 707–717, August 1989.
2. Axtell C. M., Waterson P. E. and Clegg C. W. (1997), "Problems integrating user participation into software development," International Journal of Human-Computer Studies, Academic Press Limited, Vol. 47, pp 323–345.
3. Beus-Dukic, L. and Wellings A., "Requirements for a COTS software component: a case study," Conference on European Industrial Requirements Engineering (CEIRE '98), Requirements Engineering, Springer-Verlag, Vol.3, No.2, pp. 115–120, October 1998.
4. Boloix, G. and Robillard, P. (1995), "A Software System Evaluation Framework," IEEE Computer, Vol. 28, No. 12, pp. 17–26.

5. Bravo E., "The Hazards of leaving out users," In Participatory Design: Principles and Practices, Schuler D. and Namioka A. (eds.), Lawrence Erlbaum Associates, Hillsdale, NJ, pp. 3–12, 1993.

6. Brown A. W. and Wallnau K. C., "A Framework for Systematic Evaluation of Software Technologies," IEEE Software, Vol. 13, No. 5, pp. 39–49, 1996a.

7. Brown A. W. and Wallnau K. C., "Engineering of Component-Based Systems," in Brown A. W. (ed.), "Component-based Software Engineering: Selected papers from Software Engineering Institute," IEEE Computer Society Press, Los Alamitos, California, pp. 7–15, 1996b.

8. Carney D. J. and Wallnau K. C., "A basis for evaluation of commercial software," Information and Software Technology, Vol. 40, pp. 851–860, 1998.

9. Clements P. C. (1995) From Subroutines to Subsystems: Component-Based Software Development, American Programmer 8(11), Cutter Information Corp.

10. Coppit D. and Sullivan K. J., "Multiple mass-market applications as components," Proceedings of the International conference of Software Engineering (ICSE), IEEE computer society, Los Alamitos, California, pp. 273–282, 2000.

11. Dyer J. S., "Remarks on the Analytical Hierarchy Process," Management Science, Vol. 36, No. 3, pp. 249–259, 1990.

12. Finkelstein A., Spanoudakis G. and Ryan M. (1996), "Software Package Requirements and Procurements," Proceedings 8th International Workshop on Software Specification and Design, IEEE Computer Society Press, pp. 141–145.

13. Haines G., Carney D. and Foreman J., "Component-Based Software Development/COTS Integration," Software Technology Review, Software Engineering Institute, http://www.sei.cmu.edu/str/descriptions/cbsd_body.html, 1997.

14. Harker P. T. and Vargas L. G., "Reply to – Remarks on the Analytical Hierarchy Process – by J. S. Dyer," Management Science, Vol. 36, No. 3, pp. 269–273, 1990.

15. Hokey M., "Selection of Software: The Analytic Hierarchy Process," International Journal of Physical Distribution and Logistics Management, Vol. 22, No. 1, pp. 42–52, 1992.

16. IEEE std 1209–1992 (1993), IEEE Recommended Practice for the Evaluation and Selection of Case Tools, IEEE, New York.

17. ISO/IEC 9126: 1991, "Information technology-Software product evaluation-Quality characteristics and guidelines for their use," ISO/IEC, Geneva, 1991.

18. Jirotka M. and Goguen J. A. (eds.) (1994), "Requirements Engineering social and technical issues," Academic Press Limited, London.

19. Kontio, J. (1996), "A Case Study in Applying a Systematic Method for COTS Selection," Proceedings of the 18th International Conference on Software Engineering (ICSE), IEEE Computer Society.

20. Kunda, D. and Brooks L. (2000), "Identifying and Classifying Processes (traditional and soft factors) that Support COTS Component Selection: A Case Study," European Journal of Information Systems, Vol. 9, No. 4, pp. 226–234, 2000.

21. Kunda, D. (2002), "A social-technical approach to selecting software supporting COTS-Based Systems," PhD dissertation, University of York.

22. Maiden N. A. and Ncube C. (1998), "Acquiring COTS Software Selection Requirements," IEEE Software, pp. 46–56.

23. McDermid J. A., "The Cost of COTS", IEEE Computer, Vol. 31, No. 6, pp. 46–52, 1998

24. Mollaghasemi M. and Pet-Edwards J., "Technical briefing: making multiple-objective decisions", IEEE computer society press, Los Alamitos, California, 1997.

25. Morisio M., and Tsoukis A., "IusWare: a methodology for the evaluation and selection of software products," IEEE Proceedings of Software Engineering, Vol. 144, No. 3, pp. 162–174, June 1997.
26. Mumford E. (1995), Effective Systems Design and Requirements Analysis: The ETHICS Approach, Macmillan Press Ltd, Hampshire.
27. Oberndorf P. (1997) Facilitating Component-Based software Engineering: COTS and Open Systems, Proceedings of the Fifth International Symposium on Assessment of Software Tools, IEEE Computer Society, Los Alamitos, California.
28. Oberndorf P. A., Brownsword L. and Morris E., "Workshop on COTS-Based Systems," Software Engineering Institute, Carnegie Mellon University, Special Report CMU/SEI-97-SR-019, November 1997.
29. Powell, A., Vickers, A. and Lam, W. (1997), "Evaluating Tools to support Component Based Software Engineering," Proceedings of the Fifth International Symposium on Assessment of Software Tools, IEEE Computer Society, Los Alamitos, pp. 80–89.
30. Puma Systems, Inc., "Commercial-Off-The-Shelf System Evaluation Technique (COSSET)," http://www.pumasys.com/cosset.htm, March 1999.
31. Rowley J. E. "Selection and Evaluation of Software," Aslib Proceedings, Vol. 45, pp. 77–81, 1993.
32. Roy, B., "The Outranking Approach and the Foundations of ELECTRE Methods," Theory and Decision, Vol. 31, pp. 49–73, Kluwer Academic Publishers, Netherlands, 1991.
33. Saaty, T. L. (1990), The Analytic Hierarchy Process, McGraw-Hill, New York.
34. Sledge C. and Carney D., "Case Study: Evaluating COTS Products for DoD Information Systems," SEI Monographs, http:www.sei.cmu.edu/cbs/ monographs.html, July 1998.
35. Tran, V., Liu D. and Hummel B., "Component-based systems development: challenges and lessons learned," Proceedings of the Eighth IEEE International Workshop on Software Technology and Engineering Practice incorporating Computer Aided Software Engineering, IEEE Computer Society, Los Alamitos, California, pp. 452–462, 1997.
36. Vigder M. R. and Dean J. (1997), Architectural Approach to Building Systems from COTS Software, Proceedings of the 1997 Center for Advanced Studies Conference (CASCON 97), Toronto, Ontario.
37. Vigder M. R., Gentleman W. M. and Dean J. (1996) COTS Software Integration: State of the art, National Research Council, Canada, NRC Report Number 39198.
38. Vincke P., "Multicriteria decision-aid," Wiley publishing, Chichester, 1992.
39. Walters N., "Systems Architecture and COTS Integration," Proceedings of SEI/MCC Symposium on the use of COTS in systems Integration, Software Engineering Institute Special Report CMU/SEI-95-SR-007, June 1995.
40. Williams F., "Appraisal and evaluation of software products," Journal of Information Science, Principles and Practice, Vol. 18, pp. 121–125, 1992.
41. Yoon, K. and Hwang C. (1995), "Multiple Attribute Decision-Making: an Introduction," Sage Publisher.
42. Zviran, M. (1993), "A Comprehensive Methodology for Computer Family Selection," Journal of Systems Software, Vol. 22, pp 17–26.

SCARLET: Integrated Process and Tool Support for Selecting Software Components

N.A.M. Maiden[2], V. Croce[2], H. Kim[1], G. Sajeva[2], and S. Topuzidou[3]

[1] Centre for HCI Design, City University
Northampton Square, London EC1V OHB, UK
[2] Engineering sPA, Via Dei Mille, 56 Roma 00185, Italy
[3] ATC, 1 Astronafton St., Paradissos Amaroussion 151 25, Athens, Greece

Abstract. This chapter describes the SCARLET Process Advisor, a web-enabled workflow software tool that delivers process guidance to software engineers who are selecting software components and commercial off-the-shelf (COTS) packages. It presents two forms of process guidance delivered by SCARLET – goal-based process guidance based on workflow techniques, and situated process guidance that delivers local process guidance to achieve goals in different situations. The chapter describes the software components and work flow engine needed to guide software component selection using requirements, and how it provides inputs to BANKSEC's Systems Integration Manager tool. The chapter ends with a summary of the expected innovation and future exploitation by the originating BANKSEC project.

1 Introduction

SCARLET (Selecting Components Against Requirements) is a tool-supported process that the EU-funded BANKSEC consortium has developed to guide software component selection. It integrates the use of scenarios, prototypes and measurable fit criteria into an iterative process of acquiring requirements and selecting components using these requirements as selection criteria.

In this chapter we describe SCARLET's integrated process description and software tool that, together, provide process guidance to a component procurement team (CPT). The tool, called the SCARLET Process Advisor, integrates workflow and internet technologies with situated process models to offer such a team the right advise at the right time during a component selection process. In most component selection activities it is difficult to prescribe sequences of lower-level processes to achieve higher-level goals, let alone what are the best techniques to use to achieve them. For example, information about customer requirements, components, suppliers, and procurement contracts is often not available in the order in which it is needed, so the sequence of the acquisition, analysis and decision-making processes cannot be preordained. Furthermore, information acquisition and software selection processes are often interwoven, in that the successful completion of one process often depends on the successful completion of the other. Therefore the SCARLET Process Advisor guides the

A. Cechich et al. (Eds.): Component-Based Software Quality, LNCS 2693, pp. 85–98, 2003.

procurement team using information about current selection situation. It implements the SCARLET process guidance model to recommend technique(s) that the CPT should use to undertake processes by inferring general properties about the state of the customer requirements and their compliance to candidate components. Unlike existing methods, the Process Advisor is not an add-on to the SCARLET process but an integral part of it – the process cannot be implemented effectively without the software tool.

The remainder of this chapter will be in 4 sections. Section 2 describes related work on selecting software components, then Section 3 describes the SCARLET process in sufficient detail to understand the its Process Advisor software tool. Sections 4 and 5 describe the SCARLET Process Advisor itself and its linked Software Integration Manager tool. The chapter concludes with a review of the reported research and future exploitation directions.

2   Related Work

Although there has been considerable research on COTS software package and component selection, little of it has addressed the need to integrate process and software tool support for selection activities. Burgues et al. [1] report methodological process guidance for COTS package selection but do not report software tools to support the process. Likewise component selection and evaluation methods such as EPIC and PICA [2] do not address software tools to aid selection. Elsewhere multi-criteria decision-making techniques such as the AHP have been used to select software [3] – software tools such as *ExpertChoice* are available to apply these techniques but do not support acquisition or evaluation activities.

In contrast, integrated process and software tools are central to SCARLET. We believe that effective situated process guidance cannot be given without software tools, while tailored software tool support is not possible without the precise process guidance found in SCARLET. The next section introduces the SCARLET approach in more detail.

3   The SCARLET Process

SCARLET provides process guidance for procurement teams during a concurrent systems development process, in which stakeholder requirements, the system architecture and solution components are all determined at the same time [4]. Stakeholder requirements inform the architecture design and component selection, and the designed architecture and selected components generate and constraint current stakeholder requirements. Although process guidance for acquisition, modeling and decision-making is driven by the current procurement situation, SCARLET also provides a higher-level procurement process that is goal-driven, prescriptive, and common to all procurement processes.

3.1   Goal-Driven Process Guidance

SCARLET prescribes 4 essential goals for any component selection process. These goals are to reject candidate components according to non-compliance with different types of customer requirements:

1. Simple customer requirements – high-level services and functions, requirements on the supplier or procurement contract, basic features of the software component such as price and source, adherence to international standards;
2. Simple customer requirements that require access to the software component through demonstration or use – lower-level services and functions, demonstrable attributes of the software component such as interface features, simple dependencies between customer requirements and component features;
3. Simple customer requirements that are demonstrable through short-term trial use of the software component – non-functional requirements such as performance, throughput, usability and training (where appropriate);
4. More complex customer requirements with dependencies to other requirements and legacy systems – non-functional requirements that require more extensive trial use, such as maintenance and reliability requirements, interdependencies with other software components, systems and legacy systems.

The rationale for this decision-making sequence is a simple and pragmatic one – to make the right and most simple decision at the most appropriate time in the procurement process using reliable information that is available to the CPT. As such the sequence relies on a set of assumptions – that information about components that enables the team to determine compliance with simple customer requirements is more readily available that the information needed to assess compliance with complex, interdependent non-functional requirements.

3.2   Situated Process Guidance

SCARLET prescribes four processes to achieve the 4 decision-making goals listed above:

1. Acquire information about customer requirements, software components, suppliers and procurement contracts;
2. Analyze acquired information for completeness and correctness;
3. Use this information to make decisions about component-requirement compliance;
4. Reject one or more candidate products as non-compliant with customer requirements.

Unlike the high-level decision-making objectives, the order in which these 4 processes are undertaken is situation-driven, that is the order is determined by the current state of customer requirements and compliance mappings between these requirements and component features. The achievement of each essential goal is a broad sequence, in which the first process is acquisition of information from stakeholders and the last is selection of one or more candidate components, but the sequence of the intervening processes is not predetermined and each process can be repeated many times.

However, during component procurement a large number of situations may arise at any point in the process and many techniques from different disciplines

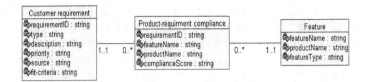

Fig. 1. The basic structure of the situation model, and the relationships between customer requirements, software components and compliance associations between requirements and component features

are available to achieve each situation. This large space of possible situations requires tool support to search it and recommend the correct process guidance. As a basis for delivering this process guidance SCARLET provides a situation model for process guidance through this complex space of situations and techniques. A situation is modelled in three parts shown in Fig. 1. We use the industry standard Unified Modelling Language (UML) [5] to represent a situation. The first part models the current state of the customer's requirements. The second part models compliance relationships between customer requirements and component features. The third part models specific features of software components. This meta-model is specified at length in [6].

SCARLET delivers situated process guidance through the Process Advisor tool by retrieving Process Chunks that link different techniques to different situations that the CPT encounters during an instance of the SCARLET process. These Process Chunks encapsulate much of the authors' expertise about requirements engineering and component selection that we have built into SCARLET process. The current version of the process specifies Process Chunks that provide guidance 53 situations using queries that act on process repositories. Each Process Chunk is defined using attribute values that make it distinctive from other chunks. These attributes include the numbers of totals of stakeholder requirements, candidate components and component features that have been acquired and specified, and the number and nature of compliance mappings between stakeholder requirements and component features. For most projects this space is too large to search manually, and the correct process guidance cannot be offered unless the method experts are available. Rather, the search mechanisms and knowledge-based advice must be software tool-based. The remainder of this chapter outlines this software tool.

4   The SCARLET Process Advisor

The SCARLET Process Advisor is part of a software product that has been developed as part of the BANKSEC consortium to support component-based software engineering. It integrates data management with decision-making support tools and has 6 components:

1. The **Process Designer** is an external tool used to design the SCARLET process that will be implemented by SCARLET Process Advisor. The process is represented using a proprietary Process Definition Language;

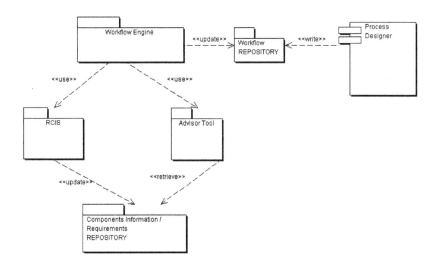

Fig. 2. The SCARLET Process Advisor's Architecture

2. The **Workflow Repository** contains the formalized data about the process undertaken to select the right software components;
3. The **Workflow Engine** is the central feature of the software package. It is responsible for the execution of the process and includes the interface used by the system to interact with members of the CPT;
4. The **Requirements-Components Integration System**, or **RCIS** for short, implements the interface that the CPT uses to populate the repository based on the SCARLET meta-model;
5. The **Requirements-Components Repository** stores information about all of the processes under execution and information about customer requirements, candidate components and their features, and established compliance mappings between requirements and component features;
6. The **Process Advisor** tool is the module which implements the SCARLET process according to its workflow specification and situation meta-model. The process is specified as a rule set that controls the execution of the process.

The overall architecture of the SCARLET Process Advisor is shown in Fig. 2. The architecture describes the interaction among Process Advisor components. The BANKSEC team uses the Process Designer tool to populate the Workflow Repository with the Workflow model of the SCARLET process, which is then published to the Workflow Engine. The Workflow Engine controls each instance of the SCARLET process by invoking the RCIS and Process Advisor tools according the SCARLET process stored in workflow Repository.

The principal output from the SCARLET Process Advisor is process advice for the CPT members on demand, in terms of:

- The next process goals to achieve (e.g. acquire more functional requirements);
- Techniques to use to achieve these process goals (e.g. brainstorming sessions
  and use case walkthroughs), and information and sources of information
  about these techniques presented as web-pages;
- Information about individual requirements, software components and component features to consider when applying the techniques (e.g. component
  features that might comply with the functional requirements being acquired).

BANKSEC's workflow engine, a workflow management system called FORO
[7], supports the management of processes and their constraints in a co-operative,
distributed environment. FORO was originally developed and distributed by
SchlumbergerSema. It supports the whole process from analysis and development
to execution of workflow processes. Analysis is carried out on a graphical manner
in a very easy to use way with the design tool. Once the design is done, FORO
provides a number of tools to implement the process and execute it.

4.1   The Process Designer Tool

The Process Designer tool was originally included in the FORO-WF tool produced by SchlumbergerSema. FORO-WF is a tool designed and built as part of
the European-funded WIDE and IB projects. The Process Designer tool provides
an intuitive graphical flow-diagram language for defining workflow processes.
Furthermore it enables users to export processes into a proprietary Process Definition Language (PDL). Processes represented using this PDL are then parsed
and published so that they can be executed using the Workflow Engine.

As above mentioned, we have used FORO's Process Designer tool to design
the SCARLET process as a workflow model. FORO tool is a self-contained
package for workflow design and management. It has a client-server architecture
and the FORO server, including its workflow engine, runs under the Linux-
Unix operating system. The SCARLET Process Advisor runs with the Workflow
Engine under Windows OS to provide sufficient but limited functionality from
FORO-WF needed for the SCARLET process.

4.2   The SCARLET Workflow

An instantiation of the main SCARLET workflow starts with the CPT defining
the process-specific parameters described later in section 4.3.1. Once the parameters have been set up, the next step is to execute C-Preview. In the BANKSEC
solution we determine high-level stakeholder and system requirements that are
independent of component selection process using the PreView method [8] that
is independent of the SCARLET process. We also use C-PreView to establish a
high-level system architecture that imposes technical requirements for component selection in SCARLET.

SCARLET also prescribes the 4 essential goals described in section 3.1. Each
goal is achieved using a workflow task. Fig. 3 shows part of the workflow diagram

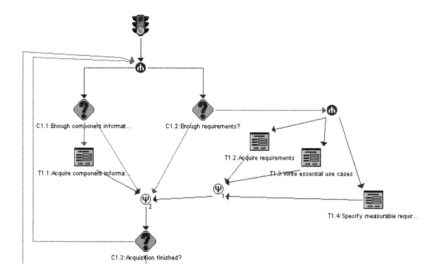

Fig. 3. A part of the workflow diagram of Goal1

for Goal 1. SCARLET encourages the concurrent acquisition of component information and requirements. SCARLET instructs the CPT to acquire component information (task T1.1) as long as the test that enough component information (C1.1) has been acquired is false. Acquiring stakeholder requirements is more complex. SCARLET recommends 3 concurrent but related tasks to acquire requirements (T1.2), write essential use cases (T1.3) and specify measurable requirements (T1.4), all controlled by the condition C1.2, which tests whether enough requirements of certain types have been acquired. The parameter values that control conditions C1.1 and C1.2 are described in Section 4.3.1.

The use of a repository, implemented as a database, allows permanent maintenance of both the process instructions and information. Furthermore it enables a CPT to support several procurement process into the same SCARLET Process Advisor tool.

4.3 The SCARLET Workflow Engine

The bespoke SCARLET workflow engine acts as an interpreter to execute instructions coded into the SCARLET process workflow definition. For each instance of the SCARLET process the workflow engine instantiates both data collection and a program counter. It also provides baseline process guidance to the CPT, and delegates task execution to software tools that make up the Process Advisor. For example, it delegates execution to the RCIS for managing information about stakeholder requirements, candidate components and requirements-component compliance mappings, and to the SIM tool used in the final phase to verify the syntactic compatibility of the selected components.

Parameterizing the SCARLET Process. Component selection processes can differ. If the CPT is selecting a large ERP-type package [9] there might only be 2 or 3 candidates to select from, whereas there are numerous software virus checkers available on the market [10]. In some cases the CPT will have a large number of established stakeholder requirements but little understanding of the components that are available to satisfy them – in other cases the candidate components will be well-understood but few stakeholder requirements have been established. To tailor SCARLET to these different component selection scenarios, SCARLET includes 9 parameters that are supported in the Process Advisor software tool. At the beginning of a process instance the CPT sets these parameter values to customize the execution of the workflow definition. The parameters are:

- **The SCARLET process goals to achieve**: SCARLET is composed of 4 essential goals to reject candidate components according to non-compliance with different types of customer requirements, as described in Section 2.1. The CPT can choose to achieve all 4 goals or a sequence of some of these goals. Naturally not all possible sequences are allowed;
- **Component range**: For each essential goal selected above the CPT can define the minimum and maximum number of candidate components that should be selected at the end of that goal, thus restricting the candidate component space throughout the SCARLET process. This parameter allows the CPT to adapt the Process Advisor to different domains and types of components;
- **Requirement types**: The CPT can choose the types of requirements to utilize within the process from the SCARLET requirement taxonomy [6]. The CPT can exclude requirement types that are inappropriate for their application or that should not be used as criteria for component selection;
- **Component feature types**: Likewise the CPT can select the feature types to use for the current application. Feature types are defined according to the SCARLET component meta-model [6];
- **Minimum level of requirement compliance**: This parameter defines the overall level of requirement compliance that each component needs to demonstrate in order to be categorized as compliant with stakeholder requirements for each essential process goal. The CPT can select a value on a normalized scale of [0,1]. For each requirement type the parameter represents the number of requirements that the component complies with divided by the total number of important requirements, where we define a requirement as important if the value of its customer satisfaction attribute is 4 or 5 on a scale from 1 to 5;
- **SCARLET process time scale**: For each activity the CPT can select the likely duration of the activity in terms of hours, days, weeks and months, thus enabling SCARLET to produce processes that are tailored to the project time available;
- **Process techniques**: The CPT can select the subset of all SCARLET techniques, specified in SCARLET process chunks, to use during the application

of the SCARLET process. As such the CPT can restrict itself to using a small set of tried-and-tested techniques on shorter or more focused component procurement projects;

- **Software tools**: Likewise the CPT can select a subset of available external software tools related to SCARLET techniques;
- **Process restart**: The CPT can state whether the process can be restarted after a complete session.

4.4 The SCARLET Process Advisor

The SCARLET Process Advisor delivers both goal-driven and situated process advice from the Workflow Engine to the CPT. Process advice is delivered in terms of sequences of process chunks that the CPT should follow.

Goal-Driven Process Advice. The SCARLET Process Advisor delivers goal-driven process advice to the CPT using the specified workflow models instantiated by the Workflow Engine. This advice can be thought as process advice that is independent of a domain or process situation. Fig. 4 demonstrates different features of SCARLET's process advice. It shows the Advisor's main process guidance window. The top part of the window describes the current SCARLET process goals and the active tasks in the workflow model that have been instantiated for this process. The CPT is currently seeking to achieve Goal3 by undertaking 3 tasks marked as active in the workflow engine - Evaluate components (T3.7), Select and reject these components (T3.8) and Extending the current set of use cases (T3.3b). The current live task is T3.7 - evaluate the components under selection. The CPT can then access more detailed information and process advice through the Goal-Driven Advice and Situated Advice windows. For example the current situated process advice is to recommend the use of the AHP method [11] to assist in the component evaluation process. Fig. 4 also demonstrates an example of more detailed, goal-driven process advice that is offered by SCARLET. Task T1.1 is a task specified in the SCARLET workflow model that guides the CPT to acquire information about candidate software components. Each task is divided into steps such as *what types of information to acquire from suppliers* and *how to search for software components*. This process advice is situation-independent - it is offers in all instances of the process in which the process parameters reveal that this process advice is available to the CPT.

Finally, Fig. 4 also demonstrates how the CPT can interact with the RCIS to input or edit information that is used by the Process Advisor to check whether goal-driven processes are complete, or to request more situated process guidance. Members of the CPT can add, edit and delete information about stakeholder requirements, candidate components and their features, or compliance mappings between requirements and component features. Fig. 4 shows the results of some component evaluation task, in which component features are identified as compliant or otherwise with stakeholder requirements. For example, the requirement

Fig. 4. The SCARLET Process Advisor's main control window, example goal-driven process advice, and the RCIS tool for defining requirement-component compliance relationships

"Internet banking site" complies with the feature Web-site publishing, and this compliance association has been weighted using MCDM techniques with a score of 9.

Situated Process Advice. Situated process advice is presented to the CPT using the same web-enabled interface. Whenever the CPT seeks advice, the Process Advisor fires situation queries that enable it to infer the current situation. Therefore, for each task within each goal phase the CPT receives both the goal-driven advice and situated process advice that is related to the process chunk(s) that are triggered by the current inferred situation. Fig. 5 shows an example of situated process advice – *using card sort techniques to acquire requirements that discriminate between candidate software components* in a situation where there is insufficient discrimination between components. The presented process chunk advises the CPT to use card sorts in different ways, then provides links to diverse, more detailed sources of information about and examples of such sort techniques. Fig. 5 also shows how the CPT can record the results of decision-making, i.e. which components to select and which components to reject. To support this process the RCIS provides the CPT with recommendations that are based on automatic computations from the earlier evaluation results, although the CPT may override these results if it do not agree with them.

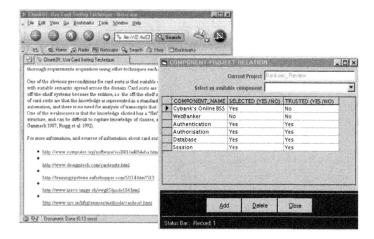

Fig. 5. Process advice on the use of card sorting techniques

The SCARLET process and Process Advisor produces different outcomes include selected software components and requirements that each component does or does not satisfy. The BANKSEC project provides an another software tool, called the Systems Integration Manager, that is linked to the Process Advisor through common data bases and enables the CPT to undertake first-cut system and architecture design using the selected components. This tool is described in the next section.

5   The System Integration Manager (SIM) Tool

The System Integration Manager (SIM) tool takes the results of the SCARLET process and guides the integration of selected components into applications. It enables the user to design applications models comprising of components and provides guidelines for subsequent implementation. Its use results in a model showing the components required for building the application, together with the essential links between these components for implementing the integrated environment. Additionally, implementation guidelines are produced that describe the derived model and the interrelationships between the components. The SIM tool is also invoked by the same Workflow Application tool which supports the SCARLET process. It passes the required process-specific parameters to SIM using an XML file.

The CPT can either open an existing application model or create a new one. SIM provides the graphical interface shown in Fig. 6 to model the component architecture. On the left side of the screen is a tree-style list of the components selected using the SCARLET process. The degree of trustworthiness of each component is represented using a simple color scheme - red indicates that the component is considered un-trusted for the application, whereas trusted components are indicated in black.

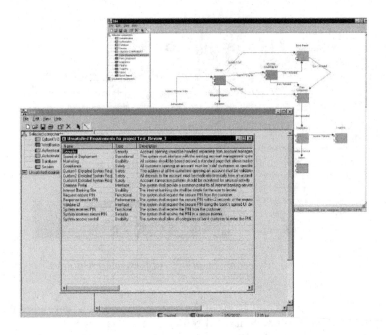

Fig. 6. Some of the SIM tool's graphical interfaces

A user starts by dragging and dropping selected components into the drawing space. The SIM tool enables the user to link the selected components using the link icon of the toolbar. The user can then add more details about the link's implied functions and component parameters. The user can also export the architecture model in XML format using UML notations into external tools such as Rational Rose. Requirements that may not have been satisfied yet through the components selected and identified are also indicated and corresponding details are provided. Finally SIM also provides a list of implementation guidelines to be subsequently used for integrating the components into applications. These guidelines include a description of the designed model, a report on the links between the components and the relationships between their functions, and a list of unsatisfied requirements, if any. These guidelines could be saved as a text file, so that they might be subsequently used during implementation for integrating the components into applications.

6   Conclusions and Future Work

The SCARLET Process Advisor is one of the first integrated component-based software engineering process environments. The SCARLET workflow, and in particular its sequence and pre-conditions, enabled us to tightly integrate processes and techniques from requirements acquisition, knowledge engineering, feature modeling and multi-criteria decision-making. The Process Advisor software tool represents an innovative mechanism for delivering process guidance to software development teams. The Advisor's web-site integrates process guidance with techniques that are specific to the SCARLET process and more general techniques that have been integrated into SCARLET, with references to external sources about these techniques.

More generally, SCARLET is one of the few implemented and industrialized examples of situated process models and process chunks for software development first reported in [12, 13]. Rolland and her colleagues define a process chunk using the NATURE process modeling formalism. A process transforms an initial situation into a result that is the target of the intention of the chunk. Although situated process models have been the subject of much academic research, there has been little empirical validation and exploitation. One innovation of the BANKSEC project was to develop and evaluate such a process advisor tool.

During the BANKSEC project we evaluated SCARLET with 2 partner banks. Both of the banks applied the SCARLET process manually rather than using the Process Advisor tool, due mainly to the unavailability of the tool before the end of the project, alas. Results from these evaluations were positive, as we will report in the future. However, the effectiveness of the SCARLET Process Advisor tool remains to be evaluated.

Acknowledgements

The authors wish to acknowledge the input and support of their colleagues in the BANKSEC consortium, and the financial support of the European Commission on IST-1999-20711 BANKSEC project.

References

1. Burgués, X., Estay, C., Franch, X., Pastor, J.A., Quer, C., 2002, "Combined Selection of COTS Components", Proceedings 1st International Conference on COTS-Based Software Systems, Springer-Verlag Lecture Notes in Computer Science 2255, 54-64.
2. Albert C., Brownsword L., "Evolutionary Process for Integrating COTS-Based Systems (EPIC): An Overview", Technical Report CMU/SEI-2002-TR-009, Software Engineering Institute, Carnegie-Mellon University, Pittsburgh.
3. Kontio, J., 1996, "A Case Study in Applying a Systematic Method for COTS Selection", Proceedings 18th International Conference of Software Engineering, IEEE, Computer Society Press, 201-209.
4. Maiden N.A.M., Kim H., 2002, "SCARLET: Light-Weight Component Selection in BANKSEC", In Business Computer-based Software Engineering", Ed. F. Barbier, Volume 705, Kluwer Academic Publishers, Boston, 49-63.
5. Booch G., Jacobson I., Rumbaugh J., 1999, "The Unified Modelling Language User Guide", Addison-Wesley-Longman.
6. Maiden N.A.M., Kim H., Ncube C., 2002, "Rethinking Process Guidance for Software Component Selection", Proceedings 1st International Conference on COTS-Based Software Systems, Lecture Notes on Computer Science 2255, Springer-Verlag, 151-164.

7. Gutiérrez G.S., 1999, "The WIDE Project: Final Report", ESPRIT Project 20280, May 1999.
8. Kotonya G., Sommerville I, 1998, "Requirements Engineering: Processes and Techniques", John Wiley & Sons.
9. Curran T.A., Ladd A., 1998, "SAP R/3 Business Blueprint", Prentice-Hall.
10. Ncube C., Maiden N.A.M., 2001, "Selecting the Right COTS Software: Why Requirements are Important", In "Component-Based Software Engineering: Putting the Pieces Together" (eds. George T. Heineman, William T. Councill), Addison-Wesley 467-478.
11. Saaty T.L., 1988, "The Analytic Hierarchy Process", University of Pittsburgh.
12. Rolland C., Grosz G., 1994, "A General Framework for Describing the Requirements Engineering Process", IEEE Conference on Systems, Man and Cybernetics, CSMC94 , San Antonio, Texas, 1994.
13. Plihon V, Rolland C. ,1994, "Modeling Ways of Working", Proceedings 7th International Conference on Advanced Information Systems Engineering, CAiSE'95, Springer Verlag.

Component-Based Software: An Overview of Testing

Auri Marcelo Rizzo Vincenzi[1], José Carlos Maldonado[1],
Márcio Eduardo Delamaro[2], Edmundo Sérgio Spoto[2], and W. Eric Wong[3]

[1] Instituto de Ciências Matemáticas e de Computação, Universidade de São Paulo
São Carlos, São Paulo, Brazil
{auri,jcmaldon}@icmc.usp.br
[2] Faculdade de Informática, Fundao Eurípedes Soares da Rocha
Marília, São Paulo, Brazil
{delamaro,dino}@fundanet.br
[3] Department of Computer Science, University of Texas at Dallas
Richardson, Texas, USA
ewong@utdallas.edu

Abstract. Component-based development makes heavy use of Object Oriented features which have motivated a major re-evaluation of software testing strategies. This chapter introduces the basic concepts of software testing focusing on the state-of-the-art and on the state-of-the-practice of this relevant area in the context of component-based software development.

1 Introduction

Software testing is a crucial activity in the software development process. Its main goal is to reveal the existence of faults in the product under testing: a program unit or a component. It is known as one of the most expensive activities in software development that can take up to 50% of the total cost in software development projects [1]. Besides its main objective—to reveal faults—the data collected during the testing phases are also important for debugging, maintenance, and reliability assessment.

Before software testing starts it is necessary to identify the characteristics of the input and output data required to make the component run (for instance, type, format and valid domain of that data), as well as how the components behave, communicate, interact and coordinate with each other. The Testing Plan is a document in a Test Design Specification that defines the inputs and expected outputs and related information like expected execution time for each run, format of the output and testing environment. Any anomaly found during testing should be reported and documented in a Test Incident Report.

In order to perform software testing in a systematic way and on a sound theoretical basis, testing techniques and criteria have been investigated. Testing techniques are classified as functional, structural, fault based, and state based, depending on the source used to determine the required elements to be exercised (the test requirements). Testing techniques and criteria are the mechanisms available to assess testing quality.

A. Cechich et al. (Eds.): Component-Based Software Quality, LNCS 2693, pp. 99–127, 2003.

Concerning the functional (black box) technique, testing requirements are obtained from the software specification. The structural technique uses implementation features to obtain such requirements, and the fault-based technique uses information about common errors that can occur during the development. In the state-based technique the requirements are obtained from a state-based specification like a Finite State Machine [2] or a Statechart [3]. These testing techniques are complementary and the question to be answered is not "Which one to use?" but "How to use them in a coordinated way, taking advantage of each one?"

According to Freedman [4], the research in software testing has been concentrated on two main problems:

− Test effectiveness: What is the best selection of test data?
− Test adequacy: How do we know that sufficient testing was performed?

Each of the above mentioned techniques has several criteria that define specific requirements that should be satisfied by the test data. In this way, requirements determined by a testing criterion can be used either for test data evaluation or test data generation. Since exhaustive testing, i.e., executing the product under test with its entire input domain, is not possible in general, test effectiveness is related with to task of creating the smallest test set for which the output indicates the largest set of faults. Testing adequacy is related to the determination of the effectiveness of a test criterion [4].

The object oriented (OO) paradigm has been extensively used, in particular because of its potential to promote component reuse. In general, component development uses much of the OO terminology. It is possible, though, to have components implemented according to the procedural paradigm, for instance, as COBOL procedures or C libraries, although, currently, most parts of software components are developed by using OO methodologies and languages.

As defined in [5], a software component is a unit of composition with contractually specified interfaces and explicit context dependencies only. A software component can be deployed independently and is subject to composition by third parties. Reusable components exist in several different types. In general, a software component can be as simple as an individual class or module, or as sophisticated as a JavaBeans, Enterprise JavaBeans [6] or COM objects [7]. It can be observed that software components inherit many characteristics of the OO paradigm, but the notion of components transcends the notion of objects. Reuse in OO in general means reuse of class library, in a specific programming language. Components can be reused without knowledge of the programming language or environment in which they have been developed [8, 9].

Encapsulation, inheritance, polymorphism, and dynamic binding bring benefits to software design and coding but, on the other hand, introduce new challenges to software testing and maintenance [10]. Software testing should incorporate the intrinsic characteristics of OO and component-based development. Considering specifically the component-based approach, two points of view related to testing can be observed: the provider's and the user's point of view.

Component providers test their components without knowledge about the context of their applications. Component users in their turn test their applications possibly without access to the component source code or data about the testing performed on them by the providers.

In the last decade, several tools and criteria have been developed for program testing [11, 12]. In the 90's researchers also started to concentrate on investigating approaches to test OO programs and components [13, 14]. With the adoption of component technology, component users observed that the quality of their component-based systems was dependent on the quality of the components they used and on the effectiveness of the testing activity performed by the component providers.

Software components may range from in-house components to Commercial Off-The-Shelf (COTS) components. The former allow clients to have complete access and control, including the development process. For the latter, on the other hand, knowledge about the development or testing processes may not be accessible. In this chapter we consider components implemented by using the OO approach. This implies that, from the provider point of view, the problems related to component testing are similar to those for OO program testing, in addition to the intrinsic problems related to the component technology. Therefore, since the component provider has access to the component source code, functional, structural, fault-based and/or state-based testing technique can be used. From the client point of view, when the source code of the component is not available, only functional and/or state-based testing techniques can be applied.

As highlighted by Weyuker [13], it is necessary to develop new methods to test and maintain components to make them reliable and reusable in a large range of software projects, products and software environments. Harrold [1] restates that the test of component-based systems, the development of effective testing processes and the demonstration of the effectiveness of testing criteria constitute the main directions to the software testing area.

In this chapter we present an overview on testing of OO software and components. In this section the basic concepts and terminology related to component testing were presented. In Section 2 the testing phases are discussed, comparing procedural and OO/component approaches. In Section 3 a classification of testing techniques is presented, as well as the definition of some testing criteria representative of each technique. Section 4 discusses more questions related to the testing of OO programs and components. In Section 5 some testing criteria specifically for OO/component testing are described. Also in Section 5 the problems to component testing automation are discussed and some existent testing tools are described. Section 6 presents an example about how to use one of the testing criteria described earlier. In Section 7 the conclusions are presented.

2   Testing Phases

As the development process is divided into several phases, allowing the system engineer to implement its solution step by step, the testing activity is also divided into distinct phases. The tester can concentrate on different aspects of

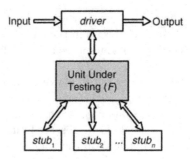

Fig. 1. Required environment for unit testing

the software and use different testing criteria in each one [15]. In the context of procedural software the testing activity can be divided into three incremental phases: unit, integration and system testing [16]. Variations in this pattern are identified for OO and component-based software, as discussed later.

Unit testing focuses on each unit, to ensure that the algorithmic aspects of each of them are correctly implemented. The goal is to identify faults related to logic and implementation in each unit. In this phase, structural testing is widely used, requiring the execution of specific elements of the control structure in each unit. Mutation testing is also an alternative to unit testing. In this phase it is common to need to develop drivers and stubs (Fig. 1). Considering F the unit to be tested, the driver is responsible for coordinating the testing of F. It gathers the data provided by the tester, passes them to F in the form of arguments, collects the results produced by F and shows them to the tester. A stub is a unit that replaces, during unit testing, another unit used (called) by F. Usually, a stub is a unit that simulates the behavior of the used unit with a minimum of computation effort or data manipulation. The development of drivers and stubs may represent a high overhead to unit testing.

After each unit has been tested, the integration phase begins and in consequence, the integration testing. But why shouldn't a program that was built from tested units that individually work as specified function adequately? The answer is that unit testing presents limitations and cannot ensure that each unit works in every single possible situation. For example, a unit may suffer from the adverse influence of another unit. Sub-functions when combined may produce unexpected results and global data structures may present problems.

After being integrated, the software works as a whole and should be submitted to system testing. The goal is to ensure that the software and the other elements that are part of the system (hardware and database, for instance) are adequately combined and the function and performance are obtained. Functional testing has been most used in this phase [16].

Fig. 2 illustrates the three phases as mentioned above, as well as the elements used in each of them, either for procedural or OO programs. According to the IEEE 610.12-1990 (R2002) [17] standard, a unit is a software component that cannot be divided. In this way, considering that testing is a dynamic activity, a

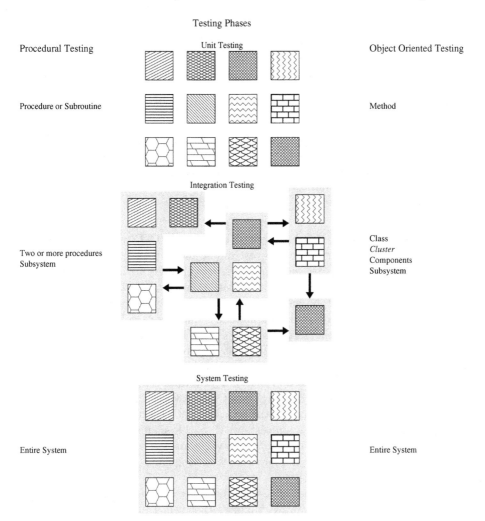

Fig. 2. Relationship between unit, integration and system testing: procedural and OO programs

unit in procedural programs is a subroutine or procedure. In OO programs, the smallest part to be tested is a method. The class to which the method belongs is seen as the driver of that method because without the class it is not possible to execute the method. In the procedural paradigm, unit testing is also called intra-procedural, and in the OO it is called intra-method [18]. By definition, a class gathers a set of attributes and methods. In this way, taking in consideration a single class it is possible to think about integration testing. Methods of the same class may interact to implement certain functionality—what characterizes the kind of integration that should be tested. This is inter-method [18] testing. In the procedural paradigm this phase is also called inter-procedural.

Table 1. Relationship between procedural and OO testing phases

Smallest Unit: Method		
Phase	**Procedural Testing**	**Object Oriented Testing**
Unit	Intra-procedural	Intra-method
Integration	Inter-procedural	Inter-method, Intra-class and Inter-class
System	Entire System	Entire System
Smallest Unit: Class		
Phase	**Procedural Testing**	**Object Oriented Testing**
Unit	Intra-procedural	Intra-method, Inter-method and Intra-class
Integration	Inter-procedural	Inter-class
System	Entire System	Entire System

Harrold and Rothermel [18] define two other types of OO testing: intra-class and inter-class. The former is used to test public method interactions through different sequences of calls to such methods. The goal is to identify possible sequences that lead the object to an invalid state. According to the authors, since the user may invoke the public method in many different orders, the intra-class testing gives one the confidence that different sequences of calls act correctly. In the inter-class testing the same concept is applied to public methods but not only those in a single class, i.e., the test requires calls among methods in different classes. After integration testing, system testing may commence. Since system testing is generally based on functional criteria, there is no fundamental difference in this phase from procedural and OO software.

A few variations regarding the testing phases for OO software are identified in the literature. Some authors understand that the smallest unit of an OO program is a class [19, 20, 10, 14]. In this way, a unit test would be composed of intra-method, inter-method and intra-class testing, and integration testing would be the same as inter-class.

Table 1 summarizes the types of testing that may be applied in each phase, either for procedural or OO software, taking either a method or a class as the smallest unit.

3   Techniques and Criteria for Software Testing

According to Howden [21], testing may be classified as specification-based or program-based testing. Such classification suggests that functional and state-based techniques are specification-based, and structural and fault-based are program-based.

In the specification-based testing the objective is to reveal faults related to the external functionality, to the communication interfaces between modules, to the required constraints (pre- and post-conditions) and to the program behavior. The problem is that often the existing specification is not formal, which makes harder the creation of test sets able to systematically exercise the component [19]. However, the specification-based criteria can be used in any context (procedural or OO) and in any testing phase without any fundamental adaptation.

Program-based testing, on the other hand, requires code handling and selection of test sets that exercise specific pieces of the code, not its specification [19]. The goal is to identify faults in the internal structure and in the component behavior. The disadvantage is that this approach may be dependent on several factors like target programming language and the need to have access to the source code. In the case of COTS, for instance, this is not always possible.

3.1 Functional Testing

Functional or black box testing (specification-based) has this name because the software is handled as a box from which the content is not known. Only the external side is visible. In this way the tester uses basically the specification to obtain the testing requirements or the test data, without any concern about the implementation [11]. A high-quality specification that matches the client's requirements is fundamental to support the application of functional criteria. Examples of such criteria are [16]: 1) Equivalency Partition, 2) Boundary Value, 3) Cause-Effect Graph, and 4) Category-Partition Method [22].

Statistical software testing can also be considered as functional testing since it is also based on the product specification. Example of such criteria are presented in [23, 24, 25, 26]. The idea behind these criteria is to exercise a program with inputs that are randomly generated according to a given distribution over the input domain, the key of its effectiveness being the derivation of a distribution that is appropriate to enhance the program failure probability. Basically, as defined in [23], the statistical test sets are defined by two parameters: (1) the test profile, or input distribution, from which the inputs are randomly drawn; and (2) the test size, or equivalently the number of inputs (i.e. of program executions) that are generated.

The use of the functional technique may make it difficult to quantify the testing activity. That is because it is not possible to ensure that certain essential parts of the product's implementation have been exercised. Another problem is that (non formal) specifications may be incomplete and so will be the test set created based on them.

On the other hand, since functional criteria are based solely in the specification, they can be used to test procedural, OO programs and software components as well [27, 28, 22, 29, 30, 10, 31].

3.2 Structural Testing

The structural testing technique, also known as white box (in opposition to "black box") fits in the class of program-based testing, since it takes into consideration implementation aspects to determine the testing requirements. Most of the criteria of the structural technique use a Control Flow Graph—CFG (also called Program Graph) to represent the program under test. A program P represented by a CFG has a correspondence between the nodes of the graph and blocks of code and between the edges of the graph and possible control-flow transfer between two blocks of code. From the CFG it is possible to select elements to be exercised during testing, characterizing the structural testing.

Structural testing faces several constraints and disadvantages as the need to determine unfeasible testing requirements such as unfeasible paths and associations [21, 32, 33, 34]. These constraints pose serious problems to testing automation. Nevertheless, this technique is seen as complementary to functional testing [16] and information obtained with its application is also relevant to maintenance, debugging and software reliability estimation [35, 36, 16, 37, 38, 1, 39].

The first structural criteria were based exclusively on control-flow structures. The most known are all-nodes, all-edges, and all-paths [40]. In the middle 70's appeared the dataflow-based criteria [41], that require interactions amongst variable definitions and variable uses to be exercised [41, 42, 43, 44]. The reasoning behind such an approach is the indication that even for small programs, control-flow-based testing is not effective for revealing even trivial faults. The use of data-flow criteria provides a hierarchy of criteria from all-edges to all-paths, trying to make the testing a more rigorous activity. Amongst the best known data-flow criteria are those introduced by Rapps and Weyuker in the middle 80's, for instance, all-defs, all-uses, all-du-paths and all-p-uses [34].

At the beginning of the 90's Maldonado [45] presented a family of criteria named Potential-Uses and the corresponding feasible criteria, obtained with the elimination of unfeasible associations. These criteria are based on associations between a variable definition and the possible points in the program where it can be used, not necessarily requiring the actual use of it.

Several extensions of data-flow criteria can be found in the literature, either for integration testing of procedural programs [46, 47, 48] or for unit and integration of OO programs [46].

3.3 Fault-Based Testing

The fault-based technique uses information about faults frequently found in software developments and also about specific types of faults that one may want to uncover [49]. Two criteria that typically concentrate on faults are Error Seeding and Mutation Testing.

Error seeding introduces in the program under test a known number of artificial faults before it is tested. After the test, from the total number of faults found and the rate between natural / artificial faults found, it is possible to estimate the number of remaining natural faults. The problems with this approach are 1) artificial faults may hide natural faults; 2) in order to obtain a statically reliable result it is necessary to use programs that can have 10,000 faults or more; and 3) it is based on the assumption that faults are uniformly distributed in the program, which in general is not the case—real programs present long pieces of simple code with few faults and small pieces with high complexity and high concentration of faults [50].

Mutation testing appeared in the 70's at Yale University and the Georgia Institute of Technology. It was strongly influenced by a classical method for digital circuit testing known as "single fault test model" [51]. One of the first papers describing mutation testing was published in 1978 [49]. This criterion uses a set of products slightly different from the product P under test, called mutants, to evaluate the adequacy of a test set T. The goal is to find a set of test cases able to reveal the differences between P and its mutants, making them to behave differently [49]. When a mutant has a behavior diverse from P it is said to be "dead"; otherwise it is a "live" mutant. A live mutant must be analyzed to check whether it is equivalent to P or it can be killed by a new test case, promoting in this way the improvement of T.

Mutants are created based on mutant operators, which are rules that define the (syntactic) changes to be done in P to create the mutants. It is known that one of the problems with mutation testing is related to the high cost to execute a large number of mutants. Besides, there is also the problem of deciding mutant equivalence, which in the general case is undecidable. Extensions of this criterion have also been proposed for integration testing as well as for program specifications. Delamaro et al. [52] defined the Interface Mutation criterion that applies the mutation concept to the integration testing phase. With that criterion a new set of mutant operators that model integration errors was proposed.

In the context of test specifications, mutation can be used to test Petri Nets [53, 54], Statecharts [55, 56], Finite state machines [57, 58] and Estelle [59, 60].

Recently, researchers have also been investigating the use of mutation testing for the OO paradigm. Kim et al. [61] proposed the use of a technique called Hazard and Operability Studies (HAZOP) to determine a set of mutant operators for Java. In general, this approach does not significantly differ from the traditional mutation with respect to mutant operators' creation, but introduces a more rigorous and disciplined way to do it. The technique identifies in the target language grammar those point candidates for mutation and then the mutant operators are created based on some predefined "guide words." A more extensive set of mutant operators for Java (inter-class mutant operators), that includes the ones proposed in [61], is defined in [62].

Researchers have also explored mutation testing in the context of distributed components communicating through CORBA [63, 64]. Yet, Delamaro et al. [65] define a set of mutant operators to deal with concurrency aspects of Java programs.

3.4   State-Based Testing

State-based testing uses a state-based representation of the unit or component under test. Based on this model, criteria to generate test sequences are used to ensure its correct behavior. One of these criteria, based on Finite State Machines (FSM), is the criterion W [2]. Other similar criteria can be found in the literature, as DS [66], UIO [67] and WP [68]. As mentioned before, mutation testing has also been used in test case generation for FSM [57, 58].

Criteria based on FSM are also widely used in OO context to represent the behavioral aspect of objects [27, 28, 29, 30, 10, 31, 14] and in the context of software components [69] since they only require a state-based representation to be applied. As can be observed, there are a large number of criteria available to evaluate a test set for a given program against a given specification. One important point to be highlighted is that the testing criteria and techniques are complementary and a tester may use one or more of these criteria to assess the quality of a test set for a program and enhance the test set, if it is the case, by constructing additional test cases needed to fulfil the testing requirements.

4   Issues Related to Component Testing

Component testing and component-based system testing face a series of particular issues, as will be discussed in this section. According to Harrold *et al.* [70], it is possible to analyze the problem from two points of view: the component user and the component provider.

4.1   Perspectives of Component-Based Testing

User's Perspective

Component users are those that develop systems by integrating third-part components. To help them, there are several initiatives to adapt traditional analysis and testing techniques to be used in the component development. However, there are issues that make this task difficult. First, the code of the components is not always accessible. Techniques and criteria based on the program implementation as data-flow-based criteria and mutation testing need the source code to determine their testing requirements. When the component source is not available to the user, such criteria cannot be used or at least an alternative setting between the parts is needed. Second, in component-based systems, even if the code is available, the components and the component-based system may have been developed in different languages and a tool to analyze/test the entire system may fail to analyze the components.

Third, a software component frequently offers more functionality than the client application needs. In this way, without the identification of the piece of the functionality that is actually required by the user, a testing tool will provide useless reports. For example, structural criteria evaluate how much a test set covers the required elements, but in a component-based system the unused part of the components should be excluded from this evaluation, otherwise the coverage assessed by the tool would be low even if the test set was a good one for the used portion of the code [71].

Developer's Perspective

The component provider implements and tests the component independently of what kind of application will use it. Unlike the user, the provider has access to the source code. Thus, testing the component is the same as traditional unit/integration testing. However, traditional criteria like control-flow-based criteria may not be enough to test the components due to its inefficiency to reveal faults [72]. Correcting a fault in a component after it is released has a high cost, many times higher than if the fault had been found during integration testing in a non-component based system because the component will probably be used in many applications.

The provider has to have mechanisms to solve two problems: first, the provider must effectively test the components as independent software units. Doing so, the provider increases the user's confidence in the component quality and reduces the testing cost for the user. Rosenblum [71] describes an approach for component unit testing that depends on the application context and so is more relevant to the user than to the provider. The second approach, proposed by Harrold *et al.* [70], separates the analysis and testing of the user application from the analysis and testing of the components.

A fundamental aspect for component or application testing is their testability. According to Freedman [4], the component's testability usually has two aspects: observability and controllability. The latter shows how easy it is to control the component in relation to its input, operation, output and behavior. The former indicates how easy it is to observe the program behavior according to its operational behavior and its output as function of its input.

As mentioned before, the features of OO programs bring a series of obstacles to the testing activity. In the next section the impact of such features in the testability of OO programs and components will be discussed. For further information the reader may refer to [19, 14, 73].

4.2   The Impact of OO on Software Testability

Encapsulation

Encapsulation means a control access mechanism that determines the visibility of methods and attributes in a class. With the access control, undesirable dependencies between client and a server class are avoided, making visible to the client only the class interface, and hiding implementation details. Encapsulation aids in the information hiding and in the design of a modular structure.

Although encapsulation does not directly contribute to the introduction of faults, it may be an obstacle to the testing activity, reducing the controllability and observability. Program-based testing requires a complete report about the concrete and abstract state of an object, as well as the possibility to change that state easily [14]. OO languages make it harder to get or set the state of an object. In the case of C++, for instance, friend functions have been developed to solve this problem. However, in the case of languages that do not provide such mechanism, other solutions must be adopted. Harrold [1] says that the solution would be the implementation of methods get and set for every attribute in a class. Another alternative would be the use of reflection (although, as highlighted by Rosa and Martins [74] not every language allows the reflection of private methods) or metadata[1] [75, 76].

---

[1] Metadata are used by the component provider to include additional information about the component without revealing the source code or other sensitive details of the component. In general, as defined in [75], metadata are *data about components* that can be retrieved or calculated by *metamethods*.

Inheritance

Inheritance is essential to OO development and component-based development. It permits the reuse by sharing features present in classes previously defined. However, Binder [14] highlights the fact that inheritance weakens encapsulation and may create a problem similar to the use of global variables in procedural programs. When implementing a class that uses inheritance it is important to know the details about the ancestor classes. Without that, it may happen that the class seems to work but it actually violates implicit constraints of the ancestor classes. Large class chains make it more difficult to understand the program, increase the chance for faults, and reduce testability.

Offutt and Irvine [22] comment that inheritance may lead to a false conclusion that aspects already tested in the super-classes do not need to be retested in the subclasses. Perry and Kaiser [19] state that even if a method is inherited from a super-class, without any modification, it has to be retested in the subclass context.

Harrold *et al.* [77] use the results from Perry and Kaiser [19] and develop an incremental testing strategy based on the class hierarchy. They propose to identify which inherited methods have to be tested with new test cases and which can be retested by using the same test cases used to test the super-class. With this strategy the testing effort can be reduced since many test cases can be reused in the subclasses. In addition, the way inheritance is implemented changes from one language to another and this can also have some influence on the testing strategy.

Multiple Inheritance

Multiple inheritance allows a class to receive characteristics from two or more super-classes that in their turn may have common features (attributes or methods with the same name, for instance). Perry and Kaiser [19] state that although multiple inheritance leads to small syntactic changes in programs, it can lead to high semantic changes, which can make the testing activity for OO programs even more difficult.

Polymorphism

Polymorphism is the ability to refer to different types of objects using the same name or variable. Static polymorphism makes such association at compilation time. For example, generic classes (C++ templates for instance) allow static polymorphism. Dynamic polymorphism allows different types of associations at execution time. Polymorphic methods use dynamic binding to determine at execution time which method should answer to a given message, based on the type of the object and on the arguments sent with the message.

Polymorphism can be used to produce elegant and extensible code but a few drawbacks can be realized in its use. For example, a method x in a super-class needs to be tested. This method is overwritten in a subclass. The correction of

x in the subclass cannot be assessed because the pre- and post-conditions in the subclass may not be the same as in the super-class [14].

Each possible binding in a polymorphic message is a unique computation. The fact that several polymorphic bindings work correctly together does not ensure that all will work correctly. A polymorphic object with dynamic bindings may easily result in sending improper messages to the wrong class, and it can be difficult to have all possible binding combinations.

Dynamic Binding

Dynamic binding allows a message to be sent to a server class that implements that message. Since server classes are frequently developed and reviewed without further concern about the client code, some methods that usually work correctly in a client class may lead to unexpected results. A client class may require a method that is no longer part of a server class, incorrectly use the methods available, or call the methods with wrong arguments.

Besides these problems, Binder [14] reports errors related to the state of the objects and sequences of messages. The packaging of methods in a class is fundamental to OO; as a consequence, messages have to be executed in some sequence, leading to the question: "Which message sequences are valid?"

Objects are created at execution time, taking memory space. Each new configuration this memory space assumes is a new state of such object. Thus, besides the behavior encapsulated by an object it also encapsulates states.

Analyzing how the execution of a method can change the state of an object, four possibilities are observed [10]:

1. It can leave the object in the same state;
2. It can take the object to a new, valid state;
3. It can take the object to an undetermined state; or
4. It can change the object to an inappropriate state;

Possibilities 3 and 4 characterize erroneous states. Possibility 1 characterizes an error if the method is supposed to behave as in possibility 2 and vice-versa.

4.3   Other Issues in Component Testing

Specifically for component testing, one additional issue that has to be considered is the kind of information that has to be included/delivered with or within the component to help, as much as possible, the testing on the user's side. As mentioned by Orso *et al.* [75], the drawbacks of component-based software technologies arise because of the lack of information about externally provided components.

Although existing component standards, including DCOM [7] and Enterprise JavaBeans [6], already provide additional information about a component by the use of metadata that are packaged with the component, it is necessary to define a standard such that, independently of the component provider, the component user can always consider that a given set of information will be available.

Moreover, such a standard makes easier the job of component testing tool developers by providing a common interface to access component features requested to perform the testing activity on a single component or on a component-based system.

Gao [78] defined a maturity model to evaluate the maturity level of a given process in an organization. The maturity model is composed by four levels focusing on the standardization of the component testing, testing criteria, management procedures and measurement activities. Although published almost five years ago, this reference is still up-to-date because not much has been done in this direction. Changes will only occur when the component user demands high-quality or certified components [79].

To achieve either a high maturity level or a certified component, the component provider has to use an incremental testing strategy that combines testing criteria of different testing techniques such as functional, structural and behavioral aspects of the component being tested. The next section presents a summary of the most relevant criteria developed for testing OO programs and software components considering both sides: component providers and component users.

5   Component-Based Testing Criteria

Testing techniques and criteria have been investigated with the aim of establishing a systematic and rigorous way to select sub-domains of the input domain able to reveal the presence of possible faults, respecting the time and cost constraints determined in a software project.

When discussing testing criteria for software components we need to consider the two perspectives of component development, because, in general, structural testing can only be performed by the component provider since such criteria require the availability of the source code. When the source code of the component is not available, the component user has to use functional and/or state-based testing criteria to perform component/system testing. Below we present different testing criteria that can be used by the component provider, component user or both.

According to Binder [80], the biggest challenge of OO testing is to design test sets to exercise combinations of sequences of messages and state interactions that give confidence that the software works properly. In some cases, test sets based on sequences of messages or states are enough. However, Binder warns that the state-based testing is not able to reveal all kinds of faults requiring also the use of program-based criteria [81, 14]. Methods in a class make use of the same instance variables and should cooperate with the correct behavior of the class, considering all the possible activation sequences. The visibility of the instance variables for all the methods in the class creates a fault hazard similar to the use of global variables in the procedural languages. Since the methods in a superclass are not explicit when a subclass is coded, this may lead to an inconsistent use of the instance variables. In order to reveal this kind of fault it is necessary

Table 2. Criteria for testing components and OO programs

Technique	Criteria	Phase[†] U	I	S
Functional	Category-Partition Method [22]	•	•	•
Structural	Data-flow [18]	•	•	
Structural	FREE [81]	•	•	
Structural	Modal Testing [80]	•	•	
Fault-Based	Class Mutation [61, 82]	•	•	
Fault-Based	Mutation on Distributed Programs(CORBA Interface) [63]		•	
Fault-Bases	Mutation on Concurrent Programs (Java) [65]	•	•	
State-Based	FREE [81]	•	•	•
State-Based	Modal Testing [80]	•	•	•

[†] Testing Phases: Unit (U), Integration (I) and System (S).

to use control-flow and data-flow criteria that ensure the inter-method (or intra-class) coverage. Table 2 shows some well known criteria to test OO programs identified in the literature, and the respective phases they are applied in.

As can be observed, functional criteria, including statistical software testing [23, 24, 25], can be applied indiscriminately to procedural, OO programs and components [11] since the testing requirements are obtained from the product specification. A case study investigating the *Category-Partition Method* in detecting faults on OO programs is described in [22]. The method provides guidelines to identify, from the product specification, different categories related to the input domain and the specific functionality that should be in the domain of these categories. Statistical software testing, in which inputs are randomly sampled based on a probability distribution representing expected field use, is also based on the specification and can also be used for testing software components [23, 24, 25]. Therefore, as mentioned in Section 3, the major problem with the functional testing technique is that, since it is based on the specification, its criteria can not assure that essential parts of the implementation have been covered.

In the case of structural testing, important work has been done by Harrold and Rothermel [18] who extended data-flow testing to class testing. The authors comment that data-flow criteria, designed for procedural programs, can be applied to OO programs both for a single method test and for interacting methods in the same class [34, 46]. They do not consider tough data-flow interactions when the users of a class make sequences of calls in an arbitrary order. To solve this problem they present an approach to test different types of interactions among methods in the same class. To test the methods that are accessible outside the class a new representation named class control flow graph was developed. From this representation new inter-method and intra-class associations can be derived. An example that illustrates this criterion is presented in the next section.

Considering the fault-based criteria, a point to be highlighted is the flexibility to extend the concepts of mutation testing to different executable entities. The criterion, initially developed for unit testing of procedural programs, has been extended to OO programs [63, 61, 62], to FSM specifications [57, 58], Petri Nets [53, 54], Statecharts [55, 56] and Estelle [59, 60].

Specifically, for OO programs mutation testing has been used to exercise aspects concerning concurrency, communications and testing of Java programs at unit and integration level: 1) Kim *et al.* [61] used a technique named HAZOP (Hazard and Operability Studies) to define a set of mutant operators for Java programs; 2) Ghosh *et al.* [63] defined a set of mutant operators aiming at testing the communications interfaces between distributed (CORBA) components; and 3) Delamaro *et al.* [65] defined mutant operators specific for concurrent Java programs. Since structural and fault-based criteria require the component source code, alternative criteria, that do not require the source code, have been proposed. Such criteria are based on metadata [76] and metacontent [75], reflection [83], built-in testing [84, 83], polymorphism [85] and state-based testing [69].

Computational reflection enables a program to access its internal structure and behavior and this is beneficial for testing by automating the execution of tests through the creation of instances of classes and the execution of different sequences of methods. In component testing, computational reflection has been used to load a class into a testing tool extracting some of the methods and invoking them with the appropriate parameters. Therefore, reflection can be used to build test cases by extracting the needed characteristics of classes [76]. Rosa and Martins [86] propose the use of reflexive architecture to validate OO applications.

Another solution, like a wrapper, is proposed by Soundarajan and Tyler [85] considering the use of polymorphism. Given the component's formal specification containing the set of pre- and post-conditions that have to be satisfied for each method invocation, polymorphic methods are created such that, before the invocation of the real method (the one implemented by the component) the polymorphic version checks if the pre-conditions are satisfied, collects method invocation information (parameters values, for example), invokes the real method, collects output information (return value, for example) and checks if the posconditions are satisfied. The disadvantage of this approach is that it requires formal specification and does not guarantee the code coverage. Moreover, to be useful, requires the implementation of an automatic wrapper generator since, once the specification changes (any pre- or post-condition), the set of polymorphic class/methods has to be regenerated/reevaluated.

Metadata are also used, in existing component models, to provide generic usage information about a component (e.g. the name of its class, the name of its methods) as well as information for testing. By using metadata, static and dynamic aspects of the component can be accessed by the component user to perform different tasks. The problem with this approach is that there is no consensus about which information should be provided and how it should be provided. Moreover, it demands more work by the component provider.

Other strategies propose an integrated approach for component-based testing generation. They combine black- and white-box information from a formal/semi-formal component's specification. The idea is to construct a graphical representation of the component using control-flow and data-flow information gathered from the specification and, from this graphical representation, control-flow- and data-flow-based criteria can be applied. The problem is that since the structural testing criteria are obtained from the component's specification, satisfying such criteria does not assure component code coverage but only component specification coverage. Moreover, they require that the component has a formal/semi-formal specification to be applied [87, 69].

The concept of auto-testable components has also been explored. The idea is to provide components with built-in testing capabilities that can be enabled and disabled, depending on when the component is working in the normal operation mode or in the maintenance mode [84, 73, 76]. Edwards [76] discusses how different kinds of information can be embedded into the component. He propose a reflexive metadata wrapper that can be used to pack more than the component itself. It also includes the component specification (formal/semi-formal), its documentation, verification history, violation checking services, self-test services, etc. Such an approach, although very useful, requires more work for the component provider since she/he has to collect and include all of this information inside the component. Moreover, which information should be provided and how it should be provided is not yet standardized, making difficult the development of a testing tool that uses such information during testing.

In general, from the user point of view, when no source code is available, only functional or state-based testing criteria can be used. This implies that, except when the component has built-in test or metacontent capabilities, no information about the coverage of that component with respect to its implementation can be obtained.

Java components, such as applets or JavaBeans, this situation can be overcome by carrying out the testing directly on the Java class file (.class) instead of on the Java source file (.java). The so called "class file" is a portable binary representation that contains class related data such as class name, its superclass name, information about the variables and constants and the bytecode instructions for each method.

Bytecode instructions resemble an assembly-like language, but a class file retains very high-level information about a program such that it is possible to identify control-flow- and data-flow-data dependency on Java bytecode [88]. Working at the bytecode level, both component provider and component user can use the same underlined representation to perform the testing activity. Moreover, the user can evaluate how much of the bytecode of a given component has been covered by a given test set, i.e, he/she can evaluate the quality of his functional test set on covering structural elements of the component [89, 90].

Besides the criteria described above, other examples can be found in the literature, among them, the work of McGregor [91], Rosenblum [71] and Harrold *et al.* [70]. Bhor [92] also carried out a survey that includes other testing techniques for component-based software. Independently of the testing criterion, it is essential that testing tools support its application. In the next section the aspects related to testing automation are discussed.

5.1   Issues on Component Testing Automation

Software component testing, as testing in general, requires several types of supporting tools: test case generators, drivers, stubs and an environment for component testing (component test bed). Taking the developer's point of view, most
testing tools for test case generation can be used to support component testing.
The main problems in component testing automation are also related with the
lack of information embedded into the component by the component providers.
The lack of a standard is a drawback since the development of a generic testing
environment, in the sense that it would be able to deal with components from
different providers and implemented in different languages, would be more difficult. Nevertheless, there are some tools in the literature that automate as much
as possible the testing of a component-based system.

A component verification tool, named Component Test Bench (CTB), is
described in [93]. The tool provides a generic pattern that allows the component
provider to specify the test set used to test a given component. The test cases are
stored in standard XML files. The component user can reuse the same test set to
retest the component to determine whether the component performs according
to its specification. The tool does not yet provide testing criteria to help the test
set generation and evaluation. It only does the conformance testing on a given
component, i.e., evaluate if the component behaves as specified.

A similar approach is used by JTest [94], a tool that automatically run tests
on Java programs. The main difference is that JTest uses the JUnit framework[2] [95] to store the test cases instead of XML file as in CTB.

Glass JAR Toolkit (GJTK) is a coverage testing tool that operates at the
bytecode level and does not require the source code to apply a white-box testing
criterion (statement or decision) on bytecodes. It can be used for testing both
compiled .jar and .class files [96].

We are also working on the implementation of a Java bytecode understanding
and testing tool, named JaBUTi[3]. The idea is to provide a complete environment
that allows both component provider and component user to carry out white-
box testing on Java bytecode. Currently, the tool supports the application of
three structural testing criteria (all-nodes, all-edges and all-uses) that can be
used in an incremental testing strategy for component-based testing. The idea
is 1) to evaluate the coverage of a given functional test set and then, 2) based
on the coverage information with respect to the structural testing criteria, to
identify which area of the component requires additional test cases to be covered,
improving the quality of the test set [90].

---

[2] JUnit is an open source Java testing framework used to write and run repeatable
tests. The basic idea is to implement some specific classes to store the information about test case input and expected output. After each test case execution,
the expected output is compared with the current output. Any discrepancy can be
reported.

[3] Interested readers can contact us by e-mail to obtain additional information about
JaBUTi.

6 JaBUTi: Example of Component Testing Criterion Usage

Most part of the tools developed for component-based testing focus on the functional aspects of the component (black box testing) and do not guarantee statement coverage of the component due to the unavailability of the corresponding source code. JaBUTi supports coverage analysis to test Java programs and Java components even if the Java source code is not available what enables the application of white-box testing. It is designed to support test set adequacy evaluation and to provide guidance in test case selection by using advanced control-flow-dependence analysis.

In [18] a set of testing criteria is defined based on a graphical representation of a class called Class Control Flow Graph (CCFG). Basically, after each CFG is constructed for each method, these CFGs are interconnected representing the method calls inside the class, resulting in a CCFG. Based on the CCFG, the authors consider three testing levels:

Intra-method: each method is tested alone. This level is equivalent to the unit testing for procedural programs;

Inter-method: addresses public methods interacting with other methods in the same class. This level is equivalent to the integration testing for procedural programs; and

Intra-class: tests the interactions between public methods when they are called in different sequences. Since the users of the class can call the methods in an undetermined order, intra-class testing aims at building the confidence that those invocation sequences do not put the object in an inconsistent state. The authors warn that only a subset of the possible sequences can be tested, since the complete set is infinity.

Based on these three levels, Harrold and Rotheermel [18] establish def-use pairs that allow the evaluation of data-flow relations in OO programs: Intra-method pairs, Inter-method pairs and Intra-class pair. Currently, JaBUTi supports the application of two control-flow-based criteria (all-nodes and all-edges) and one data-flow-based criterion (all-nodes) at intra-method level. We intent to implement additional testing criteria to also cover the inter-method level.

In this section we will illustrate the application of the all-uses criterion on a Java component considering the Java source code presented in Fig. 3. The example, extracted from [75], illustrates a component, Dispenser, and an application, VendingMachine, that uses the Dispenser component. Although not required by JaBUTi, we are showing the Java source code in Fig. 3 to facilitate the understanding of the example.

Fig. 4 illustrates the main screen of JaBUTi showing part of the bytecode instruction set of the method Dispenser.available(int sel). Besides the bytecode, the tool also displays the component's source code (when available) as well as the CFG for each method as illustrated in Figures 5 and 6, respectively. Observe that in the CFG, by placing the mouse over a given CFG node, specific information about the node is displayed such as: the node number, the first and

```
01 package vending;
02
03
04 public class VendingMachine {
05
06   final private int COIN = 25;
07   final private int VALUE = 50;
08   private int totValue;
09   private int currValue;
10   private Dispenser d;
11
12   public VendingMachine() {
13     totValue = 0;
14     currValue = 0;
15     d = new Dispenser();
16   }
17
18   public void insertCoin() {
19     currValue += COIN;
20     System.out.println("Current value = " + currValue);
21   }
22
23   public void returnCoin() {
24     if (currValue == 0)
25       System.err.println("no coins to return");
26     else {
27       System.out.println("Take your coins");
28       currValue = 0;
29     }
30   }
31
32   public void vendItem(int selection) {
33     int expense;
34
35     expense = d.dispense(currValue, selection);
36     totValue += expense;
37     currValue -= expense;
38     System.out.println("Current value = " + currValue);
39   }
40 } // class VendingMachine
```

```
01 package vending;
02
03
04 public class Dispenser {
05   final private int MAXSEL = 20;
06   final private int VAL = 50;
07   private int[] availSelectionVals = {2, 3, 13};
08
09   public int dispense(int credit, int sel) {
10     int val = 0;
11
12     if (credit == 0)
13       System.err.println("No coins inserted");
14     else if (sel > MAXSEL)
15       System.err.println("Wrong selection " + sel);
16     else if (!available(sel))
17       System.err.println("Selection " + sel + " unavailable");
18     else {
19       val = VAL;
20       if (credit < val) {
21         System.err.println("Enter " + (val - credit) + " coins");
22         val = 0;
23       } else
24         System.err.println("Take selection");
25     }
26     return val;
27   }
28
29   private boolean available(int sel) {
30     for (int i = 0; i < availSelectionVals.length; i++)
31       if (availSelectionVals[i] == sel) return true;
32     return false;
33   }
34 } // class Dispenser
```

Fig. 3. Example of a Java component (**Dispenser**) and one application (**VendingMachine**) [75]

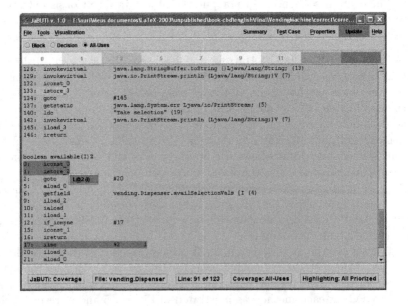

Fig. 4. JaBUTi display: Hot-spot on bytecode

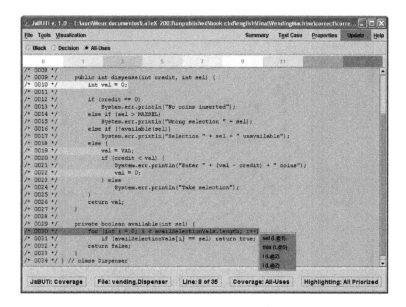

Fig. 5. JaBUTi display: Hot-spot on source code

the last bytecode instruction that compose the node, the set of defined and used variables, etc. In any representation, the tool shows which part has the highest weight [97] and should be covered first to increase the coverage with respect to a given criterion, as much as possible. Observe that, if the tester considers that another part of the component should be covered first, he/she can prioritize the coverage of that specific part and later use the recomputed hints provided by the tool to increase the coverage with respect to the other parts of the component.

For example, considering the all-uses criterion, the tool identifies the complete set of testing requirements (def-use pairs) and shows, using different background colors (weights), the set of instructions that contains a variable definition. By right clicking on one of those instructions, a pop-up menu shows the names of the defined variables at the corresponding bytecode instruction. As can be observed in Fig. 4, the method `Dispenser.available(int sel)` is the one that contains the definition with the highest weight. The same information can also be obtained from the source code or the CFG, as illustrated in Figures 5 and 6, respectively.

By selecting a given definition, the def-use pairs associated with it are shown and the graphical interface is updated. For example, considering Fig. 4, by selecting the definition of the local variable L@2[4] in the bytecode, the set of def-use pairs with respect to this variable is shown as illustrated in Fig. 7.

Observe that there are four def-use pairs with respect to L@2 defined at CFG node 0: <L@2, 0,5>, <L@2, 0,17>, <L@2, 0,(5, 15)> and <L@2, 0,(5, 17)>. The def-use pair with the highest weight is <L@2, 0,5>. By covering this

---

[4] L@2 refers to local variable number two. In case of Figure 4, L@2 corresponds to local variable i.

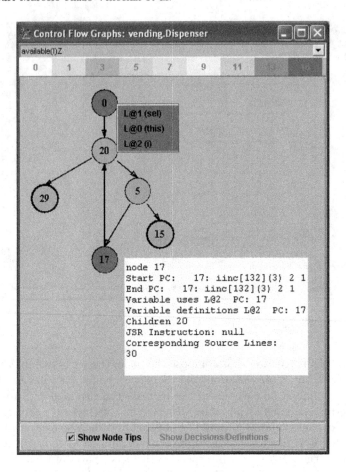

Fig. 6. JaBUTi display: Hot-spot on CFG

requirement, at least 16 other def-use pairs will be covered. For example, the test case "insertCoin, vendItem 13" that represents that a given user inserted one coin and requested the item 13 to be dispensed (a valid item) covers 38 out of the 46 def-use pairs in the two classes under testing (the Dispenser component and the VendingMachine application). By adding one more test case asking for an invalid item ("insertCoin, vendItem 15"), all the testing requirements above were covered.

The tool also generates coverage report with respect to each criterion, each class file, each method and each test case. Fig. 8 illustrates the summary with respect to each test case. The tester can enable and disable different combinations of test cases and the coverage is updated considering only the active test cases. By using JaBUTi, the component user without familiarity with Java bytecode can use the CFG to evaluate how well a given component has been tested. It is also possible to identify which areas of the component code require more test cases to increase the coverage and the confidence in the quality of the component.

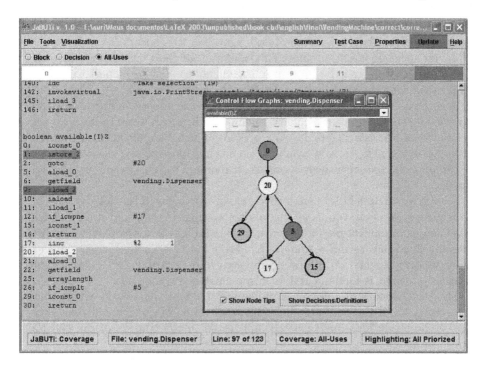

Fig. 7. JaBUTi display: Set of def-use pairs with respect to variable i defined at CFG node 0

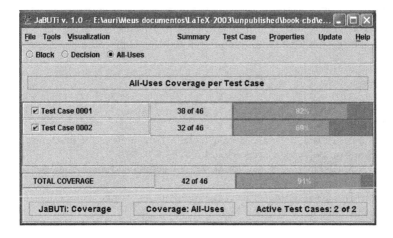

Fig. 8. Summary report by test case

7   Conclusions

This chapter highlighted the importance of the testing activity in the context of component-based system development. The component technology aims at speeding up the development process by software reuse. However, in order to ensure system quality it is necessary both to consider the concern of the developer to provide mechanisms to promote the validation of their components in their client's applications and the concern of the clients to seek developers that offer components with the quality and reliability that they demand.

In general, the client spends a large amount of time understanding how to use and evaluate the component's quality, making harder their reuse. In this way, for effective reuse it is essential to develop tools to support component testing and to encourage developers to make available, as much as possible, information about the components, reducing the cost and effort required to test a component-based system.

A large research field is open in this area, in particular in the development of techniques, criteria, and tools for component testing. In addition, standards for component communication, for documentation and for the development of built-in test mechanisms are also required. The idea of maturity models for component testing also represents an interesting research line, contributing to component certification, what is fundamental for component systems quality assurance.

The real benefits of component reuse will be achieved to the extent that components fulfill the needs of their clients in terms of quality and reliability and can be easily identified, tracked and tested in the context of the client's applications.

Acknowledgments

The authors would like to thank the Brazilian Funding Agencies – FAPESP, CAPES and CNPq – for their partial support to this research. The authors would also like to thank the anonymous referees for their valuable comments.

References

1. Harrold, M.J.: Testing: A roadmap. In: 22th International Conference on Software Engineering. (2000)
2. Chow, T.S.: Testing software design modelled by finite-state machines. IEEE Transactions on Software Engineering **4** (1978) 178–187
3. Harel, D.: Statecharts: A visual formalism for complex systems. Science of Computer Programming **8** (1987) 231–274
4. Freedman, R.S.: Testability of software components. IEEE Transactions on Software Engineering **17** (1991) 553–564
5. Szyperski, C.: Component Software Beyond Object-Oriented Programming. Addison-Wesley (1998)
6. Matena, V., Stearns, B.: Applying Enterprise JavaBeans: Component-Based Development for the J2EE Platform. 2 edn. Addison-Wesley (2001)
7. Microsoft: COM: Delivering on the promises of component technology. web page (2002) Available on-line at: http://www.microsoft.com/com/ [01-20-2003].
8. Gimenes, I.M.S., Barroca, L., Huzita, E.H.M., Carnielo, A.: The process of component development by examples. In: VIII Regional Scholl of Informatics, Porto Alegre, RS, Brazil (2000) 1–32 (in Portuguese).

9. Werner, C.M., Braga, R.M.: Component-based development. Brazilian Symposium on Software Engineering'2000 (2000) (in Portuguese).

10. McDaniel, R., McGregor, J.D.: Testing polymorphic interactions between classes. Technical Report TR-94-103, Clemson University (1994)

11. Beizer, B.: Software Testing Techniques. 2nd edn. Van Nostrand Reinhold Company, New York (1990)

12. Zhu, H., Hall, P., May, J.: Software unit test coverage and adequacy. ACM Computing Surveys **29** (1997) 366–427

13. Weyuker, E.J.: Testing component-based software: A cautionary tale. IEEE Software **15** (1998) 54–59

14. Binder, R.V.: Testing Object-Oriented Systems: Models, Patterns, and Tools. Volume 1. Addison Wesley Longman, Inc. (1999)

15. Linnenkugel, U., Müllerburg, M.: Test data selection criteria for (software) integration testing. In: First International Conference on Systems Integration, Morristown, NJ (1990) 709–717

16. Pressman, R.S.: Software Engineering – A Practitioner's Approach. 5 edn. McGraw-Hill (2000)

17. IEEE: IEEE standard glossary of software engineering terminology. Standard 610.12-1990 (R2002), IEEE Computer Society Press (2002)

18. Harrold, M.J., Rothermel, G.: Performing data flow testing on classes. In: Second ACM SIGSOFT Symposium on Foundations of Software Engineering, New York, ACM Press (1994) 154–163

19. Perry, D.E., Kaiser, G.E.: Adequate testing and object-oriented programming. Journal on Object-Oriented Programming **2** (1990) 13–19

20. Arnold, T.R., Fuson, W.A.: In a perfect world. Communications of the ACM **37** (1994) 78–86

21. Howden, W.E.: Software Engineering and Technology: Functional Program Testing and Analysis. McGrall-Hill Book Co, New York (1987)

22. Offutt, A.J., Irvine, A.: Testing object-oriented software using the category-partition method. In: 17th International Conference on Technology of Object-Oriented Languages and Systems, Santa Barbara, CA (1995) 293–304

23. Thevenod-Fosse, P., Waeselynck, H.: STATEMATE applied to statistical software testing. In: International Symposium on Software Testing and Analysis, Cambridge, MA, ACM Press (1993) 99–109

24. Whittaker, J.A., Thomason, M.: A markov chain model for statistical software testing. IEEE Transactions on Software Engineering **20** (1994) 812–824

25. Whittaker, J.A.: Stochastic software testing. Annals of Software Engineering **4** (1997) 115–131

26. Banks, D., Dashiell, W., Gallagher, L., Hagwood, C., Kacker, R., Rosenthal, L.: Software testing by statistical methods. Technical Report NISTIR 6129, NIST – National Institute of Standards and Technology (1998)

27. Hoffman, D., Strooper, P.: A case study in class testing. In: CASCON 93, IBM Toronto Laboratory (1993) 472–482

28. Turner, C.D., Robson, D.J.: The state-based testing of object-oriented programs. In: Conference on Software Maintenance, Montreal Quebec, Canada, IEEE Computer Society Press (1993) 302–310

29. Kung, D., J.Gao, Hsia, P., Toyoshima, Y., Chen, C.: On regression testing of object-oriented programs. The Journal of Systems and Software **32** (1996) 21–40

30. McGregor, J.D., Korson, T.D.: Integrated object-oriented testing and development process. Communications of the ACM **37** (1994) 59–77

31. Hoffman, D., Strooper, P.: Classbrench: A framework for automated class testing. Software Practice and Experience **27** (1997) 573–597

32. Frankl, F.G.: The Use of Data Flow Information for the Selection and Evaluation of Software Test Data. PhD thesis, Universidade de New York, New York, NY (1987)

33. Ntafos, S.C.: A comparison of some structural testing strategies. IEEE Transactions on Software Engineering **14** (1988) 868–873

34. Rapps, S., Weyuker, E.J.: Selecting software test data using data flow information. IEEE Transactions on Software Engineering **11** (1985) 367–375

35. Ostrand, T.J., Weyuker, E.J.: Using data flow analysis for regression testing. In: Sixth Annual Pacific Northwest Software Quality Conference, Portland – Oregon (1988)

36. Hartmann, J., Robson, D.J.: Techniques for selective revalidation. IEEE Software **7** (1990) 31–36

37. Veevers, A., Marshall, A.: A relationship between software coverage metrics and reliability. Software Testing, Verification and Reliability **4** (1994) 3–8

38. Varadan, G.S.: Trends in reliability and test strategies. IEEE Software **12** (1995) 10

39. Chaim, M.L.: Program Debugging Based on Structural Testing Information. Doctoral dissertation, Scholl of Computer Science and Electrical Engineering, UNICAMP, Campinas, SP, Brazil (2001) (in Portuguese).

40. Myers, G.J.: The Art of Software Testing. Wiley, New York (1979)

41. Herman, P.M.: A data flow analysis approach to program testing. Australian Computer Journal **8** (1976) 92–96

42. Laski, J.W., Korel, B.: A data flow oriented program testing strategy. IEEE Transactions on Software Engineering **9** (1983) 347–354

43. Rapps, S., Weyuker, E.J.: Data flow analysis techniques for program test data selection. In: 6th International Conference on Software Engineering, Tokio, Japan (1982) 272–278

44. Ntafos, S.C.: On required element testing. IEEE Transactions on Software Engineering **10** (1984) 795–803

45. Maldonado, J.C.: Potential-Uses Criteria: A Contribution to the Structural Testing of Software. Doctoral dissertation, DCA/FEE/UNICAMP, Campinas, SP, Brazil (1991) (in Portuguese).

46. Harrold, M.J., Soffa, M.L.: Interprocedural data flow testing. In: Third Testing, Analysis, and Verification Symposium. (1989) 158–167

47. Harrold, M.J., Soffa, M.L.: Selecting and using data for integration test. IEEE Software **8** (1991) 58–65

48. Vilela, P.R.S.: Integration Potencial-Uses Criteria: Definition and Analysis. Doctoral dissertation, DCA/FEEC/UNICAMP, Campinas, SP, Brazil (1998) (in Portuguese).

49. DeMillo, R.A., Lipton, R.J., Sayward, F.G.: Hints on test data selection: Help for the practicing programmer. IEEE Computer **11** (1978) 34–43

50. Budd, T.A.: Computer Program Testing. In: Mutation Analysis: Ideas, Example, Problems and Prospects. North-Holland Publishing Company (1981)

51. Friedman, A.D.: Logical Design of Digital Systems. Computer Science Press (1975)

52. Delamaro, M.E., Maldonado, J.C., Mathur, A.P.: Interface mutation: An approach for integration testing. IEEE Transactions on Software Engineering **27** (2001) 228–247

53. Fabbri, S.C.P.F., Maldonado, J.C., Masiero, P.C., Delamaro, M.E.: Mutation analysis applied to validate specifications based on petri nets. In: FORTE'95 – 8th IFIP Conference on Formal Descriptions Techniques for Distribute Systems and Communication Protocols, Montreal, Canada (1995) 329–337

54. Simão, A.S., Maldonado, J.C.: Mutation based test sequence generation for Petri nets. In: III Workshop of Formal Methods, João Pessoa (2000)

55. Fabbri, S.C.P.F.: The Mutation Analysis in the Context of Reactive Systems: a Constribution on the Establishment of Validation and Testing Strategies. Doctoral dissertation, IFSC-USP, São Carlos, SP, Brazil (1996) (in Portuguese).

56. Sugeta, T.: Proteum-rs/st: A tool to support the validation of statecharts based on mutation analysis. Master's thesis, ICMC-USP, São Carlos, SP, Brazil (1999) (in Portuguese).

57. Fabbri, S.C.P.F., Maldonado, J.C., Masiero, P.C., Delamaro, M.E.: Mutation analysis based on finite state machines. In: XI Brazilian Symposium on Computer Networks, Campinas, SP, Brazil (1993) 407–425 (in Portuguese).

58. Fabbri, S.C.P.F., Maldonado, J.C., Masiero, P.C., Delamaro, M.E.: Mutation analysis testing for finite state machines. In: 5th International Symposium on Software Reliability Engineering (ISSRE'94), Monterey – CA (1994) 220–229

59. Probert, R.L., Guo, F.: Mutation testing of protocols: Principles and preliminary experimental results. In: IFIP TC6 – Third International Workshop on Protocol Test Systems, North-Holland (1991) 57–76

60. Souza, S.R.S., Maldonado, J.C., Fabbri, S.C.P.F., Lopes de Souza, W.: Mutation testing applied to estelle specifications. Software Quality Journal **8** (1999) 285–301

61. Kim, S., Clark, J.A., Mcdermid, J.A.: The rigorous generation of Java mutation operators using HAZOP. In: 12th International Conference on Software & Systems Engineering and their Applications (ICSSEA'99). (1999)

62. Ma, Y.S., Kwon, Y.R., Offutt, J.: Inter-class mutation operators for Java. In: 13th International Symposium on Software Reliability Engineering - ISSRE'2002, Annapolis, MD (2002).

63. Ghosh, S., Mathur, A.P.: Interface mutation. Software Testing, Verification and Reliability **11** (2001) 227–247 (Special Issue: Mutation 2000 - A Symposium on Mutation Testing. Issue Edited by W. Eric Wong).

64. Sridhanan, B., Mundkur, S., Mathur, A.P.: Non-intrusive testing, monitoring and control of distributed corba objects. In: TOOLS'33 – 33rd International Conference on Technology of Object-Oriented Languages, Mont-saint-Michel, France (2000) 195–206

65. Delamaro, M.E., Pezzè, M., Vincenzi, A.M.R., Maldonado, J.C.: Mutant operators for testing concurrent Java programs. In: Brazilian Symposium on Software Engineering'2001, Rio de Janeiro, RJ, Brazil (2001) 272–285

66. Gönenç, G.: A method for design of fault-detection experiments. IEEE Transactions on Computers **19** (1970) 551–558

67. Sabnani, K.K., Dahbura, A.: Protocol test generation procedure. Computer Networks and ISDN Systems **15** (1988) 285–297

68. Fujiwara, S., Bochmann, G.V., Khendek, F., Amalou, M., Ghedamsi, A.: Test selection based on finite state models. IEEE Transactions on Software Engineering **17** (1991)

69. Beydeda, S., Gruhn, V.: An integrated testing technique for component-based software. In: AICCSA ACS/IEEE International Conference on Computer Systems and Applications, Beirut, Libanon, IEEE Computer Society Press (2001) 328–334

70. Harrold, M.J., Liang, D., Sinha, S.: An approach to analyzing and testing component-based systems. In: First International ICSE Workshop on Testing Distributed Component-Based Systems, Los Angeles, CA (1999)

71. Rosenblum, D.S.: Adequate testing of component-based software. Technical Report UCI-ICS-97-34, University of California, Irvine, CA (1997)

72. Ural, H., Yang, B.: A structural test selection criterion. Information Processing Letters **28** (1988) 157–163

73. Martins, E., Toyota, C.M.: Construction of autotestable classes. In: VIII Symposion of Fault Tolerance Computation, Campinas, SP (1999) 196–209 (in Portuguese).

74. Rosa, A.C.A., Martins, E.: Using a reflexive architecture to validate object-oriented applications by fault injection. In: Workshop on Reflexive Programming in C++ and Java, Vancouver, Canada (1998) 76–80

75. Orso, A., Harrold, M.J., Rosenblum, D., Rothermel, G., Do, H., Soffa, M.L.: Using component metacontent to support the regression testing of component-based software. In: IEEE International Conference on Software Maintenance (ICSM'01), Florence, Italy, IEEE Computer Society Press (2001) 716–725

76. Edwards, S.H.: Toward reflective metadata wrappers for formally specified software components. In: OOPSLA '01 Workshop on Specification and Verification of Component-Based Systems, Tampa, Florida, ACM Press (2001)

77. Harrold, M.J., McGregor, J.D., Fitzpatrick, K.J.: Incremental testing of object-oriented class structures. In: 14th International Conference on Software Engineering, Los Alamitos, CA, IEEE Computer Society Press (1992) 68–80

78. Gao, J.: Tracking component-based software. Technical report, San Jose State University, (San Jose, CA)

79. M.Voas, J.: Certifying off-the shelf-components. IEEE Computer **31** (1998) 53–59

80. Binder, R.V.: Modal testing strategies for OO software. Computer **29** (1996) 97–99

81. Binder, R.V.: The free approach to testing object-oriented software: An overview. Pgina WWW (1996) Available on-line at:
`http://www.rbsc.com/pages/FREE.html` [01-20-2003].

82. Kim, S., Clark, J.A., Mcdermid, J.A.: Class mutation: Mutation testing for object-oriented programs. In: FMES. (2000)

83. Edwards, S.H.: A framework for practical, automated black-box testing of component-based software. Software Testing, Verification and Reliability **11** (2001) 97–111

84. Wang, Y., King, G., Wickburg, H.: A method for built-in tests in component-based software maintenance. In: Third European Conference on Software Maintenance and Reengineering, Amsterdam, Netherlands, IEEE Computer Society Press (1999) 186–189

85. Soundarajan, N., Tyler, B.: Testing components. In: OOPSLA '01 Workshop on Specification and Verification of Component-Based Systems, Tampa, Florida, ACM Press (2001) 4–9

86. Rosa, A.C.A., Martins, E.: Using a reflexive architecture to validate object-oriented applications by fault injection. In: Workshop on Reflexive Programming in C++ and Java, Vancouver, Canada (1998) 76–80 (Available on-line at:
`http://www.dc.unicamp.br/~eliane`).

87. Edwards, S.H.: Black-box testing using flowgraphs: An experimental assessment of effectiveness and automation potential. Software Testing, Verification and Reliability **10** (2000) 249–262

88. Zhao, J.: Dependence analysis of java bytecode. In: 24th IEEE Annual International Computer Software and Applications Conference (COMPSAC'2000), Taipei, Taiwan, IEEE Computer Society Press (2000) 486–491

89. Zhao, J., Xiang, L., Nishimi, K., Harada, T.: Understanding java bytecode using kafer. In: 20th IASTED International Conference on Applied Informatics (AI'2002), Innsbruck, Austria, ACTA Press (2002)

90. Vincenzi, A.M.R., Delamato, M.E., Maldonado, J.C., Wong, W.E., Simão, A.S.: Jabá – a Java bytecode analyzer. In: XVI Brazilian Symposium on Software Engineering, Gramado, RS, Brazil (2002) 414–419

91. McGregor, J.D.: Parallel architecture for component testing. Journal of Object-Oriented Programming **10** (1997) 10–14 Available on-line at: `http://www.cs.clemson.edu/~johnmc/columns.html` [01-06-2003].

92. Bhor, A.: Component testing strategies. Technical Report UCI-ICS-02-06, Dept. of Information and Computer Science – University of California, Irvine – California (2001) Available on-line at: `http://www.ics.uci.edu/~abhor/` [01-06-2003].

93. Bundell, G.A., Lee, G., Morris, J., Parker, K., Lam, P.: A software component verification tool. In: International Conference on Software Methods and Tools (SMT'2000), Wollongong, Australia (2000)

94. Corporation, P.: Using design by contract to automate java software and component testing. web page (2002) Avaliable on-line: `http://www.parasoft.com/` [01-20-2003].

95. Beck, K., Gamma, E.: JUnit cookbook. web page (2002) Avaliable on-line: `http://www.junit.org/` [01-20-2003].

96. Edge, T.: Glass JAR toolkit. web page (2002) Available on-line at: `http://www.testersedge.com/gjtk/` [01-04-2003].

97. H. Agrawal. Dominators, super blocks, and program coverage. In *Proceedings of the 21st Annual ACM SIGPLAN–SIGACT Symposium on Principles of Programming Languages (POPL'94)*, Portland, OR (1994) 25–34.

Setting a Framework
for Trusted Component Trading

John Morris[1], C. Peng Lam[2], Gary A. Bundell[1], Gareth Lee[1], and Kris Parker[1]

[1] Centre for Intelligent Processing Systems, University of Western Australia
WA 6009, Australia
{morris,bundell}@ee.uwa.edu.au, gel@cs.uwa.edu.au,
kjparker@murdoch.edu.au
[2] School of Computer & Information Science, Edith Cowan University
WA 6050, Australia
c.lam@ecu.edu.au

Abstract. Software engineers constructing systems from third-party components need to be able to assess the quality of those components in order to have any confidence in the final system. We argue that the most effective and economic way to do this is for developers to supply test specifications along with the components that they offer to the market. We describe a simple, portable test specification based on XML documents. When a test specification is packaged with a purchased component, system builders are efficiently able to not only verify a component developer's claim for quality but also use the test specification to elucidate fine details of a component's capabilities that may be missing or not manifest in a natural language specification. A system builder selecting a component for integration into a new system needs to consider more than its ability to perform the required functions: the degree of testing can be an important indication of its reliability. Thus we propose an index, describing the degree of testing that a component has undergone, which can be used to rate components and aid selection decisions. Combined with a test specification, a purchaser can efficiently determine whether a component meets claims for its quality.

1   Introduction

With the growth of networking and computing power, the complexity of software systems has also increased dramatically, thus making them increasingly more expensive to develop and to maintain as well as more error prone. In order to keep the software development cost down, many software companies are using third party software components (Commercial Off The Shelf or COTS), thus introducing a set of problems that are different to those that occur in building software systems from scratch. The problems associated with the use of COTS components stem from these characteristics:

- COTS components are black boxes as purchasers do not have access to the source code;
- Software developers have no control over the evolution of COTS components;

A. Cechich et al. (Eds.): Component-Based Software Quality, LNCS 2693, pp. 128–158, 2003.

- Limited documentation can make COTS components difficult to use;
- COTS components have limited interface mechanisms for interaction with other components.

While formal verification is gaining acceptance as a technique for verifying the correctness and quality of software systems, it is usually applied in the development of safety-critical systems. Other commonly used approaches are process-based and involved use of standards such as ISO9000 and SEI-CMM as well as use of the Testing Maturity Model (TMM) [1]. The TMM is used to complement the CMM, specifically in addressing issues related to software testing and quality assurance. It consists of a set of maturity levels, a set of recommended practices at each level and an assessment model that can be used to evaluate and improve testing within an organization.

This chapter details a two-pronged approach that attempts to address the issues associated with the quality of software components: Developer Self-Certification and a Testing Index. We argue that "the quality of the whole can only be as good as that of the weakest component" and thus it is important that the quality of these software components are verifiable in some way by the component consumers who use them for software system development. The Developer Self-Certification approach involves a model for software component certification, which is based on test specifications or certificates supplied by component producers. The test specifications are in a standard portable form so that purchasers (or consumers) may evaluate the quality and suitability of purchased software components with minimal effort. The approach reduces the cost generally borne by component consumers—an amount which is deemed to be quite significant [2], where the component consumer generates the inputs, develops the test oracle and builds the test driver for testing the component. Note that in the context of our proposed approach, the term "component" refers to any piece of software with a well-defined interface and thus includes components satisfying any of the plethora of definitions of the term found in the literature [3] as well as simple functions or procedures, such as those found in a mathematical library.

We have argued previously [4] that the most effective mechanism for ensuring purchasers' satisfaction requires component producers to provide test specifications with the components they sell. These test specifications should have two vital characteristics:

1. they should be easily read and interpreted by the purchaser because the test specifications form an extension of the component's specifications, enabling the component consumers to verify that the component does in fact meet the application's requirements, and
2. component consumers should be able to run the tests themselves in order to ensure (a) that the component producer's claims are correct; and (b) the component will run correctly in the target environment, i.e. it does not rely on some unique "feature" of the component producer's environment.

It is important to emphasize that the scope for the work described in this chapter is a marketplace for small, generally non-safety critical components.

This tends to exclude large, complex testing languages such as TTCN-3 [5]. We identify some issues that we believe are vital for an orderly marketplace and propose solutions. However, marketplace strategies tend to evolve over time and our purpose is to accelerate this evolution.

Section 3.2 describes an XML-based test specification format and a system for executing these specifications. The content of the test specification is defined by a publicly available DTD [6]. It has only twelve major elements and thus is very simple to learn and adopt. We have also built a Test Pattern Verifier (TPV) in Java which executes these test specifications. The test specification has been thoroughly tested: we used a student class to see how easy it was to learn to use the specification effectively—a single lecture and a practical class sufficed to introduce them to the basic concepts.

We also believe that a mechanism is required to assess the risk associated with using a third party component. Component-Based Software Engineering (CBSE) assumes a source of reliable components: productivity gains depend not only on time saved in re-use but on the ability to omit unit testing from the system lifecycle and reliability gains depend on the degree to which units (components) may be trusted. If some parts of a system are not under the direct control of software component consumers then they need to have a means of generating a risk model for the use of the system containing those components. The testing index will aid a software consumer to estimate parameters for a risk model for a complete system. The testing levels described in Section 4 are designed to provide this. Our scale recognizes that testing is expensive and that various criteria (cost, time, etc.) will be used to determine the level of testing justified for any component.

Issues associated with the use of the test specifications and testing index are discussed in Section 5. In Section 6, we briefly describe the future trends associated with the use of trusted components and conclude in Section 7.

2   Background

2.1   Component-Based Software Engineering

Component-Based Software Engineering (CBSE) is a methodology that supports the compositional approach to building software applications involving "plug-and-play" software components (custom-built or Commercial Off-the-Shelf (COTS)) in a framework. This paradigm is becoming increasingly important owing to the maturation of several underlying technologies such as OMG's CORBA [7], Microsoft's .NET framework [8] Sun's Enterprise Java Beans framework [9]. Recent developments such as the shift from centralized mainframe-based to distributed applications and the need to reuse existing resources in the business and organizational contexts [10] are accelerating the use of CBSE for application development. However, reuse of components in CBSE differs from conventional reuse in that components are:

- required to interoperate with other components as well as the frameworks,
- required to hide their implementation details and thus their interfaces are separated from their implementations,
- usually designed on a pre-defined architecture to permit interoperability.

Component development and integration are the two key processes in CBSE. The component-based enterprise software process model [11] for application development consists of the following sequential stages: Analysis and Component Acquisition, Component-Oriented Design, Component Composition, Integration Test and System Test. The unit testing phase is missing in this methodology. This is due to the fact that often developers do not have access to the source code and thus can only work with the components in a totally black box manner. CBSE must also take into account (*i*) the mismatch which can arise between components from several sources [12], (*iii*) incomplete or incorrect behavioral specifications for the components, and (*iii*) high volatility of components as they are often upgraded—leading to cases where upgrades may not have the required capability or bug fixes. All these factors contribute to making integration an error prone process producing systems that are difficult to test and debug.

Many large industrial systems that have very high reliability and availability requirements are being developed using components. In fact, Boehm states that 99% of all executing instructions come from COTS products—based on limited analysis of data from the Department of Defence [13]. Formal methods can be used to deal with the issues we have mentioned above to ensure a reliable system, for example, Profeta III *et al.* incorporated formal methods in the design of relay-based systems for the rail transport industry to ensure that they will operate in a fail-safe manner [14]. However this approach is not a silver bullet: formal methods are not widely used in industry for a number of reasons [15]. Among these are needs for standards as well as support tools. Wileden [16] suggested that a significant investment in formal methods tools is required for industrial applications just as the significant investment in compiler technology resulted in the widespread take-up of high-level languages by the industry. An alternative to formal methods uses a visual modelling language such as UML to attempt to capture component requirements and design the component classes and the interface more accurately. The use cases can be used to derive test cases and the provision of a requirement and design model with the component will provide a more complete picture of the component's capabilities and functions.

Another approach suggested by Weyuker [17] involves testing the components for each new environment so that developers and users can predict behavior and performance. This is not a very feasible approach as it may incur significant cost.

CBSE cannot be used effectively until it can be employed within the context of well-understood methods for designing, assembling and maintaining component-based systems [12]. The development of effective strategies to support the development of trusted components—components that are certifiable in terms of their conformance to both their behavioral and interface specifications—constitutes an important step forward that we address in this chapter.

2.2   Third-Party Software Certification

Currently quality certification of most software products is based on adherence to specified processes—requiring software authors to "take oaths concerning which development standards and processes they will use". Third party software testing laboratories—or software certification laboratories (SCLs)—which certify components have been proposed by Voas: he argues that *"completely independent product certification offers the only approach that consumers can trust"* [18]. Independent SCLs would certify products. They would:

(a) receive instrumented software from developers,
(b) arrange for pre-qualified users to deploy the instrumented software,
(c) collect and analyze data from user sites,
(d) generate statistics on usage and performance in the field, and
(e) provide limited warranties for the software based on these statistics.

Over time, the operational profile of the software would generally broaden, enabling the SCLs to similarly broaden the warranty. Limitations associated with the SCL approach include:

Cost. The development cost of products certified in this way will be burdened by the significant costs of the completely independent certification process. The certifiers are unlikely to provide any form of warranty to purchasers unless (potentially expensive) liability insurance is built in to their costs. There is a possibility that insurers may be prepared to factor the amount of operational data available into their calculation of risk and lower the premium accordingly, but this will not happen unless this approach becomes common and insurers start to compete for large markets in this area.

Liability. Purchasers will not pay for the services of third party certifiers if they do not provide additional value in some form of precisely stated warranty. Whilst testing a component certainly adds value, it is doubtful whether testing alone—without some form of guarantee of the completeness of it—will add sufficient value to make a SCL viable. Although it follows some "operational profile", user-based testing is essentially random. An SCL would thus be susceptible to damage claims from unexercised "time-bombs" embedded in code. Developers simply disclaim liability: SCLs may be in a more invidious position: they are providing professional assessment of the risk of using a component. As Voas notes, courts have not been kind when such advice has been proven faulty.

Developer Resources. Much successful, widely used software has been written by a single programmer or small groups of programmers working independently: Linux is one well-known example. A thriving component market would certainly include many such products. These—generally self-financed individuals or groups—could not be expected to

(a) have the capacity to pay for SCL services,
(b) relinquish a share of their production in the early stages to attract capital to pay for SCL services,

(c) distract themselves from their creative endeavors for contract negotiations with an SCL, or

(d) be willing to invest the time to instrument their products for residual testing [19] if they were using any other formal methods for testing.

Safety-critical Systems. Voas, noting that SCLs will likely have some difficulty persuading testers to fly in software-controlled aircraft or submit to software-controlled medical devices, suggests the software might be certified in non-critical environments first. Once "noncritical certification" has been achieved, safety-critical applications could use the product. However (a) many key components of safety-critical systems will not be used in noncritical systems; and (b) operational profiles will not satisfy the applicable software product standards—for example, for airborne [20] or defence systems [21], statement coverage is required. Thus additional testing will still be needed to meet legal or contractual obligations. Furthermore, this additional testing may be the larger part of the total testing effort. Statement coverage requires the generation of test cases for many rare situations not likely to be encountered in any reasonable period of "normal" use.

Examples of the SCL approach include Underwriter Laboratories [22] where third party certification of software is based on the "UL Standard for Safety for Software in Programmable Components". A new ANSI/UL planning panel has already been set up to upgrade and to expand the existing standard to deal with safety-critical components and beyond.

On the other hand, Stafford and Wallnau [23] proposed distribution of the responsibilities associated with third party certification among the other key players in the component market place. They identified five basic players: (a) the component technology specifier, (b) the component technology implementer, (c) the reasoning framework developer, (d) the component implementer, and (e) the system developer. They also introduced an active component dossier—"an abstract component that defines certain credentials, and provides benchmarking mechanisms that, given a component, will fill in the values of these credentials" [23]. The component implementer uses the dossier to package the software component. A dossier can also be specialized to different types of systems so that it can cater to different types of analysis associated with these systems. It however will minimally contain "a postulated credential that provides an expected range for a latency measure, a test harness that is adaptable to the environment in which the component is to be deployed so that the validity of the latency measure can be tested in locus" [23].

2.3   Software Engineering Standards

Fenton and Neil [24] report discovering over 250 software engineering standards—primarily process standards [24, 25] that do not provide much assistance for testing. They compared a British standard for pushchairs[1] (BS 4792) with a defence

---

[1] Previously known as "perambulators" but more recently as "baby strollers" in some countries that claim to use English as the primary language.

software safety standard (DEF-STAN 00-55) [21]. 28 requirements in BS 4792 are entirely product requirements and 11 of these were external product requirements. In contrast, 88 of the 115 requirements in DEF-STAN 00-55 are process requirements and internal product and resource requirements made up the remainder. Not a single external product requirement was included in DEF-STAN 00-55. The British Standard BS 7925-2 [26] is a standard for software component testing but is still primarily a process standard. It requires that a tester choose one of 13 defined strategies for developing test sets. A section "other technique" was included in the standard which allows standard-conforming testing to use an unspecified technique which is appropriate to check the software being tested. Although the limitations of statement coverage are well known, it appears to be the only testing strategy that is prescribed in any other standard [27, 21, 20]. Other testing standards, including D0178B [20] that relates to white-box testing on compiled code, IEC/Nuclear—another white box approach and IEC/WG9, all involve recommendations for white-box testing methods.

Rapps and Weyuker have classified testing strategies based on the paths taken through a section of code [28]. Their classification examined paths from definitions to uses of variables. They prove various subsumption relationships which rank testing strategies in their family of strategies according to their relative strengths. However their classification covers only a very narrow band of strategies: we believe that a wider, standard scale—that can be applied to a component tested by any strategy—is needed (cf. Section 4).

Many other reliability metrics based on testing have been proposed, e.g. fault discovery rates [29]. Most of these metrics are appropriate for large systems where the number of required tests precludes fully testing to any criterion. In this work, we focus on components, which will in general be much smaller units of code for which it is practical to achieve 100% testing with some chosen strategy.

3   Strategies and Tools
for Supporting Developer Self-certification

To try to obtain some measures of trust for components, we have proposed strategies that allow purchasers to estimate component reliability via a testing index [30] as well as the idea of a component test bench [31] and developer self-certification [4] for trusted software components. This section describes concepts and a tool for developer self-certification.

3.1   What Is Developer Self-certification?

We base our model for software component certification on test specifications supplied in a standard portable form by developers so that purchasers may determine the quality and suitability of purchased software with minimal effort. The integrated circuit market was used as a model by some early proponents of component software—to the extent of calling components "software integrated circuits (ICs)". Most IC manufacturers' data sheets are structurally similar, with separate sections for DC and AC characteristics. Device parameters such as propagation delays are reported with similar notations and structures. Circuit designers benefit greatly from this de facto standardization; they can rapidly find and understand the information on data sheets from different manufacturers.

The additional information in tests clearly adds to the value of a component. Creating the test data is a time-consuming process and a viable business model would need to ensure that developers are rewarded for providing it. Although a developer may be concerned that valuable information about the internal structure of a component is being given away in the tests, we suggest that in the framework for small component trading that we are discussing here, it would rarely be economic for a third party to reverse engineer the component. In many cases, a developer will need to realism that—to establish trust—there is no alternative to providing more information and that confirmation that the internal structure has been verified will be essential.

3.2   Standard Test Specification

Numerous testing "languages" have been proposed [32, 33, 5]. However, design of a new language poses several difficulties: it must be either so simple that it lacks many necessary capabilities or it becomes as complex as the language in which the components under test are written. Alternatively, one can simply augment an existing language with some classes that perform many of the routine, repeated operations of testing: JUnit is one example of this approach [34]. We have adopted an entirely different approach: our test specifications are simple, structured documents. When complex iterative steps are required, for example in generating large test data sets, a tester writes "helper" classes in the same language as the component under test.

If developers are to supply test sets to purchasers, it becomes necessary to provide a standard, portable way of specifying the tests, so that a component user may assess the reliability of the component or alternatively, the degree of risk associated with its use in an arbitrary target system. Orso et al.'s proposal [35] is similar in concept although they do not provide formal definitions of what they refer to as "meta-data"[2]. We also believe that the requirement for instrumented code for regression tests has significant performance implications [36].

Requirements for a Standard Test Specification. To become an accepted standard many requirements should be met. The developer community is diverse and—regrettably—often puts expediency before standards and other disciplines that have beneficial long-term effects. We have listed those that we consider to be a minimum set to render a test specification format likely to gain wide acceptance and thus be suitable for a standard.

---

[2] The authors of this paper really mean "data" as they are simply adding additional data to a component. The added data does not describe other data and so does not warrant the "meta" tag!

1. *Portable.* Clearly, the format should be usable on a wide variety of operating systems, architectures and communications infrastructures.
2. *Able to handle components with state or dataflow functions in any widely used language.* A system should be to test object-oriented software as well as simple side-effect free functions, such as those found in libraries of functions for scientific, engineering and statistical applications, e.g. NAG [37].
3. *Independent of specific tools.* No specific tools should be needed to read, interpret or execute the test specifications: specifications and formats should be open and readily available.
4. *Multiple tools.* There should be no barriers to the creation of tools: users should be able to create tools which target particular needs. Any tools that are needed, e.g. parsers, should be available from multiple sources for multiple operating systems and architectures.
5. *Readily edited.* The form of the test specification should be readily edited by multiple tools. ASCII text, which can be edited by common text editors, obviously satisfies this requirement.
6. *Small.* The size of the total set of support tools should be reasonable to ensure that the system can run on a wide range of computers, including embedded devices.
7. *Easy to learn.* To be widely accepted, any system must be easy to learn: it must not have a large set of terms or elements that must be learnt before the system can be used.
8. *Able to handle GUI software.* Since much modern software hides behind graphical user interfaces (GUIs), the ability to handle GUI software is clearly a major advantage. Furthermore, there should be no ties to a specific GUI infrastructure.
9. *Able to handle the repetitive nature of tests.* Thorough testing is repetitive—requiring the application of many minor variations of a single test to the same software module.
10. *Automatically insert common tests—invariants.* Rigorous testing should involve the application of standard tests at every point in the testing process: by "standard tests", we mean invariants that should hold at all points in the life of an object or other software artifact.
11. *Users able to write their own processors.* Users should be able to write their own processors that will either provide specific capabilities for a particular type or style of software or improve and extend the capabilities of our TPV.
12. *Regression testing.* Re-testing after defects have been discovered[3] or enhancements have been made should be facilitated. Testers should be warned if one execution's results differ from a previous execution with the same inputs.

3.3   Software Component Laboratory Test Specification

Our test specification is based on W3C's Extensible Markup Language (XML) that satisfies most of the requirements stated in Section 2. XML abides by a

---

[3] Resulting from inadequate initial testing!

standard developed by an independent organization responsible for a number of other widely accepted standards; it has achieved wide acceptance; editors and parsers are available on a wide variety of hardware platforms and operating systems and it was designed to provide structured documents. XML documents are laid out with some simple rules, making them easy to read and interpret. Understanding the documents is made easier by several readily available editors which highlight the structure and provide various logical views.

By defining a minimal number of elements in the proposed test specification, we ensured that it is simple and easy to use. Rather than make the test specification complex, we allow testers to write "helper" classes in the language of the system being tested. This gives testers the power of a programming language in which they already have expertise, thus avoiding the need to learn an additional language for testing purposes only.

There are three documents associated with a component under test:

- Component Descriptor —describes an individual component
- Test Specification —specifications for individual tests
- Result Set — results obtained by executing test specifications.

These documents allow test specifications to be shared between components which have essentially identical capability but, for example, provide different space/time tradeoffs or are written in different languages. In Java's Collection framework, several classes have common behaviors defined in the Collection interface that may be tested with common test specifications. It is also easy to imagine a Java and C++ component performing the same task and having sufficiently close structures that common tests could be used. Generating complete test sets is an expensive and time consuming task and this allows the re-use of test sets. Multiple test specifications can be associated with any component, so test specification re-use is possible even if only some of a component's methods are duplicated in another one. Note that this represents a significant advantage over testing languages such as JUnit [34] or TTCN-3 [5].

Result sets could have been added to a component descriptor document but they are also kept separate because:

1. Component descriptors contain version information. However, a new version of a component will almost invariably want to use results from a previous version as a benchmark.
2. The information needed to support different development needs might be quite diverse and variable. A separate descriptor which can be customized for differing needs allows execution systems to simply copy whole structures (e.g. the <DocHeader> element can be copied without concern for internal detail) when needed. The critical test specifications remain unchanged.
3. Result sets very quickly become very large—with results from multiple executions of the same tests (when there are discrepancies)—so simply copying old result sets when creating new versions may not be desirable.
4. Management (e.g. archival) of large result sets may be simplified by keeping them in documents distinct from the component descriptors.

ComponentDescriptor Element. This element contains all the identifying information for a component: name, author, owner, version, modification history, etc. It also contains names of <TestSpecification> which are relevant to this component. An example component descriptor might contain the following information:

```
<ComponentDescriptor>
  <DocHeader>
    <Author Name="J Brown" Org="SCL" />
    <Author Name="R Smith" Org="SCL" />
    <Copyright>SCL, CIIPS</Copyright>
    <History>
      <Created Date="25.2.99" Who="JB" />
      <Mod Date="21.1.99" Who="RS" Ver="0.01">
      Bug #1 exterminated</Mod>
    </History>
  </DocHeader>
  <Implementation Name="AClass.java" Lang="Java"
                  IntName="Collection">
    <Desc>AClass models ... </Desc>
  </Implementation>
  <Interface Name="Collection">
    <Desc>Collection models general containers
          ... </Desc>
  </Interface>
  <TestSetName>AClass_TS1</TestSetName>
  <TestSetName>AClass_TS2</TestSetName>
</ComponentDescriptor>
```

The contents of the <ComponentDescriptor> may be varied according to a developer's or an application's needs so we only suggest a possible structure here. As noted above, tools can be set up to copy, for example, the whole of <DocHeader> element without being concerned about its content. With XML, some high level elements can be required (e.g. a <DocHeader> element) and the actual content of the element left to a user without affecting portability of documents. Thus details of the <ComponentDescriptor> element are not critical to the main theme of this chapter and we omit further discussion of it.

TestSpecification Document. The root element of a specification is the <TestSpecification> element. It has a name for identification and cross-referencing purposes but no other information about the component under test: this information is stored in the <ComponentDescriptor> document to facilitate re-use of test specifications.

TestSet and TestGroup Elements. These two elements are provided so that testers may group individual tests into logical hierarchies relevant to the com-

```
<TestSpecification>
  └ <TestSet Name="...">+
     ├ <TestGroup Name="...">*
     │  ├ <TestGroup>*
     │  ├ <Invariant DataType="...">*
     │  └ <Operation Name="..." Pre="op_name ">*
     │     ├ <Invariant>*
     │     ├ <Constructor>*
     │     └ <MethodCall Target="...">*
     ├ <Operation>
     └ <Invariant>
```

Fig. 1. TestSpecification document structure showing the major elements. * = 0 or more occurrences permitted, + = 1 or more occurrences permitted

ponent under test. No prescriptions are made about how they should be used, for example, a `<TestSet>` might contain all the tests for a single class and `<TestGroup>`s contain tests for individual methods of that class, but a tester is free to group the tests in other ways.

Operation Element. An individual test will usually require a number of actions to set up the test scenario—constructing objects with specific attributes in order to test one of its methods, constructing arrays of test values, etc.. All the calls that constitute a test are grouped into an `<Operation>`. Thus a skeleton of a test specification might be:

```
<TestSpecification Name="ClassA_BasicTests">
  <TestSet Name="ClassA">
    <TestGroup Name="Add tests">
      <Operation Name="Add null">
      ...
      </Operation>
      <Operation Name="Add identity">
      ...
      </Operation>
    </TestGroup>
    <TestGroup Name="Remove tests">
    ...
    </TestGroup>
  </TestSet>
</TestSpecification>
```

Our TPV displays a "tree" showing the names of the test sets, test groups and operations and allows a tester to select individual operations, whole test groups or an entire test set for execution.

The `Pre` (Prefix) attribute of an operation allows a tester to specify an operation which creates a common initial environment for multiple tests and invoke it by name as needed in other operations.

`<Operation>` attributes	
`Name`	Identifies the operation
`Pre`	Predecessor operation: the value of the Pre attribute must be an operation that has already been defined. This operation will be run as a predecessor to this one: any "values" generated by the predecessor are available to this operation. `Pre` permits a tester to define a scenario which is used by a number of tests, place it in an operation which is run as a predecessor to a number of "real" test operations.

When each operation is run, a run-time environment (RTE)—similar to a stack frame in conventional programming environments—is created which captures results from constructors and method calls. The RTE is a list of (name, value) pairs. Operations inherit RTEs from their predecessor operations.

Constructor and MethodCall Elements. Each constructor or method call may have arguments and return a result. Results are captured so that they can be compared with expected values or verified by "helper" methods. The "helper" methods allow the test specification itself to be kept simple and portable: no language-specific features were added. Furthermore implementations of functions which are essentially the same in different languages can re-use the same test specification and reduce the significant effort that test set generation requires.

These two elements cause constructors or methods to be invoked and the return value captured. They are exactly like the equivalent calls in a high level language: we could have inserted "program like" statements—as found in many other test scripts [38, 39] here, but chose the "pure" XML approach to avoid designing a new language and helping to meet requirements for ease of learning (cf. requirement 7), portability (had we used a subset of one language as a base) and the size of the TPV (with many more constructs to parse).

`<Constructor>`, `<MethodCall>` attributes	
`Name`	Class name for a constructor, method name otherwise.
`Target`	The object on which this method will be invoked. The target must have been created by a previous `<Constructor>` or `<MethodCall>` and stored in the RTE.
`Static`	Optional—designates a class method, e.g. a Java static method. The `Name` attribute must be present and names the class containing the class method.

Constructor and MethodCall elements contain `<Arg>` and `<Result>` elements which may best be described by reference to an example:

```
<Operation Name="add standard">
  <Constructor Name="ContainerA">
    <Arg Name="init_capacity" DataType="Integer">10</Arg>
    <Result Name="c"></Result>
  </Constructor>
  <MethodCall Name="add" Target="c">
    <Arg Name="a" DataType="Integer">57</Arg>
    <Result DataType="boolean"><Exp>true</Exp>
    </Result>
  </MethodCall>
  <MethodCall Name="contains" Target="c">
    <Arg Name="a" DataType="Integer">57</Arg>
    <Result DataType="boolean"><Exp>true</Exp>
    </Result>
  </MethodCall>
</Operation>
```

In this example, an operation named **add standard** will appear in the TPV's directory of executable operations. Its first action is to invoke the constructor for a container class called **containerA** with an **Integer** argument with value 10^4. The object created is stored in the TPV's runtime environment (which it creates for each operation) under the name c. Then the **add** method is invoked on the object named c (already stored in the RTE following the constructor) with argument 57. This method should return a Boolean **true**, so the <Result> element contains an <Exp> element containing the expected result. Then, to verify that the previous **add** method was successful, **contains** is called with an **Integer** argument having value 57. Again, a **true** result is expected, so the <Result> element has an <Exp> element with the value **true**.

Arg Elements. Arguments can be either literals or objects already stored in the RTE: attributes of an <Arg> element distinguish the two cases:

<Arg> attributes	
Name	Formal name of argument (present for consistency—ignored for Java test specifications)
Source	Name of an object already stored in the RTE.
DataType	Argument type: the execution system should read the data of the <Arg> element and convert it to this type before invoking the method.
Static	Specifies that a Java method is static—the **Name** attribute must be present and names the class containing the static method.

---

[4] The TPV, which works with Java classes, searches for a constructor for the target class which takes a string argument. This gives a tester the flexibility to add simple constructors to assist testing.

Result Element. If complex objects are being tested, it is often not possible to know what the expected "value" is, but some properties or invariants of the complex object can be checked with subsequent method calls. For example, with a balanced tree, such as a red-black tree, the internal structure of the tree may not be easy to determine—nor of any particular interest—as long as the rules for red-black trees are not violated. So, in a constructor for a red-black tree, the <Result> element does not have an <Exp> child, it simply provides a name for the result via the Name attribute of the <Result>. This named object can be the target of further method calls which verify the object's properties.

In either case, if the Save attribute of <Result> is Y, the returned value is saved as part of a <ResultSet> document and compared with new results in regression testing.

<Result> attributes	
Name	If present, result is saved with this name in the RTE
DataType	Data type of the returned value: the execution system should read the data of the <Exp> element and convert it to this type before comparing with the actual returned value.
Save	Save="Y" indicates that this result is to be saved in the <ResultSet> document for comparison against values produced by this operation in subsequent executions.

Exp Element. The "value" of the returned value is the data of this element. It will be assumed that the data type (as specified by the DataType attribute of the result element) has a constructor which takes a string as an argument[5]. When verifying floating point values, precise matching is not generally possible, so an <Exp> element may have a Tol attribute, which specifies a fractional tolerance. For an Exp element:

$$< \text{Exp Tol} = "\delta" > x < \backslash \text{Exp} >$$

a result value, y, is considered correct if:

$$|y - x| < \delta |x|$$

Exceptions. A complete set of tests will verify that expected exceptions are thrown or raised when the software specification requires them. An <Exception> element within a <Constructor> or <MethodCall> specifies that invocation of that constructor or method should throw an exception and the TPV reports an error if an exception of the specified type (DataType attribute of <Exception>) is not thrown. It is possible to verify the properties of the exception in the same way that the properties of any other returned object are checked: if it is given a name, then it can become the Target of subsequent method calls, which could,

---

[5] Testers can supply factory methods in helper classes if necessary.

for example, invoke the exception's `get...` methods to discover the values of its attributes. The following fragment tests for an exception thrown when the argument to `add` is `null`.

```
<Operation Name="Check Exceptions">
  ...
  <MethodCall Name="add">
    <Arg DataType="Integer">null</Arg>
    <Exception Name="add_exception">
    </Exception>
  <MethodCall>
  <MethodCall Name="getMessage"
    Target="add_exception">
    <Result DataType="String">
      <Exp>add: null argument</Exp>
    </Result>
  </MethodCall>
</Operation>
```

Note that the exception is treated like any other object once it is "captured" by the RTE.

Invariant. Commonly, there will be one or more properties of an object being tested that will be invariant, i.e. objects of a class will always have these properties—no matter what operations are applied to them. A robust testing strategy would verify these invariants after every method on an object for which an invariant was known. However, adding all the necessary code to perform all these checks is tedious and—as a consequence—often omitted to speed up test code generation. However, when an error is discovered at the end of a long sequence of method invocations in an operation, one has to trace back through many steps to locate the source of the error. One mechanical—and often effective—way of localizing the error is simply to insert all the invariants that were omitted when the test was built.

To make testing robust *ab initio*, we allow a test to specify an invariant for a class. This takes the form of a method which, if called, will always return a known result. For the red-black tree, for example, one could add a `isValidRBTree()` method which checks the behavioral rules for an object and returns true if all are obeyed. Then an `<Invariant>` element is added to the test specification:

```
<Invariant Name="RBTree">
  <MethodCall Name="isValidRBTree">
    <Result DataType="boolean"><Exp>true</Exp>
    </Result>
  </MethodCall>
</Invariant>
```

This causes the execution system to record an invariant for objects of the
RBTree class. Whenever an RBTree is passed as an argument to a method or
returned from a method (or constructor), the isValidRBTree method will be
called on the argument object or returned object. If it does not return a true,
the execution system should flag an error. This feature effectively automatically
inserts large amounts of repeated code—relieving the tester of the need to add it
explicitly and, possibly more importantly, ensuring that—when an error occurs—
the problem is flagged as close to its source as possible, i.e. as soon as the
invariant fails.

ResultSet Document. To support regression testing, results that are captured by executing any operation are stored in a <ResultSet>. This is kept as a
separate document, because the test specification may be shared between components which have the same capabilities—each component will have its own
result set. The structure of a result set mimics that of a test specification with
sets, groups and operations.

```
<ResultSet Name="ClassA_OrderTests">
  <TestSetRes Name="ClassA">
    <TestGrpRes Name="Ordering Tests">
      <OpnRes Name="Add in order"
            SWVersion="1.0" Date="24.3.99">
        <Actual Name="first"
              DataType="Integer">12</Actual>
        <Actual Name="last"
              DataType="Integer">99</Actual>
      </OpnRes>
      ...
    </TestGrpRes>
    ...
  </TestSetRes>
</ResultSet>
```

This result might have been generated from tests on a container iterator: in
the <Operation> named "Add in order", two results—named first and last—
were marked for saving (Save="Y") in the result set. The TPV will compare
values for these two variables in subsequent executions of this operation. If the
results are identical, nothing will happen. If there are discrepancies, they will be
highlighted and both results stored in the result set for later checking. It is likely
that one of the results will be identified as the desired result and "promoted"
to an <Exp> element of the method call which generated the result. In this way,
the result set forms a history of the component's operation over time.

3.4   Keeping It Simple

Our test specification does not attempt to be yet another language that a programmer must learn. It provides a minimal number of XML elements which

are easily learnt in a short time (cf. section 3.6). In general, testers will need more capabilities—for example, to facilitate building large test data structures. Rather than expand the test specification with looping and other constructs to facilitate this, we allow testers to build "helper" classes in the same language as the original components were built. This avoids any significant learning curve: we consider it reasonable to presume a good knowledge of the language in which the component under test was written! It also provides the full capabilities of a standard language rather than the limited capabilities that might be designed into a "subset" language for testing purposes.

Thus for the test which starts with, say, a container class containing 10 integer elements, the tester builds a simple factory method that takes a string argument and, in a simple loop, splits it into individual tokens, converts them to integers and adds to the container, which is then returned once the end of the string has been reached. The helper methods, being written in the target language, have access to the file system and even communications channels. Testing is inherently repetitive, so a small set of well-designed helper methods will generally suffice for even a complex component under test.

3.5   Test Pattern Verifier

The Test Pattern Verifier (TPV) enables component users to run tests on the target machine, capture and compare results from an older version of a component with a newer one. It was written in Java, in order to meet our portability goal. The Java version directly invokes methods of components under test using the Java reflection interface. However the test specifications are not constrained to Java components and work has started to extend the TPV so that it emits C++ code which is then compiled and linked with the component under test.

The TPV allows the tester to select a test specification, which is then opened, parsed and stored in an internal structure mimicking the XML document. Fig. 2 shows the TPV's main screen after a test specification has been loaded and a group of tests run. The main frame contains three panels: the left-most one displays the content of the test specification as a *test set:test group:operation* hierarchy. Testers can navigate through this hierarchy—opening and closing test sets or groups as needed—in the same way that they can navigate through a file system.

Selecting a test set, group or operation following by selection of the run option causes the appropriate set, group or single operation to be executed. The middle panel presents a history of executions to date combined with simple pass/fail statistics for each one. Selecting any one of these causes the data accompanying it to appear in the right most panel. This panel has several tabs, allowing the tester to view the execution history for individual method invocations, the state of the run time environment, error reports and results from each constructor or method call invocation.

The first time a test specification is run, only results found in <Exp> elements are checked. However each execution will produce a <ResultSet> document containing results marked for saving. This may be saved at any point. When a

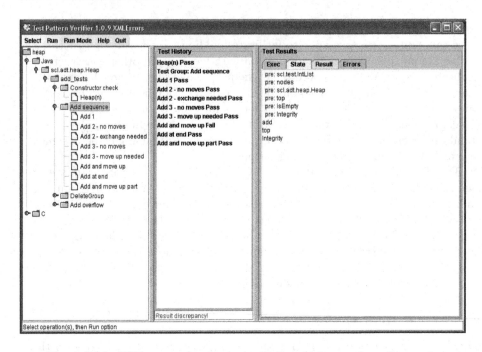

Fig. 2. Main TPV screen showing test selection, history and results panels

test specification is loaded again, if a matching result set document is found, it will also be loaded. Results from previous executions are now compared against those from the current execution and discrepancies highlighted. A history of discrepancies is also stored in the result set document.

The total size of the TPV itself is 118Kbytes. The XML parser that we routinely use adds 1Mbyte to this, but we have tested "mini" parsers that use less than 100Kbytes—the test specification does not use all the facilities of XML, so minimal parsers are acceptable. This small size means that it is practical for a developer to supply (or expect a purchaser to download) a copy of the TPV without significant additional expense. Complete test sets are likely to require more space[6] for even moderately complex components!

We emphasize that our TPV is not the only program that could be written to execute the test specifications proposed here. Users with differing needs, e.g. for reporting test results, may readily write a TPV of their own. XML parsers are available which may be directly called from programs in most major languages, so only the execution module and the result capturing and reporting modules need to be adapted to specific requirements.

---

[6] A possible criticism of the use of XML in this application is related to its "verbosity" and consequent resource usage. However, the high frequency of occurrence of a small number of XML tags means that compressors can achieve impressive results!

3.6   Usage Experience

Evaluation of the test specification and the associated TPV involved a class of 250 object-oriented programming students. The associated concepts were introduced via a single lecture and a laboratory session. These students were able to learn and effectively use the test specification and the TPV. This would not be possible in such a short time frame with a more complex testing language such as TTCN-3 [5]. They worked in groups to produce over 50 components, all accompanied by thorough sets of tests.

4   Component Testing Index

We previously argued for a mechanism to assess the risk associated with using third party components and proposed a testing index. This index is designed to allow a component purchaser to understand the degree to which a component has been tested. It may act as a basis for estimating parameters of a risk model for a complete system[7]. Developers would attach the testing level to their components and these levels would be justified by the scope of tests supplied.

This section introduces our testing level table and explains how a software system would acquire a "rating" at the various levels in the table. Some of the issues associated with using the proposed testing levels are also discussed.

The term "method" is used here with the meaning normally attributed to it in object-oriented systems. However, our discussions and rankings apply equally well to any procedure, function or subroutine in a procedural language. No distinctions are made here between methods; constructors and destructors associated with object-oriented systems—the term method encompasses all of them.

4.1   Reliability Ranking of Components and Testing Levels

The risk associated with the use of a specific component, is associated with the degree to which the component has been tested. We define "reliability" as the degree of proof that an implementation adheres to its specification[8]. We have assigned numeric indices to testing strategies: these indices can be used as parameters in risk models. The testing strategies and their associated indices are shown in Table 1. Seven basic levels were assigned values ranging from 0 to 6, with the value of 0 representing no testing being carried out and the value of 6 representing program code derived by formal transformation from the specification. This implies that in practice, components with test indices below level 1 are of no interest to component consumers and only components used in life-critical systems would need to be level 5 and above, as intensive effort would need to be

---

[7] There has been little previous work establishing precise relationships between the level of testing and the risk and clearly more research is needed in this area.

[8] Note that we assume that the specification is correct, i.e. this rating scheme does not attempt to say anything about validation—matching the specification with any user's requirements.

Table 1. Levels in the testing index

Level	Description
0	Totally untested
0.1	Passes an ad hoc set of tests generated with no defined strategy.
1	Passes test set which exercises critical capabilities. Critical capabilities should be identified in the specification as vital to the operation of a system in which this component would be embedded.
2	Passes test set based on analysis of ranges of input parameters and enumeration of possible exceptions. (a) at least one value chosen from the legal range of every input parameter, (b) at least one value chosen from the illegal range of every input parameter
2.2	Nulls: For each input for which a null value can be identified, a test case includes that null value.
2.5	Exceptions: Each exception in the specification is raised by at least one test case.
3	A formal equivalence class analysis has been conducted for every input and output parameter. For inputs, equivalence classes include classes of illegal values defined in the specification and for which method behavior is undefined. For outputs, equivalence classes include exceptions and other error outputs or states which are not necessarily reflected in values of output parameters. Test cases include: * at least one representative of each equivalence class (both input and output, legal and illegal values)
	Below Level 4, testing is "black box", i.e. based on a precise specification only. Level 4 and above implies that implementation details are checked also.

4	Test cases have been chosen using the criteria at Level 3 and a coverage tool has been used to ensure execution of every program statement. Coverage includes "missing branches". A statement of the form:
	`if ( cond ) statement;`
	has a missing branch: it is "executed" when cond is false. Test cases should make cond both true and false. Similarly, a switch statement with an empty default part has a missing branch, e.g.
	
	`switch( a ) {`
	`  case x: statement1;`
	`  case y: statement2;`
	`  }`

4.5	Inputs should be chosen such that a evaluates to x, y and a value which is neither x nor y.
5	Coverage has been achieved at Level 4 and every definition-use path in the code has been executed at least once in the course of testing.
5.5	Every identifiable path through the code has been executed. (This level considered impractical for all but the simplest pieces of code.)
6	Code derived by provably correct formal transformation from specification.
R	An "R" may be added to any rating: it signifies that a component has been tested for errors in resource usage.

applied to reach that level. Levels of verification are expressed as real numbers so as to accommodate variations in testing procedures, partial compliance as well as for insertion of new strategies.

As the proposed index is primarily based on equivalence class analysis, it is necessary to correlate other test generation techniques with equivalence class based techniques in order to use the proposed index effectively. In previous work [30], we related all the techniques found in BS7925-2 to the levels in the Table. Each of those techniques are described in terms of equivalence classes that effectively "covered" them, thus enabling an assessor to readily determine a level from our table that would apply to a component tested by each of the techniques in BS7925-2.

The various testing levels are briefly described below—full details can be found in Morris et al. [30]. For a component to pass at any other level, it must also pass at all the lower levels. Level 6 represents an approach where the software requirements are expressed in some formal notation and subsequently transformed by provably correct steps into the final code. Thus there is no formal testing and it differs from the other ratings that involve progressively more stringent testing

Level 1 is the lowest level where a component would be considered as having been tested: it requires the identification of "critical" functions from a specification. At Level 2, each input must be examined and a tester must identify legal, illegal and null values for that input. Test cases associated with legal inputs would have been included at level 1 and this level adds tests involving illegal values of inputs. Assertion mechanisms—found in programming languages like C, C++ and Eiffel—would be the simplest ways to achieve this. In languages that do not provide an inbuilt mechanism for this, a simple function taking a boolean parameter along with some mechanism for compiling it will suffice. More elaborate versions that can provide logging, stack tracing and other useful output are available, for example, in Sun's 1.4 release of Java.

Testing a component at Level 3 involves performing a full equivalence class analysis on the specification and deriving a test set from this analysis. As this level is independent of any particular implementation, artifacts associated with any implementation will only be explicitly tested if the implementation constraints are a part of its specification.

Testing a component at Level 4 involves full code coverage testing which can be achieved using a variety of tools that can provide coverage metrics of varying accuracy [40, 41, 42]. Level 5 uses Rapps and Weyuker's notion of definition-use paths [28] to identify cases which may have escaped coverage analysis. In cases where it is practical to identify and verify every possible path through the code for a method, we allow a rating of 5.5 to be claimed.

A component may need to be verified with respect to resources that it uses. Resource requirements or bounds may be defined in the component specification so these can be verified directly. At each testing level, available resource bounds may be violated (e.g. memory leakage) and thus must be verified. An "R" (Resource) tag is attached to the numeric rating when resource bounds have been checked for each test used to achieve the numeric rating. Even though resource requirements may not be an explicit part of a component's specifications they still need to be checked for unwanted or unexpected side effects the component may induce on available resources.

4.2   Issues Associated with Using the Testing Levels

Full Component Ratings. The ratings in Table 1 are specified for a single method of a component. However, components usually possess interfaces with more than one method. Each method associated with the component is tested and the minimum rating achieved for any one of its methods will be deemed to be the component's rating. However, this method of ranking may not be very relevant in practice and the frequency of use of each method could be more appropriate. Often a user's requirements (or high level software specification) will explicitly describe behavior that is actually achieved by making a sequence of method calls on an object. Operation elements in our test specification allow such sequences to be part of the test specification and labelled in a way that facilitates cross-referencing between the test specification and the software specification. In our rating, the successful completion of an operation contributes to the rating of the final method in the operation (excluding methods from "helper" classes which are invoked to verify the output of this final method.) The methods preceding this final method are simply there to provide a convenient way of producing a representative of one of the input equivalence classes for the final method. This input equivalence class is clearly one that must be tested, so that a focus on the testing of individual methods does not affect the reliability of the component viewed from a user's requirements—the user's requirements force the inclusion of the input to the final method in the operation into the full set of inputs for that method.

100% Compliance. A possible criticism of our levels is that we require 100% compliance at every stage and do not allow partial compliance: failing to reach 100% at level x results in the component being rated at level $x - \delta$. This is partly to address a weakness noted by Pfleeger *et al.* [25] when reviewing software engineering standards:

> "The first and most startling result of our work is that many standards are not really standards at all. Many 'standards' are reference or subjective requirements, suggesting that they are really guidelines (since degree of compliance cannot be evaluated)."

Secondly, the ratings are designed for components—not systems. The relatively small size of an individual component makes it feasible to attain full compliance at a target level.

Completeness of Test Sets. Purchasers needing high degrees of reliability will remain responsible for determining whether claims by vendors are valid.

However in our market model, they will start with an extensive set of tests, so, even if they find faults with a vendor's claim to completeness, they will still have fewer tests to generate.

5   Discussion

Section 3 and 4 detailed our two-pronged approach—providing tools and techniques to be used by both component producers and component consumers. When component producers provide test data to component purchasers, we see a number of advantages:

- Cost reduction. The incremental cost to developers is small as they already have to produce extensive tests as part of their own verification procedures.
- Trust is provided through the supply to component consumers of test data and the means to interpret it (the XML DTD can be used by most XML editors to display a test specification's structure and content) as well as the means to run the tests and verify that the component producer's claims for correctness are sustainable.
- Testing levels claimed by component producers as a result of their testing can be confirmed by examination of the tests.
- The test specifications augment the functional specifications (usually written in natural language and therefore potentially ambiguous). The test specifications and accompanying test results provide a precise (if voluminous!) specification for the actual behavior of the component.

Voas' Software Certification Laboratory model [18] may suit large developers producing major software packages, but a very significant section of the software industry has many small independent "manufacturers" of high quality products. The model that we propose here clearly targets small components and does not necessarily imply that the SCL model has no place: firstly, there are many situations where the cost of a software failure is high and third party certifications by specialist testing organizations be the only acceptable model and secondly, SCL certification may be the only practical alternative for large software systems. Our model is extremely effective: component producers write test specifications in a standard portable form and component consumers examine and execute those tests so that they have some degree of certainty that the larger product they are building will be reliable. In addition, while the proposed approach does not explicitly require the use of process models, it does not preclude them as they will clearly enhance the quality of the resulting products.

The testing levels discussed in Section 4 have been used to classify components in the VeriLib library [43] for reliability. Our strategy involved assigning a rating to a component as a whole using the level reached by the lowest rated functional method in its interface. A practical component will contain additional methods solely for diagnostic or integrity checking purposes. It is reasonable that these methods may be excluded for the purpose of rating the whole component. These excluded methods must be identified clearly in a class specification.

We believe our testing index addresses a need of prospective component consumers:

1. to assess the likelihood that a given component will function without error in actual use.
2. to assess the overall risk of using a system composed of numerous third party components.
3. to select components—when a number of components appear to meet a specific need, the proposed rating scheme supports the evaluation of:
   (a) the relative risk of using one component versus another.
   (b) the possible commercial consequence of using one component.
   (c) the relative value of two components, i.e. whether a component with a higher price will, in fact, justify its premium.

Component producers can also use the proposed strategies to support their claims about the reliability of their components—in terms of the provision of testing information associated with the Software Component Laboratory test specification, TPV and the provision to allow the consumer to rerun these tests. In addition, a link to the testing level will provide a recognized indication of the amount of testing that has been carried out by the producer and justifies the asking price of a component. Obviously a well tested component should cost more than another that only has limited testing.

We also argue here that in practical use, the testing index provides a clear and recognized basis for discussing a level of testing that is to be achieved for a specific component or software system. It provides a set of testing targets that were proposed and defined by an independent third party, thus allowing the negotiations between the involved parties to be centered on the decision of the desired level of testing. Although, it was not the original intention of the testing index, we observed a software development company using the testing index as a basis for contract negotiation with a client: discussions were much faster as they could focus on which level to offer or require rather than on defining the levels.

When failure is associated with some economic consequence, the reliability of non-software components as well as that of the assembled systems is commonly expressed in measures such as Mean-Time-Before-Failure. As CBSE becomes increasingly used for software system development and more components becoming available, similar risk models will be needed for these software systems. The proposed testing levels could be used as the foundation for a risk model where an appropriate risk parameter based on the mode of usage can be assigned to each level, thus providing an initial step to useful risk analysis for systems built by CBSE with COTS components.

As one final observation, we note that—as far as the software component market is concerned—supplying portable, executable test specifications can make the currently raging software professional certification argument [44, 45] somewhat irrelevant in non-safety-critical environments. We certify the product, not the producer. A professional producer will certify him or herself by providing verifiable test specifications with all of his or her output!

6   Future Trends

We believe that CBSE will not fully realize its potential until mechanisms are established by which component consumers can establish the reliability of components. Weyuker [46] discussing component reuse, concludes

> " ... that developers and potential users should be aware that components likely will not have been adequately tested for their infrastructure."

Effective and practical strategies for evaluating the reliability of components and their impact on the overall software system will need to be developed. We believe that there is a need for a uniform and recognized approach for rating the quality of software components which can be used by both component producers and consumers. Voas and Payne have proposed a "Test Quality rating" metric [18] which can be used as a dependability score for a component. The testing index proposed in this chapter is another attempt to address this need. The software industry will need to work towards some consensus on acceptable testing metrics if we are to produce trusted systems with CBSE. Component ratings will be able to be used in risk models for assessing risks associated with using those components and determine, for example, whether a component may be used "as is", whether it needs more testing or whether a more reliable one should be substituted. Development of risk models involving these metrics and tailored for CBSE will greatly aid the overall progression of CBSE.

In addition to reliability, CBSE requires economic sources of quality components. Small component producers have the opportunity to develop high quality software component in certain application domains by leveraging particular skills or knowledge and to find a market for these components. These small component producers can operate very efficiently with low overheads. They can ably develop components that target non-critical software systems as well as those systems where the cost of failure is relatively small. Since predicting whether any one component will generate high volume of sales is a difficult task, they will be quite reluctant to incur additional costs of third party certification. Third party SCL's will only add to costs unnecessarily—and be impractical for these small producers.

The market needs of component consumers should drive the development of strategies that component producers will use in delivering proofs of reliability for components. There is obviously a place for third party certification of components as there will be complex or safety critical components destined for systems for which reliability is an overriding goal and third party certification is economically justified. However, we consider that such situations are not likely to be the most common: in the majority of commercial software developments the cost of failure is relatively smaller and only a small premium (i.e. the cost of generating tests and inspecting them) for reliability can be justified. We believe that the use of the developers' self-certification approach as well as the application of the testing index is more appropriate in these cases. Tools to support the developers' self-certification approach should be developed to aid the process of producing components economically in addition to providing evidence of the level of testing.

In addition to the use of self-certification, a hybrid approach involving the concept of the active dossier [23] and incorporation of test certificates is worthy of investigation for components used in systems with higher economic impact of system failures. Strategies are needed for producing tamperproof test certificates and dossiers for components. In addition, if the dossier is to evolve over the life span of the component, we need to determine how the information relating to its evolution and usage should be incorporated into the dossier.

7   Conclusion

Currently, systems developers using CBSE can not confidently select COTS components from the large mass that is available. If the final system needs to be reliable, then its developers must know the reliability of individual components: trusting an unknown author to have thoroughly verified his or her work is not an acceptable strategy when there is any cost associated with failure. We propose two measures that would provide the needed trust: a testing index and developer written test, executable specifications or certificates. The testing index (a) assists initial selection of components; and (b) gives information about the degree of testing that could subsequently be used for risk assessment. The test specifications enable claims regarding the level of testing to be verified. These claims need to be verified manually, but, with well-organized test certificates, the cost of this should be only a fraction of that needed to generate the tests. Correct operation can be verified automatically by simply running the test specifications with a suitable tool, for example our TPV.

Developer-written test certificates will have the least impact on the final cost of a reliable component: the component's developers need to carry out the tests anyway. The only additional cost is capturing them in a regular way—and many project leaders would agree that this will often actually reduce final costs! Moreover, any extra effort is adding value to a component, as a tested component is certainly a more marketable commodity, with relatively small investments in additional time. SCL certification would also add value to a component, but it is likely that many more sales would be needed to recover the cost of generating the additional value in this way.

The test certificates have a further significant benefit; they augment and formalize the natural language functional specifications for the component as well as providing examples of its capabilities and use. The use of XML to structure the test certificates ensures portability and means that the many tools that work with it can be used to read and examine the test certificates.

Furthermore, we intended that this chapter should highlight the need for some universally accepted testing index that enables system integrators to compare different components and assess the risk associated with them. In addition, a system integrator, faced with a component that has a low rating, has a basis on which to make a rational "make or buy" decision. The likely cost to reproduce a component of higher rating can be balanced with the alternative cost. "Alternative cost" here includes not only the purchase price, but also the cost of the possible testing effort to confirm that a component meets a higher standard, for example, a desired overall system rating and possible costs to rectify or enhance a failing component.

We have proposed a rating which requires 100% compliance at its various levels because we believe that

1. compliance with a rating is more easily verified,
2. the rating is more suited to "black-box" components,

whose owners may not be willing to expose internal details and thus permit assessments based on lines of code, estimates of undiscovered errors, etc. to be used.

Whilst the software industry has shown itself to be quite adept at dealing with multiple standards, an orderly component market will need a single quality index that enables competing components to be assessed fairly. Thus a single, well accepted quality rating should assist the industry to grow—and, by providing the source of qualified, reliable components that CBSE needs to use as building blocks, increase the reliability of component-based systems as well as reducing their cost. We have put forward a simple testing index as a first step towards a generally accepted index; we would probably be surprised if this final consensus index looked much like our proposal, but CBSE practitioners need it and this process must start somewhere!

Acknowledgments

This work was supported by a grant from Software Engineering Australia (Western Australia) Ltd through the Software Engineering Quality Centres Program of the Department of Communications, Information Technology and the Arts.

References

1. Burnstein, I., Suwannasart, T., Carlson, C.R.: Developing a testing maturity model: Part I. Crosstalk: The Journal of Defense Software Engineering **9** (1996)
2. Voas, J.: A Defensive Approach to Certifying COTS Software. Reliable Software Technologies Corporation (1997)
3. Sampat, N.: Components and Component-Ware Development; A collection of component definitions. `http://www.cms.dmu.ac.uk/~nmsampat/research/subject/reuse/components/index.html` (1998)
4. Morris, J., Bundell, G., Lee, G., Parker, K., Lam, C.P.: Component Certification. IEEE Computer **34** (2001) 30–36
5. European Telecommunications Standards Institute: Testing and Test Control Notation (TTCN-3). `http://www.etsi.org/ptcc/ptccttcn3.htm` (2003)
6. Software Component Laboratory: DTD for a Test Specification. Centre for Intelligent Processing Systems (2001)

7. Object Management Group: CORBA FAQ and Resources.
   http://www.omg.org/gettingstarted/corbafaq.htm (2002)

8. Microsoft: .NET. http://www.microsoft.com/net/ (2002)

9. Thomas, A.: Enterprise JavaBeans: Server Component Model for Java.
   http://www.javasoft.com/products/ejb (1997)

10. Brown, A.W., Wallnau, K.C.: The current state of CBSE. IEEE Software **15** (1998) 37–46

11. Aoyama, M.: New age of software development: How component-based software engineering changes the way of software development. In: International Conference on Software Engineering. (1998)

12. Garlan, D., Allen, R., Ockerbloom, J.: Architectural Mismatch or Why it's Hard to Build Systems out of Existing Parts. In: Proceedings of the 17th International Conference on Software Engineering. (1995) 179–185

13. Boehm, B.: Managing software productivity and reuse. IEEE Computer **32** (1999) 111–113

14. Profeta III, J.A., Andrianos, N.P., Yu, B., Johnson, B.W., Delong, T.A., Guaspari, D., Jamsek, D.: Safety-critical systems built with cots. IEEE Computer **29** (1996) 54–60

15. Hinchey, M.G.: To formalize or not to formalize. IEEE Computer **29** (1996) 18–19

16. Wileden, J.: Programming languages and software engineering: past, present and future. ACM Computing Surveys **28** (1996) 202–242

17. Weyuker, E.J.: Testing component-based software: A cautionary tale. IEEE Software **15** (1998) 54–59

18. Voas, J.: Developing a usage-based software certification process. IEEE Computer **33** (2000) 32–37

19. Pavlopoulou, C., Young, M.: Residual test coverage monitoring. In: Proceedings of the 1999 International Conference on Software Engineering, IEEE Computer Society Press / ACM Press (1999) 277–284

20. Radio Technical Commission for Aeronautics: Software Considerations in Airborne Systems and Equipment Certification: DO-178B. RTCA, Inc (1992)

21. Ministry of Defence Directorate of Standardisation: Defence Standard 00-55: The Procurement of Safety Critical Software in Defence Equipment. HM Government (1997)

22. Underwriters Laboratories: UL Standard for Safety for Software in Programmable Components. Underwriters Laboratories (1998)

23. Stafford, J., Wallnau, K.: Is third party certification necessary? In: 4th ICSE Workshop on Component-Based Software Engineering: Component Certification and System Prediction. (2001)

24. Fenton, N.E., Neil, M.: A strategy for improving safety related software engineering standards. IEEE Transactions on Software Engineering **24** (1998) 1002–1013

25. Pfleeger, S.L., Fenton, N., Page, S.: Evaluating software engineering standards. Computer **27** (1994) 71–79

26. British Standards Institution: Standard for Software Component Testing. BS7925-2 (1998)

27. ANSI/IEEE: ANSI/IEEE standard 1008-97: IEEE Standard for software unit testing. IEEE (1987)

28. Rapps, S., Weyuker, E.: Selecting software test data using data flow information. IEEE Trans Software Engineering **11** (1995) 367–375

29. Weerahandi, S., Hausman, R.E.: Software quality measurement based on fault-detection data. IEEE Transactions on Software Engineering **20** (1994) 665–676

30. Morris, J., Lam, C.P., Lee, G.E., Parker, K., Bundell, G.: Determining component reliability using a testing index. In: Australasian Computer Science Conference. (2002)
31. Bundell, G., Lee, G.E., Morris, J., Parker, K., Lam, C.P.: A software component verification tool. In: Software Methods & Tools (SMT 2000). (2000)
32. Hoffman, D., Strooper, P.: Prose + test cases = specifications. In Li, Q., Firesmith, D., Riehle, R., Pour, G., Meyer, B., eds.: Proceedings 34th International Conference on Technology of Object-Oriented Languages and Systems (TOOLS34), IEEE Computer Society (2000) 239–250
33. SourceForge: JXUnit Test Scripting Language. `quickutil.sourceforge.net/view/Main/JXU` (2001)
34. JUnit: JUnit. `www.junit.org` (2002)
35. Orso, A., Harrold, M.J., Rosenblum, D.: Component metadata for software engineering tasks. In: Proceedings of the 2nd International Workshop on Engineering Distributed Objects (EDO 2000). Volume 1999 of LNCS., Springer-Verlag (2001) 129–144
36. Harrold, M.J., Orso, A., Rosenblum, D., Rothermel, G., Soffa, M.L., Do, H.: Using component metadata to support the regression testing of component-based software. Technical Report GIT-CC-01-38, College of Computing, Georgia Institute of Technology (2001)
37. Hopkins, T., Phillips, C.: Numerical methods in practice: using the NAG Library. Addison-Wesley (1988)
38. Firesmith, D.G.: Pattern language for testing object-oriented software. Object Magazine 5 (1996) 32–38
39. Murray, L., McDonald, J., Strooper, P.: Specification-based class testing with classbench. In: Asia Pacific Software Engineering Conference, IEEE Computer Society Press (1998) 164–173
40. Codework Ltd: C-Cover. Codework Ltd (2000) C/C++ coverage tool.
41. Horgan, J.R., London, S., Lyu, M.R.: Achieving software quality with testing coverage measures. IEEE Computer 27 (1994) 60–69
42. Lyu, M.R., Horgan, J.R., London, S.: A coverage analysis tool for the effectiveness of software testing. IEEE Transactions On Reliability 43 (1994) 527–535
43. Software Component Laboratory: VeriLib: A Source of Reliable Components. `http://www.verilib.sea.net.au/` (2000)
44. Kolawa, A.: Certification will do more harm than good. IEEE Computer 35 (2002) 34–35
45. Trip, L.L.: Benefits of certification. IEEE Computer 35 (2002) 31–33
46. Weyuker, E.J.: The trouble with testing components. In Heineman, G.T., Councill, W.T., eds.: Component-Based Software Engineering: putting the pieces together, Addison-Wesley (2001)

Appendix A. Test Specification DTD

```
<!-- title:  TestSpecification.dtd
     author: John Morris
     date:   01-06-2001
-->
<!-- VeriLib Component Test Specification DTD            -->
<!ELEMENT TestSpecification (TestSet*) >
  <!ATTLIST TestSpecification Name ID #REQUIRED >
<!ELEMENT TestSet (Desc?, (Operation | TestGroup | Invariant)*) >
   <!ATTLIST TestSet Name ID #REQUIRED >
   <!ELEMENT Desc (#PCDATA) >
   <!ELEMENT TestGroup (Desc?,(Operation | TestGroup | Invariant)* ) >
       <!ATTLIST TestGroup Name ID #REQUIRED >
       <!ATTLIST TestGroup TargetMethod CDATA #IMPLIED >
   <!ELEMENT Invariant ( Arg*, (Result | Exception)? ) >
       <!ATTLIST Invariant DataType CDATA #REQUIRED >
       <!ATTLIST Invariant MethodCall CDATA #REQUIRED >
   <!ELEMENT Operation ( (Constructor | MethodCall | Invariant)* ) >
       <!ATTLIST Operation Name ID #REQUIRED >
       <!ATTLIST Operation Pre IDREF #IMPLIED>
       <!ATTLIST Operation Version CDATA #IMPLIED>
       <!ELEMENT Constructor ( Arg*, (Result | Exception)? ) >
           <!ATTLIST Constructor Name CDATA #REQUIRED >
       <!ELEMENT MethodCall ( Arg*, (Result | Exception)? ) >
           <!ATTLIST MethodCall Name CDATA #REQUIRED >
           <!ATTLIST MethodCall Target CDATA #REQUIRED >
           <!ATTLIST MethodCall Static ( Y | N ) "N" >
           <!ELEMENT Arg (#PCDATA) >
               <!ATTLIST Arg Name CDATA #IMPLIED >
               <!ATTLIST Arg Source CDATA #IMPLIED >
               <!ATTLIST Arg DataType CDATA #IMPLIED>
           <!ELEMENT Result (Exp?) >
               <!ATTLIST Result Name CDATA #IMPLIED>
               <!ATTLIST Result DataType CDATA #IMPLIED>
               <!ATTLIST Result Qualification CDATA #IMPLIED >
               <!ATTLIST Result    Save ( Y | N ) "N" >
               <!ELEMENT Exp (#PCDATA) >
                   <!ATTLIST Exp Tol CDATA #IMPLIED >
                   <!ATTLIST Exp SpecVersion CDATA #IMPLIED >
           <!ELEMENT Exception (Exp?) >
               <!ATTLIST Exception Name CDATA #IMPLIED >
               <!ATTLIST Exception DataType CDATA #REQUIRED >
               <!ATTLIST Exception Qualification CDATA #IMPLIED >
               <!ATTLIST Exception Save ( Y | N ) "N" >
```

Fig. 3. Test Specification DTD

An extensively commented version may be found on the Software Component Laboratory's web site: http://ciips.ee.uwa.edu.au/Research/SCL/TestSpec.

Component Integration
through Built-in Contract Testing

Hans-Gerhard Gross[1], Colin Atkinson[2], and Franck Barbier[3]

[1] Fraunhofer Institute for Experimental Software Engineering
Sauerwiesen 6, D-67661 Kaiserslautern, Germany
`grossh@iese.fhg.de`
[2] University of Mannheim, D-68131, Mannheim, Germany
`atkinson@pi1.informatik.uni-mannheim.de`
[3] LIUPPA, Université de Pau et des Pays l' Adour, F-64013 Pau cedex, France
`Franck.Barbier@univ-pau.fr`

Abstract. This chapter describes a technology and methodology referred to as built-in contract testing that checks the pairwise interactions of components in component-based software construction at integration and deployment time. Such pairwise interactions are also referred to as contracts. Built-in contract testing is based on building test functionality into components, in particular tester components on the client side and testing interfaces on the server side of a pairwise contract. Since building test software into components has implications for the overall component-based development process, the technology is integrated with and made to supplement the entire development cycle starting from requirements specification activities and modeling. The chapter outlines typical specification concepts that are important for built-in contract testing, provides a guide on how to devise built-in contract testing artifacts on the basis of models, and discusses issued involved in using this approach with contemporary component technologies.

1 Introduction

The vision of component-based development is to allow software vendors to avoid the overheads of traditional development methods by assembling new applications from high-quality, prefabricated, reusable parts. Since large parts of an application may therefore be constructed from already existing components, it is expected that the overall time and costs involved in application development will be reduced, and the quality of the resulting applications will be improved. This expectation is based on the implicit assumption that the effort involved in integrating components at deployment time is lower than the effort involved in developing and validating applications through traditional techniques. However, this does not take into account the fact that when an otherwise fault-free component is integrated into a system of other components, it may fail to function as expected. This is because the other components to which it has been connected are intended for a different purpose, have a different usage profile, or are themselves faulty. Current component technologies can help to verify the syntactic

A. Cechich et al. (Eds.): Component-Based Software Quality, LNCS 2693, pp. 159–183, 2003.
© Springer-Verlag Berlin Heidelberg 2003

compatibility of interconnected components (i.e. that they use and provide the right signatures), but they do little to ensure that applications function correctly when they are assembled from independently developed parts. In other words, they do nothing to check the semantic compatibility of inter-connected components, so that the individual parts are assembled into meaningful configurations. Software developers may therefore be forced to perform more integration and acceptance testing in order to attain the same level of confidence in the system's reliability. In short, although traditional development time verification and validation techniques can help assure the quality of individual components, they can do little to assure the quality of applications that are assembled from them at deployment time.

1.1   Contracts in Component-Based Development

The correct functioning of a system of components at run time is contingent on the correct interaction of individual pairs of components according to the client/server model. Component-based development can be viewed as an extension of the object paradigm in which, following Meyer [12], the set of rules governing the interaction of a pair of objects (and thus components) is typically referred to as a contract. This characterizes the relationship between a component and its clients as a formal agreement, expressing each party's rights and obligations. Testing the correct functioning of individual client/server interactions against the specified contract therefore goes along way towards verifying that a system of components as a whole will behave correctly.

1.2   Contract-Based Integration Testing

The testing approach described in this chapter is therefore based on the notion of building contract tests into components so that they can validate that the servers to which they are "plugged" dynamically at deployment time will fulfill their contract. Although built-in contract testing is primarily intended for validation activities at deployment and configuration-time, the approach also has important implications on other development phases of the overall software lifecycle. Consideration of built-in test artifacts needs to begin early in the design phase as soon as the overall architecture of a system is developed and/or the interfaces of components are specified. Built-in contract testing therefore needs to be integrated with an overall software development methodology. In this chapter we explain the basic principles behind built-in contract testing, and how they affect component-based development principles. Additionally we show how it can be integrated with model-based development.

Since we are talking about components and component-based development, it is important that we initially define the term component and its usage throughout this chapter. We choose to define a software component as a unit of composition with explicitly specified provided, required and configuration interfaces, plus quality attributes [8]. This definition is based on the well known definition of the 1996 European Conference on Object-Oriented Programming [16], that defines a component as a unit of composition with contractually specified interfaces and context dependencies only that can be deployed independently and is subject to composition by third parties. We have intentionally chosen a broader definition that avoids the terminology *independently deployable*, since we are not specifically restricting ourselves to contemporary component technologies such as CORBA, .NET or EJB/J2EE. In this respect we are closer to Booch's definition which sees a component as a logically, cohesive, loosely coupled module that denotes a single abstraction [7]. From this it becomes apparent that components are basically built upon the same fundamental principles as object technology. The principles of encapsulation, modularity, and unique identities are all basic object-oriented principles that are subsumed by the component paradigm [3].

1.3 Structure of This Chapter

Since built-in contract testing is primarily dependent upon specification documents and models we initially introduce (Section 2) typical specification concepts that are required for its application. These represent the basis from which all built-in contract testing concepts are derived and specified. Section 3 introduces functional test generation techniques that may be used for test case design and discusses how the test cases may be derived from the specification documents. These test cases make up the tester components that are integral part of built-in contract testing. The following Section (Section 4) describes the concepts of the technology in detail, the tester components that comprise the tests and are built into the client, and the testing interface that is built into the server of a client/server relationship. Additionally, the Section provides a guide for the development of these artifacts from models. Section 5 discusses the implications of using built-in contract testing with typical component concepts such as reuse, commercial third-party components, and Web-services, and Section 6 summarizes and concludes this chapter.

2 Component Specification

The initial starting point for a software development project is typically a system or application specification derived and decomposed from the system requirements. Requirements and specifications are also the primary source for acceptance and integration testing. Requirements are collected from the customer of the software. They are decomposed in order to remove their genericity in the same way as system designs are decomposed in order to obtain finer grained parts that are individually controllable. These parts are implemented and later composed into the final product. The decomposition activity aims to obtain meaningful, individually coherent parts of the system, the components. It is also referred to as component engineering or component development. The composition activity tries to assemble already existing parts into a meaningful configuration that reflects the predetermined system requirements. In its purest form, component-based development is only concerned with the second item, representing a bottom-up approach to system construction. This requires that every single part of the overall application is already available in a component repository in a form that exactly maps to the requirements of that application. Typically, this is not the case, and merely assembling readily available parts into a configuration will quite likely lead to a system that does not conform to its original requirements. Component-based development is therefore usually a mixture of top-down decomposition and bottom-up composition activities.

A specification is a set of descriptive documents that collectively define what a component can do. Typically, each individual document represents a distinct view on the subject component, and thus only concentrates on a particular aspect. Whichever notation is used for the documents, a specification should contain everything that is necessary in order to fully use the component and understand its behavior, for composition with other components. As such, the specification can be seen as defining the provided interface of the component. It therefore describes everything that is externally knowable about a component's structure (e.g. associated components) in the form of a structural model, functionality (e.g. operations) in the form of pre- and post conditions, and behavior (e.g. states and state transitions) in the form of a behavioral specification. Additionally, a specification may contain non-functional requirements which represent the quality attributes stated in the component definition. They are part of the quality assurance plan of the overall development project or the specific component. A complete set of documentation for the component is also desirable, and a decision model that captures the built-in variabilities that the component may provide. These variabilities are supported through configuration interfaces.

2.1   Structural Specification

The structural specification defines operations and attributes of the considered subject component, the components that are associated with the subject (e.g. its clients and servers), and constraints on these associations. This is important for defining the different views that clients of component instances can have of the subject. Essentially, this maps to the prospective configurations of the subject, and thus its provided configuration interfaces. A structural specification is not traditionally used in software projects, but the advent of model driven development approaches has increased its importance as a specification artifact. In the form of a UML class or object model, the structural specification provides a powerful way of defining the nature of the classes and relationships by which a component interacts with its environment. It is also used to describe any structure that may be visible at the subject's interface [3].

To illustrate the concepts described in this chapter we will use the well known example of an Automated Teller Machine (ATM). Fig. 1 depicts the structural model of an ATM component (the subject) as a UML class diagram. The structural model only depicts the direct environment of the subject. These are the components with which the ATM interacts.

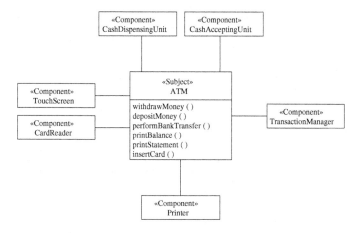

Fig. 1. UML-style structural specification of an ATM application

2.2   Functional Specification

The purpose of the functional specification is to describe the externally visible effects of the operations supplied by the component - that is, its provided interface. Example operation specifications for a *BankingCard* component in the context of the *CardReader* component are depicted in Tables 1 and 2. These provide a full functional specification of the banking card. The respective structural and behavioral models are depicted in Fig. 2.

The most important elements of a functional specification are the *Assumes* and *Result* clauses which represent the pre- and post-conditions for the operation. These are also essential for testing. The *Assumes* clause defines what must be true for the operation to guarantee correct expected execution, and the *Result* clause describes what is expected to become true as a result of the operation if it executes correctly. It is possible to execute an operation if its *Assumes* clause is false, but then the effects of the operation are not certain to satisfy the postcondition (compare with *design by contract* [12]). The basic goal of the *Result* clause is the provision of a declarative description of the operation in terms of its effects. This means it describes what the operation does, and not how. Pre- and post-conditions typically comprise constraints on the provided inputs, the provided outputs, the state before the operation invocation (initial state), and the state after the operation invocation (final state) [3, 11].

2.3   Behavioral Specification

The object paradigm encapsulates data and functionality in one single entity, the object. This leads to the notion of states, and the transitions between states, that typically occur in objects when they are operational. The component paradigm subsumes these. Components may have states too. If a component does not have states, it is referred to as functional object or functional component, meaning

Table 1. Example operation spec. for the banking card component, event *validatePIN*

Name	validatePIN
Description	Validates a given Pin and, on success, returns the stored customerDetails. After three unsuccessful invocations (invalid Pin) the card is locked.
Constraints	cardLockRequest from card locks the cardReader (card is not returned to customer)
Receives	Pin: Integer.
Returns	On success: customer details. On failure: invalid Pin error.
Sends	None.
Reads	None.
Changes	None.
Rules	Unless card is locked: return customer details. After third unsuccessful invocation [invalid Pin AND card not locked]: lock the card. After second unsuccessful invocation [invalid Pin AND card not locked]: allow one last unsuccessful attempt. After first unsuccessful invocation [invalid Pin AND card not locked]: allow two more unsuccessful attempts. After no unsuccessful invocations [invalid Pin AND card not locked]: allow three more unsuccessful attempts. One successful invocation clears the card from previous unsuccessful invocations.
Assumes	card not locked AND Number of unsuccessful attempts < 3
Result	(card locked AND Number of unsuccessful attempts = 3) XOR (card not locked AND Number of unsuccessful attempts < 3)

Table 2. Example operation spec. for the banking card component, event *unlockCard*

Name	unlockCard
Description	Unlocks a previously locked card, so that it may be used again.
Constraints	Only locked cards can be unlocked.
Receives	SecurityPin: Integer.
Returns	On success [valid SecurityPin]: CustomerDetails stored on the card.
Sends	On failure [invalid SecurityPin]: Security Pin Error.
Reads	None.
Changes	None.
Rules	On success [valid SecurityPin]: set card to cleared.
Assumes	Card locked AND (valid SecurityPin OR invalid SecurityPin).
Result	(Card cleared AND valid SecurityPin) XOR invalid SecurityPin.

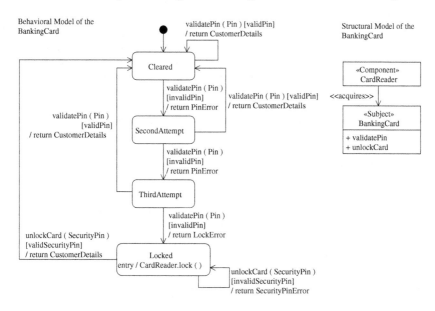

Fig. 2. UML-style behavioral specification and structural specification of an ATM banking card component

it has no internal attributes that are exhibited through its provided interface. In other words, a pure functional component does not exhibit externally visible states and transitions. It may, however, have internal states that are not externally visible.

The purpose of the behavioral specification (or the behavioral model) is to show how the component behaves in response to external stimuli [3] and changes its externally visible states. It concentrates on the *Assumes* and *Result* clauses of the functional specification that define the pre- and post-conditions of the operations (Tables 1 and 2). If the component has externally visible states, and most components do, the behavioral model succinctly expresses much of the complexity that is collectively contained in the pre- and post-conditions of the component's operations.

The behavioral model describes the instances of a component in terms of their observable states, and how these states change as a result of external stimuli that affect the component instance [11, 6]. A state is a particular configuration of the data values of an object's internal attributes. A state itself is not visible. What is visible or externally observable is a difference in behavior of the component from one state to another when stimuli are sent. In other words, if the same message is sent to a component instance twice, the instance may behave differently, depending on its original state before the message is received. A transition, or change from one state into another is triggered by an event, which is typically a message arrival. A guard is a condition that must be true before a transition can be made. Guards are used for separating transitions to various states that are based on the same event [11]. A behavioral specification may be represented

Table 3. Behavioral specification according to the model in Fig. 2.

Initial State	Pre Condition	Event	PostCondition	Final State
Cleared	[Valid Pin]	validatePin (Pin)	CustomerDetails returned	Cleared
Cleared	[Invalid Pin]	validatePin (Pin)	PinError returned	Second Attempt
Second Attempt	[Valid Pin]	validatePin (Pin)	CustomerDetails returned	Cleared
Second Attempt	[Invalid Pin]	validatePin (Pin)	PinError returned	Third Attempt
Third Attempt	[Valid Pin]	validatePin (Pin)	CustomerDetails returned	Cleared
Third Attempt	[Invalid Pin]	validatePin (Pin)	LockError returned	Locked
Locked	[Valid SecurityPin]	unlockCard (SecurityPin)	CustomerDetails returned	Cleared
Locked	[Invalid SecurityPin]	unlockCard (SecurityPin)	SecurityPinError	Locked

through one or more UML state diagrams or state tables. Fig. 2 displays the behavioral model (plus the structural model) for the *BankingCard* component with two public operations, and Table 3 displays the corresponding state table.

2.4 Component Realization

The specification does not provide sufficient information to implement a component. Before that is possible it is necessary to define how a component will realize its services. The component realization is a set of descriptive documents that collectively define how a component realizes its specification. A higher-level component is typically realized through, and composed of, a combination of lower-level components that are contained within, and act as servers to, the higher-level component. Once it has been defined which parts of a logical higher level component will be implemented through which sub-components, the implementation of the higher level component can be started.

A component realization describes the items that are inherent to the implementation of the higher-level component. This is the part of the functionality that will be local to the considered component and not implemented through sub-components. These items correspond to the component's private design that the user of the component does not see. The user or the system integrator only cares about a component's provided and required interfaces, because these define the context into which the component will be integrated.

3   Specification- and Model-Based Component Testing

The previous Section described the initial starting point for using and applying built-in contract testing in component development - namely a sound specification, ideally in the form of documents that directly support the generation of the built-in testing architecture and the built-in test suites. In this Section we discuss how the specification can be used for the generation of test artifacts for integration testing.

Since component specifications are the primary source of information for the development of built-in contract test architectures and test suites, built-in contract testing is primarily concerned with functional testing techniques that view an integrated component as a black box. However, black and white-box testing cannot be strictly separated in component testing. Component engineering takes a fractal-like view of software systems in which components are made of other components that in turn are made of other components in a recursive manner. The terminology of black and white boxes has only a meaning for the level of abstraction that we are looking at. A white box test for a super-ordinate component maps to a black box test for a sub-ordinate component and so on. Thus, testing in the traditional code-based-testing sense has no meaning in component integration testing since we are only concerned with the testing of interfaces.

3.1   Functional Testing

Functional testing techniques completely ignore the internal mechanisms of a system or a component (its internal implementation) and focus solely on the outcome generated in response to selected inputs and execution conditions [10].

Domain Analysis and Partitioning Testing. Typical representatives of functional testing techniques are domain analysis testing and partitioning techniques. A domain is defined as a subset of the input space that somehow affects the processing of the tested component. Domains are determined through boundary inequalities, algebraic expressions that define which locations in the input space belong to the domain of interest [5]. Domain analysis is used for and sometimes also referred to as partitioning testing. Many functional test case generation techniques are based upon partition testing. Equivalence partitioning is a strategy that divides the set of all possible inputs into equivalence classes. The equivalence relation defines the properties for which input sets are belonging to the same partition, for example equivalent behavior (state-transitions). Proportional equivalence partitioning, for example, allocates test cases according to the probability of their occurrence in each sub-domain.

State-Based Testing. State-based testing concentrates on checking the correct implementation of the component's state model. Test case design is based on the individual states and the transitions between these states. In object-oriented or component-based testing effectively any type of testing is state-based as soon as the object or component exhibits states, even if the tests are not obtained from the state model. In this case, there is no test case without the notion of a state or a state-transition. In other words, pre- and post-conditions of every single test case must consider states and behavior. State-based testing comprises a number of test coverage strategies: Piecewise coverage concentrates on exercising distinct specification pieces, for example coverage of all states, all events, or all actions. This technique is not directly related to the structure of the underlying state machine that implements the behavior, so it is only accidentally effective at finding behavioral faults [6]. Transition coverage is achieved through a test suite if every specified transition in the state model is exercised at least once. As a consequence, this covers all states, all events and all actions. Transition coverage may be improved if every specified transition sequence is exercised at least once [6]. This is also a method sequence based testing technique. Round-trip path coverage is defined through the coverage of at least every defined sequence of specified transitions that begin and end in the same state. The shortest round-trip path is a transition that loops back on the same state. A test suite that achieves full round-trip path coverage will reveal all incorrect or missing event/action pairs [6].

Method-Sequence-Based Testing. This test case generation technique concentrates on the correct implementation of a component's combinations, or sequences of provided operations. Test case design is based on the behavioral model, such as a UML state chart diagram. Here, the paths through the state model are checked. This may also include multiple invocations of the same operation. Method sequences are typical representatives of usage profiles, that is a profile of how a client uses the services of a component. Table 4 shows an excerpt of a typical test suite based on method sequences for the *BankingCard* component.

3.2   Model-Based Testing

Model-based testing concentrates on how tests may be derived from graphical specification notations such as the UML. Such techniques are traditionally used in the development of safety critical and real-time systems (e.g. Petri Nets), and more recently it concentrates upon approaches for how to derive test information from individual UML models.

Models represent a solid foundation for test case generation that is primarily based on the specification, and are therefore mainly functional. Models use powerful (semi-) formal abstract notations in order to express requirements specifications. Having good requirements is crucial not only for the development of a system but additionally for the development of its testing infrastructure. If requirements are additionally testable they are the perfect source for instant test scenario generation.

Class and Package Diagrams. Class diagrams represent structure, that is associations between entities plus externally visible attributes and operations of classes (or components). They are a valuable source for testing. Specification class diagrams (server) represent the interfaces that individual components export to their clients and therefore show which operations need to be tested, which operations support the testing and which external states are important for a unit. These can directly guide the construction of tester components for a server component. Realization class diagrams (client) represent the operations of the servers that a client is associated with. They only contain externally visible server operations and attributes that a client is actually using. It means such a diagram restricts the operational profile of a client in terms of operations. This helps to determine the range of operations that a tester component must consider. Class diagrams may be used to generate test cases according to boundary conditions and component interaction criteria [6]. Package diagrams represent a similar source as class diagrams although on a coarser grained level of abstraction. In built-in contract testing such component diagrams (component trees) are used to indicate variability in an application and therefore mark the associations between components that need to be augmented with built-in contract testing artifacts.

State Diagrams. State diagrams are a valuable source for testing in many ways. This is also demonstrated in Table 4. State diagrams are the primary source for test case generation in built-in contract testing for development of tester components as well as testing interfaces. State diagrams concentrate on the dynamics of components in terms of externally visible states and transitions between the states. State chart diagrams may also be used to generate test cases according to class hierarchy and collaboration testing criteria [6].

Collaboration Diagrams. While state diagrams concentrate on the behavior of individual objects, UML collaboration diagrams represent the behavioral interactions between objects. They describe how the functions of a component are spread over multiple collaborating entities (i.e. sub-components) and how they interact in order to fulfill higher-level requirements. Collaboration diagrams represent two views on an entity, a structural view, and a behavioral view. Additionally, they pose constraints on a system. Since collaboration diagrams realize a complete path for a higher-level use case they may be used to define complete message sequence paths according to the use case [1].

Use Cases, Operational Profiles, and Scenarios. Many organizations define use cases as their primary requirements specifications, for example [13]. Additionally, they use operational profiles in order to determine occurrences and probabilities of system usage. Use case models thereby map to operations in an operational profile. Another application of use cases is the generation of state chart diagrams [14] from use-case driven requirements engineering, or the generation of collaboration diagrams. Use cases may be used to generate test cases according to combinational function and category partitioning criteria [6]. Scenarios are used to describe the functionality and behavior of a software system

Table 4. Test case design based on method sequences according to the behavioral model of the banking card

#	Initial State	Pre Condition	Event	PostCondition	Final State
1	Cleared	[Valid Pin]	validatePin (Pin)	CustomerDetails returned	Cleared
2	Cleared	[Invalid Pin]	validatePin (Pin)	PinError returned	
		[Valid Pin]	validatePin (Pin)	CustomerDetails returned	Cleared
3	Cleared	[Invalid Pin]	validatePin (Pin)	PinError returned	
		[Invalid Pin]	validatePin (Pin)	PinError returned	
		[Valid Pin]	validatePin (Pin)	CustomerDetails returned	Cleared
4	Cleared	[Invalid Pin]	validatePin (Pin)	PinError returned	
		[Invalid Pin]	validatePin (Pin)	PinError returned	
		[Invalid Pin]	validatePin (Pin)	PinError returned	
		[Invalid SecurityPin]	unlockCard (SecurityPin)	Invalid SecurityPin returned	
		[Valid SecurityPin]	unlockCard (SecurityPin)	CustomerDetails returned	Cleared
5	...	...	...	...	...

from the user's perspective in the same way as use cases. Scenarios essentially represent abstract tests for the developed system that can be easily derived by following a simple process. This is laid out in the SCENT Method [15].

4   Specification of the Contract Testing Artifacts

The previous Section described which specification documents may be used to generate test data for the test suites of built-in contract testing. This Section concentrates on the description of the contract testing architecture and explains the nature of the contract testing interface on the server side, and the contract tester component on the client side of a component relationship. The test suites are contained within the tester components.

Meyer [12] defines the relationship between an object and its clients as a formal agreement or a contract, expressing each party's rights and obligations in the relationship. This means that individual components define their side of the contract as either offering a service (this is the server in a client-server relationship) or requiring a service (this is the client in a client-server relationship). Built-in contract testing focuses on verifying these pairwise client/server interactions between two components when an application is assembled. This is typically performed at deployment time when the application is configured for the first time, or later during the execution of the system when a re-configuration is performed.

The previous sections have laid out the foundations for the development of the built-in contract testing artifacts. They can be seen as an entry criterion for using built-in contract testing. This is a sound development process that is ideally based on models, though other notations may be acceptable as long as they provide similar contents, plus a testable requirements specification (that is part of the method) from which the tests may be derived. Additionally, we need to define the test target in terms of a quality assurance plan [3] that determines the testing techniques for deriving the individual test cases. This may be a selection of the test case generation techniques that we have introduced in the previous Section (Section 3).

The two primary built-in contract testing artifacts are the *server tester component* that is built into the client of a component in order to test the server when it is plugged to the client, and the *testing interface* that is built into (extends) the normal interface of the server and provides introspection mechanisms for the testing by the client.

4.1   Built-in Server Tester Components

Configuration involves the creation of individual pairwise client/server relations between the components in a system. This is usually done by an outside "third party", which we refer to as the context of the components (Fig. 3). This creates the instances of the client and the server, and passes the reference of the server to the client (i.e. thereby establishing the clientship connection between them). This act of configuring clients and servers may be represented through a special association that is indicated through an ≪acquires≫ stereotype as illustrated in Fig. 2 or in Fig. 3. The context that establishes this connection may be the container in a contemporary component technology, or it may simply be the parent object.

In order to fulfill its obligations towards its own clients, a client component (e.g. *CardReader* in Fig. 3) that acquires a new server (e.g. *BankingCard* in Fig. 3) must verify the server's semantic compliance to its clientship contract. In other words, the client must check that the server provides the semantic service that the client has been developed to expect. The client is therefore augmented with in-built test software in the form of a server tester component (e.g. *BankingCardTester* in Fig. 3), and this is executed when the client is configured to use the server. In order to achieve this, the client will pass the server's reference to its own in-built server tester component. If the test fails, the tester component may raise a contract testing exception and point the application programmer or system integrator to the location of the failure.

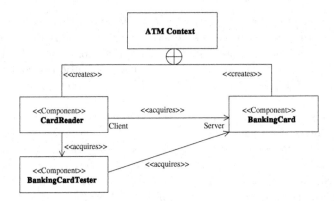

Fig. 3. Structural model of built-in contract testing *server tester component* for the *BankingCard/CardReader* example

4.2   Built-in Contract Testing Interfaces

The object-oriented and component-based development paradigms build on the principles of abstract data types which advocate the combination of data and functionality into a single entity. State transition testing is therefore an essential part of component verification. In order to check whether a component's operations are working correctly it is not sufficient simply to compare their returned values with the expected values. The compliance of the component's externally visible states and transitions to the expected states and transitions according to the specification state model must also be checked. These externally visible states are part of a component's contract that a user of the component must know in order to use it properly. However, because these externally visible states of a component are embodied in its internal state attributes, there is a fundamental dilemma.

The basic principles of encapsulation and information hiding dictate that external clients of a component should not see the internal implementation and internal state information. The external test software of a component (i.e. the built-in contract tester component) therefore cannot get or set any internal state information. The user of a correct component simply assumes that a distinct operation invocation will result in a distinct externally visible state of the component. However, the component does not usually make this state information visible in any way. This means that expected state transitions as defined in the specification state model cannot normally be tested directly.

The contract testing paradigm is therefore based on the principle that components should ideally expose externally visible (i.e. logical) state information by extending the normal functional server as displayed in Fig. 4. In other words, a component should ideally not only expose its externally visible signatures, but additionally it should openly provide the model of its externally visible behavior. A testing interface therefore provides additional operations that read from and write to internal state attributes that collectively determine the states

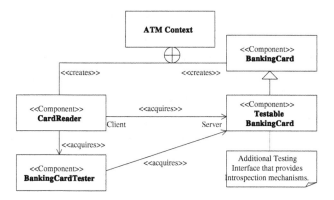

Fig. 4. Structural model of a *testing interface* or *testable component* for the ATM example

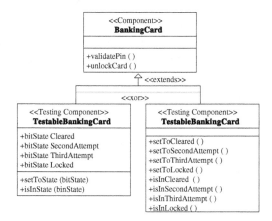

Fig. 5. Class diagram of a testable *BankingCard* component with testing interface operation that reflect the behavioral model. Two alternative implementations are feasible

of a component's behavioral model. A component that supports its own testing by external clients through an additional testing interface in this way is called *testable component*. Fig. 5 displays two alternative implementations for a *TestableBankingCard* component that exposes a testing interface according to its behavioral model depicted in Fig. 2. The first implementation type defines a number of public state variables that represent the states of the behavioral model and act as input parameter for the *setToState* and *IsInState* testing interface operations. The first operation sets the component to one of the defined states and the second one checks whether the component is in a particular state. The second implementation type defines an individual *setToState* and *isInState* operation per state in the behavioral model.

4.3   Component Associations in Built-in Contract Testing

The previous sub-sections have introduced the two primary artifacts that must be generated for built-in contract testing: tester component and testing interface. These represent additional functionality whose focus is testing. The first one extends the client component and contains the actual test cases that check the client's deployment environment. The second extends the interface of the server in order to make the server more testable.

If a server does not provide a testing interface (e.g. a COTS component) it does not mean that contract testing may not be used. It is simply limited with regard to testing controllability and observability. The test cases in the client must be designed differently as well according to the missing testing interface.

The Client and the Client's Tester Component. In the client role, a component may own and contain its tester component. This means that the test cases, typically organized as components in their own right, are permanently encapsulated and built into the client. This is the simplest form of built-in contract testing, and it provides no direct run-time configurability with respect to the type and amount of testing the client component will perform when it is connected to its server components. This association can be expressed through the UML composition relationship.

A more flexible way of built-in contract testing is realized through a loosely associated tester component that may be acquired by the testing client in the same way it acquires any other external resources. Here, the component provides a configuration interface through which any arbitrary tester component that represents the client's view on a tested server may be set. This provides flexibility in terms of how much testing will be performed at deployment time, and additionally it provides flexibility as to which type of tester will be applied according to an instantiated product line. Such an association may be represented through a UML aggregation association, or more specifically through the stereotype ≪acquires≫ that identifies the tester component as an externally acquired server (e.g. Fig. 3 and 4).

The Server and the Server's Testing Interface. In a server role, a component must be much more closely connected to its testing interface because its implementation must be able to access the server's internal variables (i.e. for setting and getting the states). The testing interface is therefore directly built in to the component and extends its normal functionality with additional testing functionality.

More flexible is a typical extension (inheritance) mechanism. Enabling and disabling the built-in testing interface can then be achieved simply by instantiating the desired type of object accordingly. Such an association can be indicated through the UML extension symbol plus the ≪extends≫ stereotype. In any case, the testing interface of a component must be visible at its external boundary. For components with nested objects it means that each of these sub-objects must be dealt with individually inside the component.

The Client's Tester and the Server's Testing Interface. The tester component of the client and the server's testing interface inter-operate in the same way as their respective functional counterparts. Since testers and testing interfaces are directly built into the system, testing represents only additional functionality that happens to be executed at component integration. The tester component must only "know" the reference of the tested server, and this is simply passed into the tester component when the clientship relation is established. Testing in this respect is only executing some additional code that uses some additional interface operations. Therefore, built-in contract testing is initially only a distinct way of implementing functionality that is executed when components are interconnected during deployment. This only concerns the architecture of a system (i.e. which components will expose additional interfaces, which components will contain tester components). The test cases inside a tester component are arbitrary, and they can be developed according to traditional criteria or any of the criteria introduced in Section 3.

4.4   Fitting It All Together – The Contract Testing Method

In a development project where no built-in contract testing is applied at the component level, the following steps may be applied in order to add built-in integration testing artifacts to test the individual semantic component interactions. Once these artifacts have been introduced, they can be reused in the same way as the components' functionality is reused in subsequent projects. In other words, every repeated integration of such an augmented component with other components in a new project can be automatically verified.

Step 1 – The Tested Interactions and the Contract Testing Architecture. In general, any client-server interaction may be augmented with built-in testing interfaces and tester components. Such interactions are represented through any arbitrary association in a structural diagram.

Associations between classes that are encapsulated in a reusable component are likely to stay fixed throughout a component's life cycle. Such associations may be augmented with removable built-in contract testing artifacts for development-time component integration testing. Such variability in testing may be implemented through a development- or compile-time configuration mechanism (e.g. include in C++), or through a run-time configuration interface that dynamically allocates tester components, and testable components with testing interfaces.

Components as units of integration will have permanent built-in testing interactions at their boundaries. This means that every external association that requires or imports an interface will be permanently augmented with a built-in contract tester component whose tests reflect its expectations towards its servers, and every external association that provides or exports an interface will be permanently augmented with a built-in testing interface.

The stereotype ≪acquires≫ represents dynamic associations that may be configured according to the needs of the application (i.e. component boundaries). The decisions about where contract testing artifacts will be built in are documented in the structure of the system. This is simply an additional software construction effort in the overall development process that adds functionality to the application. For any client-server relationship we will have to add testing interface and tester component as modeled in Fig. 4.

Step 2 – Specification of the Testing Interface and the Tester Component. The testing interface is used to set and retrieve state information about the tested server component. This is defined in the server's behavioral model. Each state in this model represents a setting for which the behavior of some operation is distinctively different from any other settings. The individual states that the behavioral model defines is therefore an ideal basis for specifying state setting and checking operations. Each state in the state model therefore maps to one state setting and one state checking method, according to which strategy is used (compare with the class diagram in Fig. 5).

The tester components are developed according to the expectation of the testing client. In other words, a client's specification (e.g. its behavioral model) represents a description of what the client needs from its environment in order to fulfill its own obligations. It represents the expectation of the testing component on its environment. So, the tests are not defined by the specification of the associated server - in this case it would only be a unit test of the server that the producer of such component may already have performed.

For example, the tester component for a *BankingCard* component that is built into the client *CardReader* component may comprise tests according to method sequence testing criteria as defined in Table 4. If the associated server component *BankingCard* exports a built-in contract testing interface according to the structural definition in Fig. 5 (first/left alternative implementation) the tester component can apply an integration test sequence as displayed in Table 5. This corresponds to the specification of test case # 4 in Table 4.

Step 3 – Component Integration. Once all the functional component artifacts and the built-in contract testing component artifacts on both sides of a component contract have been properly defined and implemented, the two components can be integrated (plugged together). This follows the typical process for component integration, i.e. a wrapper is defined and implemented for the client or the server, or an adaptor is designed and implemented that realizes the mapping between the two roles. Since the testing artifacts are integral parts of the individual components on either sides of the contract they are not subject to any special treatment, they are just treated like any normal functionality. For example, an adaptor takes the operation calls from the client and transforms them to into a format that the server can understand. If the server produces results, the adaptor takes these and translates them back into the format of the client. Since the built-in contract testing artifacts are part of the client's and server's contracts they will be mapped through the adaptor as well. Component platforms such as CORBA Components already provide support for this type of mapping.

Table 5. Example test case for a *BankingCard* Tester Component that will be built into the *CardReader* component

Initial State Setup	Operation Invocation & Parameter Constraints	Expected Outcome & Final State
SetToState(Cleared)	validatePin (Pin) AND [Invalid Pin]	PinError expected
	validatePin (Pin) AND [Invalid Pin]	PinError expected
	validatePin (Pin) AND [Invalid Pin]	PinError expected
	unlockCard (SecurityPin) AND [Invalid SecurityPin]	SecurityPinError expected
	unlockCard (SecurityPin) AND [Valid SecurityPin]	CustomerDetails expected AND IsInState(Cleared)

5 Built-in Contract Testing and the Component Paradigm

The previous Section introduced the basic principles that guide the development of built-in contract testing artifacts for the two roles in a client/server-relationship between components. These are valid for both object-oriented and component-based development. In this Section we describe how these ideas can be integrated with mainstream industrial component technologies.

5.1 Built-in Contract Testing and Reuse

Testing takes a big share of the total effort in the development of large and/or complex software. Nevertheless, component-based software engineering has mainly focused on cutting development time and cost by reusing functional code. If the components cannot be used in new target domains without extensive re-work or re-testing, the time saving becomes questionable [9]. Hence, there is a need to reuse not only functional code but also the tests and test environments that verify a component's interactions on the target platform. To attain effective test reuse in software development, there are several aspects that must be taken into account.

Contract testing includes a flexible architecture that focuses on these aspects. It is the application of this architecture that makes reuse possible. In the initial approach of built-in testing as proposed by Wang et. al. [17], complete test cases are put inside the components and are therefore automatically reused with the component. While this strategy seems attractive at first sight, it is not flexible enough to suit the general case. A component needs different types of tests in different environments and it is neither feasible nor sensible to have them all built-in permanently.

Under the contract testing paradigm test cases are separated from their respective components and put in separate tester components. The components still have some built-in test mechanisms, but only to increase their accessibility for testing by clients. The actual testing is done by the tester components that are associated with the client components through their interfaces. In this way, an arbitrary number of tester components can be connected to an arbitrary number of functional components. This offers a much more flexible way to reuse tests as they do not have to be identical to the ones originally delivered with a component. The tests can be customized to fit the context of the component at all stages in the component's life cycle.

The overall concept of test reuse in built-in contract testing follows the fundamental reuse principles of all object and component technologies. Because testing is inherently built into an application or parts thereof (the components) testing will be reused whenever functionality is reused. In fact testing in this respect is normal functionality. Only the time when this functionality is executed distinguishes it from the other non-testing functionality, that is at configuration or deployment time.

5.2   Built-in Contract Testing
and Commercial Off-the-Shelf (COTS) Components

The integration of commercially available third party components into new applications represents one of the main driving factors for component-based software development since it greatly reduces the effort involved in generating new applications. Such components are aimed at solving typical problems in distinct domains, and ideally they can be purchased off-the-shelf and simply plugged into an application. However, this ideal scenario is still some way from reality. Although they reduce the effort involved in achieving new functionality, third party components typically increase the effort involved in integrating the overall application, since they are typically available in a form that presents some integration difficulties. For example, they may provide syntactically or semantically different interfaces from what is expected and required, or they may not be entirely fit for the intended purpose. In any way, the usage and integration of third party components typically requires either the development of wrappers or adaptor components that hide and compensate for these differences, or changes in the design and implementation of the integrating client component.

Once a new component can communicate syntactically with a provided COTS component through some mechanism, the next step is to make sure that they can also communicate semantically. In other words, the fact that two components are capable of functioning together says nothing about the correctness of that interaction. This is where built-in contract testing provides its greatest benefits.

Ideally, all commercially available components should provide testability features such as the introspection mechanism that is realized through built-in contract testing interfaces. Such components will naturally fit into applications that are driven by the built-in contract testing paradigm. They simply need to be interconnected syntactically, and this of course includes the functionality as well as the testing aspects of the two components. The built-in contract testing paradigm not only suggests that testing interfaces should be provided with commercial components but also that these should be provided according to well-defined templates, so that the syntactic integration effort may eventually be removed completely. However, since the technology has not yet penetrated into the component industry, it is likely that component vendors will not provide their components with such testability features.

Commercial third party components cannot typically be augmented with an additional built-in contract testing interface that provides a client with an introspection mechanism for improved testability and observability. This means that COTS components can only be tested through their provided functional interface, as is traditionally the case in object and component testing. However, modern object languages or component platforms such as Java do provide mechanisms that enable internal access to a component. They can break the encapsulation boundary of binary components in a controlled way and offer internal access. Such mechanisms can be used to realize testing interfaces according to the built-in contract testing philosophy for any arbitrary third party component. [4] describe how this can be achieved using Java's reflection mechanism in the form of a suitable Java Library. Here, we only give a brief overview. The architecture of the library is displayed in Fig. 6. Built-in contract testing can initially be carried out by using three primary concepts. These are the testability contract, the tester and test case. These are the fundamental features that support the assessment of test results, control of the execution environment, and actions to be taken if faults are encountered. Additionally, the library provides state based testing support that is more essential to built-in contract testing. These concepts are the state-based testability contract, the state-based tester, and the state-based test case. The state-based concepts abide by the principles of Harel's state machines [4].

5.3   Built-in Contract Testing and Web-Services

Web-Services are commercial software applications that are executed on remote hosts and provide individual services which are used to realize distributed component-based systems. Web-Services fulfill all the requirements of Szyperski's component definition [16], that is a service is only described and used based on interface descriptions and more importantly, it is independently deployable. This means that a Web-Service provides its own run-time environment, so that a component-based application is not bound to a specific platform. Every part of such an application is entirely independent from any other part, and there is no overall run-time support system but the underlying network infrastructure. Web-Services represent the ultimate means of implementing component-based systems.

Contract testing provides the ideal technique for checking dynamic and distributed component-based systems that are implemented through Web-Services. In fact this is the scenario for which built-in contract testing provides the most benefits. The syntactic compatibility between a client and a Web-based server

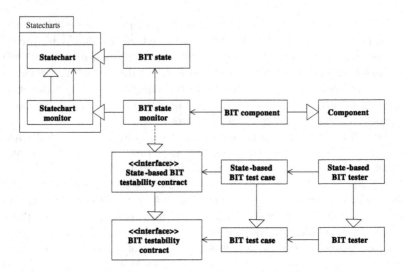

Fig. 6. Organization of the built-in contract testing Java support library [4]

is ensured through an XML mapping between their interfaces. Their semantic compatibility is checked through the built-in server tester components inside the client that are executed to validate the associated server. These tests are performed when the client is registering with a service for the first time (i.e. during configuration,) or if the client requests the same specification of the server from a different Web-Service provider (i.e. during re-configuration).

Fig. 7 displays a sample containment hierarchy of a remote connection between the ATM component (in the teller machine) and the bank's transaction manager that collects all ATM transactions. The ≪remotely acquires≫-relationship indicates that the *TransactionManager* (in this case a testable component) is not locally available. This means that this relationship will be implemented through some underlying networking infrastructure. The stereotype ≪remotely acquires≫ hides the underlying complexity of the network implementation and only considers the level of abstraction that is important for testing. This technique is termed stratification [2]. As soon as the connection between the two interacting components is established, a normal contract test may be initiated regardless of how the connection is realized in practice. The server provides a suitable test interface that the client's built-in tests can use. The client and server do not "know" that they are communicating through Web-Interfaces. This connection is established through their respective contexts when the context of the *ATM* component registers with the context of the *TransactionManager* component (Fig. 7).

Web-Services typically provide instances that are ready to use. As a result, the server component that is provided through the remote service is already configured and set to a distinct required state. A run-time test is therefore likely to change or destroy the server's initial configuration, so that it may not be usable by the client any more. Clearly, for the client, such a changed server is of

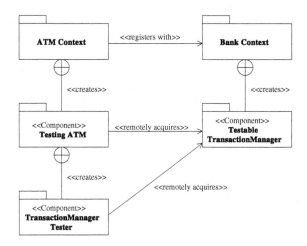

Fig. 7. Association between two remotely connected components based on a WEB-Service implementation

no use and this creates a fundamental dilemma for built-in contract testing of Web-Services.

Under object-oriented run-time systems the client can solve this dilemma by simply creating a clone of the tested component and passing the clone to the test software. This works because client and server are handled by the same run-time environment. For example, in Java this is performed through the *Object.clone* method. In this case, the test software may completely corrupt the newly created clone without any effect on the original instance, it is simply thrown away after the test, and the original is used as working server. However, in a Web-Service environment the run-time system of the client is different from that of the server, so that the client cannot construct a new instance from an existing one. The client and server are residing within completely different run-time scopes on completely different network nodes. Contract testing can therefore only be applied in a Web-Service context if the Web-Service provides some way for the client to have a clone created and accessed for testing. Some contemporary component technologies such as CORBA Components are capable of doing exactly that.

6 Summary and Conclusions

This chapter has described the methodology and process of built-in contract testing for component integration in model-driven component-based application construction. It is a technology that is based on building the test software directly into components - built-in tester components at the client side of a component interaction and built-in testing interfaces at its server side. In this way, a component can check whether it has been brought into a suitable environment, and an environment can check whether each component provides the right services. This enables system integrators who reuse such components to validate immediately and automatically whether a component is working correctly in the environment of a newly created application.

Built-in contract testing delivers the same basic benefits as any reuse technology. The effort of building test software into individual components is paid back depending on how often such a component will be reused in a new context, and a component is reused depending on how easily it may be reused in new contexts. Built-in contract testing greatly simplifies the reuse of a component because once it has been integrated syntactically into a new environment its semantic compliance with the expectations of that new environment may be automatically assessed.

Current and future work focuses on the integration of built-in contract testing with an abstract test description notation, the TTCN-3 technology, and the extension of the contract term to cope with non-functional (i.e. response time) requirements.

Acknowledgements

This work has been partially supported by the EC IST Framework Programme under IST-1999-20162 Component+ project, and the German National Department of Education and Research under the MDTS project acronym.

References

1. A. Abdurazik and J. Offutt. Using UML collaboration diagrams for static checking and test generation. In *3rd Intl. Conf. on the Unified Modeling Language (UML'00)*, pages 383–395, York, UK, October 2000.
2. C. Atkinson, C. Bunse, H.-G. Gross, and T. Kühne. Component model for web-based applications. *Annals of Software Engineering*, 13, 2002.
3. C. Atkinson and et al. *Component-Based Product-Line Engineering with UML*. Addison-Wesley, London, 2001.
4. F. Barbier, N. Belloir, and J.M. Bruel. Incorporation of test functionality in software components. In *2nd Intl. Conference on COTS-based Software Systems*, Ottawa, Canada, February, 10.-12. 2003.
5. B. Beizer. *Black-box Testing, Techniques for Functional Testing of Software and Systems*. John Wiley & Sons, New York, 1995.
6. R. Binder. *Testing Object-Oriented Systems - Models, Patterns and Tools*. Addison-Wesley, 2000.
7. G. Booch. *Software Components with Ada: Structures, Tools and Subsystems*. 1987.
8. Component+. Built-in testing for component-based development. Technical report, Component+ Project, http://www.component-plus.org, 2001.
9. D.S. Guindi, W.B. Ligon, W.M. McCracken, and S. Rugaber. The impact of verification and validation of reusable components on software productivity. In *22nd Annual Hawaii International Conference on System Sciences*, pages 1016–1024, 1989.
10. IEEE. *Standard Glossary of Software Engineering Terminology*. IEEE Std-610.12-1990, 1999.

11. J. McGregor and D. Sykes, editors. *A Practical Guide to Testing Object-Oriented Software*. Addison-Wesley, 2001.
12. B. Meyer. *Object-oriented Software Construction*. Prentice Hall, 1997.
13. S. Meyer and R. Sandfoss. Applying use-case methodology to SRE and system testing. In *STAR West Conference*, October 1998.
14. Quasar. German national funded quasar project. Technical report, http://www.first.gmd.de/quasar/, 2001.
15. J. Ryser and M. Glinz. A scenario-based approach to validating and testing software systems using statecharts. In *12th Intl. Conf. on Software and Systems Engineering and their Applications (ICS-SEA'99)*, Paris, France,, 1999.
16. C. Szyperski. *Component Software: Beyond Object-Oriented Programming*. Addison-Wesley, 1999.
17. Y. Wang, G. King, M. Fayad, D. Patel, I. Court, G. Staples, and M. Ross. On built-in test reuse in object-oriented framework design. In *ACM Journal on Computing Surveys*, volume 32, March 2000.

Quality Characteristics for Software Components: Hierarchy and Quality Guides

Régis P.S. Simão and Arnaldo D. Belchior

Masters Course in Applied Informatics
Universidade de Fortaleza (UNIFOR) Av. Washington Soares
1321 CEP 60.811.341 - Fortaleza - CE - Brasil
regis.simao@secrel.com.br, belchior@unifor.br

Abstract. The success of software component applications depends upon a number of factors, one of the most important being the quality of components. According to the ISO/IEC 9126 standard, quality characteristics can be used both as goals to be attained in the processes of developing, selecting or acquiring components and as criteria for predicting the properties of final applications. This chapter identifies the quality characteristics and sub-characteristics most relevant for software components and organizes them in dimensions that are critical to their assessment. A quality guide is presented, which was elaborated through a field research carried out with developers of components and component-based applications. A software quality evaluation model was used to treat collected data.

1 Introduction

Traditional software development has presented several problems. A large percentage of software systems have been delivered late and over budget. They usually have low quality levels and high maintenance [8]. With the globalization of markets, and the consequent increase in competitiveness, companies are becoming more concerned about the problems presented in traditional forms of software development. Large investments are being made to reformulate existing methods, and especially to elaborate new software product construction techniques.

Component-Based development (CBD) appears as a promising technique for solving the problems mentioned above. In general, this technique consists of dividing monolithic blocks into interrelated modules. This granulation of applications reduces complexity. Developers start out by building independent modules and then combine them into final applications. The reuse of existing modules can reduce development time and cost and increase productivity. Such modules are called components [20, 35, 37].

The word "component" has been largely used in relatively different meanings, depending on the relevance of specific properties for the context at hand. The definition used in this work for software components is not a new different one. It has been given by Villela, based on Sametinger [30] with Karzan's remarks about

A. Cechich et al. (Eds.): Component-Based Software Quality, LNCS 2693, pp. 184–206, 2003.
© Springer-Verlag Berlin Heidelberg 2003

software architecture [21]: "Reusable components are self-contained, clearly identifiable artifacts that describe or implement a specific function and that have clear interfaces in conformity with a given software architectural model, an appropriate documentation, and a defined degree of reuse" [35]. This definition focuses a component as a services supplier unity, from a thorough perspective (self-containment), within an application domain. It also emphasizes the conformity of interfaces with an architectural model, which enforces a set of standards and conventions, thus allowing for the integration of components. Furthermore, this definition stresses the component's maturity being based on its degree of reuse as well as the importance of an appropriate documentation. It is a good concept to work with for it comprises several important properties of components, such as conformity with an architecture, ease of learning, appropriate documentation, and self-containment.

Several factors influence the quality of a component-based application [2, 6, 15, 17, 20, 28, 37]. Bachman *et al.* [2] state that software quality depends on the quality of its components and on the component framework used. Woodman *et al.* [37] add that the development process and the maturity of an organization also influence the quality of component-based software products. In software systems built by assembling components, it is easy to perceive that the quality of its components, directly or indirectly, influences the quality of the final software. The *compositional reasoning* emphasizes that the properties of a system are influenced more by the interaction of its components than by the properties of a single component [2]. Crnkovic *et al.* [13] treat the *prediction theory.* This theory consists of predicting the properties of the assemblies of components before they are acquired and used. This theory is based on assumptions about the environment in which the assembly will run and on information about the components involved. The research model for the prediction theory suggests that component properties, directly or indirectly, involved in any research need to be defined along with the means that may be established and measured [13].

This chapter identifies and organizes relevant quality characteristics for software components and proposes a quality guide for them [31]. This guide was elaborated through a field research carried out with developers of components and component-based applications. A software quality evaluation model was used to treat collected data.

2   The Quality Model for Software Components

The software component quality model is based on the four-part ISO/IEC 9126 standard [18]. The first part of ISO/IEC 9126 defines the quality model for software products. The other three parts discuss the metrics that are used to evaluate the quality characteristics defined in part 1: internal metrics, external metrics, and quality in use metrics.

The quality model proposed by the first part of the ISO/IEC 9126 standard is subdivided into two parts: the quality model for internal and external characteristics, and the quality model for quality in use. A quality characteristic is a property of the software product that enables the user to describe and appraise some product quality aspect. A characteristic can be detailed out into multiple subcharacteristic levels.

External quality characteristics are observed when software products are run, that is, they are measured and appraised when the products are tested, resulting in a dynamic view of the software. Evaluation of internal quality characteristics is accomplished by verifying the software project and source code, resulting in a static view.

Quality in use is the combined effect of the internal and external quality characteristics, and it measures the degree to which users can reach their goals by using the software product. *The quality model for quality in use divides quality properties into four characteristics: Effectiveness, Productivity, Safety, and Satisfaction.*

The quality model for internal and external characteristics categorizes quality attributes into six characteristics: *Functionality, Reliability, Usability, Efficiency, Maintainability, and Portability.* Each of these characteristics is subdivided into quality subcharacteristics. These quality characteristics and their respective metrics can be used as goals to be reached in development, selection and acquisition of components and also as factors in predicting properties of component-based applications.

2.1   Software Component Quality Characteristics

A number of publications on components mention quality attributes that components should have [14, 18, 19, 35, 37]. However, most of these works do not specifically treat this theme, nor do they deal with it in an extensive or thorough manner. For instance, Preiss *et al.* [27] present a small group of quality characteristics organized through a simple classification model. Bertoa and Vallecillo [6] present a list of characteristics and their possible metrics for Commercial-Off-The-Shelf (COTS) components in accordance with ISO/IEC 9126 standard.

To identify and organize software component quality characteristics, an extensive bibliographical research was done in the CBD field. These characteristics were organized according to the proposal of the ISO/IEC 9126. Subsequently, new quality subcharacteristics were added to the existing characteristics in ISO/IEC 9126 so that software component quality might indeed be reached based on the bibliographical research done. In this context, 124 quality attributes (characteristics and subcharacteristics) for software components are presented and defined in Appendix A.

The proposed quality model deserves some especial notes, as it comes to be used. First of all, there is no absolute criterion for the hierarchical placement of subcharacteristics. One specific subcharacteristic might be placed in multiple branches of the hierarchy tree. Nevertheless, for the sake of factoring, each subcharacteristic is defined only once, being placed in the branch where its influence is mostly remarkable.

Second, the ISO/IEC 9126 Standard [18] aims at the quality of final software products, usually as perceived by end-users, whereas the main scope of software components is the development process in general. Therefore, some of the terms used herein extend their meaning as proposed by the ISO standard and corresponding literature. For instance, *Usability* refers not only to the interaction with end-users, but also with handling the component along the development of a component-based application [6]. The interpretation of *Portability*, as well, is extended from product transference among different environments to component reuse in several applications.

The present model defines a relatively large set of quality characteristics for software components, but it can be just partially used for the definition of quality guides and for the evaluation of software components' quality. It is also open to the addition of new subcharacteristics, such as for the mapping of quality attributes in particular settings like mobile or distributed objects.

Users interested in quality characteristics for components - may they be software architects, designers, developers of components and component-based applications, or CBD researchers - can all make use of the quality guides of this model in order to either define a new quality model or to evaluate and certify components.

2.2   Quality Dimensions for Software Components

Various factors can influence the degree of importance assigned to software component quality subcharacteristics. For example, consider the *Attractiveness* subcharacteristic, being evaluated for two software components: one for interface and the other for data. Clearly, the importance that *Attractiveness* has for an interface component is much greater than for a data component.

Also consider the *Security* subcharacteristic being evaluated for business components in two different application domains: multimedia and financial transactions domains. It is clear that the importance of *Security* in a business component for financial transactions would be greater than in a multimedia application.

Finally, consider the *Time Behavior* subcharacteristic evaluated for the same component in a specification and in executable code abstraction levels. This subcharacteristic is more important in executable component code form than in a specification form.

Therefore, the degree of importance of a quality characteristic or subcharacteristics can vary in three different dimensions:

- **The application domain**. Corresponds to the application domain where the component is used.
- **The architectural function**. The component may be distributed by the interface, business, data, and infrastructure layers.
- **The abstraction level**. The component may be reused in its specification, project and code forms (software life-cycle stages).

Several quality guides can be elaborated for software components, such as: guides for interface, data, business, and infrastructure components, guides for components of a particular application domain, abstraction level guides (software life-cycle stages), guides for business components of a particular application domain, and so on.

The influence of the *Architectural Function* dimension (considering the four layers: interface, data, business, and infra-structure) on the degree of importance of quality characteristics for software components was investigated and corroborated through a field research. Its consolidated findings are presented in the next Section in the format of a quality guide for software components.

3   A Quality Guide for Software Components

A quality guide aims to identify the quality characteristics for a particular product and to define quality levels that such characteristics should have to get a satisfactory level of quality.

Defining quality guides is an important activity in elaborating and selecting software products, especially in building and reusing components. Guides can be used as parameters so that more attention can be paid to aspects that more quickly and more cheaply raise components to expected quality levels. Consequently, developers can build their components, aiming to reach values stipulated in the guides, and thus obtaining products with satisfactory quality level, avoiding component properties with values far different from those expected.

According to Boegh [7], reaching high degrees of quality characteristics is expensive due to the large amount of necessary resources. Therefore, just attaining the quality levels that meet user needs is sufficient. In the reuse activity, guides can be used as parameters for acceptance or rejection of the components.

Guides aim to identify the importance of the quality characteristics in a software product. They can be obtained through field research conducted with specialists in the application domain. This kind of research usually uses evaluation questionnaires that collect the degrees of importance of the software product quality characteristics.

Thus, a questionnaire was developed from the hierarchical tree of the software component quality characteristics and subcharacteristics presented and described in the previous Section with the idea of elaborating a quality guide for software components. In this sense, a group of specialists evaluated the degree of importance for each quality subcharacteristic in the lowest level of the hierarchical tree. These subcharacteristics are called measurable quality subcharacteristics. The specialist group was composed of component-based application developers (component reuse) and/or component developers.

The data from the questionnaires, collected in field research, were treated by the Fuzzy Model for Software Quality Evaluation [5].

3.1   The Fuzzy Model for Software Quality Evaluation (FMSQE)

In representing imprecise reasoning models, such as for quality, fuzzy theory has been used. This theory has been applied in several areas of human knowledge and serves as the connecting link between imprecise (subjective) real-world models and their mathematical representation [5, 39].

FMSQE, developed by Belchior [5], defines various concepts and stages for elaborating quality guides and software evaluations that range from determining quality models to executing the evaluation. In [25], FMSQE was adapted to enable the ISO/IEC 9126 standard to be used as the quality model for software product quality evaluation.

FMSQE can be used in three distinct situations [5]:

- Quality Standard (QS) Determination for software product or application domain. In this context, the "quality standard" can be understood as a guide to quality evaluation in a specific application domain;
- Evaluation of a software product quality, based on a predefined QS;
- Evaluation of a software product, without predefined QS.

FMSQE defines five stages that must be used in any of the three situations mentioned above [5]:

1. The identification of the object to be evaluated, the considered quality model (characteristics and subcharacteristics) and the institutions that the product will be tested;
2. The choice of all the specialists who will participate in the evaluation process and the identification of their profile;
3. The rank determination of each measurable quality subcharacteristic, identified in the First Stage;
4. The fuzzy treatment of data provided by the specialists in the evaluation of each measurable quality subcharacteristic;
5. The fuzzy aggregation of the software quality characteristics and subcharacteristic, in each hierarchical level of the quality model.

A fuzzy set is characterized by a membership function, which maps the elements of a domain or universe of discourse X for a real number to $[0, 1]$. Formally, $\hat{A} : X \rightarrow [0, 1]$. Thus, a fuzzy set $\tilde{A}$, for instance, is a set of ordered pairs, where the first element is $x \in X$. The second, $\mu_{\tilde{A}}(x)$, is the degree of membership or the membership function of x in $\tilde{A}$, that maps x to the interval $[0, 1]$, that is, $\hat{A} = \{(x, \mu_{\tilde{A}}(x)) \mid x \in X\}$. The membership of an element within a certain set becomes a question of degree. In extreme cases, the degree of membership is 0, indicating that the element is not a member of the set, or the degree of membership is 1, if the element is a 100% member of the set [4].

In evaluating measurable quality subcharacteristics, specialists attribute grades from 0 (zero) to 4 (four) to each of them. These grades are linked to a set of linguistic terms and go through a *fuzzification process*, that is, they are transformed into normal triangular fuzzy numbers, according to Table 1. The membership functions are shown in Fig. 1.

A normal triangular fuzzy number can be represented by $\tilde{N} = (a, m, b)$, where the values a and b respectively identify the lower and upper limits of the base of a triangle, where the degree of membership $\mu_{\tilde{A}}(x) = 0$. The value of m

Table 1. Normal triangular fuzzy numbers for the software component quality evaluation

Scale	Fuzzy Number	Linguistic Term	Meaning
0	$\tilde{N}_1=(0.0, 0.0, 1.0)$	Not Important (NI)	It indicates, in an absolute way, that the existence of the quality subcharacteristic is not important.
1	$\tilde{N}_2=(0.0, 1.0, 2.0)$	Little Important (LI)	It indicates, in an absolute way, that the existence of the quality subcharacteristic is little important.
2	$\tilde{N}_3=(1.0, 2.0, 3.0)$	Desirable (D)	It indicates, in an absolute way, that the existence of the quality subcharacteristic is desirable.
3	$\tilde{N}_4=(2.0, 3.0, 4.0)$	Very Important (VI)	It indicates, in an absolute way, that the existence of the quality subcharacteristic is very important.
4	$\tilde{N}_5=(3.0, 4.0, 4.0)$	Indispensable (I)	It indicates, in an absolute way, that the existence of the quality subcharacteristic is indispensable.

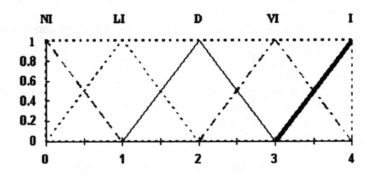

Fig. 1. Membership functions

corresponds to the height of the triangle, where $\mu_{\tilde{A}}(x) = 1$, which is the desirable quality value.

The interpretation of triangular fuzzy numbers in the context of quality characteristics can be summarized in the following rules:

- a quality (sub-)characteristic will reach acceptable level if its value falls in the interval [a, b];
- values below a mean the (sub-)characteristic does not have the least desirable quality level; values above b mean an excess of quality, i. e., an extra effort might have been uselessly spent;
- m is the most desirable quality value for a (sub-)characteristic; it means a 100% degree of belonging (1). This is the optimal point in the cost-benefit scale of the effort necessary to yield quality.

For example, consider the following triangular fuzzy number $\tilde{N} = (2.20; 3.25; 3.70)$ for a given quality characteristic. The values $a = 2.20$ and $b = 3.70$ mean the lowest and the highest level of acceptable quality for the characteristic, respectively, and $m = 3.25$ corresponds to the desirable quality value. Analyzing the value of m, according to the set of membership functions in Fig. 1, the appraised characteristic is between 3, *very important*, and 4, *indispensable*, meaning 25% *indispensable* and 75% *very important*. In this way, real-world subjective information is mapped to mathematical representations.

Specialist profiles for those who participated in this field research were obtained through a Specialist Profile Identification Questionnaire (SPIQ) (second stage of FMSQE). These profiles were treated by the fuzzy model generating weights, which influenced the final result of the software component quality evaluation by giving greater weights to specialists with more knowledge or experience. The field research was done by sending out questionnaires to a group of 30 (thirty) specialists from Brazil.

Only one of the 30 questionnaires was not considered because its respective specialist was not engaged in CBD activities, as shown by his SPIQ. The profile of the other 29 surveyed specialists can be summarized as follows:

- *CBD experience:* 56.25% of the specialists are component developers and have participated in building component-based applications; 50% have worked as software architects; 31.25% have been CBD projects managers (these percentage figures are not mutually exclusive).
- *CBD Complexity:* 37.50% of them have participated in high complexity CBD projects; 87.50% and 68.75% have respectively developed medium and low complexity applications.
- *Graduation Level:* all of the specialists are at least graduates - 31.25% of them have a PhD in Computer Sciences or similar named course; 37.50% are Masters; 12.50% have a post-graduation specialization; and the remaining 18.75% are just plain graduates.
- *CBD Publications/Lectures:* 31.25% have published CBD papers in proceedings of international conferences. 18.75% have lectured in scientific meetings.

Below, the results of this research, which generated a quality guide for software components, will be presented.

3.2   The Quality Guide for Software Components

The software component quality guide, organized according to ISO/IEC 9126, is shown in Table 5, in Appendix B, together with the triangular fuzzy numbers, which were obtained from the field research and further appraised and aggregated according to the FMSQE.

To proceed, a more select evaluation of the results obtained for each quality characteristic, Table 2, and for some software component quality subcharacteristics from Table 5 will be done. To do this, only the values of m (desirable quality values) for the normal triangular fuzzy numbers, represented by $\tilde{N}=(a, m, b)$, and based on the set of linguistic terms from Table 1 were considered.

Table 2. The software component quality characteristics summary

Characteristic	Fuzzy Number	Meaning
Portability	(2.16, 3.16, 3.77)	15.99% *indispensable*, 84.01% *very important*
Reliability	(2.08, 3.08, 3.68)	7.80% *indispensable*, 92.20% *very important*
Functionality	(2.04, 3.04, 3.63)	4.17% *indispensable*, 95.83% *very important*
Efficiency	(2.02, 3.01, 3.72)	1.04% *indispensable*, 98.96% *very important*
Maintainability	(1.91, 2.91, 3.64)	90.54% *very important*, 9.46% *desirable*
Usability	(1.67, 2.64, 3.43)	64.11% *very important*, 35.89% *desirable*

The idea of using software components is strongly correlated to properties such as adaptability without internal changes, compatibility with new versions or other components, and portability to environments other than the development one. The survey's subjects have considered the *Portability* characteristic to be the most important one when dealing with software components. That characteristic obtained a 3.16 degree of importance, interpreted as 15.99% *indispensable* and 84.01% *very important*.

Reusing software components is a CBD solution to increase the productivity and quality of final applications. It depends on components' maturity, fail tolerance and recoverability, aspects highly ranked by specialists. Components must have mechanisms to directly or indirectly recover from failure. Indeed, *Reliability* was the second most important component characteristic, as shown by the aggregate findings, with a value of 3.08, interpreted as 7.80% *indispensable* and 92.20% *very important*.

The pre-condition for using a software component, particularly when developed by a third party, is that it meet user needs, at least partially, with the required precision level, and that it conform to the application's architecture and technology. That is represented by the characteristic of *Functionality*, evaluated to a 3.04 degree, being 4.17% *indispensable* and 95.83% *very important*.

Response time is a common software requirement, subject of many investigations aimed at predicting the final performance of component-based applications. Storage media and communication networks are critical resources, demanding rational usage. Such problems raise the issue of *Efficiency*, the fourth best appraised characteristic, with a 3.01 degree, being 1.04% *indispensable* and 98.96% *very important*.

Maintainability was ranked fifth, with a 2.91 degree of importance (90.54% *very important*, 9.46% *desirable*). It is a very important characteristic, indeed. Its relatively low ranking does not mean an underestimation of component maintenance activities, but rather a specialists' preference to reuse off-the-shelf components instead of building them up and assuming the burden of maintaining them. However, the importance of this characteristic must be stressed when it comes to software houses.

The least important characteristic, as evaluated by subjects, was *Usability*, being yet 64.11% *very important* and 35.89% *desirable*, with a resulting degree of 2.64. The specialists do find non-technical aspects of software components to

Table 3. The component quality subcharacteristics most highly appraised

Subcharacteristic	Fuzzy Number	Meaning
1.2. Accuracy	(2,65; 3,65; 3,98)	37.99% *very important,* 62.01% *desirable*
4.4. Scalability	(2,56; 3,56; 3,92)	27.85% *very important,* 72.15% *desirable*
1.1. Suitability	(2,51; 3,51; 3,87)	98.27% *little important,* 1.73% *not important*
6.4. Replaceability	(2,41; 3,40; 3,83)	98.27% *little important,* 1.73% *not important*
3.4. User friendliness	(2,34; 3,34; 3,90)	98.27% *little important,* 1.73% *not important*
2.5. Reliability compliance	(2,33; 3,33; 3,90)	98.27% *little important,* 1.73% *not important*

be important, but not yet so much as they appraise the other characteristics under consideration.

Only the six more relevant and the three less relevant subcharacteristics (in the hierarchical level immediately below that of quality characteristics) will be appraised in any detail. Table 3 presents, in decreasing order of degree of importance, the six subcharacteristics most highly appraised.

For the specialists, services provided by components must meet user needs, at least partially, with the required precision level. That is indicated by the subcharacteristic of *Accuracy*, considered the most important one, with a 3.65 degree, being 64.98% *indispensable*, 35.02% *very important*.

Just below in the rank of subcharacteristics is *Scalability*, evaluated to 3.56, being 5.96% *indispensable* and 44.04% *very important*, which shows a strong concern about components' capability to respond to large volumes of requests.

Next comes *Suitability*, with a 3.51 degree, interpreted as 50.89% *indispensable* and 49.11% *very important*, meaning the component must be compatible both with the application's architecture and the development technology, and also be complete and consistent in providing the required services.

One component may also be expected to be replaceable by another or by a new version of itself. The subcharacteristic *Replaceability* was ranked at the fourth level of importance, with a 3.40 degree, being 40.26% *indispensable* and 59.74% *very important*.

Fifth in the rank of subcharacteristics, *User friendliness* was relatively a little better off than its corresponding characteristic, *Usability*, sixth in the rank of characteristics. The capability of the component to enable the user to easily use it was evaluated to 3.34, considered to be 34% *indispensable* and 66% *very important*.

An application's reliability requirements must somehow be met by its components. *Reliability compliance* is the sixth most important subcharacteristic, with a 3.33 degree, being 32.96% *indispensable* and 67.04% *very important*.

Table 4 presents, in decreasing order of importance, the three quality subcharacteristics with the lowest degrees of importance, as viewed by developers.

Table 4. The component quality subcharacteristics with the lowest degrees of importance

Subcharacteristic	Fuzzy Number	Meaning
5.5. Testability	(1,38; 2,38; 3,32)	37.99% *very important*, 62.01% *desirable*
4.3. State Behavior	(1,41; 2,28; 3,05)	27.85% *very important*, 72.15% *desirable*
3.7. Attractiveness	(0,54; 0,98; 1,87)	98.27% *little important*, 1.73% *not important*

The subcharacteristic of *Testability* obtained the third lowest degree of importance (2.38), interpreted yet as 37.99% *very important* and 62.01% *desirable*. The specialists mean that testing is important, and so is the component's capability to be tested, but in a decreasing degree to the extent that components are reused over and over, having their results frequently verified, especially if they are certified.

Finally, *State Behavior* and *Attractiveness*, with the respective degrees of 2.28 and 0.98, were the least important subcharacteristics. They are rather domain-specific, being particularly important for data components and interfaces, respectively. In general, *State Behavior* is just 27.85% *very important* and 72.15% *desirable*, and *Attractiveness* ranges from 1.73% *not important* to 98.27% *little important*.

4   Uses for Software Component Quality Characteristics and Guides

Quality characteristics and guides may be used within the various development stages of component-based applications.

Quality characteristics are very important for describing software products, while guides are important in establishing comparison parameters, either in constructing or in selecting products.

Initially, in a CBD process, developers can plan the construction of components and the application, establishing or selecting quality guides that will serve as parameters for constructing new components or in selecting others for reuse.

The FMSQE specifies rules to evaluate a component's quality [4]. First, you obtain the component's triangular fuzzy number, $\tilde{N}$. Then, $\tilde{N}$ is compared with a quality guide's fuzzy number. The final result is the component's quality level.

Complementing the construction activity, the certification of components aims to guarantee that the artifacts developed possess the desired quality levels. The quality characteristics can be used as basic information to describe component quality, and the guides can be used to validate the quality level of the components.

In the activity of selecting components, the quality characteristics can be used as basic information for indexing components in repositories and, consequently, for their recovery. Recovery can be guided by established quality guides for the constituent elements of the application.

Further, as part of the selection activity, there is the properties prediction that the final application will have. The prediction theory consists of foreseeing the quality characteristics of the final application based on the characteristics of the components and their assemblies [2, 11, 13].

However, much research is still necessary in order for quality characteristics and guides to be fully used:

– Elaborating guides, considering quality dimensions;
– Identifying or elaborating metrics for the subcharacteristics of a software component quality model;
– Elaborating a quality in use quality model for software components;
– Relating to the prediction theory and the fact that a quality subcharacteristic can influence other subcharacteristics, beyond those specified in the quality model, makes identifying these patterns of influence necessary.
– Incorporating the theories related of software component quality to CBD processes.

5   Summary

The success of component-based software applications depends upon various factors, among which, component quality is one of the most important. This chapter presented a quality model and a guide that can help identify and document the quality level of general software components.

Along with the desire of higher levels of productivity and quality, and the reduction of costs intended by CBD, it also increases the need for parameters that allow for building and selecting components at appropriate quality levels.

The proposed model presents a set of quality characteristics and subcharacteristics for software components based on ISO/IEC 9126 standard and on the specialized literature in this filed of knowledge. From this set, a quality guide for software components was proposed based on a field research accomplished with developers of components and component-based applications, and whose results were obtained through the use of a fuzzy model for software quality evaluation.

Three quality dimensions were also defined: application domains, architectural functions, and abstraction levels. These dimensions influence the degree of importance of the quality characteristics and subcharacteristics, thus allowing for the creation of more specific quality guides.

References

1. Albuquerque, A. B.: Qualidade de websites de comércio eletrônico (E-Commerce website quality). University of Fortaleza. Master's Thesis, Fortaleza, Ceará, Brazil. (2001)
2. Bachman, F., Bass, L., Buhman, C., Comella-Dorda, S., Long, F., and Robert, J.: CMU/SEI-2000-TR-008. Volume II: Technical Concepts of Component-Based Software Engineering (2nd ed.) Pittsburgh: Software Engineering Institute, Carnegie Mellon University. (2000)
3. Bashir, I., Serafini, E. and Wall, K.:Securing networks software application: introduction. Communications of the ACM, 44(2). (2000) 28-30

4. Belchior, A. D.: Controle da qualidade de software financeiro (Control of the quality of financial software). COPPE/Federal University of Rio de Janeiro. Master's Thesis, Rio de Janeiro, Brazil. (1992)
5. Belchior, A. D.: Um modelo fuzzy para avaliação da qualidade de Software (A fuzzy model to software quality evaluation). University of Fortaleza. Doctoral Thesis, Rio de Janeiro, Brazil. (1997)
6. Bertoa, M. F. and Vallecillo, A.: Atributos de calidad para components COTS (Quality attributes for COTS components). Proceedings of the 5th Wokshop Iberoamericano de Ingeniería de Requisitos y Ambientes Software. (2002) 352-363
7. Boegh, J.: A practitioners guide to evaluation of software. Proceedings of the Software Engineering Standards Symposium. (1993)
8. Bosch, J.: Design and use of software architectures: Adopting and evolving a product-line approach. Addison Wesley. (2000)
9. Campos, F.: Qualidade de aplicações hipermídia (Hipermedia application quality). COPPE/Federal University of Rio de Janeiro. Master's Thesis, Rio de Janeiro, Brazil. (1994)
10. Carvalho, O. C.: Qualidade de sistemas de informação hospitalar (Quality of hospital information systems). COPPE/ Federal University of Rio de Janeiro. Master's Thesis, Rio de Janeiro, Brazil. (1997)
11. Chen, S., Gorton, I., Liu, A. and Liu, Y.: Perform prediction of COTS components-based enterprise applications. Proceedings of the 5th ICSE Workshop on Component-based Software Engineering. (2002)
12. Clunie, C. E.: Avaliação da qualidade de especificações orientadas a objeto (Evaluation of the quality of object-oriented specifications). COPPE/ Federal University of Rio de Janeiro. Doctoral Thesis, Rio de Janeiro, Brazil. (1997)
13. Crnkovic, I., Schmidt, H., Stafford, J., and Wallnau, K.: Anatomy of a research project in predictable assembly [White paper]. Proceedings of the 5th ICSE Workshop on Component-based Software Engineering. (2002)
14. D'Souza, D. F. and Wills, A. C.: Object, components, and frameworks with UML: The catalysis approach. Addison Wesley. (1998)
15. Fuggetta, A.: Software process: A roadmap. Proceedings of the 22nd International Conference on Software Engineering. (2000)
16. Gao, J.: Component testability and component testing challenges. Proceedings of the 3rd ICSE Workshop on Component-based Software Engineering. (2000)
17. Gómez-Perez, A. and Lozano, A.: Impact of software components characteristics above decision-making factors. Proceedings of the 3rd ICSE Workshop on Component-Based Software Engineering. (2000)
18. ISO/IEC 9126: Software engineering - Product quality - Part 1: Quality model. International Organization for Standardization and International Electrotechnical Commission. (2001)
19. Jacobson, I., Griss, M. and Jonsson, P.: Software reuse: architecture, process and organization for business success. Addison Wesley. (1997)
20. Kallio, P. and Niemelä, E.: Documented quality of COTS and COM components. Proceedings of the 4th ICSE Workshop on Component-Based Software Engineering. (2001)
21. Karzan: http://www.sei.cmu.edu/cbs/papers/evalᵦib.html (2000)
22. Lima, R., Oliveira, K., Sampaio, F., Menezes, A., Blaschek, B. and Rocha, A. R.: Evaluating web sites for an educational environment target for cardiology. Proceedings of the 3rd European Software Measurement Conference. (2000)

23. Lycett, M.: Understanding variation in component-based development: case findings from practice. Information and Software Technology Journal, 43. (2001) 203-213

24. Oliveira, K. M.: Avaliação da qualidade de sistemas especialistas (Evaluation of the quality of specialist systems). COPPE/Federal University of Rio de Janeiro. Master's Thesis, Rio de Janeiro, Brazil. (1995)

25. Oliveira, K. R.: AdeQuaS: Ferramenta fuzzy para avaliação da qualidade de software (AdeQuaS: Fuzzy tool for software quality evaluation). University of Fortaleza. Master's Thesis, Fortaleza, Cear, Brazil. (2002)

26. Olsina, L., Godoy, D., Lafuente, G. and Rossi, G.: Quality characteristics and attributes for academic web sites. Web Engineering Workshop at WWW8. (1999)

27. Preiss, O., Wegmann, A. and Wong, J.: On quality attribute based software engineering. Proceedings of the 27th Euromicro Conference. (2001) 114-120

28. Preiss, O. and Wegmann, A.: A systems perspective on the quality description of software components. Proceedings of the 6th World Multiconference on Systemics, Cybernetics and Informatics, 7. (2002) 250-255.

29. Pressman, R. S.: Software engineering: A practitioner's approach (5th ed.) McGraw Hill. (2000)

30. Sametinger, J.: Software engineering with reusable components. Springer. (1997)

31. Simão, R. P. S.: Características de qualidade para componente de software (Quality characteristics for software components). University of Fortaleza. Master's Thesis, Fortaleza, Ceará, Brazil. (2002)

32. Szyperski, C.: Component object-oriented programming. Addison Wesley. (1998)

33. Valle, C., Ximenes, A. A., Campos, G., Rocha, A. R. and Rabelo, JR.: Educação de pacientes através de sistemas de acesso público (Education of patients through public access systems). Brazilian Magazine on Education Computing, 1(1). (1997)

34. Vieira, M. E., R, Dias, M. S. and Richardson, D. J.: Describing dependencies in component access points. Proceedings of the 4th ICSE Workshop on Component-Based Software Engineering. (2001)

35. Villela, R. M. B.: Busca e recuperação de componentes em ambientes de reutilização de software (Components searching and retrieving in software reuse environments). COPPE/Federal University of Rio de Janeiro. Doctoral Thesis, Rio de Janeiro, Brazil. (2000)

36. Wile, D. S., Ensuring general-purpose and domain-specific properties using architectural styles. Proceedings of the 4th ICSE Workshop on Component-Based Software Engineering. (2001)

37. Woodman, M., Benediktsson, O., Lefever, B. and Stallinger, F.: Issues of CBD product quality and process quality. Proceedings of the 4th ICSE Workshop on Component-Based Software Engineering. (2001)

38. Yacoub, S., Ammar, H. and Mili, A.: A model for classifying component interfaces. Proceedings of the 2nd ICSE Workshop on Component-Based Software Engineering. (1999)

39. Zadeh, L. A.: Fuzzy logic. IEEE Transaction Computer. 25. (1988)

A – The Software Component Quality Characteristics Definitions

The quality characteristics for software component are listed below.

1. **Functionality** – The capability of the component to provide functions which meet stated and implied needs when the software is used under specified conditions [18].

1.1. **Suitability** – The capability of the component to provide an appropriate set of functions for specified tasks and user objectives [18].

1.1.1. **Technological suitability** – The capability of the component to provide functions with a technology compatible with that used in the development of the application [1, 24].

1.1.1.1. **Methodological suitability** – The capability of the component to provide functions with a methodology compatible with that used in the development of the application [24].

1.1.1.2. **Technological infrastructure suitability** – The capability of the component to provide functions using a technological infrastructure (hardware, programming language and component technology) compatible with that used in the development of the application [1, 10].

1.1.1.3. **Appropriateness of development environment** – The capability of the component to provide functions in a development environment (tools) compatible with that used in the development of the application [24].

1.1.2. **Architectural Suitability** – The capability of the component to provide elements (interface, implementation) with an architectural style compatible with that used in the development of the application [36].

1.1.3. **Coverage** – The capability of the component to provide services that meet user needs, with specification, project and implementation [4, 6, 10].

1.1.4. **Completeness** – The capability of the component to provide all services offered, with specification, project and implementation [4, 10, 22].

1.1.5. **Correctness** – The capability of the component to assure that the results obtained are coherent with the issues raised by the user [4].

1.1.6. **Consistency** – The capability of the component to yield coherent information, without contradictions and/or ambiguities [4].

1.2. **Accuracy** – The capability of the component to provide the right or agreed results or effects with the needed degree of precision [18].

1.3. **Self-Containment** – The capability of the component to accomplish by itself alone the function that it is expected to perform [14, 19, 32, 35].

1.4. **Functional cohesion** – The capability of the component to make use of all its elements in performing its services [4].

1.5. **Interoperability** – The capability of the component to interact with one or more specified components [18].

1.5.1. **Data Compatibility** – The capability of the component to represent input and output data in a de facto standard or international format [6].

1.5.2. **Interactivity** – The capability of the component to maintain a clear and concise dialogue with other components and/or users [35].

1.5.3. **Internal interoperability** – The capability of the component to provide quality interfaces among its various parts and that they may easily be adapted to accommodate new needs [10].

1.6. **Security** – The capability of the component to protect information and data so that unauthorized persons or systems cannot read or modify them and authorized persons or systems are not denied access to them [18].

1.6.1. **Confidentiality** – The capability of the component to not make information available to unauthorized individuals, entities, or processes [1, 3].

1.6.2. Accountability – The capability of the component to provide mechanisms that make an individual or entity responsible for the use of its services [1].

1.6.3. Privacy – The capability of the component to provide mechanisms to assure user privacy in terms of outside access to handled information [1, 10, 33].

1.6.4. Vulnerability – The capability of the component to protect itself against certain types of attacks [1].

1.7. Functionality compliance – The capability of the component to adhere to standards, conventions or regulations in laws and similar prescriptions relating to functionality [18].

2. Reliability – The capability of the component to maintain a specified level of performance when used under specified conditions [18].

2.1. Maturity – The capability of the component to avoid failure as a result of faults in the software [18].

2.1.1. State Memory – The capability of the component to always execute its services as if for the first time, without knowledge of previous execution (for example: correct initialization of variables) [4].

2.1.2. Absence of errors – The capability of the component to operate without interruption of its functionality [1, 9].

2.1.3. Data entry signalizing – The capability of the component to provide alerts for input data that fall outside of specified norms or for combinations of data that indicate problems [1, 10].

2.1.4. Integrity – The capability of the component to preserve its data and processing in abnormal situations [1, 10, 33].

2.1.5. Version non-volatility – The capability of the component to be used without frequent version substitution [6].

2.1.6. Degradability – The capability of the component to detect when its integrity is being degraded [6].

2.2. Fault tolerance – The capability of the component to maintain a specified level of performance in case of software faults or infringement of its specified interface [18].

2.2.1. Robustness – The capability of the component to deal with hostile situations, and can recover from them without loss of control [1].

2.2.2. Contingency planning – The capability of the component to retrocede, in case of flaws or damage, to a simpler method of processing. In the worst case, allowing manual operation procedures [10].

2.3. Recoverability – The capability of the component to re-establish a specified level of performance and recover the data directly affected in the case of a failure [18].

2.3.1. Undo facilities – The capability of the component to provide mechanisms that enable to undo services already processed [1].

2.3.2. Help for correcting errors – The capability of the component to provide support to users in correcting errors [33].

2.3.3. Auditability – The capability of the component to create trails and a history (log) of processing already completed with a view toward subsequent auditing [1, 10].

2.3.4. Error Handling – The capability of the component to provide mechanisms to detect, handle or flag errors [6].

2.4. Evaluability – The capability of the component to enable the user to evaluate its form and/or its content [12].

2.4.1. Verifiability – The capability of the component to enable the user to evaluate its specification, project or implementation, to verify if it was built in accordance with the pre-established norms and standards of the development method utilized by the organization and/or user [12].

2.4.2. Validity – The capability of the component to enable the user to evaluate its content, by adequately describing the problem or the solution proposed, that is, by permitting an evaluation of whether or not it meets the user needs [12].

2.5. Reliability compliance – The capability of the component to adhere to standards, conventions or regulations relating to reliability [18].

3. Usability – The capability of the component to be understood, learned, used and attractive to the user, when used under specified conditions [18].

3.1. Accessibility – The capability of the component to enable the user to easily locate, identify and access it [1, 22, 35].

3.1.1. Component identification – The capability of the component to enable the user to identify it uniquely and unambiguously (for example, an ISBN for components) [4, 35].

3.1.2. Component classification – The capability of the component to provide classification data that may be used by various classification methods (free text, key word classification, numerical classification, facet and attribute pairs), enabling the user to use them to locate it [35].

3.2. Legibility – The capability of the component to enable the user easily understand it [1].

3.2.1. Clarity – The capability of the component to provide clear specification, project, implementation and documentation, avoiding information that would otherwise make it complex or difficult to understand [1, 10, 22].

3.2.2. Conciseness – The capability of the component to provide services implemented with a minimum amount of code and, specified and modelled in a non-redundant manner, containing only the essential [1, 4, 10, 22].

3.2.3. Style – The capability of the component to provide specification, project and implementation with resources that facilitate its understanding (indentation, appropriate comments and standardized identification) [1, 22].

3.2.4. Correct use of method – The capability of the component to provide specification, project and implementation with correct usage of languages adopted, in terms of notation, semantics, syntax and documentation format [12].

3.2.5. Terminology uniformity – The capability of the component to use a uniform terminology in naming entities such as variables, blocks, files, etc. [1, 4, 22].

3.2.6. Abstraction uniformity – The capability of the component to provide its documentation in a uniform level of detail at any particular stage of development [1, 10, 22].

3.3. Understandability – The capability of the component to enable the user to understand whether it suitable, and how it can be used for particular tasks and conditions of use [18].

3.3.1. Contextualization – The capability of the component to enable the user to understand the context of its use within the application domain [23].

3.3.1.1. Commonality – The capability of the component to enable the user to understand the common elements between the applications within the same domain, that are represented by the component [19, 23].

3.3.1.2. Variability – The capability of the component to enable the user to locate where that component may be varied, and to identify its variability mechanisms [19, 23].

3.3.1.3. Dependencies – The capability of the component to enable the user to understand the contextual, architectural, and environmental requirements upon which it depends to render its services [19, 32, 34].

3.3.1.3.1. Contextual dependencies – The capability of the component to enable the user to be aware of the necessary contextual requirements in its use (for example: other components, component initialization data, etc.) [32, 34].

3.3.1.3.2. Architectural dependencies – The capability of the component to enable the user to be aware of the architectural style utilized by it [32, 34].

3.3.1.3.3. Technological dependencies – The capability of the component to enable the user to be aware of the necessary technological requirements in its use (for example: methodology, software and hardware environment used in development and execution) [32, 34].

3.3.2. Justifiability – The capability of the component to enable the user to justify its construction or use, by the context in which it will be inserted [24].

3.3.3. Utility – The capability of the component to enable the user to understand the reasons that its use will bring about significantly beneficial consequences [24].

3.3.4. Relevance – The capability of the component to enable the user to understand the reasons that its construction and use are important to accomplishing the task [24, 33].

3.4. User friendliness – The capability of the component to enable the user easily use it [1].

3.4.1. Behavior uniformity – The capability of the component to provide services that always behave in a similar way, remaining comprehensible and familiar to the end user [33].

3.4.2. Interface uniformity – The capability of the component to enable the user to utilize only standardized interfaces [10, 14].

3.5. Learnability – The capability of the component to enable the user to learn its application [18].

3.5.1. User-oriented content – The capability of the component to provide its content geared toward users (for example: specific sections for maintainers and specific sections for developers) [1, 22].

3.5.2. Help availability – The capability of the component to make help information available to users [1, 10, 22, 26].

3.5.3. User support – The capability of the component to provide technical support services to the user.

3.6. Operability – The capability of the component to enable the user to operate and control it [18].

3.6.1. Manipulability – The capability of the component to enable the user locate and retrieve information from the existing documentation [1, 10, 22].

3.6.1.1. Artifact availability – The capability of the component to provide up-to-date artifacts and ready to use whenever necessary (example artifacts: models, documentation, source and executable code) [1, 4, 22].

3.6.1.2. Architectural style – The capability of the component to make use of an appropriate and well-defined pattern in the construction and composition of its components [1, 4, 10, 22].

3.6.1.3. Traceability – The capability of the component to enable the user to track its artifacts through crossed references, facilitating the search for information among the various forms of representation [1, 10, 22].

3.6.2. Controllability – The capability of the component to enable the user to control the influx and outflow of data, interface usage operations, and behavior [16].

3.7. Attractiveness – The capability of the component to be attractive to the user, such as the use of color and nature of the graphical design [18].

3.8. Usability compliance – The capability of the component to adhere to standards, conventions, styles guides or regulations relating to usability [18].

4. Efficiency – The capability of the component to provide appropriate performance, relative to the amount of resources used, under stated conditions [18].

4.1. Time behavior – The capability of the component to provide appropriate response and processing times and throughput rates when performing its function, under stated conditions [18].

4.1.1. Binding time – The capability of the component to provide various kinds of appropriate implementation bindings, examples of them are Coding time binding, Compile time binding, Link time binding, Dynamic linking time binding, Runtime binding or Reflective binding [14].

4.1.2. Capacity – The capability of the component to receive and to process an amount of appropriate information without bottlenecking [6].

4.1.3. Throughput – The capability of the component to produce an amount of appropriate information without bottlenecking [6].

4.2. Resource utilization – The capability of the component to use appropriate amounts and types of resources when the software performs its function under stated conditions [18].

4.3. State behavior – The capability of the component to preserve, to transport (movable objects) or to recover its state.

4.3.1. Statefull capability – The capability of the component to maintain its state between various interactions [38].

4.3.2. Serialization capability – The capability of the component to provide serializable code and state, that is, their representations in memory to be able to be converted to a byte sequence that they can be transferred to various agents for later recovery [6].

4.3.3. Persistence support – The capability of the component to provide mechanisms (code or standardization) that enable to save its state in a persistent storage device [6].

4.3.4. Transactional support – The capability of the component to provide mechanisms that enable transactional control of its state [6].

4.4. Scalability – The capability of the component to accommodate larger volumes of processes without the necessity of modifying the implementation [23, 37].

4.5. Appropriateness of the granularity level – The capability of the component to provide an appropriate granularity level to be functionally useful, updateable, and maintainable at high performance levels.

4.6. Efficiency compliance – The capability of the component to adhere to standards or conventions relating to efficiency [18].

5. Maintainability – The capability of the component to be modified. Modifications may include corrections, improvements or adaptation of software to changes in environment, and in requirements and functional specifications [18].

5.1. Analyzability – The capability of the component to be diagnosed for deficiencies or causes of failures in the software, of for the parts to be modified to be identified [18].

5.1.1. Architectural correctness – The capability of the component to assure that its modelling and construction are coherent with the component-based development technique used, including the disposition, composition and relations of its parts (components) [12].

5.2. Implementation feasibility – The capability of the component to be implemented in terms of readiness of resources [1, 10, 12, 22].

5.2.1. Economic feasibility – The capability of the component to be built at an acceptable cost/benefit ratio [1, 10, 12, 22].

5.2.2. Financial feasibility – The capability of the component to be built according to the availability of the necessary capital for its development [1, 10, 12, 22].

5.2.3. Market feasibility – The capability of the component to built opportunely; offering the right product at the right time [1, 22, 29].

5.2.4. Schedule feasibility – The capability of the component to be built within the planned time limit with flexibility for the introduction of non-projected and/or contingency activities, and maintaining the defined quality level for the product [12].

5.2.5. Human resources feasibility – The capability of the component to be built considering the existence and the readiness of the labor necessary for its development [1, 10, 12, 22].

5.2.6. Technology feasibility – The capability of the component to be built considering the existence and the readiness of the necessary technology for its development [1, 12, 22].

5.3. Changeability – The capability of the component to enable a specified modification to be implemented [18].

5.3.1. Changeability to correct errors – The capability of the component to enable modification for the correction of existing errors [12].

5.3.2. Evolvability – The capability of the component to enable modification for its evolution, through successive refinements that represent increasingly more complete knowledge [12, 24].

5.3.3. Extensibility – The capability of the component to enable modification for extensions, with a minimum of work as a way of accommodating new requirements of the user [19, 32].

5.4. Stability – The capability of the component to avoid unexpected effects from modifications of the software [18].

5.5. Testability – The capability of the component to enable modified software to be validated [18].

5.5.1. Start-up self-test – The capability of the component to accomplish self- and environmental tests to assure correct operation [6].

5.5.2. Test suite – The capability of the component to provide test packages (test cases, tools, etc.), that allow for the verification of the functionality of the component and the measurement of its properties (for example: performance) [6].

5.5.3. Generation of test reports – The capability of the component to supply information relating to test results.

5.6. Maintainability compliance – The capability of the component to adhere to standards or conventions relating to maintainability [18].

6. Portability – The capability of the component to be transferred from one environment to another. Environment means organization, hardware or software environment [18].

6.1. Adaptability – The capability of the component to be adapted for different specified environments without applying actions or means other than those provided for this purpose for the software considered [18].

6.1.1. Generality – The capability of the component to provide a minimum number of restrictions, so that it may be used in different contexts [4].

6.1.1.1. Typification – The capability of the component to be used in the construction of other components or to form part of component libraries.

6.1.2. Configurability – The capability of the component to be configured or customized without the need of modifications [35].

6.2. Installability – The capability of the component to be installed in a specified environment [18].

6.3. Co-existence – The capability of the component to co-exist with other independent software in a common environment sharing common resources [18].

6.4. Replaceability – The capability of the component to be used in place of another specified component for the same purpose in the same environment [18].

6.5. Portability compliance – The capability of the component to adhere to standards or conventions relating to portability [18].

B – The Quality Guide for Software Components

The quality guide for software components is presented in Table 5 below.

Table 5. The quality guide for software components

Quality Characteristic	Fuzzy Number
1. Functionality	**(2.04; 3.04; 3.63)**
1.1. Suitability	(2.51, 3.51, 3.87)
1.1.1. Technological suitability	(1.78, 2.77, 3.58)
1.1.1.1. Methodological suitability	(1.91, 2.91, 3.69)
1.1.1.2. Technological infrastructure suitability	(1.87, 2.87, 3.63)
1.1.1.3. Appropriateness of development environment	(1.39, 2.35, 3.28)
1.1.2. Architectural suitability	(2.27, 3.26, 3.85)
1.1.3. Coverage	(2.52, 3.52, 3.85)
1.1.4. Completeness	(2.56, 3.56, 3.86)
1.1.5. Correctness	(2.94, 3.94, 4.00)
1.1.6. Consistency	(2.71, 3.71, 3.97)
1.2. Accuracy	(2.65, 3.65, 3.98)
1.3. Self-Containment	(2.09, 3.09, 3.67)
1.4. Functional cohesion	(1.59, 2.59, 3.46)
1.5. Interoperability	(1.84, 2.84, 3.53)
1.5.1. Data compatibility	(1.71, 2.71, 3.44)
1.5.2. Interactivity	(2.10, 3.10, 3.68)
1.5.3. Internal interoperability	(1.79, 2.78, 3.52)
1.6. Security	(2.19, 3.19, 3.62)
1.6.1. Confidentiality	(2.46, 3.46, 3.72)
1.6.2. Accountability	(1.59, 2.59, 3.31)
1.6.3. Privacy	(2.00, 3.00, 3.65)
1.6.4. Vulnerability	(2.39, 3.38, 3.67)
1.7. Functionality compliance	(1.73, 2.72, 3.44)
2. Reliability	**(2.08, 3.08, 3.68)**
2.1. Maturity	(2.04, 3.02, 3.62)
2.1.1. State Memory	(2.20, 3.18, 3.69)
2.1.2. Absence of errors	(2.53, 3.51, 3.88)
2.1.3. Data entry signalizing	(2.05, 3.01, 3.61)
2.1.4. Integrity	(2.12, 3.12, 3.68)
2.1.5. Version non-volatility	(1.80, 2.76, 3.54)
2.1.6. Degradability	(1.63, 2.60, 3.37)
2.2. Fault tolerance	(2.18, 3.18, 3.77)
2.2.1. Robustness	(2.39, 3.39, 3.85)
2.2.2. Contingency planning	(1.97, 2.97, 3.68)
2.3. Recoverability	(2.00, 2.99, 3.56)
2.3.1. Undo facilities	(1.67, 2.64, 3.37)
2.3.2. Help for correcting errors	(1.74, 2.74, 3.45)
2.3.3. Auditability	(2.34, 3.33, 3.66)
2.3.4. Error Handling	(2.59, 3.58, 3.93)
2.4. Evaluability	(1.95, 2.95, 3.64)
2.4.1. Verifiability	(1.91, 2.91, 3.68)
2.4.2. Validity	(1.99, 2.99, 3.60)
2.5. Reliability compliance	(2.33, 3.33, 3.90)

Table 5. The quality guide for software components (Continuation)

Quality Characteristic	*Fuzzy* Number
3. Usability	**(1.67, 2.64, 3.43)**
3.1. Accessibility	(1.59, 2.56, 3.34)
3.1.1. Component identification	(1.63, 2.57, 3.23)
3.1.2. Component classification	(1.55, 2.55, 3.45)
3.2. Legibility	(1.74, 2.74, 3.51)
3.2.1. Clarity	(1.93, 2.93, 3.65)
3.2.2. Conciseness	(1.66, 2.66, 3.44)
3.2.3. Style	(1.54, 2.54, 3.33)
3.2.4. Correct use of method	(2.02, 3.02, 3.93)
3.2.5. Terminology uniformity	(1.74, 2.74, 3.47)
3.2.6. Abstraction uniformity	(1.63, 2.63, 3.39)
3.3. Understandability	(1.61, 2.58, 3.36)
3.3.1. Contextualization	(2.01, 3.01, 3.62)
3.3.1.1. Commonality	(1.87, 2.87, 3.49)
3.3.1.2. Variability	(2.06, 3.06, 3.67)
3.3.1.3. Dependencies	(2.07, 3.06, 3.66)
3.3.1.3.1. Contextual dependencies	(2.37, 3.37, 3.87)
3.3.1.3.2. Architectural dependencies	(1.89, 2.89, 3.57)
3.3.1.3.3. Technological dependencies	(2.04, 3.02, 3.60)
3.3.2. Justifiability	(1.54, 2.53, 3.39)
3.3.3. Utility	(1.67, 2.59, 3.37)
3.3.4. Relevance	(1.32, 2.27, 3.11)
3.4. User friendliness	(2.34, 3.34, 3.90)
3.4.1. Behavior uniformity	(2.36, 3.36, 3.87)
3.4.2. Interface uniformity	(2.33, 3.32, 3.92)
3.5. Learnability	(1.44, 2.43, 3.31)
3.5.1. User-oriented content	(1.32, 2.31, 3.21)
3.5.2. Help availability	(1.66, 2.66, 3.48)
3.5.3. User support	(1.38, 2.38, 3.29)
3.6. Operability	(2.00, 3.00, 3.68)
3.6.1. Manipulability	(1.98, 2.98, 3.66)
3.6.1.1. Artifact availability	(2.06, 3.06, 3.83)
3.6.1.2. Architectural Style	(2.13, 3.13, 3.66)
3.6.1.3. Traceability	(1.28, 2.28, 3.11)
3.6.2. Controllability	(2.02, 3.01, 3.69)
3.7. Attractiveness	(0.54, 0.98, 1.87)
3.8. Usability compliance	(1.54, 2.43, 3.36)

Table 5. The quality guide for software components (Continuation)

Quality Characteristic	*Fuzzy* Number
4. Efficiency	**(2.02, 3.01, 3.72)**
4.1.Time behavior	(2.18, 3.18, 3.71)
4.1.1. Binding time	(1.39, 2.39, 3.12)
4.1.2. Capacity	(2.30, 3.30, 3.80)
4.1.3. Throughput	(2.25, 3.25, 3.75)
4.2. Resource utilization	(1.87, 2.86, 3.66)
4.3. State behavior	(1.41, 2.28, 3.05)
4.3.1. Statefull capability	(1.60, 2.51, 3.35)
4.3.2. Serialization capability	(1.07, 1.95, 2.78)
4.3.3. Persistence support	(0.65, 1.31, 2.21)
4.3.4. Transactional support	(2.05, 3.00, 3.53)
4.4. Scalability	(2.56, 3.56, 3.92)
4.5. Appropriateness of the granularity level	(2.11, 3.11, 3.89)
4.6. Efficiency compliance	(1.86, 2.86, 3.77)
5. Maintainability	**(1.91, 2.91, 3.64)**
5.1. Analyzability	(2.01, 3.01, 3.70)
5.1.1. Architectural correctness	(2.01, 3.01, 3.70)
5.2. Implementation feasibility	(1.88, 2.86, 3.60)
5.2.1. Economic feasibility	(1.79, 2.77, 3.52)
5.2.2. Financial feasibility	(1.60, 2.56, 3.46)
5.2.3. Market feasibility	(1.77, 2.77, 3.51)
5.2.4. Schedule feasibility	(1.99, 2.99, 3.68)
5.2.5. Human resources feasibility	(1.94, 2.93, 3.65)
5.2.6. Technology feasibility	(2.32, 3.31, 3.90)
5.3. Changeability	(2.07, 3.06, 3.70)
5.3.1. Changeability to correct errors	(2.24, 3.24, 3.73)
5.3.2. Evolvability	(1.76, 2.75, 3.63)
5.3.3. Extensibility	(2.12, 3.12, 3.73)
5.4. Stability	(1.99, 2.99, 3.62)
5.5. Testability	(1.38, 2.38, 3.32)
5.5.1. Start-up self-test	(1.46, 2.46, 3.41)
5.5.2. Test suite	(1.54, 2.54, 3.47)
5.5.3. Generation of test reports	(0.87, 1.87, 2.83)
5.6. Maintainability compliance	(1.86, 2.86, 3.75)
6. Portability	**(2.16, 3.16, 3.77)**
6.1. Adaptability	(1.95, 2.95, 3.61)
6.1.1. Generality	(1.94, 2.93, 3.61)
6.1.1.1. Typification	(1.94, 2.93, 3.61)
6.1.2. Configurability	(1.96, 2.96, 3.61)
6.2. Installability	(2.31, 3.31, 3.87)
6.3. Co-existence	(2.25, 3.25, 3.87)
6.4. Replaceability	(2.41, 3.40, 3.83)
6.5. Portability compliance	(1.70, 2.69, 3.53)

Driving Component-Based Software Development through Quality Modelling

Colin Atkinson[1], Christian Bunse[2], and Jürgen Wüst[2]

[1] University of Mannheim, D-68131, Mannheim, Germany
colin.atkinson@ieee.org
[2] Fraunhofer Institute for Experimental Software Engineering
Sauerwiesen 6, Kaiserslautern, D-67661 Germany
christian.bunse@iese.fhg.de

Abstract. With the advent of the OMG's new Model Driven Architecture (MDA), and the growing uptake of the UML, the concept of model-driven development is receiving increasing attention. Many software organizations have identified the MDA as being of strategic importance to their businesses and many UML-tool vendors now market their tools as supporting model-driven development. However, most UML tools today support only a very limited concept of model driven development—the idea of first creating platform independent models and then mapping them into executable code. In contrast, true model-driven development implies that the development flow of a project is in some way "driven" (i.e. guided) by models. Quality attributes of models (e.g., measures derived from structural attributes) could be used in this regard, but although many different types of measures have been proposed (e.g. coupling, complexity, cohesion) they are not widely used in practice. This chapter discusses the issues involved in supporting this more general view of model driven development. It first presents some strategies for deriving useful quality-related information from UML models and then illustrates how this information can be use to optimize project effort and develop high-quality components. We pay special attention to how quality modelling based on structural properties can be integrated into the OMG's Model Driven Architecture (MDA) initiative.

1 Introduction

Software organizations are attracted to Component-Based Development (CBD) [16] because it offers the prospect of significant improvements in productivity. By assembling new applications from pre-fabricated and pre-validated components, rather than building them from scratch using traditional developing techniques, organizations can achieve significant savings in cost and time. At present, however, industrial component-technologies such as COM+/.NET, EJB/J2EE and CORBA only support components in the final implementation and deployment stages of development, leaving analysis and design to be organized in traditional, non-component-oriented ways. This not only reduces the potential impact

A. Cechich et al. (Eds.): Component-Based Software Quality, LNCS 2693, pp. 207–224, 2003.

of component-based development, since the design phase of development is precisely where the most critical decisions about software architecture and reuse are made, but also forces notions and metrics for component quality to be highly implementation- and deployment oriented. A more abstract representation of components is desirable because it would allow CBD issues to be considered earlier in the development process and thus to cover a wider part of the software lifecycle.

The software industry has in fact been moving towards more abstract representations of software artifacts for some years, although not specifically in connection with component-based development. Fuelled by the popularity of the Unified Modelling Language (UML) [15], the Object Management Group has recently adopted "Model Driven Architecture" (MDA) [8] as its unifying vision for software engineering. Like component-based development, the aim of MDA is to promote reuse. By separating the description of key application abstractions and logic from the details of specific implementation platforms these key artifacts can be made more stable over time and thus can deliver a greater return on investment. MDA therefore emphasizes the distinction between Platform Independent Models (PIMs), which capture key application abstractions and logic in a platform independent way, and Platform Specific Models (PSMs) which represent the concrete mapping of these artifacts to specific implementation technologies.

Although CBD and MDA offer alternative strategies for reuse, they are in fact complementary and can be used to reinforce each other. MDA addresses the previously mentioned shortcoming of industrial component technologies, namely their focus on the implementation/deployment phases of development, by providing a framework for a model-based (i.e. UML based) representation of components. Several component-oriented development methods, such as Catalysis [9], KobrA [1] and UML Components [6], now emphasize the modelling of logical components in terms of UML diagrams in the early (analysis and design) phases of development. CBD, in turn, addresses a major weakness of the MDA approach — namely its lack of prescriptive support for the modelling process. Although the theoretical advantages of model-driven development are generally accepted, and many companies claim to be using the UML in their software engineering activities, the state-of-the practice is still very primitive. For most companies and tool-vendors model-driven development simply means creating platform independent UML models and then mapping them (as automatically as possible) into platform specific code. While this separation of concerns is valuable, however, it falls far short of the full vision of model-driven development. In particular, there is little attempt to use the information in models developed early in the lifecycle to actually "drive" the development of later models or artifacts. "Model-based development" would thus be a far more accurate term for the current state of the practice rather than "model-driven development".

Adopting a component-based strategy for organizing platform independent models can help address this problem by facilitating the measurement and use of concrete metrics to help move the development process forward. This chapter elaborates on this opportunity by showing how metrics derived from component-

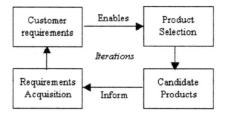

Fig. 1. Component Modelling

oriented models created early in a development project can be used to "drive" activities performed later in the project. The activities that we consider are those associated with quality assurance, since these play a particularly important role in the success of a project. In Section 2 we explain our model of components and composition, and how they can be captured using the UML, while in Section 3 we outline the motivation for quality assurance in software development projects and explain the fundamental role that a quality model can play. Then, in Section 4 we describe in detail how structural properties such as coupling, complexity, and size can be measured for UML artifacts, (i.e., how these quality measures are defined), and give an example based on the component-description models defined by the KobrA method [1]. Section 5 uses the concepts defined in section 4 to show some examples of how information garnered from UML models can be used for decision making in later parts of a project. Section 6 describes some future trends in component-based development. Finally, Section 7 concludes.

2   UML-Based Component Modelling

The techniques explained in this chapter will work with any approach for the UML-based modelling of components, but in this chapter we use the KobrA method [1] as the underlying foundation. Within the KobrA method, all behavior-rich abstractions, including entire systems, are viewed as components and are modelled in the same basic way. Moreover, the assembling of components is regarded as creating a larger component at the next level of granularity. Thus, a complete application architecture is viewed as a recursive structure in which larger components are realized in terms of smaller components, which in turn are composed of even smaller components, and so on.

The general set of models used to describe a single component is illustrated in Fig. 1. This shows that the models are organized into two groups, those making up the *specification* of the component that describes its externally visible properties, and those making up the *realization* that describe how the component is constructed from other objects and components (i.e. its design). The specification consists of three models which present different, but interrelated, views of the components properties: the structural model describes the data types that the component manipulates and the external component types with which it interacts, the functional model describes the semantic properties of the component's operations in terms of pre and post conditions, and the behavior model presents the abstract states and transitions exhibited by the component. The realization also consist of three models which present different, but integrated views of how the component is realized: the structural model, which elaborates on the specification structural models to describe the architecture of the component, the interaction model which shows how each of the component's operations is implemented in terms of interactions with other components, and the activity model, which shows the algorithms used to implement the operations. In all cases, strict rules ensure that the various models are internally and externally consistent with one another.

The concept of composition appears in the KobrA method in two basic ways, both derived from the semantics of the UML. At run-time, component instances (created from the abstract component types modelled in the way described above) interact with one another through the traditional client-server model. Client-server (or in KobrA, clientship) relationships are generally loosely coupled, but it is also possible for clientship relationships to imply some form of whole-part relationship. Aggregation is a loose form of the whole-part relationship, in which there is a general notation of the server being a part of the client, but there is no concept of binding or related life-times. The stricter form of whole-part relationship is composition, which as well as indicating that the server is a part of the client also captures the idea that the server is private to the client, and its lifetime is tied to that of the client.

As well as this form of composition, at development time there is also the concept of structural whole-part relationships in which the definition of one component forms a part of the definition of another. In the UML this is captured though the containment (or ownership) relationship between packages. One package contains another package if all the elements within one package are also contained in the other. Packages play the role of name-spaces in the UML, so the nesting of packages serves as the basis for the hierarchical naming of model elements.

Both UML notations of composition are adopted in the KobrA method. Each logical component has an associated UML package, which contains the various models (and model elements) that document the properties of the component (Fig. 1). The model elements in the specification of the component are viewed as public members of the package, while those in the realization are viewed as private. By nesting component packages inside one another, the overall structure of a system can be represented as a tree-based hierarchy of components, each modelled in the way illustrated in Fig. 1. The desired client-server structure of the run-time instance of the components (including any run-time composition or aggregation relationships) is documented explicitly within the components' structural models.

3   Quality Assurance

Quality assurance (QA) encompasses the activities involved in maximizing the quality of the software artifacts developed in a project based on the available resources. In a quantitative sense, therefore, the goal of quality assurance is to ensure that certain desired quality attributes or properties are attained or exceeded. The ISO9126 standard for software product quality [12] defines a set of six quality attributes: functionality, reliability, usability, efficiency, maintainability, and portability, each broken down into several sub-characteristics. These are intended to cover all quality needs of all stakeholders in a software product. For each quality attribute, specific QA techniques exist, e.g., inspections and testing to ensure functionality and reliability, or change scenario analysis to assess the maintainability of software design. The QA approach in this chapter is the measurement of structural design properties, such as coupling or complexity, based on a UML-oriented representation of components. UML design modelling is a key technology in the MDA, and UML design models naturally lend themselves to design measurement.

In the context of the ISO9126 product quality framework, structural properties are internal quality attributes. Internal attributes can be measured in terms of the product itself. All necessary information to quantify these internal attributes is available from the representation (requirements, design document, source-code, etc.) of the product. Therefore, these attributes are measurable during and immediately after the creation process. Internal quality attributes describe no externally visible quality of a product, and thus have no inherent meaning in themselves. In contrast, the six quality attributes ("-ilities") mentioned above are *external attributes*. Such quality attributes have to be measured with respect to the relationship between the product and its environment; measuring these attributes *directly* requires additional information. For example, maintainability can only be measured directly when the product actually undergoes maintenance, in terms of time spent. Reliability can be measured in terms of mean-time-to-failure (MTTF) of the operational product. External attributes can only be measured directly some time after the product is created (i.e., post-release, when the detection and removal of quality problems is time and cost intensive).

An artifact's internal attributes are assumed to have a causal impact on its external attributes. For instance, systems with loosely coupled components are expected to be more maintainable than highly coupled components, while components with high structural complexity are more fault-prone than those of low complexity. Making the link from internal attributes to their impact on external attributes is the purpose of a quality model.

Measurement of structural properties is attractive because it is objective and automatable, and thus fast to perform at low cost. Using a quality model, we can identify areas in a design with potential quality problems, and make these the focus of (more expensive) QA activities such as reviews and testing.

3.1 Quality Measures

A large number of measures have been defined in the literature to capture internal quality attributes such as size and coupling for OO systems [2]. Most of these measures are based on plausible assumptions, but, in the light of the discussion of the previous section, the two key questions are to determine whether

- They are actually useful, significant indicators of any relevant, external quality attribute, and how they can be applied in practice
- They lead to cost-effective models in a specific application context.

These questions have not received sufficient attention in the current literature. All too often design measurement is treated not as a means to an end, but as an end in itself. Answering the questions stated above requires a careful analysis of real project data. Some 30 empirical studies have been performed and reported in order to address the above-mentioned questions [2]. The results of these studies can be summarized as follows:

- Most of the studies are concerned with the prediction of class fault-proneness or development effort based on design measurement taken from source code.
- Data sets with fault or effort data at the class level are rare. As a consequence, these data sets tend to be repeatedly used for various studies. Instead, we find a large number of different studies using a small number of data sets. These data sets often stem from small industrial projects or academic environments (student labs).
- Only about half of the studies involve some attempt to build an accurate prediction model for the quality to predicted. The remaining studies only investigate the impact of individual measures on system quality, but not their combined impact.
- From the studies that build quality prediction models, only half of these studies investigate the prediction performance of the model in a relevant application context. Those results, however, look promising. For instance, in the context of fault-proneness prediction, prediction models that pinpoint the location of 80% of post-release faults are possible. Such models can be used to focus other quality assurance activities (inspections, testing).

4   Measurement of Structural Properties

The internal quality attributes of relevance in model-driven development are structural properties of UML artifacts. The specific structural properties of interest are coupling, complexity, and size. These are well understood, and as shown by empirical studies are indicators of various external qualities in OO design [3, 4, 5, 7, 10, 14]. To support the definition of coupling, complexity, and size measures we provide a "plan" for coupling, complexity, and size measurement.

4.1   Size Measurement

Size measures are counts of elements in UML diagrams and are good candidates for developing cost estimation models for designing, implementing, inspecting, and testing modelled entities. Such estimates are used as input for effort planning purposes and the allocation of personnel. The definition of such measures requires the resolution of three questions related to the overall measurement goal.

Table 1. Building Blocks for Size Measures

Entity	Constituent elements within
Component	Subcomponents, Packages, Subsystems, Classes, Interfaces
Package	Packages, Subsystems, Classes, Interfaces
Subsystem	Packages, Subsystems, Classes, Interfaces, Operations
Class	Classes, Operations, Attributes, States
Interface	Operations
Object	
Operation	Parameters

Question 1: What entities are to have their size measured?

Question 2: What constituent elements contribute to the size of these entities?

Question 3: How is the size of the entity to be quantified in terms of its constituent elements?

Ad Questions 1 and 2: Table 1 summarizes the possible choices for the first two decisions in the context of component-based development. The left column states the entities for which size is measured, the right column indicates what elements make up each entity and contribute to its size.

Components and classes are likely to be the most useful entities. Investigating size at a lower abstraction level requires an investigation of the external quality properties at that level (e.g., accounting for development effort per operation). However, this may be impractical. When defining size measures, it is not recommended to count entities of different types within one measure, since this would assume that the entities have equal impact on the quality. Therefore, we suggest that entities be measured separately, and that separate measures be used as building blocks for quality models as described in Section four.

Ad Question 3: For the quantification of entity-size there are two options. The size of a "higher-level" entity can be measured in terms of (1) the *number* of a certain type of countable element within it, or (2) the *sum of the size* of certain countable elements. In general, the first option results in a more coarse-grained measurement than the second option. The choice therefore depends on the stability of the number of counted elements at the time when the measurement is performed.

As an example, consider a KobrA [1] class diagram for the realization of a simple banking system of the form illustrated in Fig. 2. To measure the size of the bank component the following steps are performed:

- **Question 1:** entity to measure – the *components*.

  Question 2: constituent elements – component is constituted by a set of *classes*.

  Question 3: count the *number* of constituent elements.

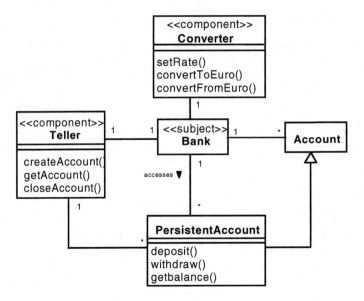

Fig. 2. Class Diagram for Bank

The resulting measure is simply the number of classes in the component. Considering the component Bank depicted in Fig. 2, the measure of this component is 5, since it is composed by 5 classes (Converter, Teller, Bank, Account and PersistentAccount).

- **Question 1:** entity to measure – the *components*
  Question 2: constituent elements – *classes* of the component
  Question 3: *sum of the size* of the constituent elements.

We need a size measure for classes, which we define in the following.
  - **Question 1:** entity to measure – the *classes*
    Question 2: constituent elements – the operations they *contain*
    Question 3: count the *number* of constituent elements.

The resulting measure is the number of operations in the classes of the component. In Fig. 2, the size of the Bank component is 9 operations (only operations for three classes have been identified at this stage).

Considered in isolation, these numbers give us little, if any, useful information. However, when compared they can help allocate resources. For example, measuring the size of all entities (e.g., components) in the banking system allows us to make statements of the form "Bank" is twice as large as some other system or component. Such information can be used as input for the allocation of personnel. If empirical data is available, size measures can also be used to predict the effort for implementation and testing, thus supporting project planning and management.

4.2   Coupling Measurement

Coupling is the degree to which various entities are connected. These connections cause dependencies between the entities that have an impact on various external system quality attributes. Examples are maintainability (a modification of an entity may require modifications to its connected entities), testability (a fault in one entity may cause a failure in a completely different, connected entity), and fault-proneness (dependencies usually define a client-server relationship in which the client developer needs to know exactly how to use the service). Thus, a common design principle is to minimize coupling. The definition of such measures requires six questions to be answered:

Question 1: What entity is to have its coupling measured?

Question 2: By what mechanism is the entity coupled to other elements?

Question 3: Should multiple coupling connections between two elements (e.g. multiple associations between two classes) be counted separately or not?

Question 4: What is the direction of coupling (import or export coupling)?

Question 5: Should direct and/or indirect connections be counted?

Question 6: Are there any special relationships that should exist between connected entities?

For each question there are a number of options to choose from. These are detailed in the following: The actual selection should be driven by the measurement goal in mind and the design practices at hand.

Ad Question 1: the entities for which we may quantify coupling are the same as for size measures (see column "Entity" in Table 1): components, packages, subsystems, classes, interfaces, objects, or operations.

Ad Question 2: the possible types of links between a client and a server entity[1] (operation, class, component) are:

- Associations, e.g., between two classes. Aggregations and compositions may be subsumed under "associations" or measured separately as unique coupling mechanisms.
- UML Dependencies between any two elements.
- UML Abstractions (e.g., between interfaces and implementing classes).
- Operation invocation (object instance of class C sends message to object instance of class D).
- Parameter type (operation of class C receives/returns parameter of type class D).
- Attribute type (attribute of class C has attribute of type class D).

Ad Question 3: If there can be multiple coupling connections between a pair of elements, we have to decide whether to count these connections individually, or whether to just take into account the fact that there are connections

---

[1] Most, but not all connectors are directed and thus impose client and server roles on the connected items. For undirected connectors, the connected items are just two equal peers.

between the element pair, regardless of their precise number. The answer depends on the stability of the number of connections. If it is likely to change, a precise count is not needed.

Ad Question 4: For directed connectors, it is possible to count import or export coupling. Import coupling analysis the entities in their role as clients of other attributes, methods, or classes, while export coupling analysis the entities in their role as servers. High import coupling indicates that an entity strongly relies on other design elements to fulfill its job. Thus, import coupling has to be considered together with the following external attributes: understandability, fault-proneness, and maintainability. High export coupling states, that one entity is heavily used by others. Thus, it has to be considered together with the following external attributes: criticality and testability.

Ad Question 5: A yes/no decision has to be made as to whether the coupling measure should only count direct connections between elements or indirect ones as well. Indirect connections can be relevant when estimating the effort of run-time activities such as testing and debugging or the impact of modifications (ripple effects). Direct connections are sufficient for the analysis of understandability. To understand a component it is sufficient to know the functionality of directly used services. In contrast, knowledge about their implementation is not needed.

Ad Question 6: In some cases, we may only want to count coupling between entities that have a special relationship. For example, only coupling between classes with an inheritance relationship may be counted; or coupling to classes that are variation spots in a framework or product line architecture.

As an example of a coupling measure, we use the above schema to count operation invocations for the classes of a component.

Q1: entity to measure – the classes
Q2: coupling mechanism – messages invoking operations
Q3: direction of coupling – import coupling (outgoing messages)
Q4: multiple connections – multiple invocations of the same operation are counted individually
Q5: direct/indirect connections – count direct connections only
Q6: no special relationships between caller and callee.

Assuming the following collaboration diagrams for the withdraw() and deposit() operations of the Bank component (Fig. 3), the import coupling of class Bank is 7 (2 × getAccount(), 2 × convertToEuro(), 1 × getBalance(), 1 × deposit(), 1 × withdraw()).

If we change the definition of the coupling measure to count export coupling (Question 3), the resulting coupling values are 2 for classes Teller and Converter, 3 for PersistentAccount.

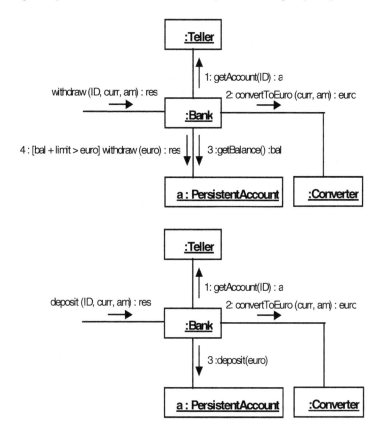

Fig. 3. Collaboration Diagram for the withdraw() and deposit() operations

4.3 Complexity Measurement

Whereas coupling is concerned with how a design entity is connected to other design entities, complexity measures are concerned with how connected the elements within a design entity are (e.g., associations between classes of a component, or invocations between operations of a class). The higher the connectivity of elements within the design entity, the higher its complexity. The questions to be answered when defining complexity measures are therefore similar to those for coupling measurement:

Question 1: What entity is to have its complexity measured?
Question 2: By what mechanism are the elements in the design entity connected with each other?
Question 3: Should multiple connections between two elements be counted separately or not?
Question 4: Should direct and/or indirect connections be counted?
Question 5: Are there any special relationships that should exist between connected entities?

Ad Question 1: the entities for which we may quantify complexity are the same as for size measures (see column "Entity" in Table 1): components, packages, subsystems, classes, interfaces, objects, or operations.

Ad Question 2: The mechanisms by which elements in the design entity are connected are the same as the coupling connectors in listed in Question 2 of Section 4.2. In addition, transitions between states contribute to the complexity of a class.

The options for the remaining questions are the same as for coupling measurement as described in Section 4.2. As an example of a complexity measure for a component, we count the number of associations between classes of the component:

Q1: Entity to measure – the component

Q2: Connection mechanism between design elements – associations between classes of the component

Q3: multiple connections – multiple associations between the same two classes are counted as one, not individually

Q4: direct/indirect connections – count direct connections only

Q5: no special relationships between associated classes.

Applying this measure to the class diagram for Bank (Fig. 2) we see that there are 2 associations between classes of the component.

5   Example Quality Models

The previous Section identified several internal quality attributes that can be measured directly from UML diagrams. However, these internal attributes are of little direct value by themselves. In the following the use of different quality models to assess various quality attributes is discussed. We show how such models can be used to identify potential risk areas in the system models and how this information can be used to drive the inspection and testing activities.

5.1   Prediction Models

Prediction models try to estimate the future quality of a system from internal quality attributes. This is achieved by exploring the relationships between internal and external attributes from past systems as well as by applying insights into the system under development. In the following the construction and usage of such a prediction model is described in the context of fault-proneness and structural properties of a class. Fig. 4 depicts the steps involved in building the quality model.

A measurement tool is applied to a set of previously created documents to obtain the relevant structural properties. This results in a set of documents enriched with structural properties. In addition, fault data (e.g., from inspections) has to be selected for these documents. Statistical analysis (e.g. classification

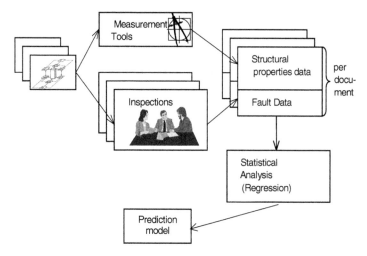

Fig. 4. Building a Prediction Model

or regression analysis) is then used to explore the relationship between fault data and structural properties. The result is a prediction model (i.e., a regression equation) that computes a predicted fault-proneness or predicted number of faults. This model can be used to make predictions for new entities as depicted in Fig. 5.

For a new entity the measurement tool is reapplied to obtain data on structural properties. This is an automatable, cheap, and fast process. The resulting data is fed into the prediction model, which uses the now known relationships between coupling, complexity and faults to calculate, for instance, a predicted fault-proneness for the document — that is, the probability that a fault will be found in the document upon inspection[2].

The resulting output is useful for deciding what activities to perform in the ensuing development process and what these activities should focus on. For instance, if the predicted fault-proneness is below 25%, it is not necessary to inspect the document but to proceed immediately to the next development activity. However, if the predicted fault-proneness is above 25% an inspection can be triggered. Thus, effort can be focused on the artifacts that are more likely to contain faults. Prediction models for other system qualities (e.g., models to predict implementation and test effort from size) can be built in the same way.

The advantage of prediction models is that they provide a mapping from non-interpretable internal quality data to interpretable external qualities. The result is an absolute, quantitative statement about the external quality of a system, which can be understood by developers and expressed in the same units in which the external quality is measured. However, a disadvantage is that the data requirements are high, and that the building and use of such models requires expertise in statistics.

---

[2] The kind of prediction depends on the used regression analysis, which in turn depends on the type of (fault) data collected.

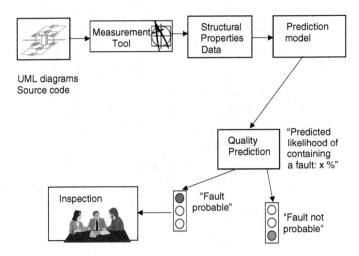

Fig. 5. Using the Prediction Model

Industrial experience with prediction models for fault-proneness/effort prediction in the context of OO system development (not limited to component development) is encouraging [3, 4, 7, 10, 14]. When predicting fault-proneness for classes, the best models have consistently obtained a percentage of correct classifications of about 80% and find more than 80% of faults (these figures assume that classes predicted fault-prone are inspected, and all faults are found during the inspection). Overall, the results suggest that design measurement-based models for fault-proneness predictions of classes may be very effective instruments for quality evaluation and control of components. From the results presented in studies predicting development effort, we may conclude that there is a reasonable chance that useful cost estimation models can be built during the analysis and design of object-oriented systems. System effort predictions with relative errors below 30% (an acceptable level of accuracy for cost estimation models) seem realistic to achieve.

The empirical results also indicate that prediction models are highly context-sensitive, affected by factors such as project size, development processes at hand, and so forth. Therefore, prediction models need to be built and validated locally in the development environment in which they are used. Also note that the above results were achieved performing measurement on source code artifacts, not UML design artifacts. A demonstration of these principles using UML design measurement remains future work.

5.2   Quality Benchmarks

The idea of benchmarks is to compare structural properties of an entity with properties of previous systems that are 'known to be good'. To this end, measurement values for selected size, coupling, and complexity measures are stored in a database. If a new or modified component has to be evaluated, the same

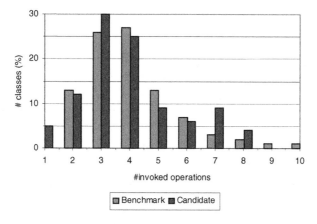

Fig. 6. Benchmark

measurements are applied. Afterwards the distribution of each size, coupling, and complexity measure is compared to the distribution of those stored in the database.

As an example, Fig. 6 shows a (fictitious) distribution of the number of operations invoked by the classes of a component. The vertical axis indicates, for each value on the horizontal axis (number of invoked operations), the percentage of classes in the component that have that particular value. In the example, the distribution of the new component follows closely the distribution of the benchmark, except for values 7 and 8, which occur more frequently. Such deviations pinpoint potential risk areas. The example also illustrates that the examination of distributions provides more information than simply defining thresholds for each measure. Although the number of invoked operations is not exceedingly high (the benchmark suggests 10 as an upper value), there are more than an average number of classes with 7/8 invoked operations. This may point to a problem.

Unlike the prediction model approach, benchmarking does not require external quality data. No absolute statement about the quality of entities can be made. A database of past 'known to be good' entities has to be acquired before the approach can be used operationally. However, a quality benchmark can be used to:

1. provide guidance for design decisions — a simple example, a quality benchmark for the size of class, object, or interaction diagram provides objective criteria as to whether the diagram is too big.
2. define design exit criteria. For instance, deviations from the quality benchmark must either be justified, or the design reworked.
3. identify potential trouble spots in the system that should be the focus of inspection and testing.

An industrial application of quality benchmarking in the context of large-scale software acquisition (COTS, outsourced development) is reported in [13].

Table 2. Example of a Simple Ranking Model

Component	Rank Measure 1	Rank Measure 2	Rank Measure 3	Average Rank
Component2	24	3.5	12	13.17
Component18	9	16	14	13
Component7	17	3.5	7	9.17
...	...			

5.3   Simple Ranking Models

The ranking model approach uses selected structural property measurements to select potentially critical areas in a design. Although it does not require the measurement of external quality data, it is important that the measures are indicators of specific qualities (see Section 5.1). The steps involved are as follows:

1. Apply design measurement to the system
2. Rank entities in decreasing order, independently for each measure, and assign ranks. The entity with the lowest value is assigned rank 1, the entity with the next lowest value is assigned rank 2, etc.
3. For each entity, take the average rank of that entity for all measures.
4. Sort the entities in decreasing order of their average rank.

An example application is shown in Table 2. The first column indicates the entity name, the next three columns the ranks for three selected measures, and the last column the average of these ranks. Rows are sorted in decreasing order. Entities at the top are potentially critical, because they display less desirable structural properties. Thus, such entities should be selected first for inspections or testing until the allocated resources are depleted.

The advantage of this approach is that it is immediately applicable — neither external quality data nor a database of past 'known to be good' systems is required. Unfortunately, there is no absolute statement about the quality of the system. In addition, it is not possible to make statements about the quality of individual entities in isolation since only relative rankings of entire sets of entities are possible. Furthermore, the creation of such a ranking may result in lost information since measures are not usually defined on an interval or even ratio scale but are only used on an ordinal scale. In summary, this approach is therefore less powerful than the others. To use this approach effectively it must be ensured that the used measures are related to the external quality in mind.

6   Future Trends

The use of structural measures to help drive the allocation of resources in software development projects will undoubtedly increase in the future. However, further research is needed to improve the usefulness of measures derived from early, analysis and design artifacts of the kind usually associated with platform independent models.

Most of the measurement activity reported to date is actually based on measurement of source-code. Early analysis and design artifacts are, by definition, not complete and only represent early models of the actual system to be developed. The use of predictive models based on early artifacts and their capability to predict the quality of the final system still largely remains to be investigated.

One reason for the lack of empirical work carried out on design artifacts to date is missing tool support to automatically collect design measures. While there are many static analyzers for source-code of all programming languages, tools to collect design measures from UML diagrams are scarce. Some commercial UML modelling tools have measurement capabilities, though often limited to size measures. SDMetrics[3], a flexible tool using the XMI standard to read UML designs and calculate user-specified design measures as outlined in Section 4, was released only recently.

Future research needs to focus on collecting large data sets involving large numbers of systems from the same environment. In order to make the research on quality prediction models of practical relevance, it is crucial that these models be usable from project to project. Their applicability depends on their capability to accurately and precisely predict quality attributes (e.g., class fault-proneness) in new systems, based on the development experience accumulated from past systems. Though some studies report the construction of such models, few report their actual application in realistic settings. Our understanding has now reached a sufficient level to enable such studies to be undertaken.

Cost-benefit analysis related to the use of quality prediction models are scarce. Little is known about how the predictions made by statistical models compare with those made by system experts in terms of correctness and completeness. Furthermore, there might be a way to combine expert opinion with object-oriented design quality models to obtain more reliable statements about system quality. Future empirical studies should also take this into account to improve the case for the use of design-measurement-based quality prediction models.

7   Summary and Conclusions

The model driven architecture (MDA) is a powerful approach for improving long-term productivity by increasing the return on investment derived from software development effort. Although its theoretical advantages are widely accepted, however, the state-of-the practice is still very primitive. For most companies and tool-vendors model-driven development simply means creating platform independent UML models and then mapping them (as automatically as possible) into platform specific code. There is currently very little support for using platform independent model created early in the software lifecycle to "drive" ensuing development activities. Much of the potential benefits of model <u>driven</u> development therefore remain to be realized.

---

[3] SDMetrics – software design measurement tool for the UML, see
  http://www.sdmetrics.com

This chapter has pointed the way towards true model driven development by briefly illustrating how the measurement of UML structural properties can help drive the quality assurance activities in component-based development. Such measures are objective, can be collected automatically and provide early feedback on the quality of entities (e.g., components). This feedback can help an organization allocate quality assurance effort and thus "drive" part of the overall development process from model-derived data.

References

1. C. Atkinson, J. Bayer, C. Bunse, E. Kamsties, O. Laitenberger, R. Laqua, D. Muthig, B. Paech, J. Wüst, J. Zettel. *Component-based Product Line Engineering with UML*. Addision-Wesley, Component Series, 2001.
2. L. Briand, J. Wüst. Empirical Studies of Quality Models in Object-Oriented Systems. *Advances in Computers*, 59:97–166, 2002.
3. L. Briand, J. Wüst, J. Daly, V. Porter. A Comprehensive Empirical Validation of Product Measures for Object-Oriented Systems. *Journal of Systems and Software*, 51:245–273, 2000.
4. L. Briand, J. Wüst, H. Lounis, S. Ikonomovski. Investigating Quality Factors in Object-Oriented Designs: an Industrial Case Study. In *Proc. of ICSE'99*, pages 345–354, Los Angeles, USA, 1999.
5. L. Briand, C. Bunse, J. Daly. A Controlled Experiment for Evaluating Quality Guidelines on the Maintainability of Object-Oriented Designs. *IEEE Transactions on Software Engineering*, 27(6), 2001.
6. John Cheesman and John Daniels. *UML Components: A simple process for specifying component-based software*. Addison-Wesley, 2000.
7. S. Chidamber, D. Darcy, C. Kemerer. Managerial use of Metrics for Object-Oriented Software: An Exploratory Analysis. *IEEE Transactions on Software Engineering*, 24(8):629–639, 1998.
8. Desmond F. D'Souza. OMG's MDA - An Architecture for Modeling, OMG MDA. Seminar, October 2001. Available at www.omg.org
9. Desmond F. D'Souza and Allan Cameron Wills. *Objects, Components, and Frameworks with UML. The Catalysis Approach*. Addison-Wesley, Object-Technology Series, 1999.
10. N. Fenton, S. Pfleeger. *Software Metrics, A Practical and Rigorous Approach*. International Thompson Computer Press, 1996.
11. W. Li, S. Henry. Object-Oriented Metrics that Predict Maintainability. *Journal of Systems and Software*, 23(2):111-122, 1993.
12. ISO/IEC FCD 9126-1.2, "Information Technology – Software Product. Quality– Part 1: Quality Model". 1998.
13. C. Mayrand, F. Coallier. System Acquisition Based on Software Product Assessment. In *Proc. of ICSE'96*, pages 210–219, Berlin, Germany, 1996.
14. P. Nesi, T. Querci. Effort estimation and prediction of object-oriented systems. *Journal of Systems and Software*, 42:89–102, 1998.
15. Object Management Group (OMG). *Unified Modeling Language (UML)*. Version 1.4, 2001. Available at www.omg.org
16. Clemens Szyperski. *Component Software. Beyond Object-Oriented Programming*. Addison-Wesley, 1998.

Towards a Quality Model for the Selection of ERP Systems

Pere Botella[1], Xavier Burgués[1],
Juan P. Carvallo[1], Xavier Franch[1], Joan A. Pastor[2], and Carme Quer[1]

[1] Universitat Politècnica de Catalunya (UPC)
c/ Jordi Girona 1-3 (Campus Nord, C6)
08034 Barcelona
{botella,diafebus,carvallo,franch,cquer}@lsi.upc.es
http://www.lsi.upc.es/~gessi/
[2] Universitat Internacional de Catalunya (UIC)
c/ Immaculada 22 (Campus Iradier)
08017 Barcelona
jap@unica.edu

Abstract. ERP systems are a category of COTS products that offers extensive support to the management of business processes in most kind of companies and organizations. Due to their increasing adoption and the risks coming from their incorrect selection, efforts towards effective and reliable selection methods should have a positive impact in the community. This chapter proposes the adoption of quality models as a means for structuring the description of the capabilities of such type of products. The ISO/IEC 9126-1 quality standard is chosen as a framework, and a methodology for tailoring it to this specific domain is followed. The chapter also shows the formalization of the quality model by using a formal language. Last, the use of the quality model for processing quality requirements is also addressed.

1 Introduction

A paradigm shift suddenly emerging during the last few years is the clear tendency taken by both private companies and public administration offices with regard to software product acquisition. Rather than generally taking on bespoke software development projects, which was the rule not so long ago, public and private enterprises now prefer more and more to buy, adapt and integrate software components in the form of *Commercial-Off-The-Shelf (COTS) products* [6, 19], an option which was before the exception but that is now generalizing across organizational functions, industries and countries.

Within the COTS worldwide movement, a particular type of global product has gained its role as one of the insignia warships of such a tendency, at least in terms of business functional, geographic and economic success. We refer to the so-called *Enterprise Resource Planning (ERP)* systems [7, 8, 16]. ERP systems are COTS products designed to cover business processes common to many

A. Cechich et al. (Eds.): Component-Based Software Quality, LNCS 2693, pp. 225–245, 2003.

companies and industries (sales, manufacturing, services, etc.) that take place across common areas (operations, human resources, financials, etc.). ERP systems are also tailored to specific vertical markets such as education, healthcare or logistics; therefore ERP systems (or specific versions of the same family) may be highly different from each other.

Famous products from global companies such as SAP, Oracle, JD Edwards, Pepperwort, Baa o Navigio, to name just a few, are currently available in the ERP systems market. These and other similar products have already helped many enterprises, either public or private, either big-, small- or medium-sized, to overcome technological barriers such as the Y2K problem and the shift to the Euro currency. Further than these serious but circumstantial problems, many companies are trying to use ERP systems as their informational base upon which to build their global business effort, which implies dealing with many currencies, languages and time zones. In terms of overall business volume generated by ERP systems and their implied services, this is how the strategic executive consulting and publishing firm IDG Group evaluated their impact just in Europe:

"... the Western European market for services around Enterprise Resource Planning (ERP) applications will grow from $15 billion in 2001 to $24 billion by 2005. ERP services are services provided for consulting, implementing, supporting, training and operating an ERP application. In 2001, 61% of ERP services spending has been concentrated in Western Europe's four largest economies: Germany, UK, France and Italy."

IDG Group (www.idg.com), 2001.

Besides the big numbers and the success stories, there has also been a significant number of companies which have reported significant problems in adapting their selected ERP system and in obtaining returns on their investment, which extreme cases where the company survivability has been put into question. Certainly, while not doing a good job in selecting an appropriate ERP system may put a big company into trouble, it can easily kill a small- or medium-sized one. This has raised the interest on the topic of ERP selection, from both researchers and practitioners as well.

In this chapter we build upon our prior research on the topics of selection of COTS products and more specifically of ERP systems, by concentrating on the use, extension and formalization of a generic public quality model to deal with the particular case of ERP products. This task may be undertaken partly before and partly during a particular ERP selection process. With this effort we hope to add new perspectives in dealing with the product evaluation inherent within ERP selection processes.

The rest of the chapter is organized as follows. Section 2 introduces with detail the key concepts of COTS product and quality model for a COTS product. Section 3 is the core of the chapter, aimed at building the quality model for ERP systems. In Section 4 a formalization of the quality model in the NoFun language is depicted. Section 5 addresses the applicability of the quality model for stating quality requirements. Last, Section 6 gives the conclusions.

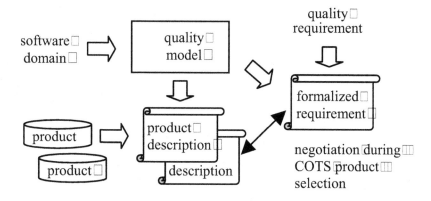

Fig. 1. Use of a quality model during COTS product selection

2   Quality Models for COTS Products

Commercial-Off-The-Shelf (COTS) products are software components that are available in the market to be purchased, interfaced with or integrated into other software systems. More precisely:

> A COTS product is a [software] product that is: (1) sold, leased, or licensed to the general public; (2) offered by a vendor trying to profit from it; (3) supported and evolved by the vendor, which retains the intellectual property rights; (4) available in multiple, identical copies; (5) used without internal modification by a consumer.

> B. Meyers, P. Oberndorf. *Managing Software Acquisition*, Addison-Wesley, 2001.

This embraces a large amount of existing software components, from a tiny ActiveX component to a huge financial system or an ERP system as defined in the introduction.

Intensive use of COTS products during software development requires adapting some traditional practices of software engineering, such as requirements elicitation and testing. Also some specific activities arise in this new context, among which selection of COTS products [14] plays a prominent role.

Some approaches have been proposed for conducting a COTS product selection process [18, 20, 2]. All of them identify some factors that influence the process, among them we mention: managerial issues, company policies, confidence on the vendors and quality of the COTS product. In this chapter, we focus specifically on this last issue, by proposing *quality models* as a framework for assessing product quality. The main purpose of quality models is to support the negotiation between user requirements and product capabilities during COTS product selection (see Fig. 1).

But, what is a quality model? We may consider, for instance, the following definition:

A product quality model, therefore, must comprehensively identify the tangible (measurable and/or assessable) internal product characteristics that have the most significant effect on external quality attributes. And it must establish the dependencies between the two.

R.G. Dromey. "Concerning the Chimera", IEEE Software, Jan. 1996, pp. 33–43.

This point of view in the above definition is clearly oriented to the evaluation of bespoke software systems, whose internal structure is accessible and exposed to analysis. But this is not the usual case for COTS products, as it becomes obvious if we consider their definition, because the internal features of COTS products are usually hidden. For this reason, we aim at using a more general description of quality model, such as the following:

Software product quality should be evaluated using a defined quality model. [...] Software product quality should be hierarchically decomposed into a quality model composed of characteristics and subcharacteristics which can be used as a checklist of issues related to quality.

ISO/IEC 9126-1 Software Engineering–Product Quality–Part 1, June 2001.

In fact, the ISO/IEC Standard 9126-1 provides a good framework for determining a quality model for a given domain of COTS products. The standard fixes six characteristics that are decomposed into subcharacteristics (see Fig. 2). This provides a very flexible departing quality model that can be tailored to any specific domain by adding, adapting, decomposing or discarding some of the subcharacteristics, and then identifying some quality attributes of the COTS products in the domain, as well as the metrics for measuring them.

Due to the strategic nature of ERP systems selection, we may say that any organization pursuing a successful ERP experience should start by following a well-established ERP system selection process, defined in terms which should be as systematic and affordable as possible [12, 21]. We advocate that the definition of a quality model for ERP systems can play a crucial role in this process and thus we aim at its definition in the next section.

3   A Quality Model for ERP Systems

We adopt the ISO/IEC Quality Standard 9126-1 [15] as the framework for defining a quality model for ERP systems. Due to its generic nature, the departing quality model defined in this standard must be completed by adding some more appropriate elements, their interdependencies and their metrics.

With this in mind, we take advantage of previous experiences on the use of the ISO/IEC 9126-1 standard [4]. We use a methodology that consists of six steps as defined in [10, 11]. The methodology may be summarized as follows:

Functionality	
suitability	presence and appropriateness of a set of functions for specified tasks
accuracy	Provision of right or agreed results or effects
interoperability	capability of the software product to interact with specified systems
security	prevention to (accidental or deliberate) unauthorized access to data
functionality compliance	adherence to application of functionality related standards or conventions
Reliability	
maturity	capacity to avoid failure as a result of faults in the software
fault tolerance	ability to maintain a specified level of performance in case of faults
recoverability	capability of reestablish level of performance after faults
reliability compliance	adherence to application of reliability related standards or conventions
Usability	
understandability	effort for recognizing the logical concept and its applicability
learnability	effort for learning software application
operability	effort for operation and operation control
attractiveness	capability of the product to be attractive to the user
usability compliance	adherence to application of usability related standards or conventions
Efficiency	
time behavior	response and processing times; throughput rates
resource utilization	amount of resources used and the duration of such use
efficiency compliance	adherence to application of efficiency related standards or conventions
Maintainability	
analysability	identification of deficiencies, failure causes, parts to be modified, etc.
changeability	capability to enable a specified modification to be implemented
stability	capability to avoid unexpected effects from modifications
testability	capability to enable for validating the modified software
maintainability compliance	adherence to application of maintainability related standards or conventions
Portability	
adaptability	opportunity for adaptation to different environments
installability	effort needed to install the software in a specified environment
co-existence	capability to co-exist with other independent software in a common environment sharing common resources
replaceability	opportunity and effort of using software in the place of other software
portability compliance	adherence to application of portability related standards or conventions

Fig. 2. ISO/IEC 9126-1 characteristics and subcharacteristics

- **Step 1.** *Determining first-level quality subcharacteristics.* This step aims at adding new subcharacteristics specific to the domain, refining the definition of some existing ones, or even eliminating some.
- **Step 2.** *Defining a hierarchy of subcharacteristics.* Subcharacteristics may be further decomposed into new ones with respect to some factors.
- **Step 3.** *Decomposing subcharacteristics into attributes.* The abstract subcharacteristics must be decomposed into more concrete entities, the quality attributes, which keep track of particular observable features of COTS products.
- **Step 4.** *Decomposing derived attributes into basic ones.* High-level attributes (derived attributes) may still be abstract enough to require further decomposition in terms of others.

- **Step 5.** *Stating relationships between quality entities.* Relationships between attributes are explicitly stated. The model becomes more exhaustive and as an additional benefit, implications of quality user requirements become clearer.
- **Step 6.** *Determining metrics for attributes.* Not only the attributes must be identified, but metrics for all the basic attributes must be selected, as well as metrics for those derived attributes whose definition does not depend on any particular selection process (i.e., attributes of generic nature).

Although the above steps have been presented as they were to be applied in a sequential way, in fact they may be iterated or intertwined at any acceptable extent.

Needless to say, before starting the quality model construction, the domain of interest must be thoroughly analyzed and understood. In [4] we propose the use of conceptual models as an aid for supporting this comprehension.

3.1 Step 1: Determining First-Level Quality Subcharacteristics

It was mentioned in Section 2 that the ISO/IEC 9126-1 standard provides six quality characteristics and their subcharacteristics. After some experiences, we have confirmed that the basic set of subcharacteristics provided by this standard is complete and accurate enough to be used as a starting point and thus it may be naturally adopted when building quality models for COTS products in most the domains, including ERP systems. But in a particular quality model, we may add new subcharacteristics specific to the domain, refine the definition of some existing ones, or even eliminate some. For instance, we have slightly changed the definition of the *Operability* subcharacteristic, to make explicit that tailoring tasks affect the way in which users operate and interact with the system. But the most important effect of step 1 takes place when considering the *Functionality* subcharacteristic.

Many software manufacturers tend to offer additional applications with their products to enhance their functionality. Such applications are not usually shipped within the original product; they are usually offered separately, as extensions of the product. In the case of ERP systems, these applications include graphical-statistical and reporting tools, web service components or workflow and project management engines. These added features may become relevant in particular selection processes and so it is important to include them as attributes inside a separate *Suitability* subcharacteristics, namely *Added Suitability*.

On the other hand, as mentioned in Section 1, ERP systems not only cover functional areas common to many enterprises, but also integrate some industry-specific functional modules. Those modules (which may be highly different from each other) are not common to all ERP systems, but they need to be evaluated anyway. Therefore, a quality model to be used during an ERP system selection process should include a part of its hierarchy specifically defined for this purpose.

But because of the number of available modules and their heterogeneous nature, it is impossible and useless to create a quality model to include all of them. As a way of dealing with this problem we identify a new *Suitability* subcharacteristic, called *Industrial Specific Suitability*. The lower levels of the hierarchy bound to this subcharacteristic (including its further decomposition into specific subcharacteristics for each industrial module) have to be refined when completing the quality model in a particular selection process.

As a result, we have finally split the *Suitability* subcharacteristic into three: *Basic Suitability, Industrial Specific Suitability* and *Added Suitability*.

3.2   Step 2: Defining a Hierarchy of Subcharacteristics

Subcharacteristics may be further decomposed into new subcharacteristics with respect to some factors. Let us focus again on *Suitability* and, more precisely, on *Basic Suitability*. Because ERP systems are products covering many functional areas and business processes, two approaches may be followed when building the quality model:

- To create separate quality models for each type of basic functionality and then to bring them together into *Basic Suitability*;
- To split *Basic Suitability* into several subcharacteristics, one to represent each functional area and each business process in the domain.

The first approach behaves better from the extensibility and reusability point of view. For instance, consider those contexts where the selection is open for the inclusion of vertical applications that offer specific functionalities which are not included in the usual ERP systems; the quality models for these applications may be reused and integrated into the one for the ERP systems. The second approach can be more adequate when aiming at selecting a fully integrated ERP system, in which case a great deal of attributes such as those related with security and data coding schemas, as well as those concerning general behavior (e.g., verification on data inputs, querying of master files, definition of function keys and error management mechanisms) have to be common to all the areas in the product.

In our proposal we follow the second approach. As a result, we split the *Basic Suitability* subcharacteristic into twelve subcharacteristics representing the main functional areas commonly found in most companies. As we are illustrating a generic model for ERP systems, we have selected these areas without considering a particular business model.

After all those considerations the top level hierarchy of the model has been structured as shown in Fig. 3.

Because of the extend of the ERP systems domain, we will drive the construction of the model and the explanation of the next steps focusing mainly on one single subcharacteristic of *Basic Suitability*, namely *Logistics*. Also, given that tailoring ERP systems is also a highly important aspect, we will also pay attention to the *Operability* subcharacteristic from *Usability*.

Subcharacteristics			Definitions
Level 1	Level 2	Level 3	
Suitability	Basic Suitability	Sales & Receivable Accounts	Presence and appropriateness of a set of functions for the given functional areas
		Production & Quality	
		Purchases & Payable Accounts	
		Financials	
		Fixed Assets	
		Inventories	
		Maintenance	
		Marketing	
		Payrolls & Human Resources	
		Accounting	
		Logistics	
		Cross-Applications	
	Industry Specific Suitability		Presence and appropriateness of a set of functions specific to the industrial nature of the enterprise to be evaluated
	Added Suitability		Additional functions provided to the package by adding applicational extensions to it
Operability			Effort for operation and operation control. This includes the tailoring activities required to configure the environment and the application behavior

(Leftmost labels: **Characteristics** / **Functionality** for the Suitability rows; **Usability** for the Operability row.)

Fig. 3. Quality model for ERP systems: detail of *Suitability* and *Operability* subcharacteristics

3.3 Step 3: Decomposing Subcharacteristics into Attributes

The abstract subcharacteristics must be decomposed into more concrete concepts, the quality attributes, which keep track of particular observable features of the products in the domain.

Identifying the appropriated quality attributes is not an easy task. In fact it may not be possible to identify all of them but just a significant group of the most relevant ones. This general sentence becomes specially important in the domain of ERP systems, whose number of attributes may grow to be really high. Many well-known sources may be used for this purpose including product manuals, demos, interviews, on-line documentation, technical reports, etc. Experience is also a key factor for avoiding or solving the typical problems related to the selection of quality attributes.

Just to mention some of them and their occurrence in our context:

 - The lack of standard terminology leads to problems such as the identification of attributes with different names but representing the same concept, or even worst, attributes with the same name but representing different concepts in two different packages. For example, the concept of adding to the inventory products which have been shipped from providers is named *Stock Reposition* in some systems and *Purchase Reception* in others.

– The confusion of attribute values with attributes themselves. Some ERP packages may transfer information to other applications such as spreadsheets or word processors. An attribute to represent each of the possible output formats or supported applications may be defined. But a more careful analysis reveals that those attributes are actually the set of values that may take a single attribute representing the supported interfaces (connectors) to external applications.

– The right classification of attributes suitable for more than one subcharacteristic. That is, attributes may be suitable for more than one subcharacteristic, and therefore the hierarchy of the model may take a graph-like form. This is not a problem by itself, although management of the quality model becomes a bit more difficult. This happened when considering some attributes from two different, orthogonal points of view: business processes and company areas.

Not only attributes have to be identified but also their definitions have to be provided in order to clarify the concepts that they represent and also as a way to link them to the subcharacteristics into which they have been classified.

Many attributes selected for the model are context-dependent. This means that their metrics must be defined in relation to the particular context which the ERP product has to be selected for. For instance, if a company business model is more oriented to logistics than to manufacturing, then more importance should be given to the evaluation of attributes related to that functional area. Even among enterprises with the same business model there may be contextual differences affecting the evaluation of attributes. As an example, let us consider two furniture manufacturing companies. One of them produces all the parts for its products from the basic materials while the other builds its products by assembling parts that have been previously ordered to different suppliers. As a result, the quality model for first company should be tailored to be more concerned on the control and reduction of manufacturing costs, while the other should be more concerned on the control of the logistics related to the process of buying the parts and their timely reception. Other similar situations may be found at [16].

3.4   Step 4: Decomposing Derived Attributes into Basic Attributes

Many derived attributes have been identified for the ERP systems model. For instance the *Support for Multi-Currency* derived attribute (which appears in some *Suitability* subcharacteristics) has been decomposed into some basic ones: *Support for the Definition of Currencies; Currencies Exchange Rates; Support for the Registration of Transactions in Multiple Currencies; Support for Emitting Multicurrency Statements*; and *Support for Automatic Currency Exchange*. We have arranged the ERP model to accommodate an attribute hierarchy down to three levels of depth, as shown in Figures 4 and 5 for the *Logistics* and *Operability* subcharacteristics. This has lead us to a highly structured quality model easier to understand, extend and use.

As in the case of decomposition of subcharacteristics, some attributes may play a part in more than one derived attribute.

3.5 Step 5: Stating Relationships between Quality Entities

To obtain a really complete quality model, the relationships among attributes and their dependencies must be explicitly stated. The model becomes more exhaustive, and, as an additional benefit, the implications of quality user requirements might become clearer (see Section 5). These relationships were already identified as important when building quality models for small and medium COTS products, but become really crucial in this huge domain.

A tabular representation of some relevant attribute relationships that we have identified is shown in Fig. 6. Attributes in rows contribute to attributes in columns, with either a positive (+) or a negative (-) partial support, while some attributes simply depend on others (D); see [5] for a similar, more expressive approach that could eventually be integrated into our methodology. For instance, we may notice the final representation in the table of the cooperation of *Priorization (of Purchase Orders)* with *Production Schedules*; the conflict of *Cancellation (of Purchase Orders)* with *Automatic Purchase Orders Generations*; and the dependency of *Creates Work Order Automatically* on *Automatic Generation Based on Customer Orders*.

As it happened with attributes, relationships may also be context-dependent. An illustrative sample is the dependency relationship between the sales invoices (*Sales & Receivable Accounts* subcharacteristic) and the production orders (*Production & Quality* subcharacteristic) attributes. Some companies may generate production orders based on the actual sales (e.g., a customized manufacturing company which needs the particular customer specifications to build their products). Others may not care about this fact and generate their production order based on some planning (e.g., a manufacturing company which produces mass consumption, not perishable products). While others may sale only what has been already produced or available on stock (e.g., a flowers production company, whose products are perishable and the daily production depends on external factors such as the weather and lighting conditions). This kind of relationship can be formally stated in the model but may later be redefined depending on the context.

3.6 Step 6: Determining Metrics for Attributes

Not only the attributes must be identified, but metrics for all the basic attributes must be selected, as well as metrics for those derived attributes whose definition does not depend on their context of use.

Some attributes can be evaluated by simple boolean values to state presence or absence of a product feature (e.g., the support for adding new records to

Subcharacteristic	Attribute Level 1	Attribute Level 2	Attribute level 3	Definition
Logistics (partial)	Master Files			Attributes related to the management of basic data required for the module functioning.
		Customers		Maintenance of the customers master file.
		Freight Carriers		Maintenance of the freight carriers master file.
		Postal Zones		Maintenance of the postal zones master file.
		Countries		Maintenance of the countries master file.
		Regions		Maintenance of the country regions master file.
	Shipping Management			Attributes related to the management of picking and dropping shipments.
		Create Shipping Order		Support for the registration of shipment orders (heading and detail information).
		Prints Shipping Documents		Attributes related to the capability of the package for printing shipping documents.
			Inventory Pick Lists	Support for printing inventory pick lists (both for picking and dropping shipments).
			Packing Lists	Support for printing packing lists (both for picking and dropping shipments).
			Shipping Labels	Support for printing shipping labels (both for picking and dropping shipments).
		Consolidate Items into Boxes/Crates		Support for automatically or manually organize the items to be shipped into shipment packaging units (boxes, crates, containers, etc.).
		.....	.....	
	Shipment Picking			Attributes related to the management of picking shipments.
		Multiple Ship-From Contacts		Possibility to record multiple ship-from contacts for a single picking shipment.
		Multiple Purchase Addresses		Possibility to record multiple purchase addresses for a single picking shipment.
		.....		
	Shipment Dropping			Attributes related to the management of dropping shipments.
		Multiple Ship to Addresses		Possibility to record multiple ship to addresses in a single order.
		.....	.....	
.....				

Fig. 4. ERP Quality Model; quality attributes for the *Logistics* subcharacteristic (partial)

Subcharacteristic	Attribute Level 1	Attribute Level 2	Attribute level 3	Definition
Operability (partial)	Users Management			Attributes related to the management of basic data required for the module functioning.
		Individual Users		Maintenance of the system users master file.
		Groups		Maintenance of user groups master file.
		User Privileges		Maintenance of user privileges master file.
		User Profiles		Maintenance of the user profiles master file.
		......	......	
	Password Management			Attributes related to the management of password protected options on the system.
		System Protection		Possibility to restrict user access to the system by password.
		Modules		Management of password restrictions to forbid users access to modules
		Functions		Management of password restrictions to forbid users from executing specific functions of the system.
		Files		Management of password restrictions to forbid users access to system files.
		Reports		Management of password restrictions to forbid users from executing specific reports.
		Transaction Types		Management of password restrictions to forbid users from executing specific transactions of the system.
		Data Input Fields		Management of password restrictions to forbid users from changing specific fields of screens on the system.
		System Auditing Functions		Management of password restrictions to forbid users access to some system auditing functions.
	Management of Fields Lengths and Formats			Attributes related to the tailoring of data fields on the system.
		User-Defined Field Formats		Possibility to redefine default field formats (e.g.: telephone numbers, postal codes, etc.).
		Coding		Attributes related to the tailoring of identification codes for data on the system (e.g.: accounts codes, document numbering, master files identifiers, etc.)
			User-Defined Coding Schemes	Possibility to define structure of codes across the system (e.g. number of code digits, code prefixes and suffixes, etc.).
		......	......	

Fig. 5. ERP Quality Model; quality attributes for the *Operability* subcharacteristic (partial)

masters on-the-fly). Others may be represented by simple units such as integer or float values of a particular unit (e.g., the average response time of a particular function in milliseconds or the maximum number of decimal digits for numeric values). A number of attributes require a more complex representation such as fixed or open sets (e.g., the languages supported by the interface or the list of DBMS supported by the system).

Metrics for some quality attributes may be difficult to define. This is the case of attributes whose values are not absolute, but depend on some other values. A typical case happens when the attributes depend on the underlying platform. For instance, many attributes related to the time behavior subcharacteristic may fall into this category. Any restriction in the function domain or range should be stated.

It should be clear that defining the metrics is the only way to have an exhaustive and fully-objective quality model. As stated by the ISO/IEC 9126-1 standard [15, p. 16], having rigorous metrics is the only way to obtain a quality model useful for doing reliable comparisons.

In the case of basic attributes, metrics must be quantitative; in derived attributes, they could be either quantitative or qualitative, with explicit formula computing their value from their component attributes. It is worth remarking the qualitative label metrics, with values such as "good", "fair", "poor" and so on, which are referred to as *rating levels* in the ISO/IEC standard. Some examples of metrics appear in the next section.

4   Formalizing the Quality Model

Once the quality model is built as we have seen in the last section, we must decide if it is worthwhile to take the final step of formalizing all or part of it. The benefit of formalization is twofold: on the one hand, some weak points such as ambiguities, inconsistencies and incompleteness in the quality model are expected to be detected, as it is the usual case in any formalization process; on the other hand, formal descriptions of quality models are necessary for providing some tool support to the ERP selection problem. Furthermore, formal descriptions become a useful way to record technical decisions and requirements that can be communicated among experts as we will show in the next section.

At a first glance, formalization may seem a difficult and costly task with no revenue, but this is not true in all circumstances. Concerning the effort, we remark that the transition from a structured quality model (as ISO/IEC-9126-1-based ones are) to a formal language can be automated to a great extend. Also, return of investment is an important factor to be considered. A formal description of (a part of) the ERP domain, together with the formal description of particular ERP systems, is a means to make ERP selection faster (searches and queries—representing requirements—may be formally stated and solved using ERP descriptions as solution space) and more reliable (tool support lessen the risk of forgetting parts of the model to be properly analyzed). Anyway, we remark that we propose formalization as an optional activity, to be carried out when appropriate.

The table below transcribes the matrix shown in the figure. Top‑level subcharacteristic groups are given across the top; attribute rows are listed down the left. Cell values are **D** or **+** or **-**.

Column key (left→right):
C1 = Production schedules / *Automatic generation based on customer orders*;
C2 = Production orders / *Automatic purchase orders generation*;
C3 = Purchase orders / *Purchase proposals*;
C4 = Purchase order tracking / *Purchase order state*;
C5 = Purchase order tracking / *Shipment dates control*;
C6 = Inventory Management / *Receiving Schedule*;
C7 = Shipment Dropping / *Delivery route scheduling per carrier*;
C8 = Shipping Schedule / *Specify Delivery Date Per Line Item*;
C9 = Shipping Schedule / *Calculates Ship-by Date*.

Group	Subcharacteristic	Attributes	C1	C2	C3	C4	C5	C6	C7	C8	C9
			(Production & Quality)		*(Purchases & Payable Accounts)*				*(Logistics)*		
Sales & Receivable Accounts	Master Files	Customers							D		
	Purchase Orders	Cancellation				-		-	D	D	D
		Confirmation	D	D	+		+		D	D	D
		Prioritization of Orders	+	+					+	+	
		Creates Work Order Automatically		D						+	+
	Inventory Management	Available Inventory reservation (by lots if required)				+		+			
Production & Quality	Production orders	Automatic consideration and compensation for standard process damage percentage				+					
		Detailed listing of needed materials and resources				D					
		Automatic purchase orders generation				+	+	+			
		Available assignment of required materials on inventory				+					
	Product recipes	Parts and supplies				D					
		Process line								D	D
		Alternative process lines								+	+
		Time tables								D	D
Purchases & Payable Accounts	Purchase order tracking	Purchase order state	+								
		Shipment dates control	+								
		Incident management	+								
		Management of products with pending shipments	+								
		Cancellation of pending remains	-								
	Inventory Management	Receiving Schedule	D								
Logistics	Shipping Schedule		D								

Fig. 6. Some relationships among quality entities

We present here an approach centered on the definition of a language called *NoFun* (acronym for "NOt-just-FUNctional" — formerly "NOn-FUNctional"), which is to be used as a formal language for the exhaustive description of software quality. The language consists of three different parts [13, 1]. The first one is specifically oriented to express an ISO/IEC-based quality model. Using the second part, particular products can be described through assignment of values to basic attributes. In the third one, quality requirements can be stated, both context-free (universal quality properties) and context-dependent (quality properties for a given framework—software domain, company, project, etc.).

Table 1. Formalization of the *Basic Suitability* subcharacteristic

```
subcharacteristic module BasicSuitability for ERPSystem
  decomposed as SalesAndReceibableAccounts, ProductionAndQuality
        PurchasesAndPayableAccounts, Financials, FixedAssets,
        Inventories, Maintenance, Marketing, PayrollsAndHumanResources
        Accounting, Logistics, CrossApplications
  imports FourValueScale
  subcharacteristic BasicSuitability[ByAreas]
        depends on subcharacteristics(BasicSuitability)
        declared as
            function from subcharacteristics(BasicSuitability)
                    to FourValueScale
        defined as
            for all x in subcharacteristics(BasicSuitability)
                    it holds that BasicSuitabilityByAreas(x) = x
  subcharacteristic BasicSuitability[ERP]
        depends on subcharacteristics(BasicSuitability)
        declared as FourValueScale deferred
end BasicSuitability for ERPSystem

domain module FourValueScale
  domain ordered FourValueScale = (None, Fair, Satisfactory, Excellent)
end FourValueScale
```

In this section, we focus on the part aimed at formalizing the quality model, while in the next section we will give an example of requirements formalization. As giving the whole formalization of the quality model would be tedious, we focus here on some of the parts presented in Section 3, namely one of the subcharacteristics (*Basic Suitability*) and two derived attributes (*Users Management* and *Password Management* from the *Operability* subcharacteristic).

We start the formalization by focusing on the *Basic Suitability* subcharacteristic. From Fig. 3, we may see that it is defined in terms of twelve other subcharacteristics, one for each type of functional area. For this reason, we conclude that the best metrics for this subcharacteristic is a function from the functional areas to a qualitative four-value scale. The definition of the metrics just applies delegation to the appropriate subcharacteristic. In addition, we include a qualitative alternative metric in case of being interested on measuring the whole basic functionality of ERP systems. This metric is clearly context-dependent, since it is not possible to determine the weights of the twelve subcharacteristics without taking the context of selection into account.

Table 1 presents the NoFun modules needed for this part of the model[1]. The *Basic Suitability* module states first the decomposition into the twelve subchar-

---

[1] For the sake of brevity, we do not include comments in the contents of the module, although they are explicitly required by the language definition.

Table 2. Formalization of the *Users Management* attribute

```
attribute module SingleUserManagement for ERPSystem
  imports UserManagementLevels
  attribute basic SingleUserManagement
        declared as UserManagementLevels
end SingleUserManagement for ERPSystem

attribute module GroupManagement for ERPSystem
  imports UserManagementLevels
  attribute basic GroupManagement
        declared as UserManagementLevels
end GroupManagement for ERPSystem

domain module UserManagementLevels
domain ordered
    UserManagementLevels = (None, Definition, Privileges, Profiles)
end UserManagementLevels

attribute module UsersManagement for ERPSystem
  decomposed as SingleUserManagement, GroupManagement
  imports UserManagementLevels
  attribute derived UserManagement
        depends on SingleUserManagement, GroupManagement
        declared as UserManagementLevels
        deferred
end UsersManagement for ERPSystem
```

acteristics, and introduces the two metrics. The domain for the four-value scale must be also declared in a separate domain module, usable in other contexts (in the same or other quality models). We remark the use of a *subcharacteristics* operation which supports the hierarchical decomposition of metrics following the layout of the model.

Next we present the formalization of the *Users Management* attribute belonging to the *Operability* subcharacteristic. This is a good example of how the formalization process may help on improving the final form of the quality model. In Section 3, we have decomposed *Users Management* into four basic attributes, each supposed to be measured as boolean metrics (see Fig. 4). However, when defining the concrete form of the metrics, we have finally rearranged the decomposition and we have identified two attributes with four possible values, depending on the type of management; two of the types correspond to two of the former attributes. The values of the attributes stand for: no management facilities available; simply definition of users or groups; facilities to assign privileges; and facilities to create profiles. See Table 2 for the NoFun modules.

Note that the *Users Management* attribute is finally left undefined because it is context-dependent; as an example, we provide in Table 3 a possible special-

Table 3. Definition of the *Users Management* attribute in a particular context

```
attribute module UsersManagementByMin for ERPSystem
  refines UsersManagement
  subcharacteristic UserManagement
      defined as min(SingleUserManagement, GroupManagement)
end UsersManagementByMin for ERPSystem
```

ization of the metrics considering that the value of the attribute is the minimum of the values of the two composing basic attributes.

Last we address to the *Password Management* attribute. Fig. 5 showed its decomposition into eight similar attributes. In this case, for each of these attributes except for the first one (*System Protection*) two different levels of information may be required: if password protection exists for each of the underlying concepts (module, function, etc.) and in this case, which are the concrete concept instances protected, if not all of them.

For this reason, we have decided to identify seven new attributes at level 3, one for each concept except system; each of them keeps track of the set of concept instances protected, being the string "AllInstances" a wildcard (i.e., full protection for this concept). Attributes at level 2 are defined as derived, being their value not just a boolean but a three-valued logic. As in the case of *Basic Functionality*, we introduce more than one metrics for *Password Management*: (1) a function implementing delegation; and (2) a qualitative metrics whose definition is not included since it is context-free. Table 4 encapsulates the NoFun definition. Since the attributes at level 3 are identical, we encapsulate them in one single module; this cannot be done in the same way with attributes at level 2 since decomposition of attributes must be stated.

5 Evaluation of Products and Expression of Requirements Using the Quality Model

Once the quality model for ERP systems is built during a selection process, it becomes possible to describe concrete ERP systems and to express quality requirements to model the needs of a company in the selection process.

When evaluating product quality, it turns out to be very difficult to find complete and reliable information about all product attributes. Manufacturers tend to give just a partial view of their products. Either they put so much emphasis on their product benefits, without mentioning the weaknesses, or they give a partial look. Some third-party reports look very independent, but some have been strongly refuted by the technical departments of involved parties, making them difficult to rely on. Other non-commercial articles compare features, but often they base their reports on evaluators' knowledge of the tools, and their particular taste, more than in rigorous technical tests. A quality model provides an independent framework to drive the evaluation process.

Table 4. Formalization of the *Password Management* attribute

---

```
attribute module PasswordSupportLevel3 for ERPSystem
  attribute basic ModulePassword3, FunctionPassword3, FilePassword3
                  ReportPassword3, TransactionPassword3
                  DataInputFieldsPassword3, AuditPassword3
        declared as set of String special value {"AllInstances"}
end PasswordSupportLevel3 for ERPSystem

attribute module ModulePassword for ERPSystem
  imports PasswordSupportLevel3
  decomposed as ModulePassword3
  attribute derived ModulePassword depends on ModulePassword3
        declared as (None, Partial, Total)
        defined as
              empty(ModulePassword3) implies ModulePassword = None
              ModulePassword3 = special implies ModulePassword = Total
              otherwise ModulePassword = Partial
end ModulePassword for ERPSystem
```

...similar attribute modules for functions, files and others[a]

```
attribute module SystemPassword for ERPSystem
  attribute basic SystemPassword declared as Boolean
end SystemPassword for ERPSystem

attribute module PasswordManagement for ERPSystem
  decomposed as SystemPassword, ModulePassword, FunctionPassword
                FilePassword, ReportPassword, TransactionPassword
                DataInputFieldPassword, AuditPassword
  imports FourValueScale
  subcharacteristic PasswordManagement[BySubject]
        depends on subcharacteristics(PasswordManagement)
        declared as
              function from subcharacteristics(PasswordManagement)
                      to boolean
        defined as
              for all x in subcharacteristics(PasswordManagement)
                      it holds that PasswordManagement(x) = x
  subcharacteristic PasswordManagement[ERP]
        depends on subcharacteristics(PasswordManagement)
        declared as FourValueScale deferred
end PasswordManagement for ERPSystem
```

---

[a] A better solution could have been provided using some refinement constructs available in NoFun. We have chosen here simplicity instead of expressive power.

Table 5. Formalization of two requirements in the ERP system selection process for the ACME company

```
requirement module SuitabilityReqts on Suitability for ACME
  definition
  globalSuitability: essential
        concerns BasicSuitability
        defined as
         for all x in subcharacteristics(BasicSuitability)
         it holds that BasicSuitability[ByAreas](x) >= Satisfactory
  economicalIssues: advisable
        concerns BasicSuitability
        defined as
          for all x
          in {SalesAndAccounts, PurchaseAccounts, Financial}
          it holds that BasicSuitability[ByAreas](x) = Excellent
  end SuitabilityReqts on Suitability for ACME
```

The quality model can be used for describing quality requirements in a structured manner. For instance, the informal and fuzzy requirement "The ERP system to be selected should cover the main functionalities of all the company areas up to an acceptable level and especially optimal behavior in the areas related to economical issues is pursued" may be expressed as the conjunction of two requirements using the *Basic Suitability* subcharacteristic and one of its metrics, interpreting "up to an acceptable level" as the *Satisfactory* value in the four-value scale unit and "optimal behavior" as *Excellent* in the same scale.

The relationships between quality entities can also be used with the same aim. Let us assume a user requirement demanding an ERP that allows creating work orders automatically. Without the defined relationships between the *Creates Work Order Automatically* and the *Automatic Generation Based on Customer Orders* attributes, the satisfaction of this requirement would depend just on the first attribute. But having the relationship, we will know that it depends on both.

Table 5 provides the formalization of the first requirement using NoFun. Once this requirements is expressed using NoFun, they may be compared to the descriptions of particular ERP systems, that could also be expressed in the same language ameliorating then the comparison of products with requirements.

6   Conclusions

One of the most critical activities required in COTS-based software development is COTS product selection. One of the factors that positively influence the success of a COTS product selection process is a deep enough knowledge about its segment of COTS market. We propose quality models as a way to characterize

COTS products belonging to a certain domain. These models are exhaustive and structured descriptions of these domains to serve as a framework in which particular COTS products may be evaluated and compared to user requirements during a selection process.

In this chapter we have described the construction of a quality model for a particular COTS domain, ERP system domain. The methodology applied that was presented in [10, 11] has been used in other domains, such as mail servers [4], e-learning, etc. Also it can be seen as the continuation of some previous experiences in the field of ERP system selection [3, 21]. We have also proposed to express the quality model in the NoFun description language, both to detect weaknesses in the quality model and to support expression of quality requirements, even allowing tool support during selection.

When applying our methodology to this particular case, we have confirmed the opinion of some authors [9, 17] saying that building the quality model is a complex activity, endangered by many factors: poor description of the domain, lack of ability when identifying the quality entities, inappropriate metrics, etc. However, once available, it becomes a real powerful tool which provides a general framework to get uniform descriptions of the great deal of ERP systems available in the market. Comparison of these products is then favored, as we have shown in this chapter with the use of the ERP systems quality model.

Finally, it is important to state that our proposal not only improves the reliability of COTS product selection but could also lower the cost of the very selection process. This is the case because the ERP system domain satisfies two conditions: (a) a great deal of companies and organizations worldwide require ERP systems for supporting their business process; and (b) there are many ERP systems available in the market. Just consider for a moment the amount of repeated work that is done in the ERP systems selection processes of different organizations. They face very similar problems, with some tasks that are exactly the same, and for those repeat the same process over and over, wasting human resources and money while doing so. The existence of a quality model for this domain may help to make the selection a simpler task, since it is not necessary to rediscover which are the factors that influence the ERP system selection, just to tailor the quality model to a specific selection context.

Acknowledgments

This work is partially supported by the Spanish research program CICYT under contract TIC2001-2165. Juan Pablo Carvallo work has been supported by an AECI grant. Also thanks to Mark Foster and Jordi Marco for their technical support with LaTeX.

References

1. P. Botella, X. Burgués, X. Franch, M. Huerta, G. Salazar. "Modeling Non-Functional Requirements". In Proceedings Jornadas de Ingeniería de Requisitos Aplicada (JIRA), Sevilla (Spain), June 2001.

2. X. Burgués, C. Estay, X. Franch, J. Pastor, C. Quer. "Combined Selection of COTS Components". In [6].
3. X. Burgués, X. Franch, J.A. Pastor. "Formalising ERP Selection Criteria". In Proceedings of the 10th IEEE International Workshop on Software Specification and Design (IWSSD), San Diego (CA, USA), November 2000.
4. J.P. Carvallo, X. Franch, C. Quer. "Defining a Quality Model for Mail Servers". In Proc. of the 2nd International Conference on COTS-Based Software Systems (ICCBSS), LNCS 2580, Ottawa (Canada), February 2003.
5. L. Chung, B. Nixon, E. Yu, J. Mylopoulos. *Non-Functional Requirements in Software Engineering*. Kluwer Academic Publishers, 2000.
6. *Proceedings of the 1st International Conference on COTS-Based Software Systems* (ICCBSS), LNCS 2255, Orlando (FL, USA), February 2002.
7. T. Davenport. "Putting the Enterprise into the Enterprise System". Harvard Business Review, July-August, 1998, pp. 121-131.
8. T. Davenport "Mission Critical: Realizing the Promise of Enterprise Systems". Harvard Business School Press, 2000.
9. R.G. Dromey. "Cornering the Chimera". IEEE Software, vol. 13, January 1996.
10. X. Franch, J.P. Carvallo. "A Quality-Model-Based Approach for Describing and Evaluating Software Packages". In Proceedings of the 10th IEEE Joint Conference on Requirements Engineering (RE), Essen (Germany), September 2002.
11. X. Franch, J.P. Carvallo. "Using Quality Models in Software Package Selection". IEEE Software, vol. 20(1), January 2003.
12. X. Franch, J.A. Pastor. "On the Formalisation of ERP Systems Procurement". In Proceedings of the 2nd International Workshop on Commercial Off-The-Shelf Software (COTS'00), Limerick (Ireland), June 2000.
13. X. Franch. "Systematic Formulation of Non-Functional Characteristics of Software". In Proceedings of the 3rd IEEE International Conference on Requirements Engineering (ICRE), Colorado Springs (CO, USA), May 1998.
14. A. Finkelstein, G. Spanoudakis, M. Ryan. "Software Package Requirements and Procurement". In Proceedings of the 8th IEEE International Workshop on Software Specification and Design (IWSSD), 1996.
15. ISO/IEC Standard 9126-1 Software Engineering – Product Quality – Part 1: Quality Model, June 2001.
16. F.R. Jacobs, D.C. Whybark. *Why ERP?*. McGraw-Hill, 2000.
17. B. Kitchenham, S.L. Pfleeger. "Software Quality: the Elusive Target". IEEE Software, vol. 20, January 1996, pp. 12–21.
18. J. Kontyo. "A Case Study in Applying a Systematic Method for COTS Selection". In Proceedings of the 18th IEEE International Conference on Software Engineering (ICSE), 1996.
19. B.C. Meyers, P. Oberndorf. *Managing Software Acquisition*. Addison-Wesley, 2001.
20. N. Maiden, C. Ncube. "Acquiring Requirements for COTS Selection". IEEE Software 15(2), 1998.
21. J.A. Pastor, X. Franch, F. Sistach. "Methodological ERP Acquisition: the SHERPA Experience". In *The Guide to IT Service Management*, Vol. I, chapter 16, edited by J. van Bon. Addison-Wesley, 2002.

Maturing Architectures and Components in Software Product Lines

Jan Bosch

University of Groningen
Department of Computing Science
P.O. Box 800, NL9700AV, Groningen, Netherlands
Jan.Bosch@cs.rug.nl
http://www.cs.rug.nl/~bosch

Abstract. Software product lines have received considerable adoption in the software industry and prove to be a very successful approach to intra-organizational software reuse. Existing literature, however, often assumes a singular transition from independent product development to a software product line approach. In this chapter, we present an overview of different approaches to architecture-centric, intra-organizational reuse of software architectures and components and organize these in maturity levels. In addition, we present the notion of hierarchical scopes in software development organizations where different scopes may have achieved different maturity levels. The claim of this chapter is that the challenge that most organizations face is not the singular adoption of a software product line, but rather the continuous maturation of the organization in terms of exploiting intra-organizational reuse at multiple levels of scope in the organization.

1 Introduction

Software engineering is concerned with the cost-effective development and evolution of software of specified quality and within predefined resource constraints. As any engineering discipline, also software engineering is constantly developing new technology, methods, tools and approaches to increase ability of software engineering professionals to improve cost-effectiveness, predictability of quality and time-to-market. Probably the most promising approach to achieve this is the use of software artefacts in multiple contexts, i.e. software reuse. One can identify two types of software reuse, i.e. inter- and intra-organizational reuse of software. Inter-organizational reuse of software is rather well established through the ever increasing amounts of functionality that is provided through the infrastructure of modern software applications. This infrastructure typically consists of numerous components such an operating system, database management system, graphical user interface, web server, et cetera.

Software product lines (or software system families) is one of the forms through which intra-organizational reuse of software has evolved during the last decade. A software product line [3, 5, 8] consists of product line architecture, a

A. Cechich et al. (Eds.): Component-Based Software Quality, LNCS 2693, pp. 246–258, 2003.

set of shared components and a set of products. Each product derives a product architecture from the product line architecture, selects, instantiates and configures product line components and adds, if necessary, product specific code. The introduction or adoption of a product line approach is, in most recent literature (including our own), a process that requires technical, process, organizational and business changes and that requires a rather fundamental rethinking of the whole approach to software development [3, 1, 14].

However, with the evolving insight into the way organizations achieve intra-organizational reuse of software artefacts, we have come to realize that this is not a black and white choice. Typically, an organization may exploit different approaches to sharing software artefacts. These approaches can be organized into a number of maturity levels, where each higher level employs more domain engineering, i.e. development of software artefacts for multiple contexts, and less application engineering, i.e. development of software artefacts for a single context. Below, we briefly discuss the product line maturity levels that we have identified. Later in the chapter, these are presented in more detail:

- **Independent products**: Initially, the organization develops multiple products as several independent entities. These products do not share software artefacts in any planned way, only by coincidence.
- **Standardized infrastructure**: The first step towards sharing is when the organization decides to standardize the infrastructure based on which a set of products is built.
- **Platform**: A subsequent development is to extend the standardized infrastructure with internally developed software artefacts, i.e. a platform, that provide functionality that is common to all products in the scope. Each product is developed on top of the platform.
- **Software product line**: The fourth level of maturity is when the organization employs a software product line. The shared artefacts in the product line contain functionality that is shared by all or a subset of the products. Products may sacrifice efficiency or other requirements for the benefits of being member of the product line.
- **Configurable product base**: The final level is the situation where the differences between the different product has been so well understood that these can be mapped to variation points that can be bound at installation or run- time. As a consequence, individual products are derived by configuring the shared software artefacts appropriately.

A second issue that is relevant in this context is the fact that, especially in larger organizations, intra-organizational reuse takes place at multiple levels of scope. In Fig. 1, this is illustrated graphically. In our example, the organization employs a number of infrastructure components. At the top level scope, three infrastructure components are used as a basis to provide shared software artefacts to the next level scopes. Scope 1.1 reuses these shared artefacts and develops some additional ones based on which three products are developed, i.e. P_A, P_B and P_C. Product P_B is used to derive three different customer products.

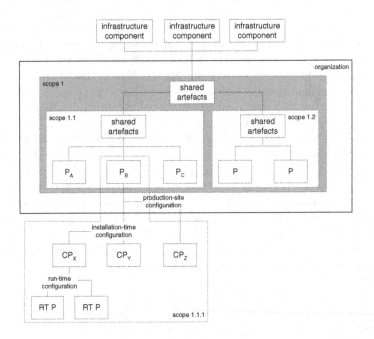

Fig. 1. Different scopes of intra-organizational reuse

Product CP_Z is derived at the developing organization itself, whereas the other products are configured during the installation of the software at the customer site. Customer product CP_X can, at run-time, be configured into two different products. If we analyze the maturity of this organization, we can conclude that the organization has reached the platform level at scope 1, the software product line level at scope 1.1 and the configurable product level at scope 1.1.1. Although it is natural for an organization to reach a higher level of maturity for smaller scopes, this is not necessarily the case. One of the approaches that we discuss later in the chapter is the programme of product lines. In that case the top level scope has a maturity level of a configurable product whereas the components are at the product line maturity level.

The claim and, we believe, contribution of this chapter is that the challenge with respect to intra-organizational reuse that most organizations face is not the singular adoption of a software product line, but rather the continuous maturation of the organization in terms of exploiting intra-organizational reuse at multiple levels of scope in the organization by increasing the product line maturity levels. In fact, we believe that moving from an independent products approach to a software product line in one step is a high risk undertaking for most organizations due to the number of the business, organizational, process and technological changes that needs to occur at the same time. An approach where the organization moves through the product line maturity levels with a clear goal of what to achieve, we believe, is more viable and closer to the actual situation in the software industry.

The remainder of this chapter is organized as follows. In the next Section, we discuss maturity for the product line artefacts, i.e. the product line architecture, components and products. For each of these, one can distinguish at least three levels of maturity. In Section 3, we discuss the maturity levels of intra-organizational software reuse that we introduced earlier in more detail. Section 4 discusses the process of maturation in organizations, whereas Section 5 discusses related work. Finally, the chapter is concluded in Section 6.

2   Product Line Artefact Maturity

One can identify three types of artefacts that make up a software product line, i.e. the product line architecture, shared components and the products derived from the shared artefacts. For each of these artefacts, one can identify three maturity levels, depending on the level of integration achieved in the product line. Below, we discuss each artefact in more detail.

The software architecture of the product line is the artefact that defines the overall decomposition of the products into the main components. In doing so, the architectures captures the commonalities between products and facilitates the variability. One can identify three levels of maturity:

- **Under-specified architecture:** A first step in the evolutionary adoption of a software product line, especially when converging an existing set of products, is to first define the common aspects between the products and to avoid the specification of the differences. This definition of the architecture gives existing and new products a basic frame of reference, but still allows for substantial freedom in product specific architectural deviation.
- **Specified architecture:** The next maturity level is to specify both the commonalities and the differences between the products in the software architecture. Now, the architecture captures most of the domain covered by the set of products, although individual products may exploit variation points for product specific functionality. The products still derive a product specific architecture from the product line architecture and may consequently make changes. However, the amount of freedom is substantially less than in the under-specified architecture.
- **Enforced architecture:** The highest maturity level is the enforced architecture. The architecture captures all commonality and variability to the extent where no product needs, nor is allowed, to change the architecture in its implementation. All products use the architecture as-is and exploit the variation points to implement product specific requirements.

The second type of artefact is the product line component, shared by some or all products in the product line. Whereas the product line architecture defines a way of thinking about the products and rationale for the structure chosen, the components contribute to the product line by providing reusable implementations that fit into the designed architecture. Again, one can identify three levels of maturity for product line components:

- **Specified component:** The first step in converging a set of existing products towards a product line is to specify the interface of the components defined by the architecture. A component specification typically consists of a provided, a required and a configuration interface. Based on the component specifications, the individual products can evolve their architecture and product specific component implementations towards the product line, thereby simplifying further integration in the future.
- **Multiple component implementations:** The second level of maturity is where, for an architectural component, multiple component implementations exist, but each implementation is shared by more than one product. Typically, closely related products have converged to the extent that component sharing has become feasible and, where necessary, variation points have been implemented in the shared components.
- **Configurable component implementation:** The third level is where only one component implementation is used. This implementation is typically highly configurable since all required variability has been captured in the component implementation. Often, additional support is provided for configuring or deriving a product specific instantiation of the component, e.g. through graphical tools or generators.

The third artefact type in a software product line is the products derived from the common product line artefacts. Again, three levels of maturity can be distinguished:

- **Architecture conformance:** The first step in converging a product towards a product line is to conform to the architecture specified by the product line. A product can only be considered a member of the product line if it at least conforms to the under-specified architecture.
- **Platform-based product:** The second level is the minimalist approach [1] where only those components are shared between products that capture functionality common to all products. Because the functionality is so common, typically little variability needs to be implemented.
- **Configurable product base:** The third level of maturity is the maximalist approach [1], where all or almost all functionality implemented by any of the product line members is captured by the shared product line artefacts. Products are derived by configuring and (de-)selecting elements. Often, automated support is provided to derive individual products.

3   Maturity Levels of Software Product Lines

As mentioned in the introduction, architecture-centric, intra-organizational reuse takes place in various forms. In our experience, these approaches can be organized in a number of levels. The approaches that we have identified are ranging from a standardized infrastructure based on which products are created to a configurable product base that can be used to derive a variety of products. Thus, for a set of products covering a defined scope and that exhibit some commonality, an organization has a number of alternatives for developing and evolving these products, in addition to developing each product from scratch. Below, we discuss the different approaches that we have identified. Starting from a situation in which each product or application is developed independently, the main maturity development path consists of a standardized infrastructure, a platform, a software product line and finally a configurable product base.

3.1   Standardized Infrastructure

Description. The first step that an organization takes when evolving towards exploiting commonality in its products is to standardize the infrastructure based on which the products are developed. This infrastructure typically consists of the operating system and the typical commercial components on top of it such as a database management system and a graphical user interface. In addition, the organization may acquire some domain-specific components from external sources. These components are typically integrated through some proprietary glue code.

Example. An example of a company exploiting this approach is Vertis Information Technology. This company develops administrative applications typically supporting some technical production systems. Vertis typically builds its applications on top of a Windows NT platform running the Oracle database system and associated tool set. They have bought a number of domain specific components specific for the Dutch taxation system. These components have been integrated with the Oracle tool set and the operating system to form a rather advanced infrastructure based on which the applications are constructed.

SPL Artefact Maturity. The standard infrastructure approach cannot impose more than an underspecified architecture. Since the infrastructure typically only provides relatively generic behavior, it cannot fully specify a software architecture for the product line. In addition, the standard infrastructure can only specify the part of component interfaces that is concerned with the functionality provided by the infrastructure. For instance, in the case of an object-oriented database being part of the standard infrastructure, persistent components need to support interfaces for persistence, queries and transactions. Products based on the standard infrastructure only need to conform to the architectural restrictions imposed, but are free otherwise.

3.2   Platform

Description. The next level in achieving intra-organizational reuse is when the organization develops and maintains a platform based on which the products or applications are created. A platform typically includes a standardized infrastructure as discussed in the previous Section. On top of that, it captures all functionality that is common to all products or applications. The common functionality that is not provided by the infrastructure is implemented by the organization itself, but typically the application development treats the platform as if it was an externally bought infrastructure.

Example. An example of a company employing the platform approach is Symbian Ltd. The company develops the Symbian OS (earlier known as EPOC), an operation system, application framework and application suite for personal digital assistants and mobile phones. The Symbian OS is distributed in three device family requirement definitions (DFRDs), i.e. a landscape display communicator (640 x 200 pixels and up), a portrait display communicator (approximately 320 x 240 pixels) and a smart phone family. Each of these DFRDs is distributed to the licensees as a platform that has to be extended with device specific functionality and licensee-specific applications.

SPL Artefact Maturity. The platform approach typically employs an under-specified architecture, because it lacks the information about specific products constructed on top of the platform. Compared to the standardized infrastructure approach, the platform architecture typically demands more conformance from products in terms of architectural rules and constraints that have to be followed. Component interfaces are typically specified at least partially and for the common behavior, component implementations may be provided by the platform. Products are constructed on top of the platform, as indicated in the table. Platforms are typically created through the efforts of a dedicated domain engineering team, but do not necessarily require the existence of a domain engineering unit during the usage and evolution of the platform.

3.3   Software Product Line

Description. Once the benefits of exploiting the commonalities between the products become more accepted within the organization, a consequent development may be to increase the amount of functionality in the platform to the level where functionality common to several but not all products becomes part of the shared artefacts. Now we have reached the stage of a software product line. Functionality specific to one or a few products is still developed as part of the product derivation. Functionality shared by a sufficient number of products is part of the shared product line artefacts, with the consequence that individual products may sacrifice resource efficiency or development effort for being part of the product line.

Example. An example of an organization employing this approach is Axis Communication AB, Lund. At the time that we studied the company, it developed a range of network devices such as scanner servers, printer servers, storage servers and camera servers. These products were developed by as many business units and based on a set of common software artefacts, i.e. a product line architecture and a set of more than 10 object-oriented frameworks that were used as configurable product line components.

SPL Artefact Maturity. The software product line approach specifies a product line architecture that captures the commonalities and variabilities of the products. For each architectural component, one or more component implementations are provided. For the more stable and well understood components, multiple implementations may have merged into one configurable component implementation. Products are based on the product line, but may deviate where necessary.

3.4 Configurable Product Base

Description. Especially if the organization develops products in relatively stable domains and derives many product instances, there is a tendency to further develop the support for product derivation. The consequence is that the organization, rather than developing a number of different products, moves towards developing only one configurable product base that, either at the organization or at the customer site, is configured into the product bought by the customer. Some companies use, for instance, license key driven configuration, shipping the same code base to each and every customer. The code base configures itself based on the provided license key, allowing access to certain parts of the functionality while blocking others.

Example. An example of an organization applying this approach is Telelarm AB, producing fire alarm systems. After several years developing and evolving an object-oriented framework for applications in the domain, the company reached the level where each customer basically received the same code base. The persons performing the installation at the customer site are supported by a configuration tool that manages the customer specific configuration of the product.

SPL Artefact Maturity. The most domain-engineering centric approach centers around a configurable product base. In this case, the architecture is enforced in that no product can deviate from the commonalities and variabilities specified in the architecture. Consequently, each architectural component typically has one associated configurable component implementation and the products are derived from these artefacts by excluding those parts not needed.

4 Multi-scope Intra-organizational Software Reuse

In the introduction to this chapter, we discussed the notion of scope and illustrated it graphically in Fig. 1. For the purpose of this chapter, we define scope as "a set of features and software artefacts, including architectures, components and/or products that is perceived and treated as related". The maturity levels that we presented in the previous Section are concerned with one scope, but within an organization multiple scopes can be present that are organized in a hierarchical fashion. However, it is also possible that multiple, unrelated scopes exist within the organization. This is, for instance, the case when two business units within the organization both employ a software product line approach, but the resulting product lines share no artefacts. In the case that an organization aims to increase the amount of intra-organizational reuse, the organization typically evolves through three phases, i.e. create a scope, mature the scope and collapse the scope. Below, these phases are discussed in more detail.

Create scope: The first step of an organization towards increased reuse is to identify that worthwhile commonalities between its products exist that should be exploited. The organization then creates a scope within which previously independent products evolve to, e.g., the first maturity level discussed in the previous Section, i.e. standardizing the infrastructure. Initially, the effect on the development organization is limited as the amount of domain engineering is minimal. The primary difference is cultural: whereas the products first were fully independent, now some coordination needs to take place.

From the perspective of variability management, one can identify that variability was, up to now, solely managed during the requirements engineering level. During requirements analysis, it was decided what features each individual product should contain. All software development was then single system development. Now, the first effects of exploiting commonalities are felt in the software development.

Mature scope: Once a basic level of sharing is in place, the second phase is to increase the amount sharing between the products in the scope. In the case of a managed, continuous evolution, the products in the scope move through the various maturity levels until the software product line level is reached. Typically, the development organization is modified to reflect the changing balance between the amount of domain engineering versus the amount of application engineering.

Variability management now more and more affects the software artefacts as these need to incorporate increasing numbers of variation points that also are bound at later and later stages in software development. Once the software product line level is reached, many variation points are bound during the product derivation step which, depending on the type of product, may have been reduced to days or hours. A second development is that an increasing number of variation points is no longer bound during software development, but rather at installation or run-time.

Collapse scope: As the understanding of the application domain increases and assuming the application domain is sufficiently stable, several organizations reach a point where all variation points within the scope can be bound at installation or run-time. At this point, the various products within the scope have merged into a single, configurable product (or product base). From a development perspective, the organization is, within this scope, now concerned with a single product and in a way the scope 'collapses' as this type of development, despite its increased complexity, resembles the development of an independent product, i.e. our starting point. Note that organizations typically still market a variety of different products based on this single, configurable product.

As mentioned earlier, among others, license key driven configuration may be used to provide the customer with different products. As mentioned, variability management has now moved completely to the final stages of the development life cycle, i.e. installation and run-time.

Although the three phases discussed above represent an ideal maturation process, in most cases, the hierarchy of the various scopes within the organization is not stable. An event that may interrupt the above process is the reorganization of the scope. For instance, the organization identifies that the initial scope has been set too wide, limiting a subset of products to fully exploit their commonalities. In response, the organization may create an additional, nested scope covering those products. Within the nested scope, the products can more easily achieve a higher maturity level.

From the above example, one might deduce that the most typical situation is where the more nested scope also has a higher maturity level. Although this indeed seems to be the case in many organizations, we have found two multi-scope approaches that show that it is possible that a broader scope has a higher maturity level than nested scope, i.e. the programme of product lines approach and the product population approach. These approaches are discussed below.

4.1 Programme of Product Lines

Description. Especially for very large systems, the program of product lines approach can be used. The approach consists of a software architecture that is defined for the overall system and that specifies the components that make up the system. Several or all of the components are software product lines. The result is a system that can be configured as the configurable product described above. However, because of its size, the configuration of the components is basically performed through product line-based product derivation or by using the configurable product base approach.

Example. An illustrative example of this approach is provided by Nokia Networks. The main product of this division are telecom switches. Each system consists of several product families. These product families are developed on top of platforms that in turn consist of reusable design blocks consisting of reusable components. A system delivered to a customer requires selection and configuration of each of the aforementioned elements. Change management in this context is a highly complex endeavor. Nokia Networks employs an approach that they refer to as System Feature Management.

SPL Artefact Maturity. In the case of a program of product lines, the overall architecture is typically fully specified or even enforced as it defines the interaction between the component product lines. The architectural components are software product lines in themselves and, as such, typically rather configurable.

Products are derived by configuring the product line components for the specific context in which these are used.

4.2 Product Populations

Description. Whereas the approach discussed above extends the set of features covered by a single system, the product population approach extends the set of products that can be derived from the shared product line artefacts. This does not refer to the situation where the same feature scope is populated with a more fine-grained set of products, but rather to the situation where the set of covered features is extended to allow for a more diverse set of products to be derived.

Example. Philips Consumer Electronics presents an excellent example of this approach. As discussed in [13], Philips has adopted an approach where a set of components can be used to derive a variety of different products, including analog televisions, digital televisions, video recorders and digital set-top boxes. A number of teams around the world develop components that adhere to a rather underspecified architecture and, especially, its underlying principles. Other teams create individual products by selecting, composing and configuring components.

SPL Artefact Maturity. The product population approach increases the scope the product line in terms of features and products. Due to the wide variety of products, the architecture cannot be enforced. In addition, depending on the type of population, the architecture may even not be fully specified, because part of the variability is achieved by creative configurations of the components. There may be multiple component implementations, although some components may need to be specifically implemented for each product.

5 Related Work

Software reuse is a long standing ambition of the software engineering community, dating back to the late 1960s [9] and 1970s [10]. The increasing popularity of the object-oriented paradigm during the 1980s lead to the definition of object-oriented frameworks. As part of this work, for instance, the REBOOT project defined reuse maturity levels [7]. Also, Roberts and Johnson [11] discuss a number of maturity levels for objects oriented frameworks in the form of a pattern language.

During the 1990s, the notion of software product lines (or software system families) was adopted and achieved increasing attention as can be judged from the existence of several large European projects, including ARES, PRAISE, ESAPS and CAFE, the software product line initiative at the software engineering institute (SEI) [3], and the first conferences in the field, e.g. [6].

Several authors published work in related to this chapter. Weiss and Lai [14] present an approach that relates to the maturity level that we refer to a configurable product base. In their approach, a generator is developed that generates the specific product derivation that is required. Czarnecki and Eisenecker [4] also employ generative techniques to minimize the amount of application engineering needed. Schmid [12] discusses the process of scoping during the adoption of software product lines. In an earlier paper [2], we introduce a first attempt to classify software product line maturity levels. In that paper, we focus on the relation between maturity levels for the overall approach and the software artefacts and the organizational model selected for software development. The existing work (including our own), however, takes a single scope perspective and do not explicitly consider a situation where a hierarchy of scopes exists, where scope may have a different maturity level.

6   Conclusions

Software product lines have received wide adoption in many software companies and have proven to be very successful in achieving intra-organizational reuse. Existing literature, however, often assumes a singular transition from independent product development to a software product line approach. However, in our experience with industry we have identified that companies employ widely different approaches and that these approaches evolve over time. These approaches can be organized in a number of maturity levels. These maturity levels include standardized infrastructure, software platform, software product line and configurable product base. For a given scope in terms of features and products, each of the approaches can be applied. The optimal approach for a company depends on the maturity of the organization, but also on the maturity of the application domain.

Next to the different approaches to software product lines, we have also presented maturity levels for the product line artefacts, i.e. the architecture, components and the products. The product line architecture can be under-specified, fully specified or enforced. The components can just consist of a component interface specification, multiple component implementations and one configurable component implementation. Finally, a product can conform to the product line architecture, be a platform-based product or be derived from a configurable product base.

In Section 4, we discussed the notion of scope and the phases of scope creation, maturation and collapse that an organization typically evolves through. In addition, we discussed the hierarchical nature of scopes, i.e. a scope is often nested in broader scope. Especially in larger organizations, several levels of scope may exist. To illustrate multi scope approaches, we discussed the program of product lines and product populations approaches.

The claim and, we believe, contribution of this chapter is that the challenge with respect to intra-organizational reuse that most organizations face is not the singular adoption of a software product line, but rather the continuous maturation of the organization in terms of exploiting intra-organizational reuse at multiple levels of scope in the organization by increasing the maturity levels. Based on the conceptual framework presented in this chapter, an organization can identify the scopes it currently employs and embark on improvement initiatives at each level.

Acknowledgements

Many thanks to Osmo Vikman from Nokia who kindly provided information about the program of product lines approach as used within Nokia Networks and to Rob van Ommering for his information on the product populations approach.

References

1. Jan Bosch. *Design and Use of Software Architectures: Adopting and Evolving a Product Line Approach.* Addison-Wesley & ACM Press, May 2000.
2. Jan Bosch. Maturity and evolution in software product lines: Approaches, artefacts and organization. In *Proc. of the Second Software Product Line Conference (SPLC2)*, pages 257–271, August 2002.
3. Paul Clements and Linda Northrop. *Software Product Lines - Practices and Patterns.* Pearson Education (Addison-Wesley), 2001.
4. Krzysztof Czarnecki and Ulrich W. Eisenecker. *Generative Programming - Methods, Tools, and Applications.* Addison-Wesley, June 2000.
5. D. Dikel, D. Kane, S. Ornburn, W. Loftus, and J. Wilson. Applying software product-line architecture. *IEEE Computer*, 30(8):49–55, August 1997.
6. Patrick Donohoe, editor. *Software Product Lines - Experience and Research Directions.* Kluwer Academic Publishers, 2000.
7. E-A. Karlsson, editor. *Software Reuse - a Holistic Approach.* John Wiley & Sons, 1995.
8. R.R. Macala, L.D. Stuckey, and D.C. Gross. Managing domain-specific product-line development. *IEEE Software*, 13(1):57–67, 1996.
9. M. D. McIlroy. Mass produced software components. In P. Naur and B. Randell, editors, *Report on a Conference Sponsored by the NATO Science Committee, 7th to 11th October 1968*, Garmisch, Germany, 1969.
10. David L. Parnas. On the design and development of program families. *IEEE Transactions on Software Engineering*, 2(1), March 1976.
11. D. Roberts and R. Johnson. Evolving frameworks: A pattern language for developing object-oriented frameworks. In *Proc. of the Third Conference on Pattern Languages and Programming*, Montecillio, Illinois, 1996.
12. K. Schmid. Software product lines: Experience and research directions. In Patrick Donohoe, editor, *Proc. of the First Software Product Line Conference (SPLC1)*, pages 513–532. Kluwer Academic Publishers, August 2000.
13. R. van Ommering. Building product populations with software components. In *Proc. of ICSE'02*, 2002.
14. D.M. Weiss and C.T.R. Lai. *Software Product-Line Engineering - A Family-Based Software Development Process.* Addison-Wesley, 1999.

Assessment of High Integrity Software Components for Completeness, Consistency, Fault-Tolerance, and Reliability

Hye Yeon Kim[1], Kshamta Jerath[2], and Frederick Sheldon[3]

[1] Bluetooth Research Group, Samsung Electro-Mechanics, HQ
314, Meatan-3Dong, Paldal-Gu, Suwon, Kyounggi-Do, South Korea, 442-743
hyekim@ieee.org
[2] School of Electrical Engineering and Computer Science
Washington State University, Pullman, WA 99164, USA
kjerath@eecs.wsu.edu
[3] Oak Ridge National Laboratory (ORNL), PO Box 2008, MS 6363
1 Bethel Valley Road, Oak Ridge, TN 37831-6359, USA
sheldon@acm.org

Abstract. The use of formal model based (FMB) methods to evaluate the quality of components is an important research area. Except for a growing number of exceptions, FMB methods are still not really used in practice. This chapter presents two case studies that illustrate the value of FMB approaches for developing and evaluating component-based software. In the first study, Zed (or Z) and Statecharts are used to evaluate (a priori) the software requirement specification of a Guidance Control System for completeness, consistency and fault-tolerance. The second study evaluates (post-priori) the reliability of a complex vehicle system using Stochastic Activity Networks (SANs). The FMB approach presented here provides further evidence that such methods can indeed be useful by showing how these two different industrial strength systems were assessed and the results. Clearly, future investigations of this nature will help to convince software system developers using component based approaches that such FMB methods should be considered as a valuable tool toward improving the software product lifecycle (quality, schedule and cost).

1 Introduction

To manage increasing complexity and maximize code reuse, the software engineering community has, in recent years, put considerable effort into the design and development of component-based software development systems and methodologies [4]. The concept of building software from existing components arose by analogy with the way that hardware is now designed and built, using cheap, reliable standard "off-the-shelf" modules. The success of component based software technology is dependent on the fact that the *effort* needed to build component based software systems can be significantly decreased compared to

A. Cechich et al. (Eds.): Component-Based Software Quality, LNCS 2693, pp. 259–286, 2003.

traditional custom software development. Consequently, component producers have to ensure that their commercial components possess trusted *quality* [39]. To achieve a predictable, repeatable process for engineering high-quality component based software systems, it is clear that quality must be introduced and evaluated at the earliest phases of the life cycle.

Developing Component-Based Software (CBS) systems is facilitated by component reusability. The development process for CBS is very similar to the conventional software development process. In CBS development, however, the requirements specification is examined for possible composition from existing components rather than direct construction. The components can be functional units, a service provider (i.e., application programs, Web-based agent or enterprise system [13]), or components of an application ranging in size from a subsystem to a single object[1]. To ensure the quality of the final product, assessment of such components is obligatory. Some form of component qualification at the earliest possible phase of system development is therefore necessary to avoid problems in the latter phases and reduce life-cycle costs.

Evaluation of the software system must take into consideration how the components behave, communicate, interact and coordinate with each other [2]. *Reliability*, a vital attribute of the broader quality concept, is defined as the degree to which a software system both satisfies its requirements and delivers usable services [12]. Quality software, in addition to being reliable, is also robust (and fault tolerant), complete, consistent, efficient, maintainable, extensible, portable, and understandable.

In this chapter, we discuss how one can evaluate the quality of the components using formal model based (FMB) methods (e.g., Z, Statecharts, and Stochastic Activity Networks). We present an FMB framework for assessing component properties like completeness and consistency of requirement specifications using Z and Statecharts; and approaches for verifying properties like reliability using stochastic modelling formalisms. Two case studies are discussed in this context based on both a mission critical (guidance control) software requirements specification and a vehicular system with various interacting components (possibly) provided by different vendors. The assessment of quality (i.e., reliability) for elements such as anti-lock brakes, steer-by-wire and traction control are considered based on empirical data. Naturally, a single example showing the complete process would be ideal. However, our group had two different projects (one with NASA and the second with a road vehicle manufacturer). Although different applications dealing with slightly different artifacts, there are convenient similarities (i.e., comparable properties) in their application domain: embedded real-time command and control responsive systems. These different but similar systems understandably interrelate and it is hoped that the reader can *bridge* the difference.

---

[1] A software component is a unit of composition with contractually specified interface and explicit context dependencies only. It can be deployed independently and is subject to composition by third parties. The most important characteristic is the separation of the component interface from its implementation.

2   Background

Component-Based Software Development (CBSD) approaches are based on developing software systems by selecting appropriate off-the-shelf components and then assembling them using a well-defined software architecture[2]. CBSD *can* significantly reduce development cost and time-to-market, and improve maintainability, reliability and overall quality of software systems. However, quality assurance technologies for CBS must address two inseparable questions: 1) How to *certify quality* of a component? 2) How to *certify quality* of software systems based on components? (Our studies focus on this aspect.) To answer these questions, models should be developed to define the overall quality control of components and systems; metrics should be found to measure the size, complexity, reusability and reliability of components and systems; and tools should be selected to test the existing components and resulting system(s). Component requirements analysis is the process of discovering, understanding, documenting, validating and managing the requirements for a component.

Hamlet et. al., address the first question for quality assurance technologies listed above: Namely, how to certify the quality of a component? They present a theory of software system reliability based on components. The theory describes how component developers can design and test their components to produce measurements that are later used by system designers to calculate composite system reliability (i.e., without having to implement and test the system being developed). Their work describes how to make component measurements independent of operational profiles, and how to incorporate the overall system-level operational profile into the system reliability calculations. In principle, their theory resolves the central problem of assessing a component. Essentially, a component developer cannot know how the component will be used and so cannot certify it for an arbitrary use; but if the component buyer must certify each component before using it, component-based development loses much of its appeal. This dilemma is resolved if the component developer does the certification and provides the results in such a way that the component buyer can factor in the usage information later, without having to repeat the certification [14].

Another natural reason for CBSD is the drive to shorten the SD lifecycle, which motivates the integration of commercial off-the-shelf (COTS) components for rapid software development. To ensure high reliability using software components as their building blocks, dependable components must be deployed to meet the reliability requirements. The process involves assembling components together, determining the interactions among the integrated components, and taking the software architecture into consideration. Black-box based approaches may not be appropriate for estimating the reliability of such systems, as it may be necessary to investigate the system architecture, the testing strategies, as well as the separate component reliabilities. In [27], the authors assume com-

---

[2] The software architecture of a program or computing system is the structure(s) of the system that comprise the software components, the externally visible properties of those components and the relationship(s) among them.

ponents are independent and can be viewed as composed of logically individual parts that can be implemented and tested independently. In addition, transfer of control among software components follows a Markov process[3]. Sherif et al. [36], propose a similar analysis technique for distributed software systems. The technique is based on scenarios that are modelled as sequence diagrams. Using scenarios, the authors construct Component-Dependency Graphs (CDG) for reliability analysis of component-based systems.

The growing reliance on COTS components for developing *large-scale projects* comes with a price. Large-scale component reuse leads to savings in development resources, but not without having to deal with integration difficulties, performance constraints, and incompatibility of components from multiple vendors. Relying on COTS components also increases the system's vulnerability to risks arising from third-party development, which can adversely affect the quality of the system, as well as cause expenses not incurred in traditional software development. The authors of [35] introduce metrics to accurately quantify factors contributing to the overall quality of a component-based system, guiding quality and risk management by identifying and eliminating sources of risk.

An artifact or component is fit-for-purpose if it manifests the required behavior(s) in the intended context(s), while the same is true for the composed system. The whole system therefore may be fit-for-purpose and, consists of some number of artifacts in some context. Furthermore, we need to know the quality of the whole system. It doesn't make any sense to talk about the quality of a single artifact as a stand-alone entity, independent of any particular context. There is no absolute (context-free) measure of quality. However (see [37]), under some special circumstances, it is possible to carry out a completely definitive test to demonstrate that a given artifact completely satisfies a given (formal) specification. Still, this does not prove that the artifact actually meets the users stated or implied needs. A requirements statement describes what an object must satisfy when used for a given purpose, in a given context (i.e., the *actual* requirements). When developing an object for reuse, however, the developer usually does not have access to the complete set of concrete requirements. Instead, the developer attempts to build reusable objects by working against a generalized statement of requirements that hopefully covers a reasonable range of *actual* requirements.

2.1   Assessing Requirement Specifications Using Z and Statecharts

As is well known, CBS development begins by specifying the requirements like any other software development effort. The Software Requirements Specification (SRS) describes what the software must do. Naturally, the SRS takes the core role as the descriptive documentation at every phase of the life-cycle. Therefore, it is necessary to ensure the SRS contains correct and complete information for the system. For that reason, employing a verification technique is necessary for the specification to provide some support of prototyping, correctness proofs, elaboration of test data, and failure detection. To avoid problems in the later

---

[3] The next transfer of control to be executed is independent of the past history and depends only on the present component.

Fig. 1. Form of axiomatic definition

development phases and reduce the life-cycle costs, it is crucial to ensure that the specification be complete and consistent.

The completeness of a specification is defined as a lack of ambiguity in terms of creating an implementation that can satisfy the specified requirements. Thus, the specification is incomplete if the system behavior is not precisely stated because the required behavior for some events or conditions is omitted or is subject to multiple interpretations [24]. On the other hand, consistency means the specification is free from conflicting requirements and undesired non-determinism [7]. The lack of information or precision presents incompleteness, while conflicting information presents inconsistency. Hypothetically, if we distill the specification down to a simple finite state system, we may discover missing states (i.e, incompleteness) or state transitions from one state to possibly different states on the same input (i.e., conflicting non-determinism, which gives inconsistency).

Typically, fault-tolerance is considered as an implementation property that provides for (1) explicit or implicit error detection for all fault conditions, and (2) backup routines to guarantee continued service of critical functions in case errors arise during operation of the primary software [33]. For the SRS, it can be defined as (1) existence of specified requirements to detect errors for all fault conditions, and (2) presence of specified requirements that support the system robustness, software diversity, and temporal redundancy for continuing service of critical system functions in the case of failure.

Most problems can be traced to the requirements specification typically due to ambiguity [10]. Formal methods unambiguously define the requirements of software with respect to its specification. They are the primary way to have a rigorous definition of correctness of the system requirements. The decision to use formal specifications mainly depends on the criticality of the component, in term of severity of fault consequences and of the complexity of its requirements or of its development [33].

Z is classified as a model-based specification language equipped with an underlying theory that enables non-determinism to be removed mechanically from abstract formulations that result in *concrete* specifications. In combination with natural language, it can be used to produce a formal specification [41]. Let's just review some of the basic elements that make Z useful and compose part of our FMB framework strategy.

Axiom is one way to define a global object in Z. It consists of two parts: declaration and predicate (see Fig. 1). The predicate constrains the objects introduced in the declaration.

Schemas are the main structuring mechanism used to create patterns and objects. The schema notation is used to model system states and operations.

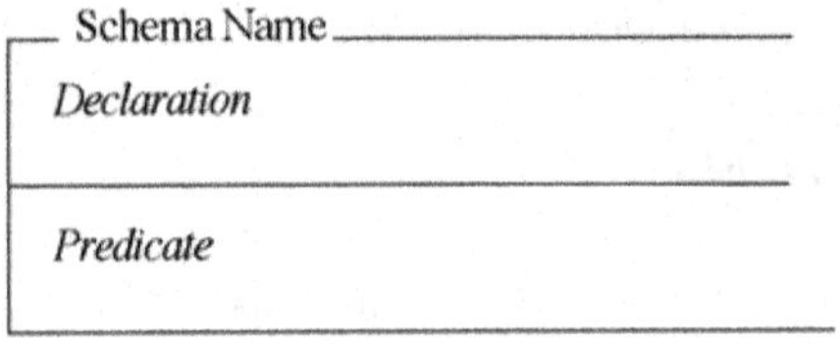

Fig. 2. Form of a schema

A *schema* consists of two parts: a declaration of variables and a predicate constraining their values (see Fig. 2). The name of a schema is optional, however, it is more convenient to give a name because it can be referenced within other schemas.

The *free type* is used to define new types similar to the enumerated types provided by many programming languages [20]. The free type in Fig. 3 introduces a collection of constants, one for each element of the set *source*. Constructor is an injective function whose target is the set *Free_type_name*. Consistency of free type can only be validated when each of the constructions (i.e., the set *source*) is involved with Cartesian products, finite power sets, finite functions, and finite sequences [41]. Axioms and abbreviations are used to define global constants and functions. The abbreviation T_n==seq $\mathcal{N}$ states that T_n is another name for sequence of natural numbers.

$$Free\_type\_name ::= constants \mid constructor \langle\!\langle source \rangle\!\rangle$$

Fig. 3. Free type notation

The state of the system and the relationship between the states of various components can be explained using the aforementioned Z formalism. The production of such a specification helps one to understand requirements, clarify intentions to identify assumptions and explain correctness. These facilities are useful and essential in clarifying ambiguities and solidifying one's understanding of the requirements.

Statecharts, a state-based formal diagrammatic language, are a visual formalism for describing states and transitions in a modular fashion, enabling cluster orthogonality (i.e., concurrency) and refinement, and supporting the capability for moving between levels of abstraction. The kernel of the approach is the extension of conventional state diagrams by AND/OR decomposition of states together with inter-level transitions, and a broadcast mechanism for communication between concurrent components. The two essential ideas enabling this extension are the provision for depth (level) of abstraction and the notion of orthogonality. In other words, Statecharts = State-diagrams + depth + orthogonality + broadcast-communication [15].

Statecharts provide a way to specify complex reactive systems both in terms of how objects communicate and collaborate and in terms of how they behave internally[4]. Together, Activity-charts and Statecharts are used to describe the system functional building blocks, activities, and the data that flows between them. These languages are highly diagrammatic in nature, constituting full-fledged visual formalisms, complete with rigorous semantics that provide an intuitive and concrete representation for inspecting and (mechanically) checking for conflicts [16]. The Activity-charts and Statecharts are used to specify conceptual system models for symbolic simulation. Using the simulation method, assumptions are verified, faults may be injected, and hidden errors are identified that represent inconsistencies or incompleteness in the specification.

Ambiguous statements in the SRS are revealed during the construction of Z schemas. When a misinterpreted specification in Z is uncovered during the execution of the Statecharts model, the Z specification can be refined using the test results.

2.2   Predicting Reliability Using Stochastic Formalisms

As with hardware systems, CBS systems can be modelled early on during the system lifecycle. A mathematical model is used to predict (estimate in the case that empirical data is available) the value of some quality attribute. For example, the reliability of the software system is based on parameters that are previously known or evaluated during integration and test of the software components [12]. Modelling and subsequent sensitivity analysis of these models can provide measurements regarding overall software-system reliability and suitability of a particular component for being used as part of the whole system context.

Stochastic Petri Nets (SPNs) and Stochastic Activity Networks (SANs) are formalisms that can be used to create concise representations/models of real-time, concurrent, asynchronous, distributed, parallel and/or non-deterministic systems. Tools exist to automatically generate and solve the underlying Markov chains from these representations.

Structurally, SANs consist of four primitive objects: *places, activities, input gates* and *output gates* [3]. Places represent the state of the modelled system. They are represented graphically as circles. Each place contains a certain number of tokens which represents the marking of the place. The set of all place markings represents the marking of the network. Activities represent actions in the modelled system that take some specified amount of time to complete. There are of two types: *timed* and *instantaneous*. Timed activities have durations that impact the performance of the modelled system, and are represented as hollow ovals. Instantaneous activities represent actions that complete in a negligible amount of time compared to the other activities in the system. *Case probabilities*, represented graphically as circles on the right side of an activity, model uncertainty associated with the completion of an activity.

Input gates control the enabling of activities and define the marking changes that will occur when an activity completes. They are represented graphically as triangles with their point connected to the activity they control. Like input

---

[4] Statecharts are utilized in this respect by way of the Statemate Magnum tool.

gates, output gates define the marking changes that will occur when activities complete. The only difference is that output gates are associated with a single case. They are represented graphically as triangles with their flat side connected to an activity or a case.

We discuss reliability modelling of component-based software systems (using SANs) emphasizing failure severity levels and coincident errors among components to predict the overall system reliability. The reliability of a CBS system is a function of the reliabilities of the individual components that compose the complete system. If the components were all independent of each other, the overall reliability would simply be the product of the reliabilities of all the individual components. However, in practice, this is hardly the case. Components interact with each other, depending on other components for control information or data. Any representation claiming to realistically model the system must take this interaction into consideration. Coincident errors have been considered and modelled for predicting system reliability in [1, 8, 9, 21, 25, 29, 34].

Further, errors and/or defects occurring in the system have varying levels of severity and pose different levels of threat to the overall system operation. A system having considerable number of high-severity defects is certainly less reliable than a system having more low-severity defects. Predicting the reliability/availability based on these characteristics of the system provides more objective and concrete information that can be used in assessing the risk tradeoffs and integrity levels. Severity is an important candidate to weight the data used in reliability calculations and must be incorporated into the model to determine the probability that the system survives, including efficient or acceptable levels of degraded operation. Severity of failures has been considered in the context of gracefully degrading systems in [11] and modelled using Markov Reward Models in [17].

Modelling and prediction of system reliability on the basis of these three characteristics is explained in the next section. Practical issues that stand in the way of developing such models include: (1) obtaining component reliability data, (2) a simple yet effective model being able to capture only limited (but significant) interactions among components, (3) the need to estimate fault correlation between components, and (4) reliability depends on how the system is used, making usage information an important part of the evaluation [26].

Further, two distinct problems that arise while using Markov processes are largeness and stiffness [32]. The size of a Markov model used for the evaluation of a system grows exponentially with the number of components in the system. If there are n components, the Markov model may have up to 2^n states. This causes the analysis to take a great deal of time. Stiffness is due to the different orders of magnitude (sometimes 10^6 different) between the rates of occurrence of performance-related events and the rates of rare, failure-related events. Stiffness leads to convergence difficulty in solving the model (i.e., numerical instability). Any attempt at modelling using Markov models must address these two problems. A case study is presented in Section 4 to illustrate the use of our technique on a real-world problem and how the challenges can be overcome.

3 A Framework for Evaluating Quality

We present two different studies that combine three formal approaches (i.e., logical analysis using Z, visualization, simulation and testing using Statecharts, and stochastic analysis using SANs) into a general FMB framework for the development of CBS systems. A CBS system is made up of numerous components that may be derived from different sources, including COTS or other proprietary components. It is important to first identify the appropriate components for the system being built, by carefully analyzing the system requirements [6]. Fig. 4 shows a process for selecting the appropriate components.

- *Identify usable components.* To investigate all possible components that may be useful in the system, a vast number of possible candidates must be available as well as tools for finding them.
- *Select components that meet system requirements.* Often the requirements cannot be fulfilled completely. A trade-off analysis is needed to adjust the system architecture and to reformulate requirements when selected, existing components do not completely cover stated requirements. This analysis will determine whether existing components may be used.
- *As necessary, create proprietary components for use in the system.* In the CBSD process this procedure is less attractive because it involves more effort and lead-time. On the other hand, components that include core-functionality of the product are likely to be developed internally as they will provide the competitive advantage of the product.
- *Adapt the selected components to the existing component model or requirement specification.* Some components may be directly integrated into the system while others will be modified through a modification and refinement process (e.g., using wrapping code for adaptation, etc.).
- *Compose and deploy the components using an appropriate framework.* Component models themselves would provide the framework needed.
- *Replace earlier versions with updated component versions.* This corresponds with system maintenance (both perfective and corrective).

This process enables the selection of suitable components for building the CBS system. The lower part of Fig. 4 illustrates the development stages of a CBS system needed to ensure quality (complete, consistent and dependable). The process starts with the *specification stage*, in which there exist only abstract notions of different components. The components are identified and requirement verification and validation of the software requirement specification can be carried out using Z and Statecharts (or other suitable formal analysis method and tools). It is important to uncover bugs and ambiguities in the requirements earlier in the lifecycle than later, to avoid having to take (more) costly corrective actions at later stages in the process.

After verifying the requirement specification, the CBS system is designed and prototyped using mathematical models (e.g., stochastic or analytic techniques) to evaluate and predict the quality and reliability of the proposed system. Reliability assessment can be carried out using stochastic modelling methods if

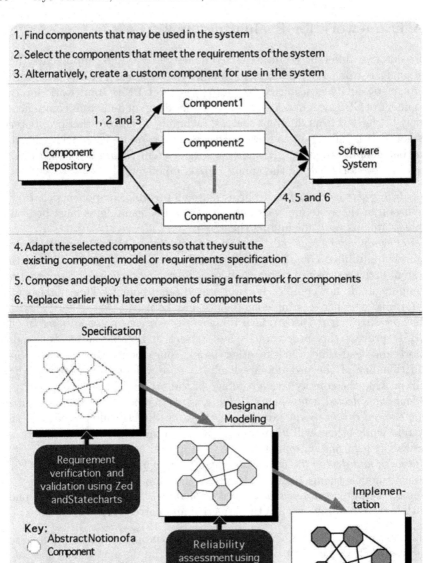

1. Find components that may be used in the system

2. Select the components that meet the requirements of the system

3. Alternatively, create a custom component for use in the system

4. Adapt the selected components so that they suit the
   existing component model or requirements specification

5. Compose and deploy the components using a framework for components

6. Replace earlier with later versions of components

Fig. 4. FMB development framework for CBS system

the reliability data for the individual components and possible correlation between components is available. Without such data, the analysis can also be conducted using hypothetical values for the purpose of determining the system sensitivities. As shown in Fig. 5, the use of these formal methods (Z, Statecharts

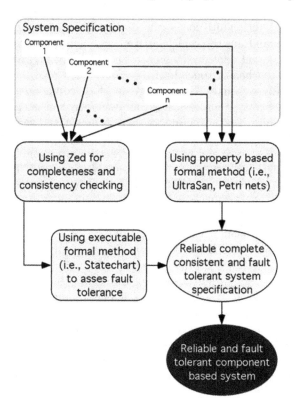

Fig. 5. Applying formal methods to CBSD

and SANs) at different stages in the CBSD lifecycle may result in the development of a dependable CBS system (assuming the model is transformed into the implementation—a significant assumption).

4   Case Studies

This section applies the concepts and framework presented above using two different case studies. The first study presents the use of both Z and Statecharts for verification and validation of software requirements of a Guidance Control Software (GCS) System for the Viking Mars Lander. The second study models and analyzes the reliability of an Anti-lock Braking System of a passenger vehicle.

4.1   Assessment of GCS System Requirements

The GCS principally provides vehicle control during the Lander's terminal descent phase[5]. After initialization, the GCS starts sensing vehicle altitude. When

---

[5] The Lander has three accelerometers, one Doppler radar with four beams, one altimeter radar, two temperature sensors, three gyroscopes, three pairs of roll engines, three axial thrust engines, one parachute release actuator, and a touch down sensor.

a predefined engine ignition altitude is sensed, the GCS begins guidance and control. The software maintains the vehicle attitude along a predetermined velocity-altitude contour. Descent continues along this contour until a predefined engine shut off altitude is reached or touchdown is sensed.

In this first study we qualified a subset (i.e., four components) of the GCS requirements in a two-step process for completeness, consistency, and fault-tolerance. Z was applied first using abstraction to detect and remove ambiguity from the Natural Language based (NL-based) GCS SRS. Next, Statecharts and Activity-charts were constructed from the Z description to enable visualization and symbolic simulation (i.e., inputs, processing and outputs). The system behavior was assessed under normal and abnormal conditions. Faults were seeded into the model (i.e., executable specification) to simulate abnormal conditions. In this way, the integrity of the SRS was assessed which identified both missing and inconsistent requirements.

Using our approach, the NL-based requirements are first re-written into the Z notation. The schema is the principle structuring mechanism (using refinement based predicate and propositional logic and set theory). Eighty percent of the SRS was completely translated into schemas thereby clarifying and concretizing the selected requirement subset. The schemas were subsequently (and iteratively) translated into Statecharts (and Activity-charts), which provided a new (executable) perspective. Simulations were performed to verify that no non-deterministic state and activity transitions exist. Some improperly defined function and data items were found in the schemas. For example, we found that correctly specified (when compared to the SRS) function and data items in both the Z and Statechart models elicited unexpected outputs during simulation. We refined the schemas, as a consequence, to avoid erroneous simulation output.

Furthermore, during the simulations, faults were injected into State and Activity-charts by changing state variable values at various breakpoints (chosen randomly). The outputs were then compared to the expected output (determined by the formula given in the SRS). This procedure enabled us to evaluate the system's ability to cope with unexpected system failures. Fig. 6 shows an example using the FRAME_COUNTER input variable that illustrates the complete translation cycle. The top box in Fig. 6 represents the NL-based SRS. The middle box of Fig. 6 represents the Z Specification while the bottom box shows the Statechart model of the ARSP (Altimeter Radar Sensor Processing) sub-module. In the SRS, the FRAME_COUNTER is defined as an integer with range $[1 - (2^{31} - 1)]$. In Z, the FRAME_COUNTER is declared as a set of natural numbers in the signature part, and the range of the variable is defined within the schema's predicate. The Statechart representation of the FRAME_COUNTER variable is presented with the direction of data transfer from EXTERNAL to the ARSP Module. Its type and value range are defined in the Statemate data dictionary (not shown)[6].

---

[6] For this case study, four components of the GCS system were assessed including the ARSP, Roll Engine Control Law Processing (RECLP), CP (Communication Processing), and GP (Guidance Processing) components. Each component was evaluated both separately and in an integrated form using our Z/Statecharts approach.

Step 1: NL-Based SRS

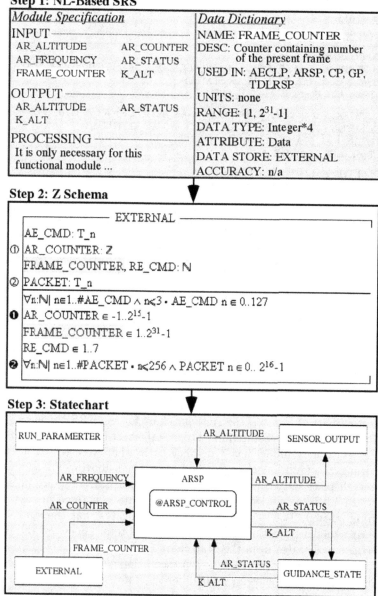

Module Specification	Data Dictionary
INPUT	NAME: FRAME_COUNTER
AR_ALTITUDE AR_COUNTER	DESC: Counter containing number
AR_FREQUENCY AR_STATUS	of the present frame
FRAME_COUNTER K_ALT	USED IN: AECLP, ARSP, CP, GP,
	TDLRSP
OUTPUT	UNITS: none
AR_ALTITUDE AR_STATUS	RANGE: [1, 2^{31}-1]
K_ALT	DATA TYPE: Integer*4
PROCESSING	ATTRIBUTE: Data
It is only necessary for this	DATA STORE: EXTERNAL
functional module ...	ACCURACY: n/a

Step 2: Z Schema

```
┌─────────── EXTERNAL ──────────────────────────┐
│ AE_CMD: T_n                                     │
① AR_COUNTER: Z                                   │
│ FRAME_COUNTER, RE_CMD: N                        │
② PACKET: T_n                                     │
├─────────────────────────────────────────────────┤
│ ∀n:N| n∈1..#AE_CMD ∧ n⩽3 · AE_CMD n ∈ 0..127   │
❶ AR_COUNTER ∈ -1..2¹⁵-1                          │
│ FRAME_COUNTER ∈ 1..2³¹-1                        │
│ RE_CMD ∈ 1..7                                   │
❷ ∀n:N| n∈1..#PACKET · n⩽256 ∧ PACKET n ∈ 0.. 2¹⁶-1 │
└─────────────────────────────────────────────────┘
```

Step 3: Statechart

Fig. 6. Translation example from NL-based SRS to Statecharts

The ARSP, as a functional unit, reads the altimeter counter provided by the altimeter radar sensor and converts the data into a measure of distance to the surface of Mars. The ARSP schema (Fig. 7) describes the function of the ARSP unit. The Schema imports the ARSP_RESOURCE and the ARSP_FUNCTION

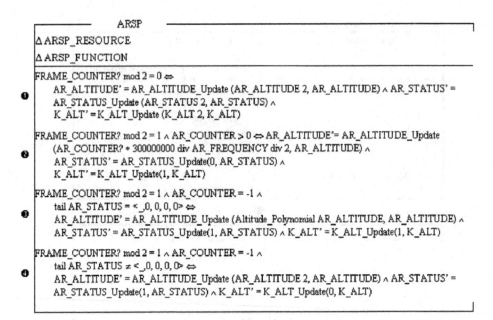

Fig. 7. ARSP schema with predicate expressions numbered 1–4

schema for modification[7]. Predicate (1) requires that the current AR_ALTITU-DE, AR_STATUS, and K_ALT element values be the same as the predecessors when the FRAME_COUNTER? is even. Predicate (2)–(4) describe the ARSP functional unit in the same manner as for predicate 1.

The bottom part of Fig. 6 is the Activity-chart for the ARSP schema shown in Fig. 7 and has one control state linked to a Statechart (@ARSP_CONTROL). This ARSP Statechart model has 4 distinct paths that were tested for fault-tolerance using the fault injection method (described above). The simulation results for each path (i.e., the state transitions shown in Fig. 8) are presented in Table 1. E_1 in Table 1 means that the given state is entered at first when the execution started. The "-" mark in Table 1 indicates that the state is not entered during model execution. The Activity and State names are the names of the activities and states from the Statechart.

Fig. 8 gives the finite state machine representation of the Statecharts model for the ARSP component showing four different state transition *paths*. To appreciate how the fault injection is performed note, for example, the simulation starts from the first state "ARSP_CONTROL". When the simulation process reaches the "ARSP_START" state, the selected variable value is altered (i.e., representing an injected fault, e.g., memory error). The simulation then continues until the "DONE" state is reached. At this point the output values are compared with the expected values.

---

[7] Note, the various "_Update" functions used in the ASRP schema are defined in the ASRP_FUNCTION schema, which is not shown.

Table 1. ARSP component simulation results

Name of Chart	Activity/State Name	Transition Paths			
		1	2	3	4
ARSP	ARSP	E_1	E_1	E_1	E_1
	@ARSP_CONTROL	E_2	E_2	E_2	E_2
ARSP_CONTROL	ARSP_START	E_3	E_3	E_3	E_3
	KEEP_PREVIOUS_VALUE	E_4	-	-	-
	ESTIMATE_ALTITUDE	-	E_4	-	-
	CALCULATE_ALTITUDE	-	-	E_4	-
	KEEP_PREVIOUS	-	-	-	E_4
	DONE	E_5	E_5	E_5	E_5

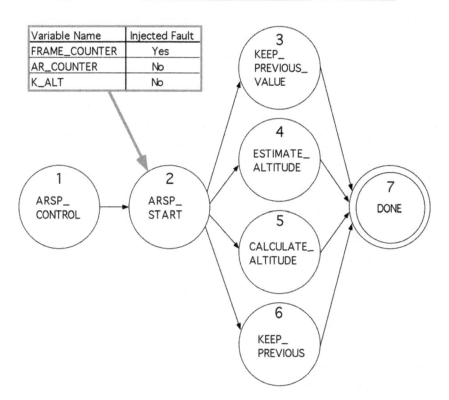

Fig. 8. State transition diagram showing fault injection locale

Table 2 details the steps used for injecting faults by altering a system state variable (e.g., FRAME_COUNTER) at a certain state or so-called breakpoint (e.g., ARSP_START) during the simulation. "-" implies don't care and "*" indicates an estimated value in the table. The expected values of the output variables are not the same as the actual values of the output due to the state variable change. Again, the expected values are determined based on equations given in the requirements specification.

Table 2. Detailed fault injection data

	Variables	Before Execution	Expected Values	After Execution
	FRAME_COUNTER	2	2	2
Input	AR_STATUS	-	[1,1,0,0,0]	[1/0,1,0,0,0]
	AR_COUNTER	-1	-1	-1
	AR_STATUS	[1,0,0,0,0]	[1,1,0,0,0]	[1/0,1,0,0,0]
Output	K_ALT	[1,1,1,1,1]	[1,1,1,1,1]	[1,1,1,1,1]
	AR_ALTITUDE	[2000, -, -, -, -]	[2000, 2000, -, -, -]	[*, 2000, -, -, -]

Table 3. ARSP fault injection results

	Altered State Variable											
State where fault is injected	FRAME_COUNTER				AR_COUNTER				AR_STATUS			
	Path				Path				Path			
	1	2	3	4	1	2	3	4	1	2	3	4
ARSP_START	x	x	x	x	x	x	x	x	x	x	x	x
KEEP_PREVIOUS_VALUE	√	√	√	√	√	√	√	√	√	√	√	√
ESTIMATE_ALTITUDE	√	√	√	√	√	N/A	√	√	√	N/A	√	√
CALCULATE_ALTITUDE	√	√	√	√	√	√	x	√	√	√	√	√
KEEP_PREVIOUS	√	√	√	√	√	√	√	√	√	√	√	√
DONE	√	√	√	√	√	√	√	√	√	√	√	√

The fault injection results are described in Table 3 (bold 'x' indicates the aforementioned example described in Fig. 8). This table shows 72 test results (outputs) from 12 different simulation runs. An "x" indicates an incorrect output, √ indicates no defect and "N/A" indicates not applicable. The "State where fault is injected" column is the same state defined in the Statecharts model (also shown in Fig. 8). The result table indicates that all output values are incorrect when faults are injected to the ARSP_START state[8]. In addition, a fault injected into the CALCULATE_ALTITUDE state produces erroneous outputs. Therefore, one can conclude these two Statechart model states are the most vulnerable.

Based on the simulation results, the SRS was determined to be incomplete. To remedy the situation, the AR_FREQUENCY value must be bounded to prevent the AR_ALTITUDE value from exceeding its limit. To do this, one of the following conditions should be included:

1. $1 \leq AR\_FREQUENCY \leq AR\_COUNTER \times 75000$
2. $AR\_COUNTER = -1 \mid$
$$(0 \leq AR\_COUNTER \leq AR\_FREQUENCY/75000)$$

Using Statemate, a GCS Activity-chart (Fig. 9) is developed inside of the GCS project. Activities are represented by rectangles and States are represented by rectangles with rounded corners. Every activity must have only one control state. The GCS activity (representing the GCS schema—see Fig. 10) interacts

---

[8] Any false/erroneous input given in the initial state causes incorrect output and the ARSP_START state is the initial state for the ARSP component.

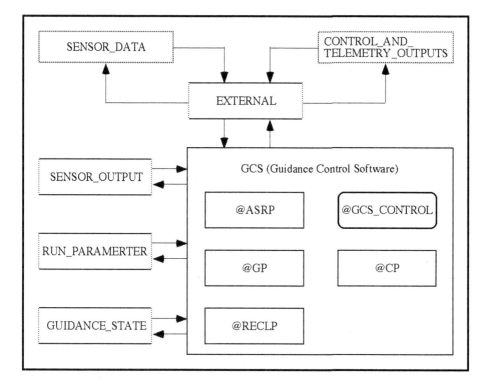

Fig. 9. GCS Activity-chart

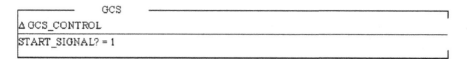

Fig. 10. GCS schema

with four data stores (represented by rectangles with dotted vertical edges), which contain data definitions. The data stores contain the same variable definitions as in the corresponding Z schemas. The "@" symbol indicates a chart linked to a particular state or activity. For example, the @GCS_CONTROL state represents a link with the GCS_CONTROL Statechart. The @ARSP, @CP, @ GP, and @ RECLP activities represent the four GCS components and are linked to their own Activity-charts respectively.

The GCS project has GCS Activity-charts and four sub-Activity-charts. Each Activity-chart has one control state that is linked to a Statechart. Most of the Statecharts used for controlling activities are divided into several Statecharts, which use super-states to reduce complexity. Table 4 gives the execution orders of the GCS Statechart model, which are equivalent to the Z specification of the GCS system. The execution test results show that the Statecharts model does

Table 4. GCS excerpt high-level activity or state charts simulation results

Name of chart	Activity/State Name	Activity/State Transition Order					
	@GCS_CONTROL	En_1	En_{33}				
	@ARSP	En_4	En_7				
GCS	@GP	En_{14}	En_{17}				
	@RECLP	En_{24}	En_{27}				
	@CP	En_9	En_{12}	En_{19}	En_{22}	En_{29}	En_{31}
	INITIALIZATION	En_2	En_3				
GCS_CONTROL	@SUBFRAME1	En_5	En_{13}				
	@SUBFRAME2	En_{15}	En_{23}				
	@SUBFRAME3	En_{25}	En_{33}				
SUBFRAME1	RUN_ARSP	En_6	En_8				
	RUN_CP	En_{10}	En_{11}				
SUBFRAME2	RUN_GP	En_{16}	En_{18}				
	RUN_CP	En_{20}	En_{21}				
SUBFRAME3	RUN_RECLP	En_{26}	En_{28}				
	RUN_CP	En_{30}	En_{32}				

not have absorbing states or activities. Moreover, all of the activities and states
are reachable and there is no inconsistency in the model. This result indicates
that it is feasible to assess the overall structure of components integration using
Z and Statecharts for completeness and consistency. The approach provides a
way to deal with a complex set of requirements for a component based embedded
control system symbiotically utilizing verification and validations tools (Z/Eves
from ORA Canada [31] and Statemate from ilogix [19]).

4.2   Reliability Assessment of the ABS of a Passenger Vehicle

The increasingly common use of software embedded in critical systems has created the need to depend on them even more than before, and to measure just
how dependable they are. Knowing that the system is reliable is absolutely necessary for safety-critical systems, where any kind of failure may result in an
unacceptable loss of human life. This case study uses an analytical approach
for estimating the reliability of a CBS system. It demonstrates our approach to
estimating the reliability of the system by taking the architecture of the CBS
system and the reliabilities of the individual components into consideration.

Anti-Lock Braking System Description. The system under study here is
an embedded vehicle sub-system (including both hardware and software components). A complex embedded vehicle system (like the Anti-lock Braking System)
is composed of numerous components and the probability that the system survives (efficient or acceptable degraded performance) depends directly on each of
the constituent components.

Anti-lock Braking System (ABS) is an integrated part of the total vehicle
braking system. It prevents wheel lockup during an emergency stop by modu-
lating the brake pressure and permits the driver to maintain steering control

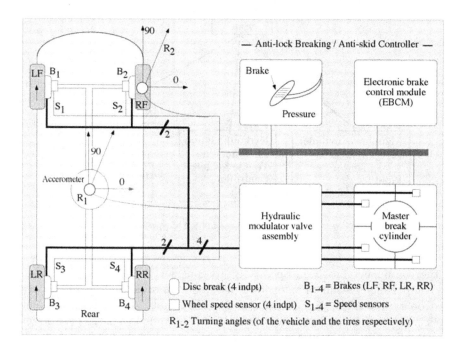

Fig. 11. Top-level schematic showing sensors/actuators and processing

while braking. Fig. 11 shows a top level schematic of the ABS. The ABS of a passenger vehicle is composed of the following components: (*i*) Wheel Speed Sensors—These measure wheel-speed and transmit information to an electronic control unit. (*ii*) Electronic Control Unit (Controller)—This receives information from the sensors, determines when a wheel is about to lock up and controls the hydraulic control unit. (*iii*) Hydraulic Control Unit (Hydraulic Pump)—This controls the pressure in the brake lines of the vehicle. (*iv*) Valves—Valves are present in the brake line of each brake and are controlled by the hydraulic control unit to regulate the pressure in the brake lines.

Stochastic Activity Network (SAN) Model. The ABS is modelled using SANs [3], which are a stochastic formalism used for performance modelling. Tools exist to automatically generate the underlying Markov chains from a high level representation of the system in the form of a SAN model. UltraSAN is an X-window based software tool for evaluating systems that are represented as SANs.

Assumptions. Modelling the ABS using SANs requires a number of simplifying assumptions. To allow a Markov chain analysis, the time to failure of all components is assumed to have an exponential distribution. This signifies that the distribution of the remaining life of a component does not depend on how

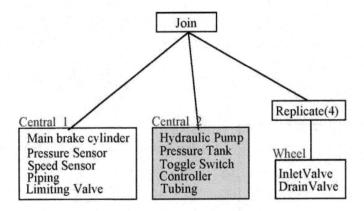

Fig. 12. The ABS composed SAN model

long the component has been operating. To consider the severity of failures, every component is assumed to operate in three modes: normal operation, degraded operation or causing loss of stability. To be able to model coincident failures, some correlation between failures of certain components (like controller and hydraulic pump) is assumed.

Composed SAN Model. The composed ABS model is shown in Fig. 12. The model consists of three individual SAN subnets: *Central_1*, *Central_2* and *Wheel*. The *Wheel* subnet is replicated four times to represent the four wheels of the vehicle. The division into these three categories is done to facilitate the representation of coincident failures. Such a distribution/categorization avoids replicating of subnets where unnecessary (for modelling severity and coincident failures) and thereby prevents the potential state explosion problem.

SAN Subnets Modelling Failure Severity and Coincident Failures. All subnets when combined to form the composed model share some common places: *degraded, LOS, LOV* and *halted*. The first three places represent the severity of failure, while the *halted* place is relevant in the context of the halting condition (i.e., system failure). The *Central_2* subnet is shown in Fig. 13. The presence of tokens in *degraded, LOS* and *LOV* represents the system operation under degraded mode, loss of stability and loss of vehicle respectively. The system is operating normally when there are no tokens in any of these three places.

The subnet is instantiated with a single token in the *central_2* place. The *central2_op* activity fires and deposits a token in each of the five places: *hydraulicPump, pressureTank, toggleSwitch, controller* and *tubing*. The portion of the subnet for the *controller* component is highlighted in Fig. 13 and discussed here in the context of severity of failures. The *controllerFail* activity models the failure of the controller. There are three possible outcomes of this activity. The *controller* either degrades (with probability 0.2, output gate *controllerDe-*

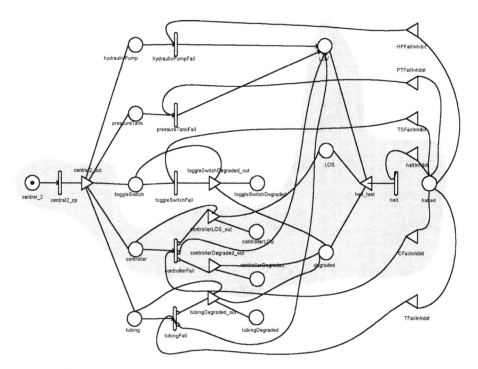

Fig. 13. Central_2 subnet with the controller component highlighted

graded_out), or causes loss of stability (with probability 0.4, output gate *con-trollerLOS_out*), or causes loss of vehicle (with probability 0.4, output to *LOV*). In the former two cases the controller continues to operate in a degraded manner, as is evident by the recycling back of the token to the *controller* place. Further, the failure rate in this situation increases by two (for degraded) and four (for loss of stability) orders of magnitude respectively. The code snippet that achieves this is shown in Table 5.

Coincident failures involving two components are represented by causing the failure of one component (degraded operation or loss of stability) to increase the failure rate of the dependent component. The degeneration of a component A to a degraded mode causes the failure rate of a "related" component B to increase by two orders of magnitude. The failure of component A to a lost stability mode causes the failure rate of a "related" component B to increase by four orders of magnitude. Table 5 shows the rates for the activities modelling the failure of the controller and the hydraulic pump (other component failure rates are modelled in a similar manner). Case 1, 2 and 3 represent the probabilities of the failure causing loss of vehicle, loss of stability and degraded mode respectively.

Since UltraSAN requires the failure rate to be specified in a single state-ment, the conditional operator available in the C programming language is used. Consider the *controllerFail* activity in Table 5. Since a degenerated tub-ing (i.e., in degraded mode) is assumed to affect the failure rate of the con-

280 Hye Yeon Kim, Kshamta Jerath, and Frederick Sheldon

Table 5. Activity rates model severity and coincident failures

Activity	Rate	Probability		
		Case 1	Case 2	Case 3
controllerFail	MARK(controllerLOS)!=0? controllerRate*10000: (MARK(controllerDegraded)!=0 || MARK(tubingDegraded)!=0 ?controllerRate*100 :controllerRate)	0.4	0.4	0.2
hydraulicPumpFail	MARK(controllerLOS)!=0? hydraulicPumpRate*10000: (MARK(controllerDegraded)!=0 ?hydraulicPumpRate*100 :hydraulicPumpRate)	1.0	-	-

troller, if the number of tokens in the *tubingDegraded* place is not zero (i.e., MARK(tubingDegraded)!=0), the failure rate for the controller increases by two orders of magnitude (i.e., controllerRate*100). Similarly, for the *hydraulicPump-Fail* activity, it is assumed that a failed controller affects the failure rate of the hydraulic pump. Thus, the failure rate for the hydraulic pump increases by four orders of magnitude if the controller has failed causing loss of stability, and increases by two orders of magnitude if the controller is operating in a degraded mode.

Reliability Measure and Halting Condition. The required reliability measure is defined as a reward rate function. The reward rates for the SAN model are defined to take the degraded operation of the system into consideration.

Reward rates are specified using a predicate and a function. The function represents the rate at which the reward is accumulated in the states when the predicate evaluates to true. Fig. 14 shows the reward rate used to calculate reliability. As long as the system is functioning (i.e., not in an absorbing state), the reward accumulates as a function of the number of tokens in the *degraded*, *LOS* and *LOV* places. The function evaluates to 1.0 when there are no tokens in any of those three places indicating normal operation. The reliability is 0 when the system has stopped functioning (in an absorbing state). For all other states, the reliability ranges from 1.0 to 0.0 depending on how degraded the system is (indicated by the number of tokens in those three places).

This SAN model recycles tokens when the system is either operating in normal mode or degraded mode. Thus, it is necessary to explicitly impose a halting condition to indicate an absorbing state. The *halted* place common to all the subnets is used to specify the halting condition. Five or more tokens in *degraded*, or three or more tokens in *LOS*, or one or more token in *LOV*, cause a token to appear in *halted*. The presence of a token in this place is the indication of an absorbing state in the corresponding SAN. This is achieved by having an input condition on each activity stating that the activity is enabled only if there are no

---

Predicate:
  MARK(halted)==0

Function:
  1.0/(1+MARK(degraded)+MARK(LOS)+MARK(LOV))

Fig. 14. Reward rate to calculate reliability

tokens in the *halted* place (i.e., MARK(*halted*)==0). The presence of a token in *halted* thus disables all the activities in the model, thereby causing an absorbing state.

Reliability Analysis Results. The reliability of the system at time t is computed as the expected instantaneous reward rate at time t. To determine the reliability of the ABS, transient analysis of the developed SAN models was carried out using the instant-of-time transient solver available in the UltraSAN tool. The reliability was measured between 0 and 5×10^4 hours. The time duration was deliberately conservative, even though the average life span of a passenger vehicle ranges from 3000–9000 hours, the reliability measures were determined for up to 5×10^4 hours.

The reliability measure was predicted at 11 different points along the range of 0 to 5×10^4 hours. The interval between the points did not remain constant along the entire time range and therefore the X-axis is not linear and should be taken into account when viewing the results graphs. The expected values of reliability at various time instances were plotted as a function of time. In Fig. 15, the Y-axis gives the measure of interest—the reliability; while the time range (0 to 5×10^4 hours) is shown along the X-axis. As expected, the reliability steadily decreases with time. The dashed line indicates the reliability function when coincident failures are modelled and the complete line indicates the reliability function when coincident failures are not modelled.

The reliability functions diverge perceptibly after around 1000 hours of operation, and the difference continues to increase with time. At 5×10^4 hours, the reliability has dropped down to 0.21 when coincident failures are modelled, and down to 0.30 when coincident failures are not modelled, a difference of 0.09 in reliability in the two cases within 5×10^4 hours. Considering the time period approximately around the expected lifetime of the vehicle (3,000-9,000 hours), the difference in reliability after 5000 hours of operation is approximately 0.0253 and after 10^3 hours is 0.0493. This clearly indicates that representing severity and coincident failures in the model contributes to predicting the system reliability that may be closer to how the real system will behave considering the underlying assumptions.

The Mean Time to Failure calculated at 5×10^4 hours in the case where coincident failures are not modelled is approximately 29,000 hours, and in the case where coincident failures are modelled is approximately 25,000 hours, a difference of 4,000 hours. It is important to realize that these results are only for

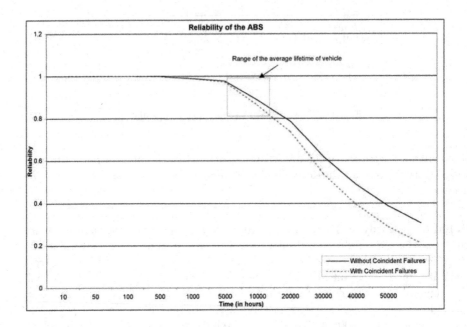

Fig. 15. Reliability results for severity and coincident failures

the limited number of coincident failures and levels of severity that have been modelled. Clearly, modelling severity and coincident failures have a significant contribution in determining the system reliability at any given instant of time.

Validity Concerns. A model is always a compromise between precision and simplicity. How closely a model mirrors its originator or the vision of the system is in direct conflict with how easily and efficiently the model can be analyzed (i.e., solved with respect to its predicted behavior). The models described were built incrementally to achieve the best balance between faithfulness to the real system and keeping the model tractable at the same time. As a result, models of higher fidelity (more realistic) were created progressively.

5   Challenges

The CBSD paradigm has emerged from the concept of building software out of components. Using components is not such a new concept, as traditional design methods have always tried to identify parts (modules, classes, functions, etc.) that are appropriate and effectively address the principle of separation of concerns (moderated by suitable measures of cohesion and coupling). Moreover, the notion of packaging software in such a way that makes it reusable is not new either (e.g., generic packages/instantiation, inheritance/polymorphism, etc.). Notwithstanding, the CBSD paradigm, as a new sub-discipline of software engineering, has been recognized as an important new development that brings support for developing dependable and maintainable high integrity systems as assemblies of components as well as strategies for developing components as reusable entities that are flexible, and extensible. CBSD faces many challenges, some of which include [6]: component trustworthiness and certification [28], composition predictability [40], requirements management and component selection [18, 22, 23], long-term management of CBS systems [6], development process models, component configurations, versioning and hierarchy (e.g., nesting that causes lack of conceptual integrity [5]), dependable safety-critical systems and CBS Engineering including trustworthy, scalable, cost-effective tool support. These are some of the current challenges. The success of CBSD will heavily depend on further research and the emergence of standard formalized frameworks (e.g., FMB methods) that can endure the aforementioned challenges in the critical disciplines that support those essential activities related to CBS systems development.

6   Conclusions and Future Work

As the demand for more flexible, adaptable, extensible, and robust high integrity CBS systems accelerates, adopting new software engineering methodologies and development strategies becomes critical. Such strategies will provide for the construction of CBS systems that assemble flexible software components written at different times by various developers. Traditional software development strategies and engineering methodologies, which require development of software systems from scratch, do not adequately address these needs. CBSD works by developing and evolving software from selected reusable software components, then assembling them within appropriate software architectures. CBSD relies heavily on explicitly defined architectures and interfaces, which can be evaluated using our FMB framework. CBSD has the potential to:

- Significantly reduce the development cost and time-to-market of enterprise CBS systems,
- Enhance the reliability of CBS systems using FMB methods where each reusable component is assessed in terms of covering and satisfying requirements (e.g., complete, consistent, etc.) and undergoes reliability analysis as deemed necessary, especially for high integrity system deployment,
- Improve the maintainability of CBS systems by allowing new, higher-quality components to replace old ones; and
- Enhance the quality of CBS systems where application-domain experts develop components, while software engineers specializing in CBSD, assemble the components.

CBSD is in the very first phase of maturity. CBSD using FMB methods is even less mature. Nevertheless, formal approaches are recognized as powerful tools that can significantly change the development of software and software use in general. Tools and frameworks for building applications and systems by means of component assembly will be tantamount in meeting the challenges ahead. Standardization of domain-specific components on the interface level will make it possible to build applications and systems from components purchased from different vendors. Work on standardization in different domains continues, (e.g., the OPC Foundation [30], is working on a standard interface to make possible interoperability between automation and control applications, field systems and devices and business and office applications)[9].

The result of the first study showed how to construct a complete and consistent specification using this method (Z-to-Statecharts). The process uncovered incomplete and inconsistent requirements that were associated with ambiguities (i.e., a reader's interpretation of the natural language and its inherent lack of precision). We have demonstrated our approach can help to identify ambiguities that result in incorrectly specified artifacts (i.e., in this case, requirements).

In the second study, the characteristics of failure severity and coincident failures were successfully incorporated into the model developed for the ABS of a passenger vehicle. The models evolved over successive iterations of modelling, increasingly refined in their ability to represent different factors that affect the measure of interest (i.e. system reliability). This refinement process, we claim, gives a (potentially) more realistic model. For example, the analyses showed that the reliability predictions were different (i.e., deteriorated) when the non-functional characteristics of severity and coincident failures were incorporated. However, because the model is an abstraction of the real world problem, predictions based on the model should be validated against actual measurements observed from the real phenomena. This study can be the basis of numerous other studies, building up on the foundation provided and investigating other areas of interest (e.g., validating predictions against field observations, or finding a more realistic level of abstraction combined with a higher degree of complexity, and solving the models using supercomputers).

Acknowledgments

The authors wish to thank Dr. Tom Potok, who is the Applied Software Engineering Laboratory Group Lead at ORNL, and Dr. Stefan Greiner at Daimler-Chrysler (RIC/AS) for their help and critique. Also, Kelly Hayhurst, who is a research scientist at NASA Langley, working in the area of design correctness and certification, provided immeasurable, crucial and essential support with respect to the GCS Requirements Specification. Her help and encouragement is *deeply* appreciated.

References

1. Arlat, J., K. Kanoun, and J.-C. Laprie, Dependability Modeling and Evaluation of Software Fault-Tolerant Systems. IEEE Transactions on Computers, 1990. 39(4):504–513.

---

[9] Support for the exchange of information between components, applications, and systems distributed over the Internet will be further developed. Works related to XML [13] will be further expanded.

2. Clements, P., Bass, L., Kazman, R., and Abowd, G., Predicting Software Quality by Architecture-Level Evaluation. Component-Based Software Engineering: Selected Papers from the Software Engineering Institute, 1995: pp. 19–25.

3. Couvillion, J., Johnson, R., Obal II, W. D., Qureshi, M. A., Rai, M., Sanders, W. H., and Tvedt, J. E., Performability Modeling with UltraSAN. IEEE Software, 1991. 8(5):69–80.

4. Cox, P.T. and B. Song. A Formal Model for Component-Based Software. in Proc. of 2001 IEEE Symosium on Visual/Multimedia Approaches to Programming and Software Engineering. 2001. Stresa, Italy: IEEE. pp. 304–311.

5. Crnkovic, I., Larrson, M., Kuster, F. J., and Lau, K., Databases and Information Systems, Fourth International Baltic Workshop, Selected Papers. 2001: Kluwer Academic Publishers. pp. 237–252.

6. Crnkovic, I., Component-based Software Engineering—New Challenges in Software Development. Software Focus, 2002. 2(4):127–133.

7. Czerny, B., Integrative Analysis of State-Based Requirements for Completeness and Consistency, in Computer Science. 1998, Michigan State University.

8. Dugan, J.B. Experimental analysis of models for correlation in multiversion software. in Proc. of 5th Int'l Symposium on Software Reliability Engineering. 1994. Los Alamitos, CA: IEEE Computer Society. pp. 36–44.

9. Eckhardt, D.E. and L.D. Lee, Theoretical Basis for the Analysis of Multiversion Software Subject to Coincident Errors. IEEE Transactions on Software Engineering, 1985. 11(12):1511–1517.

10. Fitch, D., Software Safety Engineering (S2E) Program Status. 2001. sunnyday.mit.edu/safety-club/fitch.ppt.

11. Gay, F.A., Performance Evaluation for Gracefully Degrading Systems. in Proc. of 9th Annual Int'l Symposium on Fault-Tolerant Computing (FTCS-9). 1979. Madison, Wisconsin: IEEE Computer Society. pp. 51–58.

12. Glass, R.L., Software Reliability Guidebook. 1979, Englewood Cliffs, New Jersey: Prentice-Hall. pp. 241.

13. Griss, M.L. and G. Pour, Accelerating Development with Agent Components. IEEE Computer, 2001. 34(5):37–43.

14. Hamlet, D., D. Mason, and D. Woit. Theory of Software Reliability Based on Components. In Proc. of 23rd International Conference on Software Engineering (ICSE'01). 2001. Toronto, Canada: IEEE Computer Society. pp. 361–370.

15. Harel, D., Statecharts: A Visual Formalism for Complex Systems. Science of Computer Programming, 1987. 8:231–274.

16. Harel, D. and M. Politi, Modeling Reactive Systems with Statecharts. 1998: McGraw Hill.

17. Hecht, M., D. Tang, and H. Hecht. Quantitative Reliability and Availability Assessment for Critical Systems Including Software. 12th Annual Conference on Computer Assurance. 1997. Gaitherburg, Maryland.

18. Heineman, G. and W. Councill, Component-based Software Engineering: Putting the Pieces Together. 1 ed. 2001, Boston: Addison Wesley. 818.

19. I-Logix, I-Logix Inc. Website. 2002. www.ilogix.com.

20. Jacky, J., The Way of Z: practical programming with formal methods. 1997: Cambridge University Press.

21. Kanoun, K. and M. Borrel. Dependability of Fault-Tolerant Systems—Explicit Modeling of the Interactions Between Hardware and Software Components. in Proc. of 2nd Int'l Computer Performance and Dependability Symposium (IPDS). 1996. Urbana-Champaign: IEEE Computer Society. pp. 252–261.

22. Kim, H.Y., Validation of Guidance Control Software Requirements Specification for Reliability and Fault-Tolerance, in School of Electrical Engineering and Computer Science. 2002, Washington State University: Pullman. pp. 76.

23. Kotonya, G. and A. Rashid. A strategy for Managing Risks in Component-based Software Development. in Proc. of 27th Euromicro Conference. 2001. Warsaw, Poland: IEEE Computer Society. pp. 12–21.

24. Leveson, N., Safeware – system safety and computers. 1995: Addison Wesley.

25. Littlewood, B. and D.R. Miller, Conceptual Modeling of Coincident Failures in Multiversion Software. IEEE Transactions on Software Engineering, 1989. 15(12):1596–1614.

26. Littlewood, B. and L. Strigini. Software reliability and dependability: a roadmap. in Proc. of International Conference on Software Engineering. 2000. Limerick, Ireland: ACM Press. 22. pp. 175–188.

27. Lo, J.-H., Kuo, S.-Y., Lyu, M. R., and Huang, C.-Y. Optimal Resource Allocation and Reliability Analysis for Component-Based Software Applications. Computer Software and Applications Conference, COMPSAC'02. 2002. Oxford, England: IEEE Computer Society.

28. Morris, J., Lee, G., Parker, K., Bundell, G., and Chiou, P. L., Software Component Certification. IEEE Computer, 2001. 34(9):30–36.

29. Nicola, V.F. and A. Goyal, Modeling of Correlated Failures and Community Error Recovery in Multiversion Software. IEEE Transactions on Software Engineering, 1990. 16(3):350–359.

30. OPC Foundation. 2002. http://www.opcfoundation.org.

31. ORA, ORA Canada Website. 2002. http://www.ora.on.ca/.

32. Popstojanova, K.G. and K. Trivedi. Stochastic Modeling Formalisms for Dependability, Performance and Performability. Performance Evaluation: Origins and Directions. 2000: Springer-Verlag. LNCS 1769. pp. 403–422.

33. Pradham, D.K., Fault-Tolerant Computer System Design. 1996: Prentice Hall.

34. Sahner, R.A. and K. Trivedi. A hierarchical, combinatorial-Markov model of solving complex reliability models. in Proc. of ACM/IEEE Fall Joint Computer Conference. 1986. Dallas, Texas: IEEE Computer Society. pp. 817–825.

35. Sedigh-Ali, S. and R.A. Paul. Metrics-guided quality management for component-based software systems. in Proc. of Computer Software and Applications Conference, COMPSAC'01. 2001. Chicago: IEEE Computer Society. pp. 303–308.

36. Sherif, M.Y., C. Bojan, and H.A. Hany. A Component-Based Approach to Reliability Analysis of Distributed Systems. in Proc. of the 18th IEEE Symposium on Reliable Distributed Systems. 1999. Lausanne, Switzerland. pp. 158–167.

37. Veryard, R., Software Component Quality. 1997.
    http://www.users.globalnet.co.uk/~rxv/CBDmain/DIPQUE.htm.

38. Voas, J. and J. Payne, Dependability Certification of software components. Journal of Systems and Software, 2000. 52:165–172.

39. Wallin, C., Verification and Validation of Software Components and Component Based Software Systems, in Building Reliable Component Based Systems, I. Crnkovic and M. Larrson, Editors. 2002, Artech House.

40. Wallnau, K. and J. Stafford. Ensembles: Abstractions for a New Class of Design Problem. in Proc. of 27th Euromicro Conference. 2001. Warsaw, Poland: IEEE Computer Society. pp. 48–55.

41. Woodcock, J. and J. Davies, Using Z: Specification, Refinement, and Proof. Series of Computer Science. 1996: Prentice Hall International.

Reasoning about Software Architectures with Contractually Specified Components

Ralf H. Reussner[1], Iman H. Poernomo[2], and Heinz W. Schmidt[2]

[1] Fachbereich Informatik. Carl von Ossietzky Universität Oldenburg
D-26111 Oldenburg, Germany
reussner@acm.org
[2] School of Computer Science and Software Engineering
Monash University, Caulfield East, Victoria 3145, Australia
{ihp,hws}@csse.monash.edu.au

Abstract. One of the motivations for specifying software architectures explicitly is the better prediction of system quality attributes. In this chapter we present an approach for determining the reliability of component-based software architectures.

Our method is based on RADL (Rich Architecture Definition Language), an extension of DARWIN [16]. RADL places special emphasis on component interoperation and, in particular, on accounting for the effects of interoperation on system reliability. To achieve this, our methods use a notion of design-by-contract [19] for components, called parameterized contracts [26]. Our contracts involve finite state machines that allow software architects to define how a component's reliability will react to a deployment environment. We show how a system, built from contractually specified components, can be understood in terms of Markov models, facilitating system reliability analysis.

We illustrate our approach with an e-commerce example and report about empirical measurements which confirm our analytical reliability prediction by means of monitoring in our reliability testbed.

1 Introduction

Architecture-based approaches to software design involve understanding of the coarse-grain *compositional structure* of a system. This is useful, because it facilitates compositionality. Compositionality is the ability to reason about system properties based on external abstractions of system components and the overall structure of component assembly [4]. A set of important system properties are *nonfunctional* properties: quality attributes such as reliability and performance.

In this chapter, we will examine a methodology for component-based architecture specification and the prediction of system quality attributes. Our work is based on a notion of design-by-contract [19] for components, called parameterized contracts [26].

A. Cechich et al. (Eds.): Component-Based Software Quality, LNCS 2693, pp. 287–325, 2003.
© Springer-Verlag Berlin Heidelberg 2003

1.1   Components and Component-Based Architectures

A component-based software architecture describes the usage relations between coarse-grain components and the composition of components in terms of other related components.

Commonly, architectural views of component-based software are provided by an architectural description language (ADL). An ADL models configurations of

- *components*, units of independent deployment, possibly asynchronous points of computation in a system,
- *connections* between *ports* or *services* of these components, the possible types of communication and interaction within a system, and
- *compound components*, higher-level components composed of interconnected lower-level components [14, 17].

Because components can operate asynchronously, and connections are a form of loosely coupled communication, ADLs are well suited to describe concurrent, distributed and/or event-based software. Also, most ADLs have a well-defined behavioral semantics, so that configurations have a meaning which can be analyzed (to prove, for instance, safety and liveness properties). In this way, ADLs have a syntax and semantics aimed at defining and analyzing distributed configurations of components.

Architectural description is complemented by detailed design of individual components. The former is more closely connected to requirements analysis and specification, while the latter relates to implementation and verification. For the sake of a fully integrated design process, it is important to relate both aspects of system description.

An important aspect of a detailed design is component interface specifications, via component contracts. Broadly defined, a component contract is a specification of the relation between provided and required interfaces of a component. Contracts are a vital aspect of component-based software engineering (CBSE), and, we argue, can also aid architectural description. This occurs when we treat a component contract similar to a classical contract (pre- and post-conditions) for imperative programs, yielding a notion of design-by-contract for both: run-time checks of contract conformance and also static interoperability checks between contracts.

In Section 3, we define an extension of the DARWIN ADL [16]. Our extension permits a kind of component contract, called parameterized contracts [26]. We precisely define parameterized contracts and explain our notion of design-by-contract for constructing architectures.

Then we extend these techniques to a method for modelling and predicting quality attributes based on contracts.

1.2   Modelling and Prediction of Reliability

Modelling and predicting the reliability of *component based* systems bears problems that do not occur in reliability prediction of monolithic systems.

Monolithic systems can be regarded as relatively self-contained. While some components are self-contained systems themselves, most are not and require external components to operate. Consequently, their reliability depends on other external components (i.e., its deployment context).

Taking into account the organizational or personal *separation* of the development of different components and their deployment - one of the defining properties of components [34, pp. 274-275] - then it becomes clear that the component developer has only a very limited knowledge of the component deployment context. Furthermore, the component vendor usually is not willing to restrict the re-usability of a component by strong assumptions on the deployment context. As a result, the reliability (and other quality attributes) cannot be provided directly by the component vendor. More concrete, the influence of the deployment context is twofold:

Unknown usage profile: Unlike hardware systems software does not age, i.e., one cannot model software reliability as a function of time. Furthermore, the occurrence of software failures depends on the usage of the software. (It is well experienced that the same software product may expose no error or many, depending on the functionality used.) Consequently, software reliability is commonly defined as a function of the usage profile. Of course, the usage profile is part of the deployment context, i.e., is not fixed for a component.

Unknown required context: As discussed above, most components rely on other components of its environment. The exact properties of these components are not known until deployment. Such external, components include middleware (such as servers mapping web interfaces to back-office data bases), operating systems, network and transport services, etc, each potentially a point of failure if the component relies exclusively on it.

As a consequence of these two observations, the component developer cannot state explicitly the reliability of a component.

At the same time, the component-based approach is also a blessing to the software reliability engineer due to the compositionality of component-based architectures, which holds the promise of a compositional approach to reasoning about reliability. It requires that in general components are black boxes that are executable in some form. In a component based software development process therefore some of the required components will be available and can be profiled. As a result, CBSE can take an *empirical, execution-based reliability engineering* approach easing evaluation and validation of prediction. This brings component-based software reliability engineering closer to hardware reliability engineering.

For traditional software, in practice it is much harder to determine the reliability of a system in advance, since solid data on its failure can only be collected after deployment.

The availability of (some) required components and potentially (some) usage profiles of components that are parts of the "real" environment are clearly beneficial - provided the system architecture is tightly connected with the final implementation of the system. This observation translates into the following two requirements to an architectural description language:

1. the transition from system design to implementation should be made as simple as possible. Specifically for an ADL this means that concepts of the target platform (in practice: the middleware platform) should be reflected closely in the ADL [30]. This may include, for example, context interception or context attributes, such as those in .NET [22].
2. Since software architecture evolves over time, ADLs must simplify tracking architectural changes based on changes in software configuration, packaging and binary deployment.

In Section 2 we present our approach to modelling reliability based on software architectures. To make the article relatively self-contained, we discuss some fundamental issues of reliability. This will motivate our component-oriented notions of reliability.

In Section 3 we review RADL, an extension of the DARWIN ADL [16] including components with rich interfaces and parameterized contracts. In this Section we also discuss the contractual use of components and introduce parameterized contracts as a method for computing functional and extra-functional properties of a component in dependency of its environment.

Section 4 then shows how to use the modelled reliability to predict the reliability of a component assembly, and ultimately, of whole architectures. We use parameterized contracts [26]. Parameterized contracts are used to compute the reliability of provided methods from that of required methods and ultimately the reliability of provided components from those of required ones. In other words we model reliability dependencies rather than absolute reliabilities. This method overcomes the problem of missing usage and context information for components.

The assumptions used in our model for reliability prediction are discussed in Section 5. Making these assumptions explicit, eases the decision, whether our model is applicable to a certain context and facilitates scientific discussions and further enhancements of the model.

An empirical validation of our reliability model is given in 6. How to practically apply our model, especially how to collect the data required, is discussed in Section 7. Related work is discussed in Section 8. Limitations and future extensions are presented as part the conclusion (Section 9).

2   Reliability of Component-Based Software Architectures

Usually, software reliability is defined as the *probability of failure-free operation of a software system for a specified period of time in a specified environment* (e.g., [11, 15]). It is a function of (a) the *usage profile*, i.e., the inputs to and the use of the software system and (b) of the faults in the software.

2.1 Reliability, Availability and Mean-Time between Failure

For measuring and predicting system reliability, we use the following basic notions [11, 15]:

MTTF *mean time to failure* defines the average time to the next failure;
MTTR *mean time to repair* is the average time it takes to diagnose and correct a fault, including any re-assembly and restart times.
MTBF *mean time between failures* is simply defined as

$$MTBF = MTTF + MTTR$$

Failure rate is the number of failures per time - it is the reciprocal of MTBF.

Availability is defined as *the probability of a system being available when needed*, that is the fraction of time during which a component or system is operating, i.e., the uptime over the total service time in a given period:

$$A = \frac{MTTF}{MTBF} = \frac{MTTF}{MTTF + MTTR}.$$

2.2 Basic Reliability Model for a Method Call

When calling a method, several factors influence whether the method returns the correct value or not. Hence, each of this factors contribute to the method's reliability. We model the following factors, which are also reflected in our model of component based software architectures (presented below in Section 3). As shown in the time-line in Fig. 1, we can separate the following sub-steps, each with its own reliability, when calling a method:

Method call: The actual call of a method starts in the calling process when executing the call statement and stops when the method starts its execution (possibly in a different process). The mechanism of calling a method may be as simple as a pushing return address and parameters on the stack and performing a jump-operation (in case of a local inner-process method call), but be also so complicated as setting up and using a network connection (in case of a remote procedure call (RPC)). Anyhow, each of these ways of calling a method is associated with a certain value of reliability. We model this factor as a constant of a connection between the interface offering the service and the component realizing this service. (The use of a constant is certainly a simplification, since the length of the parameter-stream to be transmitted in a RPC is also a factor, but is not known before run-time in general. Hence, we use a method and connection specific constant.)

Method execution: The phase of the method execution starts after the method call succeeded, i.e., when the thread of control reaches the code of the method and ends when the method comes to its return statement. Hence, this factor equals the reliability of the method's body. The reliability of the method execution can be modelled in a single number, but is influenced by a number of factors: it depends on the underlying execution environment (i.e, hardware, operating system, probably middleware), and, due to that, the reliability of a method execution is inversely proportional to the time consumed by a method execution. Further on, the reliability of a method execution depends also on the quality of the method's code. Also, as discussed below, other methods might be called most likely, which have their own reliability. Excluding this factor of other methods reliability, we can assume that all other factors, contributing to the method's body reliability, are constants.

Calls to external methods: In most cases, a method relies on other methods to provide its offered service. While the method's body is executed, other methods are called. This is not a constant factor, because the reliability of external methods depends on the environment, where the component is used in. This factor is crucial when relating the methods reliability to the reliability provided by its environment. This is the major issue in Section 4.2.

Return of the result: After execution of the method's body the results (if there are any) have to be transported back to the caller. This clearly depends on the length of the result stream (even if there are no explicit results, the caller has often to be notified of the end of the method call, e.g., by bringing back the thread of control). Further on, the mechanism, how the method was called (local call, inter-process call, RPC, etc.) plays an important role. We model the reliability of a method call with a method and connection specific number, as we did for the reliability of the method call.

Although the above analysis brought up a number of factors, influencing the reliability of a method call, in practice it is very hard to quantify each of them separately. From a component-oriented viewpoint, we have two kinds of factors: (a) constant factors, such as reliability of the method's body code, reliability of call and return and (b) variable factors, such as the reliability of external method calls. How we can come to actual figures for constants, is discussed in Section 7.

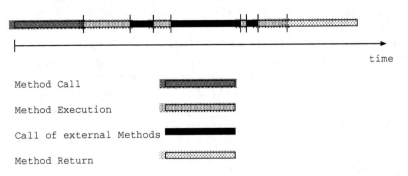

Fig. 1. Different phases of a method call

We model the reliability of a method call with three figures:

– The method and connection specific reliability r_{cr} of a method call and method return: Actually r_{cr} is the product of the reliability of the correct

call of the method and the correct return of the results. Since the reliabilities
of call and return depend on the reliability of the same calling mechanism and
the same kind of underlying hardware (e.g., network for a RPC, memory for
a local call), it is justified only to consider their product instead of modelling
them separately.

- The reliability of the method body r_{body} without considering the reliability
  of called methods: This factor reflects the quality and the length of the
  method's code and the kind of operations it performs.
- The reliability of external method calls (r_e): Since a method may call several
  external methods and may have several branches and loops, one requires a
  profile for all possible execution traces through the methods code, to obtain
  a single number for the influence of external methods reliability.

The reliability of a method call is the product of all these phases:

$$r_m := r_{cr} \cdot r_{body} \cdot r_e \qquad (1)$$

In Section 4.2 we will further elaborate factor r_e. We will be interested in
the effect of the usage profile on the reliability of external methods depends on
the usage profile. Since we base the formulation of the usage profile on provides-
protocols in interfaces, we first discuss the contractual use of software components within software architectures.

3   Modelling Architectures and Architecture Reliability with Contractual Interfaces

In this Section we briefly describe RADL (rich architectural description language) and the contractual use of software components within this ADL, concentrating on issues relevant for the reliability prediction model presented afterwards. A more detailed treatise about RADL can be found in [30, 32]. A more
detailed discussion of parameterized contracts is given in [26, 27].

3.1   Interfaces, Components, Bindings and Mappings

When constructing software systems out of components, one has to know the
components' properties without inspecting their code. This does not only demand for a standardized detailed documentation of components but also for component interfaces which contain more information as current signature-list based
interfaces. To make the information given in interfaces beneficial for component
based software development, we have to make sure that it is useful for static (i.e.,
not execution based) interoperability checks, which happen at composition-time,
that is, before the user comes in contact with the system.

Therefore, the use of enriched interfaces has often been advocated [3, 8, 13,
26]. In RADL an interface can include

- common signatures, describing how to call a component-service (i.e., method name, parameter types and their order, return type and possibly thrown exceptions),
- call sequences, i.e., information about the correct order of service calls. This models inter-service relations, e.g., before using a special service, an initialization service has to be called before. These sequence specifications are called *protocols*.
- specifications of the quality of service delivered by the components services. This affects extra-functional properties, like reliability, but also timing, security, etc.

It is commonly agreed that components not only must have an interface describing the services provided by the component, but also needs an interface, describing the services required by the components. The need of separate requires-interfaces becomes immediately obvious when facing the problem of checking the interoperability between two components A and B. If it is to be checked whether A uses correctly services provided by B, it is not sufficient to know what services B offers. One also has to know what services A expects B to provide. As described in detail in the next subsection, provides- and requires-interfaces of components play a crucial role for the contractual use of components.

It is important to note, that the arguments for enriched (provides-) interfaces given above, also carry over for requires-interfaces. If a provides-interface describes a protocol how to use its provided services (i.e., the provides-protocol), one can only use this information in interoperability checks, if requires-interfaces also describe, by which possible sequences they call the provided services. Hence, analogously to the provides-protocol, a requires-protocol has to be specified. This argument generically works for all interface models, i.e., also for interfaces with extra-functional properties.

Basing on that discussion of the necessity of enriched interfaces and requires-interfaces, we define an architectural *component* as follows.

Definition 1 (Component)
A component *is a self-contained component with one or several provides-interfaces and one or several requires-interfaces.*

Since a component may contain recursively sub-components, we differ between *basic components* (which act as black-boxes) and *composite components*, which are composed by sub-components. An example configuration is shown in Fig. 2.

Component `OnlineAccMgr`, for example, is modelled as a basic component, while `BankSystem` is modelled as composite component.

Connections appear only between interfaces. Connections between a requires-interface and a provides-interface are called *bindings*, because they actually bind components together. Connections between two provides-interfaces (or two requires-interfaces) are called *mappings*. Mappings map functionality provided in the interface of an outer component to functionality provided in inner com-

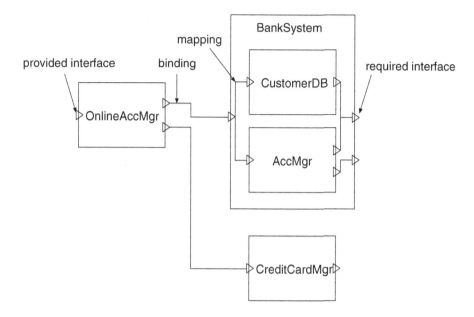

provided interface

binding

mapping

BankSystem

required interface

OnlineAccMgr

CustomerDB

AccMgr

CreditCardMgr

Fig. 2. Example: Components, Interfaces, Bindings and Mappings

ponents. (Likewise for required functionality.) The example itself is discussed in more detail in Section 6.

3.2 Component Protocols and Finite State Machines

Mostly, the term *component protocol* denotes the set of valid sequences of calls to services supported by a component (i.e., the *provides protocol* as part of the provides interface) [13, 23]. A *valid* call sequence is a call sequence which is actually supported by the component. An example of valid calls to a `OnlineAccMgr` component may be the sequence `login-listAccounts-logout`, whereas the sequence `login-firstretry-firstretry` is not supported, hence invalid.

Besides this, also the necessity of specifying the sequences of calls to external services (i.e., the *requires protocol* as part of the requires interface) is pointed out (e.g., [42] or more explicitly and generally in [1]).

Anyhow, the provides- and the requires-protocols are considered as sets of sequences. Various models have been used to describe these sets of sequences (e.g., [3, 8, 13, 23, 28, 36]), each having specific benefits and drawbacks. Examples are regular expressions, logic constraint languages, Petri-nets, etc. (see [28, 36, 37] for a more detailed discussion). State machines are one of those well-known notations for protocol specification [3, 9, 23, 42]. The benefits of a state machine specification of protocols are (a) representing protocols in a compact and precise manner, and (b) enabling automatic formal analysis of protocols. Finite state machines (FSMs) [12] comprise a finite set of states. When modelling call sequences, we model for each state which methods are callable in this state.

P-FSM and Usage-ProfileOnlineAccMgr

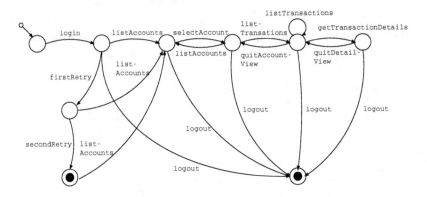

Fig. 3. P-FSM of the `OnlineAccMgr`

In many cases, a method call changes the state of the state machine, i.e., some other methods are callable after the call, while others, callable in the old state, are not callable in the new state. A change of states (from an "old" state to a "new" state) is called *(state) transition*. The UML includes the standard notion of FSMs. In the *state transition diagram* in Fig. 3 states are denoted by circles, transitions by arrows. There is one designated state in which the component is after its creation (i.e., the *start-state*). From this start-state all call sequences start. A transition is decorated with the name of the method which was called to trigger that transition.

A valid call sequence leads the FSM into a so-called *final-state*. These final-states are denoted by black cycles within the states. (In Fig. 3 one can see that the valid sequence `login-listAccounts-logout` leads the FSM in a final-state, while, for example, the invalid sequence `login-firstretry-firstretry` does not.)

Formally, a FSM can be defined as follows:

Definition 2 (Finite State Machine)
A FSM $A = (I, S, F, s_0, t)$ consists out of an input alphabet (I), a set of states (S), a set of final states ($F \subseteq S$), a start state ($s_0 \in S$), and a total transition function $t : S \times I \to S$.

(To make t a total function an FSM can use a single error state, where all invalid prefixes of words lead to.)

We call the FSM specifying the provides-protocol the P-FSM. The requires-protocol is described by a so called *requires-FSM* (R-FSM).

The P-FSMs input alphabet is the set of methods provides by the component. In the reverse, the input alphabet of the R-FSM is the set of (external) methods required by the component. Hence, the language accepted by the P-FSM are valid call sequences of the component's methods. The language accepted by the R-FSM includes all sequences of the component to other external components.

Since our implementation utilizes a state-machine based approach, in the following, we identify for sake of simplicity state-machines and protocols (like the provides-protocol and the P-FSM, etc.).

3.3 Parameterized Contracts

Interoperability Checks, Substitutability Checks and Classical Contracts for Software Components. Before defining contracts for components, we briefly review B. Meyer's design-by-contract principle from an abstract point of view. According to [19, p. 342], a contract between the client and the supplier consists of two obligations:

- The client has to satisfy the precondition of the supplier.
- The supplier has to fulfil its postcondition, if the precondition was met be the client.

Each of the above obligations can be seen as the benefit for the other party. (The client can count on the postcondition if the precondition was fulfilled, while the supplier can count on the precondition). Putting it in one sentence:

If the client fulfils the precondition of the supplier, the supplier will fulfil its postcondition.

The used component plays the role of a supplier. But to formulate contracts for components, we also have to identify the pre- and postconditions and the user of a component. But what is to be considered a precondition, postcondition and user depends whether the component is used at run-time or configuration-time. Let's first consider the component's use at run-time. Using a component at run-time is calling its services. Hence, the user of a component C is the set of all components connected to C's provides-interface(s).

The precondition for that kind of use is the precondition of the service, likewise the postcondition is the postcondition of the service. Actually, that shows that this kind of use of a component is nothing different than using a method. Therefore, we consider this case as the use of a *component service*, but *not* as the use of a *component*. Likewise, the contract to be fulfilled here from client and supplier is a *method contract* as described by B. Meyer already in 1992. This is not the contract for using the *component*!

The other case of component usage (usage at composition-time) is actually the relevant case when talking about the contractual use of components. This is the important case when architecting systems out of components or deploying components within existing systems for reconfigurations. Again, in this case a component C is acting as a supplier and the environment as a client. The component C offers services to the environment (i.e., the components connected to C's provides-interface(s)). According to the above discussion of contracts, these offered services are the postcondition of the component, i.e., what the client can expect from a working component. Also according to B. Meyer's above mentioned description of contracts, the precondition is what the component C expects from

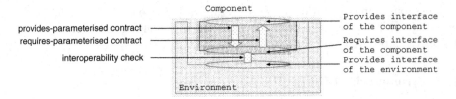

Fig. 4. Interoperability checks (1) and Requires-parameterized Contract (2) and Provides-parameterized Contract (3)

its environment (actually all components connected to C's requires-interface(s)) to be provided by the environment, in order to enable C to offer its services (as stated in its postcondition). Hence, the precondition of a component is stated in its requires-interfaces. Analogously to the above single sentence formulation of a contract, we can state:

> If the user of a component fulfils the component's requires-interface (offers the right environment) the component will offer its services as described in the provides-interface.

Let's denote with pre_c the precondition of a component c and with $post_c$ the postcondition of a component c. For checking whether a component c can be replaced safely by a component c', one has to ensure that the contract of c' is a subcontract of c. The notion of a subcontract is described in [19, p. 573] like contravariant typing for methods: A contract c' is a subcontract of contract c iff

$$pre_{c'} \trianglelefteq pre_c \wedge post_{c'} \trianglerighteq post_c \tag{2}$$

(Where $\trianglerighteq$ means "stronger", i.e., if pre_c and $post_c$ are predicates,$\trianglerighteq$ is $\Rightarrow$. In the set semantics of pre- and postcondition below, $\trianglerighteq$ is the set-inclusion $\supseteq$.)

To check the interoperability between components c and c' (see point (1) in Fig. 4), one has to check whether

$$pre_c \trianglelefteq post_{c'} \tag{3}$$

Coming back to protocol-modelling interfaces, we can consider the precondition of a component as the set of required method call sequences, while the postcondition is the set of offered call sequences. In this case, the checks described in the above formulas (2) and (3) boiled down to checking the inclusion relationship between the sets of call sequences, i.e., for the substitutability check we have:

$$pre_{c'} \subseteq pre_c \wedge post_{c'} \supseteq post_c \tag{4}$$

and for the interoperability check:

$$pre_c \subseteq post_{c'} \tag{5}$$

For arbitrary sets A and B holds $A \subseteq B \iff A \cap B = A$. Hence, the inclusion check we need for checking interoperability and substitutability can be reduced to computing the intersection and equivalence of sets of call sequences. One of the main reasons for choosing finite state machines as a model to specify these sets of call sequences was the existence of efficient algorithms for computing the intersection of two FSMs and checking their equivalence. Of course, more powerful models than FSMs exist (in the sense that they can describe protocols which cannot be described by FSMs) but for many of these models (like the various push-down automata) the equivalence is not decidable. Hence, one can use these models for specifying component interfaces, but that does not help to check their interoperability or substitutability at configuration-time.

Parameterized Contracts as Generalization of Classical Contracts.
While interoperability tests check the requires-interface of a component against the provides-interface of *another* component, parameterized contracts link the provides-interface of one component to the requires- interface of *the same* component (see points (2) and (3) in Fig. 4).

The usefulness of parameterized contracts is based on the observation that in practice often only a subset of a component's functionality is used. This is especially true for coarse-grained components. In this case, also only a subset of the functionality described in the requires-interface is actually used. That means that the component could be used without any problems in environments where not all dependencies, as described in the requires interface, are given. Vice versa, if a component does not receive all (but some) functionality it requires from the environment, it often can deliver a reasonable subset of its functionality.

These facts can be modelled by a set of possible provides-interfaces $\mathbf{P} := \{prov\}$ and a set of possible requires-interfaces $\mathbf{R} := \{req\}$ and a monotone total bijective mapping p between them $p : \mathbf{P} \to \mathbf{R}$ [1]. As a result, each requires-interface $req \in \mathbf{R}$ is now a function of a provides-interface $prov$: $req = p(prov)$ and (because p is bijective) each provides-interface $prov \in \mathbf{P}$ can be modelled as a function of a requires-interface $req \in \mathbf{R}$: $prov = p^{-1}(req)$.

This mapping p is now called *parameterized contract*, since it parameterizes the precondition with the postcondition of the component and vice versa. It can be considered as a generalization of "classical contract" which uses a fixed pre- and postcondition. The parameterized contract is bundled with the component and computes the interfaces of the components on demand.

For the following, assume component B uses component C and is used by component A. If component A uses only a subset of the functionality offered by B we compute a new requires-interface of B with the parameterized contract p_B:

$$p_B(req_A \cap prov_B) =: req'_B \subseteq req_B \qquad (6)$$

Note that the new requires-interface req'_B requires possibly less than the original requires-interface $req_B := p_B(prov_B)$ (but never more) since p_B is monotone

---

[1] p can be made total and surjective by defining $\mathbf{P} := dom(p)$ and $\mathbf{R} := im(p)$.

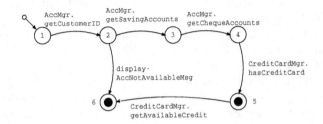

Fig. 5. Service effect FSM of service `listAccounts` of component `OnlineAccMgr`

and $req_A \cap prov_B \subseteq prov_B$. When computing the requires-interface out of a provides-interface (possibly intersected with an external requires-interface) the parameterized contract is called *provides-parameterized contract*.

Likewise, if component C does not provide all the functionality required by B, one can compute a new provides-interface $prov'_B$ with p_B:

$$p_B^{-1}(req_B \cap prov_C) =: prov'_B \subseteq prov_B \tag{7}$$

Since p_B is monotone, p^{-1} is, too. With $req_B \cap prov_C \subseteq req_B$ we have $prov'_B \subseteq prov_B := p^{-1}(req_B)$. In this case we use a *requires-parameterized contract*.

We can implement parameterized contracts for component interfaces which contain the provides-/requires-protocol. The parameterized contract, i.e., the reversible mapping between these interfaces, is specified by the so-called *method requires finite state machines* (SE-FSMs). Each method s provided by a component is associated with its SE-FSM$_s$. The SE-FSM$_s$ describes all sequences of calls to other methods, which can be made by the method s when it is called. A simple example of a SE-FSM is shown in Fig. 5. A transition of an SE-FSM corresponds to a call of an external method.

It shows that a call to method `listAccounts` of the `OnlineAccMgr` will lead to calls to certain sequences of calls to external methods. An example of a sequences is `getCustomerID`, `getSavingAccounts`, `getChequeAccounts` (all from component `AccMgr`) followed by calls to `hasCreditCard` and `getAvailableCredit` (of component `CreditCardMgr`).

To realize a provides-parameterized contract of a component C we interpret the transition functions of the P-FSM and the SE-FSMs as graphs. Each edge (transition) in the P-FSM-graph corresponds to a method. We substitute for each transition in the P-FSM-graph the SE-FSM of the corresponding method. The resulting graph contains all the SE-FSMs in exactly the orders by which their methods can be called from the component C's client. That means the resulting graph, interpreted as a FSM, describes all sequences of calls to external components, hence describes the requires-protocol.

If we ensure that the insertion of SE-FSMs into the P-FSM is reversible (e.g., by marking the "beginning" (withe a transition carrying the method name) and "ending" (done by a "return-transition") of each SE-FSM, we can generate out

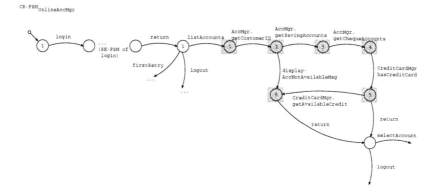

Fig. 6. Partial R-FSM of the `OnlineAccMgr`

of a given R-FSM a P-FSM, giving us a requires-parameterized contract. Fig. 6 shows this insertion with explicit marking of beginnings and endings.

To adapt a component C to an environment E, we build the intersection of the R-FSM$_C$ and the P-FSM$_E$. The result is a possibly different R-FSM$_C{}'$, which describes the call sequences emitted by C and accepted by E. From that R-FSM$_C{}'$ we generate a (possibly) new provides-protocol P-FSM$_C{}'$ using the requires-parameterized contract as sketched above. A detailed discussion of implementing parameterized contracts for protocol adaption including complexity measures, treatise of advanced issues like reentrance and recursion, can be found in [26].

In our example, the online account manager (with its provides-protocol shown in Fig. 3) has to be adapted to new specific environments which are formed by the provides-protocols of a bank system and a credit card manager. As shown in the architecture (Fig. 2) the bank system consists of an account manager and a customer-database. As an example, imagine, the customer database is not available in this environment. (This could be the case because of a temporary loss of connection but also because a down-scaled version of the system lacks this database principally.) Anyhow, by that lack of the customer database only service `getTransactionDetails` is affected. All other services of `OnlineAccMgr` make effectively only use of the `AccMgr` component of the banking system. Consequently, the requires-parameterized contract will compute the subset of functionality which still can be provided by the `OnlineAccMgr` in this environment, as shown in Fig. 7.

Although this kind of adaptation is expressible by normal signature-list based interfaces, many adaptations might only affect the protocol, hence cannot be expressed by just listing the provided methods.

Since in our approach of component protocol adaptation we compute the intersection of the requires-protocol of one component and the provides-protocol of another, our approach only works if we yield a non-empty intersection. But there are also realistic cases where this intersection is empty but still an adaptation would be possible. For example, consider a provides-protocol that needs a call

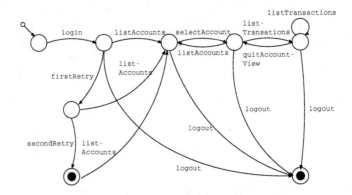

Fig. 7. Adapted P-FSM of the `OnlineAccMgr`

to an initialization method before other methods can be called and a requires-protocol which simply never performs this call to the initialization method but otherwise is compliant to the other service call sequences. In this case the intersection is empty (since no call sequence has a common prefix), but an intermediating adaptor could easily bridge the incompatibility by injecting the missing call to the initialization method. The (semi-) automatic generation of this kind of adaptors is described in [31].

The following scenarios demonstrate the application of parameterized contracts. Provides-parameterized contracts are useful when designing a new system. A software architect states the functionality a component has to fulfil. Then she finds several candidate components in a repository that deliver at least the required functionality. For all these candidate components one can compute the functionality they really need in this context via their provides-parameterized contracts. This can be done because the functionality the component has to provide in this context is known. The benefit is that only those external components have to be provided which are really needed in this usage context. As a result, less external components may be needed than requested in a maximal requires-interface if only a subset of the component's functionality is used.

Requires-parameterized contracts are useful for integrating components into existing systems. Imagine an existing system should be reconfigured with a new component, or an existing system architecture should be enhanced by an existing component. One question in this situation is which functionality the new component will deliver without changing the environment of the component. For creating fault-tolerant system architectures requires-parameterized contracts can be applied at run-time. This is useful because in fault-tolerant systems it is important to know which functionality a component can offer after other components have been failed.

Parameterized contracts are an abstract concept not tied to a specific interface model. Like most ADLs, parameterized contracts only need the explicit separation of provides- and requires-interfaces. Further on, parameterized contracts can be applied at design-time, at composition-time (e.g., to integrate components into existing systems) or at run-time (e.g., for graceful system degradation). Like classical contracts, parameterized contracts can be applied to a number of different software units, such as methods, modules, objects and components. (But parameterized contracts may prove most useful when applied to components.)

Applying parameterized contracts to software components means the interfaces of the component are recomputed dynamically. The code has not to be manipulated. For practical reasons it is most beneficial that the programmer does not have to foresee and program all possible component adaptations in advance, which are computable by parameterized contracts.

For components with strongly connected provided and required services parameterized contracts do not make sense. E.g., for a screen-saver without access to a graphic-device a requires-parameterized contract cannot compute a meaningful provides-interface.

4   Predicting Reliability of Component-Based Software Architectures

Since parameterized contracts are a general concept for component description, they can be adapted to a range of models for provides- and requires-interfaces. In our work, we include reliabilities in the parameterized contracts of components.

Parameterized contracts for components with reliability information in their interfaces mean that the reliability of the component's provided services are computed in dependency from the reliability of the component's environment. This direction of a parameterized contract is discussed in Section 4.2. But also the other direction is of practical concern: given the reliability expected from a component, one is interested in the reliability the component expects its environment to fulfil. It is not possible to state the reliability expected by the component in its requires-interfaces explicitly, but one can compute conditions, which can be checked, when composing the component in its environment.

We define some formal apparatus for defining parameterized contracts that provide protocol and reliability concepts.

4.1   Markov Models

It is now common ground to look at software reliability as a function of a usage profile, which is usually given as a Markov model [2, 39]. This means, that software reliability depends on the sequence of state transitions (in our case component method invocations). The Markov property means that the probability of executing a given method only depends on the state where it can be called from. It does not depend on the history, how one came to that state if there are multiple different ways to reach the state. The Markov model specifies the probability of occurrence for each call sequence.

P-FSM and Usage-ProfileOnlineAccMgr

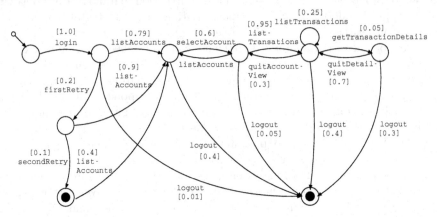

Fig. 8. Transition diagram of the P-FSM of the `OnlineAccMgr` and annotated usage profile

Due to the Markov property, one can look at a Markov model as a finite state machine with probabilities associated with each transition. This fits very well in the RADL-approach, since FSMs are already given at the interfaces for modelling call sequences. Therefore, we built our definition of Markov models on the definition of FSMs (definition 2).

Given that, we define a Markov model as a FSM with a function, associating with each transition a certain probability under the constraint that the sum of probabilities leaving a state must be one.

Definition 3 (Markov Model)
A Markov Model MM $A = (I, S, F, s_0, t, u)$ *consists out of a FSM* (I, S, F, s_0, t) *and a total function* $u : S \times I \to [0..1]$ *mapping a probability value to each transition. It must hold*

$$\forall s \in S \backslash F . \sum_{i \in I} u(s, i) = 1$$
$$\forall s \in F . \sum_{i \in I} u(s, i) \leq 1$$

The sum of the probabilities related outgoing transitions in final states may be below one, that is, there is a given probability that one remains in a final state. (For reasons of theoretical analysis, one we introduce a new state ("super-final-state" SFS), which is connected to each final-state $f \in F$ by a specific transition $t(f, \hat{e}) = SFS$ $(\hat{e} \notin I)$, with $u(f, \hat{e}) := 1 - \sum_{i \in I \wedge t(f,i) \neq SFS} u(f, i)$. With this construction one assures that also for final-states $f \in F$ holds $\sum_{i \in I} u(f, i) = 1$. The other benefit of this construction is that we have only one final state (i.e. the SFS) [38].)

The usage profile of a component is then given by its P-FSM and a probability function u, forming together a Markov model. An example is shown in Fig. 8. It shows, that everybody first performs a login. After that, 20% of users retry for the first time (because their login failed), 1% immediately logout out, and the majority of 79% proceed by listing their accounts. Analogously one can interpret the data given for the other states.

Like the representation of a FSM's transition function as a table (since the number of states and number of input symbols is finite, the table is also finite), one can represent u as a finite matrix $P = ((p_{ij}))_{ij}$, with $p_{i}j := \sum_{a \in I \wedge t(i,a)=j} u(i,a)$ with $i, j \in S$, showing the probability of coming from state i to state j within one step (i.e., without considering paths over other states).

The services of a component $(s_1, \cdots, s_n)$ form with their associated reliability values a reliability vector $R = [r_{s_1}, \cdots, r_{s_n}]$. Lets denote with r_{ij} the reliability r_m of the method $m \in I$ when $t(i,m) = j$ holds with $i, j \in S$. The values $((r_{ij}))_{ij}$ for a reliability matrix R. Given the usage-profile as a matrix P and the reliability matrix R one can compute a matrix giving the probability of successful transitions from state i to state j: $S = ((s_{ij}))_{ij}$, with $s_{ij} := r_{ij} \cdot p_{ij}$. (With denoting $\star$ the *pointwise* matrix-product, we can write $S = R \star P$.)

The probability of reaching state j from state i without an failure in k steps equals then $S^k(i,j)$.

When having loops, one cannot bound the number of transitions used to reach another state with a constant k. (The number of loop executions is finite, but arbitrarily high.) Therefore, the matrix $\sum_{k=0}^{\infty} S^k$ has to be computed. Fortunately, since all its entries are below or equal one, one can sum it up as a converting geometric series. Hence, $\sum_{k=0}^{\infty} S^k = (I - S)^{-1}$, where I is the identity matrix of size $(n \times n)$. The overall system reliability is then given by resolving the infinite sum as geometric sum:

$$r_{system} = (I - S)^{-1}(\hat{i}, \hat{j}) \qquad (8)$$

This means the reliability is given in the entry $(\hat{i}, \hat{j})$, where $\hat{i}$ is the index of the start state and $\hat{j}$ is the index of the super final state (SFS). More details are provided in [2].

Our presentation here follows Cheung, but differs in the modelling of reliability and the meaning of transitions. In Cheung's work, transitions denote the transition of the control-flow from one module to another, while in our model a transition is a change of states in a protocol automaton. Cheung models reliability as a function of states, while we model it as a function u of the transition. Our approach could be included in Cheung's work by introducing an extra state s_t for each transition t and splitting up each transition t into two: one leading to this extra state, and one leaving this extra state and leading to the state, where t lead to. While this construction shows that our model can be subsumed in his work from a theoretical point of view, the benefit of avoiding the introduction of extra states lies in the closeness of our model to provides-protocols and in keeping automata small. Both issues are important from a practical point of view

- The effort for the user modelling usage profiles should be kept as small as possible. Annotating existing provides-protocols and service effect automata

to arrive at usage-profiles is far more practical than developing yet another view of the system and keeping it consistent with other views of the system (while requirements and designs change frequently).
- The smaller the automata, the easier to comprehend for the user and the faster to process by tools.

Given this notion of bindings, mappings, and service effect automata we can now define basic and composite components more formally.

Definition 4 (Basic Component)
A basic component B is a tuple $(P - Interfaces, R - Interfaces, SEProt, u)$ of a non-empty, finite set $P - Interfaces$ of provides-interfaces, a finite set $R - Interfaces$ of requires-interfaces and a service effect automaton $SEProt$, describing the service effect protocol. The function u makes the service effect automata to a Markov model and therefore has to be specified as given in definition 3.

(Actually, the service effect protocol could be described by a variety of calculi, such as constraints formulated in temporal logic, process calculi, Petri-nets, etc. Since we can directly make use of finite state machines when specifying a Markov model, we use FSMs in this chapter.)

Definition 5 (Composite Component)
A composite component C is a tuple

$$(P - Interfaces, R - Interfaces, Components, Mappings, Bindings, r_m, r_b)$$

where $P - Interfaces$ and $R - Interfaces$ are the sets of provides- respective requires-interfaces. Components is a non-empty set of other (so-called "inner") components (composite or basic). The set Bindings contains the bindings which connect the requires- and provides-interfaces of inner components. The set Mappings contains mappings connecting all provides-interfaces of $P - Interfaces$ to provides-interfaces of inner components and requires-interfaces of inner components to all requires-interfaces of C. The rational constant $r_m \in [0..1]$ indicates the reliability of a mapping, likewise is $r_b \in [0..1]$ the reliability of a binding.

Note, that even in case of inner components, the set *Bindings* may be empty, as our example configuration in Fig. 2 shows. Not all requires-interfaces of inner components must be mapped to requires-interfaces of $R - Interface$, since some requires-interfaces of inner components might not be used in specific contexts. But all requires-interfaces of $R - Interface$ must be mapped to inner requires-interfaces. In practice often holds $r_m = r_b$, but, in general, mappings and bindings might often include different glue-code, which justifies different values.

4.2   Reliability of Basic Components

As mentioned, the reliability of a component is not given as a fixed number, but a function of the component's environment-reliability and the usage profile of

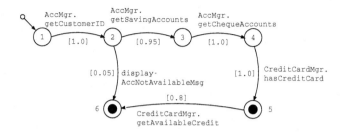

Fig. 9. Service effect protocol of the service `listAccounts` and annotated usage model

the component. Since we do not want to limit the reliability of a component to a fixed usage profile or a fixed environment (what the component developer also cannot foresee), we have to describe the reliability of a basic component as the reliabilities of its methods m_i in dependency of the reliability of the external methods which are used by m_i. If the component is set up in its usage context, we use two steps for predicting its reliability.

1. We compute numerical values for the service reliabilities (which we describe in detail in the next subsection) and
2. We compute the reliability of the overall component out of the reliabilities of its method and the context-specific usage profile (what is described at the end of this Section).

Computing the Service Reliabilities of Basic Components Using Parameterized Contracts. To link the environmental reliability information received at requires-interfaces to the reliability of methods offered at the provides-interfaces, the parameterized contracts use the service-effect FSM of each method. A service effect automaton of a service s gives the possible sequences of calls to external methods, which may be executed when s is called. This information forms a basis for a usage profile, which describes what call sequences s calls with a certain probability. In Fig. 9 we see as an example a service effect automaton and usage profile of the service `listAccounts` of our aforementioned `OnlineAccMgr` component. Given the reliability of the external methods called by `listAccounts`, we can compute the reliability of `listAccounts` by formula 8.

In general, the service effect automaton of service s provides a service specific usage profile P_s. (Note that this usage-profile is a constant of the service s, and therefore a part of the parameterized contract of the component. It is not to confuse with the usage profile of the component, which is part of the component's deployment context.) The provides-interface of the external components c gives reliability values of the external methods as a reliability matrix R. Hence, we can compute the matrix of successful transition probabilities $S_s := R \star P_s$. We

Table 1. Reliability values for services of the `AccMgr`, `CreditCardMgr` and the private service of `OnlineAccMgr` that are used by the service `listAccounts`

Component	Service	Reliability value
AccMgr	getRelGetCustomerID	0.9999
	getRelGetSavingAccounts	0.9995
	getRelGetChequeAccounts	0.9995
OnlineAccMgr	displayAccNotAvailableMsg	0.99999
CreditCardMgr	hasCreditCard	0.9999
	getAvailableCredit	0.9999

now can compute the factor r_{s_e} for each method s, i.e., the influence of external methods on the reliability of service s, using formula 8.

$$r_{s_e} = (I - S_s)^{-1}(startState, SFS) \qquad (9)$$

This means we take the element of matrix $(I - S_s)^{-1}$ which denotes the reliability of reaching the SFS from the start state, as explained in Section 4.1.

According to formula 1, the reliability of the service s requires to multiply r_e with r_{body} and r_{cr}. In our architectural model we set r_{cr} depending on the architecture of the system, i.e., to the square of the product of the reliabilities of all traversed mappings and bindings. (The square of that product, because the connections are used twice: for calling the method and for returning the result.)

We demonstrate that by computing the reliability service `listAccounts` of the `OnlineAccountMgr`-component. We can transform the probabilities given with the transition function in Fig. 9 into the following matrix P:

$$P_{listAccounts} = \begin{pmatrix} 0 & 1 & 0 & 0 & 0 & 0 & 0 \\ 0 & 0 & 0.95 & 0 & 0 & 0.05 & 0 \\ 0 & 0 & 0 & 1 & 0 & 0 & 0 \\ 0 & 0 & 0 & 0 & 1 & 0 & 0 \\ 0 & 0 & 0 & 0 & 0 & 0.8 & 0.2 \\ 0 & 0 & 0 & 0 & 0 & 0 & 1 \\ 0 & 0 & 0 & 0 & 0 & 0 & 0 \end{pmatrix} \qquad (10)$$

Note, that state number 7 plays the role of the "super-final-state" (SFS) here, where transitions from the final-states 5 and 6 lead to (with the probability of remaining in final states). As shown in equation 1, the reliability of service `listAccount` depends on (a) the reliability of the call/return mechanism (modelled in our architecture by the reliability of bindings (r_b) and mappings (r_m), (b) the reliability of the service's body (r_{body}) and (c) the reliability of external methods. Table 1 lists for each service of `AccMgr` which is called by `listAccount` the product of $r_{cr} \cdot r_{body} \cdot r'_e$ where r'_e is the reliability of external method called by the methods of `AccMgr`. (Since we do not model these external methods in our example, we simply state the product, but not the single factors which lead to it.)

The internal methods used are described in Table 1. For internal methods, we consider $r_{cr} = 1$.

These values could be rewritten in a matrix by using the transition function. The entries r_{ij} of the reliability matrix R give the reliability of performing the service call leading from state i (row-index) to state j (column-index). For example to find the value for entry r_{12} we first have to determine, by which service call this transition is triggered. From the transition function (as shown in Fig. 9) we know, that it is a call to `getCustomerID`. Its reliability is given in Table 1 as 0.9999. Performing so for all entries, we result in the following matrix $R_{listAccounts}$.

$$R_{listAccounts} = \begin{pmatrix} 0 & 0.9999 & 0 & 0 & 0 & 0 & 0 \\ 0 & 0 & 0.9995 & 0 & 0 & 0.99999 & 0 \\ 0 & 0 & 0 & 0.9995 & 0 & 0 & 0 \\ 0 & 0 & 0 & 0 & 0.9999 & 0 & 0 \\ 0 & 0 & 0 & 0 & 0 & 0.9999 & 1 \\ 0 & 0 & 0 & 0 & 0 & 0 & 1 \\ 0 & 0 & 0 & 0 & 0 & 0 & 0 \end{pmatrix} \quad (11)$$

(Note that transition into SFS have always reliability one.) Now we can compute the matrix $S_{listAccounts}$ by element-wise (pointwise) multiplication of $R_{listAccounts}$ and $P_{listAccounts}$.

$$S = R \star P = \begin{pmatrix} 0 & 0.9999 & 0 & 0 & 0 & 0 & 0 \\ 0 & 0 & 0.949525 & 0 & 0 & 0.049995 & 0 \\ 0 & 0 & 0 & 0.9995 & 0 & 0 & 0 \\ 0 & 0 & 0 & 0 & 0.9999 & 0 & 0 \\ 0 & 0 & 0 & 0 & 0 & 0.79992 & 0.2 \\ 0 & 0 & 0 & 0 & 0 & 0 & 1 \\ 0 & 0 & 0 & 0 & 0 & 0 & 0 \end{pmatrix} \quad (12)$$

The result according to formula 8 is a reliability of service `listAccount` of approx. $(I - S)^{-1}(1, 7) = 0.99877$, what results in a MTTF of 816 calls.

Computing the Reliability of Components with Component Usage-Profiles. Given a component K with its usage-profile based on its provides-protocol P-FSM$_K$ and the reliability of its provided services (as computed by equation 9), we can again form from the reliability matrix R and the usage profile P matrix $S = R \star P$. Than we apply formula 8 to compute the overall reliability of K.

4.3   Reliability of Composite Components

Like we predicted the reliability of basic components in two steps, we also approach the prediction of the reliability of composed components in two analogous steps. We first determine the service reliability and then the of overall reliability by using a usage profile and the reliability of the services. In fact, the last step, the computation of the overall reliability works for composite components exactly like for basic components.

Given a composite component

$$C = (P{-}Interfaces, R{-}Interfaces, Components, Mappings, Bindings, r_m, r_b)$$

the reliability of a composite component's service s is defined by the reliability of the mapping to the provides interface of an inner component K_{inner} realizing with an service s_{inner} the service s and the reliability of s_{inner}. Hence, we have:

$$r_s := r_m \cdot r_{s_{inner}} \tag{13}$$

Now we have to separate two cases.

1. K_{inner} is a composite component,

$$K_{inner} = (P{-}Interfaces', R{-}Interfaces', Components',$$
$$Mappings', Bindings', r'_m, r'_b)$$

   For the computation of s_{inner} we recursively apply formula 13. Note that $r'_m \neq r_m$ may be the case.
2. K_{inner} is a basic component: for computing the reliability of s_{inner} we use the service effect automaton of K_{inner} and proceed as described in Section 4.2 and apply formula 9. When constructing the matrix R out of the reliabilities of required services, once again, one has recursively to decide, whether a required service is outside of C, or realized by another component $K' \in Components$. In the first case, the reliability of the external service is given by the outer requires-interface of $R{-}Interfaces$ and the reliability r_m of the used mapping. If the required service is realized by another inner component, one computes its reliability with the above formula 13.

Lemma 1
The recursion in computing the reliability of composite components (case 2 in above) ends if the architecture is layered.

To proof this, we first note that all architectures have a finite number of refinements into composite components. At a certain level of abstraction we deal with basic components, so their reliability can be computed by their service effect automata's usage profile. Secondly, if the architecture is layered, required methods of inner methods are mapped to external methods, because the set of inner components is finite (according to definition 5 and practical considerations).

5   Assumptions

Our reliability model is built on several underlying assumptions, which restrict the applicability of the model. Making these assumptions explicit, eases the decision, whether our model is applicable to a certain context and facilitates scientific discussions and further enhancements of the model.

We have two groups of assumptions: (a) the availability of data, and (b) assumptions concerning the mathematical model.

5.1 Assumptions Concerning Required Data

To compute the reliability of basic components we need the following data:

- **From the component provider**: the usage profile of the service effect automata,
- **From the component user**: the reliability of the environmental services (i.e., the services listed in the required-interfaces of the component. This includes the reliability of the bindings (e.g., network connections, if the component is to be used in an distributed networked environment). In case the component user is interested getting the reliability of the component presented in one figure (rather than in service specific reliability figure), a usage profile of the component must be provided.

Note that persons in different roles may act as a component user: system architects, system administrators, software developers, project leaders, etc. Hence it is not necessarily the end user. Different ways of gathering that data are discussed in Section 7.

For predicting the reliability of composite components, the following data is required:

- **From the component provider**: the service effect automata of the included basic component's services, the bindings and mappings with their reliability,
- **From the component user**: the same as for basic components.

Since in our model the component user has to provide the same data for using basic or composite components, the user has not to be concerned with the inner components structure. This supports the black-box usage of components. The main difference for providing data exists for the component developer (who has usually the necessary insight into the component). The different reliability calculation methods for basic and composite components are implemented in tools, they are transparent for the component user.

5.2 Assumptions Concerning the Mathematical Model

In our model, we assume that the call of services can be modelled with a Markov process: This means that the path through the control-flow of the program is not important. When a service is called, its reliability does not depend on the methods called before. This means that failures of services are independent: The probability that a service fails, depends solely on this service, but not on the history of previous service calls.

Although this assumption is nowadays well accepted when modelling software reliability (especially in combination with statistical testing) [5, 39, 35], it is worth discussing why one can assume that the reliabilities of different service calls are independent. The reason why this assumption might not hold, is that the effect of errors propagating from one faulty service to another service, which might be correctly implemented, but fails due to a propagated error. This can happen, when due to a previous error a service is called with parameters for which its behavior is unspecified. While this certainly happens in many software systems, this propagation of errors yet another reason to use Meyer's design-by-contract principle [18]. Since contracts for services (methods) clearly specify as preconditions under which circumstances (i.e., parameter-values) a service can fulfil its specification (as given in the postcondition), this mechanism effectively prevents error propagation. In case of a faulty result returned by a faulty service, the next method using this result might detect the error in its precondition. In this case the error will not be propagated and may raise an exception shortly after the execution of the faulty service. But one still has to keep in mind, that even the tightest precondition cannot detect faulty parameter-values, if it is included in the specified range of valid parameter values. Therefore, despite the common practice of applying Markov models one still needs empirical studies justifying its assumption of independent service reliabilities.

The assumption of independent service reliability also requires the assumption of independent component reliability. While Cheung justifies this assumption by empirical investigations for modules [2], some counter examples are known as well: For increasing the reliability of airborne communications, redundant computers are installed assuming the independence of their failure. In a recent aircraft failure the triple redundant computer systems failed successively due to water leakage in the area where all three systems were installed in close proximity causing these coincident failures.

To achieve high levels of reuse and configuration flexibility, current software architecture models aim at portability, platform independence, distribution and location transparency. In an assembled and deployed system however, logically independent software components may then run on, or depend on, the same hardware/software system.

In our method we address this problem by modelling shared resources and their reliability as bindings to shared provided interfaces of such resources.

In RADL, basic components are the smallest unit of distribution. All the provided interfaces of a single basic component are considered to depend on the one physical component which becomes a single point of failure for these interfaces and its users (required-interfaces).

To support system (hardware/software) reliability calculations, we assume that all components have implicit resource mapping interfaces, such that shared hardware resources are modelled by bindings to common shared components and, ultimately, their reliability can then enter our calculus by means of appropriate bindings.

Besides this assumption relating to the Markov model, we assume, that it is sufficient to consider only service calls, but not to model parameters of methods, which may differ at run-time. Therefore the measured profiles have a relative "low resolution". If different parameters to methods give considerably different variations in the behavior, a "higher resolution" may be required. This can be achieved in our framework but may require modelling additional states (representing input parameter range profiles) and dependencies in terms of service-effect models.

6   Empirical Evaluation

In our empirical validation of the reliability model of basic components we insert a basic component (associated with its service effect protocols) into a testbed. The testbed provides all methods required by the component. There are two kinds of independent variables we can control:

- The reliability of the methods provided by the testbed. They are programmed in a way, that they throw exceptions with a given, adjustable probability.
- The usage profile of the service effect automata. At each branch of the control flow (e.g., if-statements and while-statements) we decide with a given, adjustable probability, which branch to take.

The dependent (observed) variables are the reliabilities of the services, provided by the component in the testbed.

Given that, we conduct the following experiments:

1. Validation of prediction against measurements:
   Independent variables: reliabilities of required methods
   Fixed variables: usage model of the service effect automata
   Measured variables: reliability of provided methods
2. Test of the influence of accuracy of service effect automata usage model:
   Independent variables: accuracy of the service effect automata's usage models
   Fixed variables: reliabilities of required methods
   Measured variables: reliability of provided methods
   We check the measured against the predicted reliability of provided methods which shows the influence of the accuracy of the service effect automata's usage model's accuracy.

The prediction is computed in each experiment for each method like it was done for the service listAccounts in Section 4.

6.1   Testbed for Validation

The testbed used for the empirical experiments was designed to have the maximum control over reliability and usage profiles. The main idea is to test a component (the basic component OnlineAccMgr) in an environment which has only services with a predefined reliability and to implement services of OnlineAccMgr as "dummy" methods, containing only calls to external methods and statements directing the control-flow according to a predefined usage profile.

The whole example system is implemented in Java classes. To realize external (environmental) services with a predefined reliability we implemented all services required by OnlineAccMgr as methods, throwing an exception with a predefined, adjustable probability (i.e., the reliability of the service). We deliberately omitted all other functionality to avoid other causes of exceptions, which would disturb the measurements. For example, the code of service `getSavingsAccount` of `AccMgr` is simply:

```
public void getSavingsAccounts() throws Exception
{
    if (Math.random() > relgetSavingsAccounts) {
        throw new Exception();
    }
}
```

The implementation of the `OnlineAccMgr`'s services follows the same idea of not including anything which might cause extra exceptions. The code for `listAccounts` consists only out of method calls and an `if` statement, to handle control-flow related statements:

```
public String[] listAccounts() throws Exception
{
    accMgr.getCustomerID();
    if (Math.random() > firstBranchlistAccount) {
        displayAccNotAvailableMsg();
    }
    else {
        accMgr.getSavingsAccounts();
        accMgr.getChequeAccounts();

        creditCardMgr.hasCreditCard();
        // actual if (creditCardMgr.hasCreditCard())
        // but that would mean we have to adapt the usage profile of
        // listAcounts also in CreditCardMgr.hasCreditCard
        if (Math.random() <= secondBranchlistAccount) {
            creditCardMgr.getAvailableCredit();
        }
    }
    return new String[0];
}
```

The test driver calls each service a predefined number of times N. (For the presented measurements $N = 100000$) and counts the number of exceptions thrown N_e. From that the MTTF (N/N_e) can be computed having the "time unit" of a service call. The reliability is $1 - N_e/N$.

6.2   Example System

We measure the reliability of the following `OnlineAccMgr`-component in our testbed. The `OnlineAccMgr`-component (online account manager component) is a component residing on a internet-service host of a bank, providing online

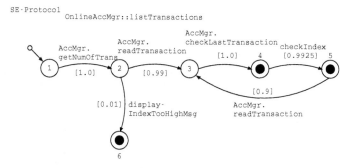

Fig. 10. Service effect protocol of the service `listTransactions` and annotated usage model

banking facilities. The model of the component is motivated by the functionality provided by the online facility of one major Australian bank. In Fig. 8 we show in form of a finite state machine the provides-protocol of this component. Also shown is a (estimated) usage profile of the component, denoted by the probabilities given in squared brackets for each state transition.

After the user has logged in the system (having the possibility of two failed trails), the system lists all accounts of the user with their balances. For a selected account, a pre-defined number of the most recent transactions are listed. The user can scroll for further transactions and look at details of transactions, like their receiver, ID, etc. At any time, the user can logout. When leaving the transaction details view, the user can further scroll through the transactions of the selected account. The user also can select other accounts to proceed with inspecting their transactions without login out.

We show for services of the `OnlineAccMgr`-component the service effect protocols with their model of usage of external methods.

The service `listAccounts` (Fig. 10) reads the bank-internal customer-ID of the user logged in. In case the ID is not provided (e.g., due to discrepancies of the online-banking department and the general customer database of the bank), an error message is issued. Otherwise, the savings- and cheque-accounts of the user are retrieved. If a credit card account (provided by a different branch of the bank or a third-party) is available, the current credit limit is also shown.

The service effect automaton of service `listTransactions` is presented in Fig. 10. This service has two parameters: the account and an index, describing which transactions to list. The user interface offers the possibility to present a fixed number (say 10) of transactions, in reversed order of their date. Calling `listTransactions` again, the next 10 transactions are listed. The service first checks whether the index is in a valid range (by retrieving the maximal number of transaction of this account). Afterwards, in a loop the availability of further transactions to display and the index is checked (to provide maximal 10 transactions).

Fig. 11 shows the service effect automaton of service `getTransactionDetails`. The routine tries to find the partner of the transaction (i.e., the persons or insti-

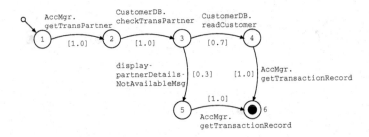

Fig. 11. Service effect protocol of the service `getTransactionDetails` and annotated usage model

Table 2. Contexts with different reliabilities for component `OnlineAccMgr`

Service	Context 1	Context 2
`accMgr.relgetCustomerID`	0.9999	0.99999
`accMgr.relgetSavingsAccounts`	0.9995	0.9
`accMgr.relgetChequeAccounts`	0.9995	0.99
`accMgr.relgetNumOfTrans`	0.9995	0.9
`accMgr.relreadTransaction`	0.9999	0.99
`accMgr.relcheckLastTransaction`	0.9995	0.999
`accMgr.relgetTransPartner`	0.9995	0.9
`accMgr.relgetTransactionRecord`	0.9995	0.9999
`customerDB.relcheckTransPartner`	0.9995	0.9
`customerDB.relreadCustomer`	0.9995	0.9
`creditCardMgr.relhasCreditCar`	0.9999	0.995
`creditCardMgr.relgetAvailableCredit`	0.9999	0.995

tutions originating or receiving money). Depending on the transaction's success, the routine includes some details (according to privacy restrictions) of this transaction partner and lists other details of this transaction (such as ID, exact date, etc.).

The reliability of external services used in different settings is given in Table 2.

6.3   Comparison of Predicted and Measured Reliability

The deviation of the prediction from the measured values is small (below 1%) as shown in Table 3. The predicted reliability is computed as described in Section 4.2. For measurements and prediction we used the values of external services' reliability of context one (as given in Table 2).

The lower accuracy of service `listTransactions` is caused by its loop. Because one cannot give an upper bound of loop executions, the prediction considers also infinite sequences by using the geometric sum in formula 8. However, since in practice loop executions are arbitrarily high but finite, a certain inaccuracy arises. Measurements also show, that the high accuracy of prediction is

Table 3. Predicted vs. measured reliability for services of `OnlineAccMgr`

Service	pred. Rel.	meas. Rel.	difference	error [%]
listAccounts	0.99877	0.99877	-	-
listTransactions	0.98705	0.99397	0.00692	0.70
getTransactionDetails	0.99800	0.99813	0.00013	0.01

also maintained if the reliability of the external methods is low (e.g., 0.85). More important is, that if the reliability of external methods is such low, the reliability of the `OnlineAccMgr`'s services is too low for any reasonable application (see Fig. 12).

The x-axis shows the factor by which the values of external reliabilities (as given in Table 2) is scaled down. A common factor is used keeping the relations between the different external reliabilities constant while scaling down. The reliability of service `listTransactions` drops faster than the other services' values, due to its internal loop. That makes clear, that (a) the control flow of an offered services matters (and hence should be provided in form of service effect automata by the component vendor) and (b) the external reliability values are crucial (at least for loop-containing services) for the provided reliability of a component's service. Even small differences in the external reliability (e.g., 0.02) may decrease the reliability of a method by 50%. This is a strong justification for deploying parameterized contracts to compute a context-dependent reliability of components. These results were taken with the external services' reliabilities of context one, as given in Table 2.

In Fig. 13 we show the difference between predicted and measured reliability varied over accuracy of the usage profile given in the service effect automata. The predicted value varies over the usage profile, while the measured reliability is fixed (i.e., are the values given in Table 3). This simulates the effect, that one performs predictions with inaccurate service effect usage profiles. Most interestingly, the accuracy of the prediction does not depend strongly on the accuracy of the usage profile given with the service effect automata of `listAccounts`. (Similar results hold for the other services.) This is even more interesting when considering the strong influence of the environmental reliability on the service reliability (as shown in Fig. 12). The reason for the weak influence of the usage profiles accuracy is caused by the fact that different call sequences still often have the same or similar reliability (especially when methods are simply called in different order the product of the reliabilities is not changed) and also when determining the reliability of a service by many single calls, chances are high, that many call sequences with similar reliability values occur.

Of course, if external methods have strongly different values for reliability, the influence of the usage profile increases. One can see that in Fig. 13 when comparing the accuracy of the prediction done in context one (with relatively similar reliability values for external methods) and context two (with relatively different values of reliabilities). (Concrete values given in Table 2). While that is no surprise, the interesting fact is, that even in context two where services'

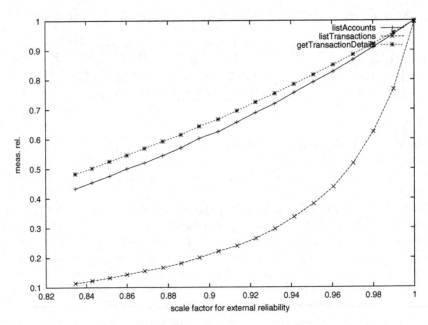

Fig. 12. Comparing the reliability of services depending of the external services' reliabilities

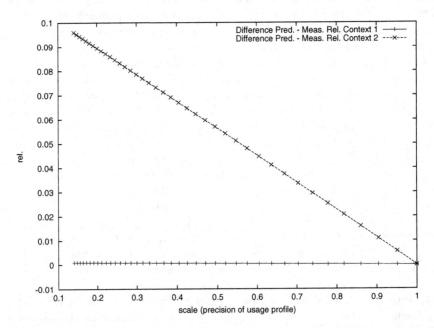

Fig. 13. Differences between predicted and measured reliability of service listAccounts varied over the accuracy of the usage profile of the service effect automata for both contexts of external reliability

failure rates differ in a magnitude of four, the influence on the reliability is still below 10%.

These findings demonstrate that also roughly estimated values of the service effect automata's usage profiles will lead to good predictions, even if they are far of the real usage profile. This is even more important, since in practice, the usage profile of a service effect automaton depends on the usage profile of the overall component, which is not known to the component developer. Opposed to that, our model assumes that the usage profiles of the service effect automata can be given by the component developer. These measurements justify this assumption. The component developer does not need to know the component's usage profile for providing usage profiles of the service effect automata.

7 Gathering Usage Profiles and Reliability Data

As mentioned in Section 5 the applicability of our model depends on the availability of data, mainly reliability figures for external services, bindings, mappings and usage profiles. There are different ways for gathering this data.

Modelling: Reliability and especially usage profiles can be modelled within the software development process. Often, explicit specified usage profiles are considered to be time-consuming and tedious and, hence, shifting the software development costs to the front stages, what many managers will not appreciate. While this is true to a certain extent, one can model profiles at all stages (analysis, design and implementation). Besides the reliability-prediction this also helps to generate realistic test cases [5] or to understand the system requirements.

Monitoring: Usage profiles and reliability data can also be obtained by monitoring user behavior and gathering data about system failures, MTTF and MTTR.

Estimating: In case of non-available specifications and if monitoring is infeasible (e.g., because an implementation of the component or the environment is missing), one still can guess reliabilities (e.g., as uniform, only component-specific figure). Likewise one can estimate usage profiles (e.g., by assuming equi-partition of all outgoing transition of each state, or by some "educated guesses", i.e., by guessing the usage profile by using some knowledge about the applications domain and frequency of errors, etc.).

In practice, a combination of these approaches is usually appropriate: for gathering data of the service effect automata's reliability the component developer might perform simple monitoring when testing the component (which should happen anyhow). But also simple estimations are of practical use. As our experiments show, even if the failure rates of the different methods varies between 10% and 0.0001%, the accuracy of the usage profile do not affect the accuracy of the predictions strongly (see for example Fig. 13). The reliability of basic external services such as operating systems primitives can also be provided by monitoring. This effort is justified, since their reliability affects the

performance of all applications using it. In case of missing data, also some estimations (like failure-free or constant values for specific service-classes) can help.
The usage profile of a component can be derived from usage models developed
in the specification phase of the software project. Although that is not common
practice in general, projects concerned with high-dependability software often
develop exact usage models. Even if exact usage profiles for the software do not
exist, one can derive good data also from usage scenarios and use cases, as for
example part of the UML [29].

8   Related Work

One of the original motivations for architecture specification is the prediction of
system quality attributes [33].

Using architectural information for predicting the reliability of the overall
system is an ongoing concern in reliability prediction, e.g., [2, 7, 38]. Cheung introduced usage profiles and build a prediction model which was concerned with
the flow of control between different modules. The deployment of usage profiles
was also strongly advocated in the cleanroom approach by Mills et al. [20]. In this
context, usage profiles and Markov models have been investigated [35, 39, 21].
Also basing on Cheung's work, Wang et al. introduced an architectural prediction
model, which predicts system reliability out by regarding different architectural
styles, such as pipelines or filters [38]. While investigating the influence of architectural styles on the system's reliability brings valuable insights, their work
is not primarily concerned with software component specific problems of reliability prediction. Although they use the Cheung's calculus in principle, they
avoid the matrix inversion by computing matrix-determinants. For large matrices, computing the determinant (with complexity in $O(n!)$) is much more costly
than inverting the matrix what can be done by a Gauss elimination and some
bookkeeping (complexity in $O(n^3)$). (For that reason, we use Cheung's matrix
inversion.) A stronger component-oriented view on software architectures was
advocated in Hamlet's work [7]. There it is also stated that the reliability of a
component can only be computed with an available usage profile and what is to
do, if that is missing to the component vendor. Hence Hamlet's work deals with
the explicit separation of component development and deployment. However, the
influence of external components reliability is not considered.

A syntax for defining and specifying quality of service attributes is given
by Frolund and Koistinen in [6]. Like in our work, they especially emphasize
the contractual use of quality of service attributes. Opposed to our approach of
context-specific computation of reliability, in their work, reliability is modelled
as a constant feature of the component.

Parameterized contracts were first introduced implicitly in [24] for computing
context-dependent component protocols. A more theoretical treatise is given
in [26].

The need of enriched component interfaces is claimed by many authors
(e.g., [3, 8, 13, 25, 36, 37]). RADL in general was introduced in [30]. DARWIN,

RADL's predecessor, advocated strongly the use of requires-interfaces [16], which was done on the programming language level already in Wirth's Modula-2 [40]. (Even more astonishing is their absence in Sun's EJB or Microsoft's .NET.) Since every analysis method depends strongly on the availability of the required data, special research has been undertaken to generate service effect automata out of code by control-flow analysis [10]. Alternately, tool support also exists for deriving finite state machines out of message sequence charts [41].

9   Conclusions and Future Work

We presented a novel approach to predict the reliability of components based software architectures. Our approach accounts for the fact that a software component's reliability cannot be determined without any context information. We model component reliability by parameterized contracts, which allow the component user to compute the reliability of a component in dependence of its environment.

The (functional and extra-functional) properties of a component always depends on the properties received from its environment. Hence, especially in those systems where many different configurations and environments exist, it is important to perform both fine-grained adaptations of functionality and computation of extra-functional properties. We presented parameterized contracts as a generalization of interoperability checks between components (i.e., classical contracts of components). In this chapter we discussed how parameterized contracts are used for adapting component protocols and predicting reliabilities automatically.

Our empirical validation shows that the reliability of a component's service may strongly depend on the reliability of its environment. This shows that reliability is not a fixed property of a component, but a function of the component's context and usually cannot be evaluated by the component vendor. Measurements show that the control-flow of a component's service strongly affects the influence of the service's environment on its reliability. This strongly advocates that the component vendor must provide some information about the component's realization. Fortunately, our model shows that this does not necessarily break the black-box principle of a component. Furthermore, it is proved sufficient to provide a so-called service effect automaton (which can be derived automatically out of the component's code) describing the sequences of calls to external methods, to which a call to the service leads. It is empirically shown that a rough estimated guess of this automaton's usage profile can lead to very accurate predictions of the components reliability. Altogether, by our measurements, it is made clear that our specifications and parameterized contracts approach (a) are justified (without them reliability could not be predicted accurately, as counterexamples show) and (b) that more detailed specifications cannot increase accuracy of predictions significantly.

By considering software architectures as composite components, we compute their reliability by recursively determining the reliability of inner components and their connections. We take into account that different connections have different reliabilities. We do this by employing connection-specific reliability parameters.

Our approach supports CBSE by supporting the separation of component design and deployment, since we give a clear separation of information which must be provided by the component developer and information to be provided by the component user. Our model overcomes the problem that the components reliability is not computable by the component developer.

As discussed in detail in Section 5 our model's applicability depends on the justification of underlying assumptions. Mainly, we require that all data required by our model is available. While we show that the accuracy of the usage profile of a service effect automata may not be significant in many cases, we also show examples for the importance to a precise knowledge of the external services' reliability.

The main mathematical assumption behind our approach is the applicability of a Markov model. This actually refers to the assumption of independent failure probabilities for services. While some work seems to justify this assumption, still an empirical evaluation of these claims is of interest.

Besides that, our model is primarily concerned with non-cyclic architectures. While many architectures in practice are falling in this category (like layered systems or bus-centered systems), an extension for cyclic dependencies is often relevant (consider for example the callbacks used in framework based architectures, often leading to cyclic dependencies).

In this chapter, we described how to compute the reliability of a component from the environment's reliability and how to infer the reliability of a component based software architecture from a component's reliability. Also, the reverse question is of practical interest: the deduction of component reliability requirements from of requirements to the overall system's reliability.

Cyclic dependencies in composite components can be resolved by the creation of an overall behavioral specification, acting as an overall service effect automaton. While this construction leads to FSMs with exponentially many states (in dependence of the number of participating automata), more intelligent ways of producing such an overall FSM seem to be available for further research.

Another promising area might be the simplification of our model in certain contexts. For example, if all components are installed locally (i.e., no network connections involved) all bindings and mappings might have the same (high) reliability. Hence, one may assume one single value for all bindings and mappings, if not simply reliability 1.0 at all. Besides these possible simplifications, the main structure of our approach will remain: the use of parameterized contracts to specify and compute a context-dependent reliability of component-based software architectures.

Parameterized contracts reflect the dependencies of a component's properties from its environment. This dependency not only affects the component's reliability but also many other functional and extra-functional properties. Therefore, as a further application, the use of parameterized contracts for modelling the components timing behavior seems to be a fruitful area for future research.

Acknowledgements

The authors would like to thank Judith Stafford for her extensive and valuable comments on drafts of this work and the anonymous reviewers for their advice in improving the presentation of our work.

References

1. Přemysl Brada. Towards automated component compatibility assessment. In Wolfgang Weck, Jan Bosch, and Clemens Szyperski, editors, *Proceedings of the Sixth International Workshop on Component-Oriented Programming (WCOP'01)*, June 2001.
2. Roger C. Cheung. A user-oriented software reliability model. *IEEE Transactions on Software Engineering*, 6(2):118–125, March 1980. Special collection from COMPSAC '78.
3. Luca de Alfaro and Thomas A. Henzinger. Interface automata. In Volker Gruhn, editor, *Proceedings of the Joint 8th European Software Engeneering Conference and 9th ACM SIGSOFT Symposium on the Foundation of Software Engeneering (ESEC/FSE-01)*, volume 26, 5 of *SOFTWARE ENGINEERING NOTES*, pages 109–120, New York, September 10–14 2001. ACM Press.
4. W.-P. de Roever, H. Langmaack, and A. Pnueli. *Compositionality: The Significant Difference. International Symposium , COMPOS'97, Bad Malente, Germany.* Springer-Verlag, 1998.
5. M. Dyer. *The Cleanroom Approach to Quality Software Development.* Series in Software Engineering Practice. Wiley & Sons, New York, NY, USA, 1992.
6. Svend Frolund and Jari Koistinen. Quality-of-service specification in distributed object systems. Technical Report HPL-98-159, Hewlett Packard, Software Technology Laboratory, September 1998.
7. D. Hamlet, D. Mason, and D. Woit. Theory of software reliability based on components. In *Proceedings of the 23rd International Conference on Software Engeneering (ICSE-01)*, pages 361–370, Los Alamitos, California, May12–19 2001. IEEE Computer Society.
8. Jun Han. Temporal logic based specification of component interaction protocols. In *Procedings of the 2nd Workshop of Object Interoperability at ECOOP 2000*, Cannes, France, June 12.–16. 2000.
9. Gerald J. Holzmann. *Design and Validation of Computer Protocols.* Prentice Hall, Englewood Cliffs, NJ, USA, 1991.
10. Gunnar Hunzelmann. Generierung von Protokollinformation für Softwarekomponentenschnittstellen aus annotiertem Java-Code. Diplomarbeit, Fakultät für Informatik, Universität Karlsruhe (TH), Germany, April 2001.
11. Anthony Iannino John D. Musa and Kazuhira Okumoto. *Software Reliability - Measurement, prediction, application.* McGraw-Hill, New York, 1987.
12. S. C. Kleene. Representation of events in nerve nets and finite automata. In C. Shannon and J. McCarthy, editors, *Automata Studies, Annals of Math. Studies 34*, pages 3–40. Princeton, New Jersey, 1956.
13. Bernd Krämer. Synchronization constraints in object interfaces. In Bernd Krämer, Michael P. Papazoglou, and Heinz W. Schnmidt, editors, *Information Systems Interoperability*, pages 111–141. Research Studies Press, Taunton, England, 1998.

14. Jeff Kramer, Jeff Magee, Keng Ng, and Naranker Dulay. Software architecture description. In *Software Architecture for Product Families: Principles and Practice*, pages 31–64. Addison-Wesley, 2000.
15. Jean-Claude Laprie and Karama Kanoun. Software reliability and system reliability. In Michael R. Lyu, editor, *Handbook of Software Engineering Reliability*, pages 27–69. McGraw-Hill, New York, 1996.
16. Jeff Magee, Naranker Dulay, Susan Eisenbach, and Jeff Kramer. Specifying distributed software architectures. In *Proceedings of ESEC '95 - 5th European Software Engineering Conference*, volume 989 of *Lecture Notes in Computer Science*, pages 137–153, Sitges, Spain, 25–28 September 1995. Springer-Verlag, Berlin, Germany.
17. Nenad Medvidovic and Richard N. Taylor. A classification and comparison framework for software architecture description languages. *IEEE Transactions on Software Engineering*, 26(1):70–93, Janurary 2000.
18. Bertrand Meyer. Applying "design by contract". *IEEE Computer*, 25(10):40–51, October 1992.
19. Bertrand Meyer. *Object-Oriented Software Construction*. Prentice Hall, Englewood Cliffs, NJ, USA, 2 edition, 1997.
20. Harlan D. Mills, Michael Dyer, and Richard Linger. Cleanoom software engineering. *IEEE Software*, 4(5):19–25, September 1987.
21. John D. Musa. Operational profiles in software-reliability engineering. *IEEE Software*, 10(2):14, March 1993.
22. Microsoft Corp., The .NET homepage. http://www.microsoft.com/net/default.asp.
23. Oscar Nierstrasz. Regular types for active objects. In *Proceedings of the 8th ACM Conference on Object-Oriented Programming Systems, Languages and Applications (OOPSLA-93)*, volume 28, 10 of *ACM SIGPLAN Notices*, pages 1–15, October 1993.
24. Ralf H. Reussner. Dynamic types for software components. In *Companion of the Conference on Object-Oriented Programming Systems, Languages, and Applications (OOPSLA '99)*, November 5–10 1999. extended abstract.
25. Ralf H. Reussner. Enhanced component interfaces to support dynamic adaption and extension. In *34th Hawaiin International Conference on System Sciences*. IEEE, January 3–5 2001.
26. Ralf H. Reussner. *Parametrisierte Verträge zur Protokolladaption bei Software-Komponenten*. Logos Verlag, Berlin, 2001.
27. Ralf H. Reussner. The use of parameterised contracts for architecting systems with software components. In Wolfgang Weck, Jan Bosch, and Clemens Szyperski, editors, *Proceedings of the Sixth International Workshop on Component-Oriented Programming (WCOP'01)*, June 2001.
28. Ralf H. Reussner. Counter-constraint finite state machines: A new model for resource-bounded component protocols. In Bill Grosky, Frantisek Plasil, and Ales Krenek, editors, *Proceedings of the 29th Annual Conference in Current Trends in Theory and Practice of Informatics (SOFSEM 2002), Milovy, Tschechische Republik*, Lecture Notes in Computer Science. Springer-Verlag, Berlin, Germany, November 2002.
29. James Rumbaugh, Ivar Jacobson, and Grady Booch. *The Unified Modeling Language Reference Manual*. Addison-Wesley, Reading, MA, USA, 1999.
30. Heinz W. Schmidt, Iman Poernomo, and Ralf H. Reussner. Trust-by-contract: Modelling, analysing and predicting behaviour in software architectures. *Journal of Integrated Design and Process Science*, 5(3):25–51, September 2001.

31. Heinz W. Schmidt and Ralf H. Reussner. Generating Adapters for Concurrent Component Protocol Synchronisation. In *Proceedings of the Fifth IFIP International conference on Formal Methods for Open Object-based Distributed Systems*, March 2002.

32. Heinz W. Schmidt and Ralf H. Reussner. Parameterised Contracts and Adaptor Synthesis. In *Proceedings of the ICSE Workshop of Component Oriented Software Engineering (CBSE5)*. IEEE, May 2002.

33. Mary Shaw and David Garlan. *Software Architecture*. Prentice Hall, Englewood Cliffs, NJ, USA, 1996.

34. Clemens Szyperski. *Component Software: Beyond Object-Oriented Programming*. ACM Press, Addison-Wesley, Reading, MA, USA, 1998.

35. Carmen Trammell. Quantifying the reliability of software: Statistical testing based on a usage model. In *Proceedings of the Second IEEE International Symposium on Software Engineering Standards*, pages 208–218, 1995.

36. A. Vallecillo, J. Hernández, and J.M. Troya. Object interoperability. In A. Moreira and S. Demeyer, editors, *Object Oriented Technology – ECOOP '99 Workshop Reader*, number 1743 in LNCS, pages 1–21. Springer-Verlag, Berlin, Germany, 1999.

37. A. Vallecillo, J. Hernández, and J.M. Troya. Object interoperability. In J. Malenfant, S. Moisan, and A. Moreira, editors, *Object Oriented Technology – ECOOP 2000 Workshop Reader*, number 1964 in LNCS, pages 256–269. Springer-Verlag, Berlin, Germany, 2000.

38. Wen-Li Wang, Ye Wu, and Mei-Hwa Chen. An Architecture-Based Software Reliability Model. In *Proceedings of the 1999 Pacific Rim International Symposium on Dependable Computing, 16-17 December, Hong Kong, China*. IEEE, 1999.

39. James A. Whittaker and Michael G. Thomason. A Markov chain model for statistical software testing. *IEEE Transactions on Software Engineering*, 20(10):812–824, October 1994.

40. Niklaus Wirth. *Programming in MODULA-2*. Springer-Verlag, 3rd Edition, 1985.

41. Bart Wydaeghe. *Component Composition Based on Composition Patterns and Usage Scenarios*. Dissertation, Department of Computer Science, Vrije Universitiet Brussel, Belgium, 2001.

42. D. Yellin and R. Strom. Protocol Specifications and Component Adaptors. *ACM Transactions on Programming Languages and Systems*, 19(2):292–333, 1997.

Reuse of Formal Verification Efforts
of Incomplete Models
at the Requirements Specification Stage[*]

Rebeca P. Díaz-Redondo, José J. Pazos-Arias, and Ana Fernández-Vilas

Departamento de Enxeñería Telemática, Universidade de Vigo, Spain
{rebeca,jose,avilas}@det.uvigo.es

Abstract. Even though verifying systems during any phase of the development process is a remarkable advantage of using formal techniques, in software engineering practice the great computing resources needed to verify medium-large and large systems entails an efficiency problem in incremental life-cycles, where each iteration implies identifying new requirements, verifying them and, in many cases, modifying the current release of the system to satisfy the new functional specifications. In order to improve the consistency checking process in this kind of life-cycles, we propose reusing formal verification information – previously obtained by a model checking algorithm – to reduce the amount of verifications. This proposal is supported by ARIFS methodology (*Approximate Retrieval of Incomplete and Formal Specifications*) which provides a classification mechanism and an approximate and efficient retrieval one (without formal proofs) to recover the verification information linked to formal and incomplete functional specifications.

1 Introduction

Building large and complex systems, like distributed ones, increases the difficulty of specifying requirements at the beginning of the software process, since these requirements continuously evolve throughout the life-cycle. What is more, at early phases designers usually have not a deep knowledge about the system and, in any case, the complexity could be excessive for a one-step design. Current software engineering practice addresses this problem by the use of incremental development techniques, which makes life-cycle models flexible enough to follow these inevitable and often continuous changes.

On the other hand, formal techniques are expected to be adapted to support this practice, outside their traditional role of verifying that a model meets certain fixed requirements. In fact, in this kind of incremental life-cycles it is usually necessary to join different kinds of formal techniques, because the necessities at each phase of the development process are different [2].

Merging these two previous tendencies (incremental life-cycles and combination of formal techniques), it is possible to obtain a formal software development

[*] Partially supported by PGIDT01PX132203PR project (Xunta de Galicia)

A. Cechich et al. (Eds.): Component-Based Software Quality, LNCS 2693, pp. 326–351, 2003.
© Springer-Verlag Berlin Heidelberg 2003

model which fits in with requirements change throughout the life-cycle and splits complexity.

On the other hand, reusability is widely suggested to be a key to improve software development productivity and quality, but, unlike other engineering fields, software engineering has not yet developed into a mature discipline where reuse is totally embedded. In fact, although software reuse has been informally practiced since programming was born (basically code), a substantial quality and productivity payoff from reuse can only be achieved if reuse is conducted systematically and formally [20] to which there have been innumerable attempts. Besides that, the notion of reuse at the requirements stage is widely accepted as a desirable aim, because reuse at the requirements level can significantly increase reuse at the later stages of development [16]. However, there is little evidence in the literature to suggest that requirements reuse is widely practiced.

ARIFS methodology [7, 6] addresses this concern proposing the reuse of formal requirements specifications at the phase of requirements acquisition of a totally formalized and incremental life-cycle. In fact, the productivity and quality payoff from requirements reuse increases in this kind of software processes because the implementation phase is semiautomatic. Therefore, reusing at the requirements specification stage directly entails reusing at the implementation stage. To be precise, ARIFS methodology supports:

- The reuse of incomplete specifications (obtained from intermediate phases of a totally formalized, iterative and incremental requirements specification process) with the aim of saving specification, synthesis and formal verification (by using a model checking algorithm) efforts [8, 9, 10].
- The reuse of formal verification results with the aim of reducing the great amount of computing resources needed to check the consistency of medium-large and large requirements specifications.

In this chapter, we only focus on this last goal, that is, on reusing formal verification information to improve the consistency checking process at the requirements specification stage. At each iteration of this stage, we need to ensure having a consistent specification, that is, it is essential to "verify" if the new identified requirements are consistent with the current model of the system. Therefore, at each iteration, a consistent (although partial) specification of the system is always available, which allows users to do "validation tasks" over the current specification of the system. Because of this, the amount of computing resources needed to formal verification dramatically increases in this kind of incremental life-cycles.

Reusing previous verification efforts entails a big reduction in these verification necessities, because we are able to minimize the number of executions of the model checking algorithm and/or to reduce the number of states of the model where the consistency checking is needed. Our proposal supplements other traditional techniques to improve model checking algorithms like increasing the efficiency of the verification algorithms or using symbolic graphs (Section 2).

This chapter is organized as follows: the next Section summarizes the most important extant research on retrieving reusable components and improvements in model checking techniques; Section 3 outlines the software development process where ARIFS methodology is included; ARIFS methodology is described in Section 4; Section 5 describes the functional relationship among reusable components which allows reusing verification information; in Section 6 we explain what verification results are going to be reused and in Section 7 the mathematical aspects which enables the reuse of verification information; Section 8 shows how the reuse process is tackled out and clarifies this process by a little example; in Section 9 we study the benefits and costs of reusing verification information in this environment; and, finally, a summary and future work are exposed in Section 10.

2   Related Work

Research on Software Reuse. Organizing large collections of reusable components is one of the main lacks in software reuse, because providing efficient and effective mechanisms to classify and retrieve software elements from a repository is not an easy problem. Retrieving mechanisms usually rely on the same idea: establishing a *profile* or a set of component's characterizing attributes which is used to classify and retrieve them from a repository. Whenever this profile is based on formal specifications, problems derived from natural language are avoided. The typical *specification matching* process starts expressing the relation between two components by using a logical formula. Then, a theorem prover checks its validity, and only if the prover succeeds, the component is considered to be suitable. The vast number of proof tasks makes a practical implementation very hard, so in many of the following works this number is usually reduced applying other techniques.

In the proposal of Zaremski and Wing [23], formal proofs are restricted to a small subset of the repository, which is previously selected by using preconditions and postconditions. In REBOUND (REuse Based On UNDerstanding) tool [19] formal proofs are reduced by applying different heuristics, based on the semantics of specifications.

In [4] a two-tiered hierarchy of the repository based on formal specifications using OSPL is proposed. The lower level is based on generality relationships; and the higher one on similarity relationships, which are assessed by a clustering algorithm. Firstly, it is selected the most suitable cluster, and secondly, a theorem prover is used to finish the search.

NORA/NAMMR tool [21] is basically a *filter pipeline* trying to ensure a *plug-in compatibility*. They use *signature matching filters*, *rejection filters* (based on model checking techniques), and, finally, *confirmation filters* (based on Setheo theorem prover). One of its main problems is that recursive specifications management which is not supported by Setheo.

To sum up, current research lines focus on reusing components at latest stages of the development process, like code, and on using formal descriptions to allow an exact retrieval by applying formal proofs. On the contrary, we propose reusing formal components at early stages, like requirements specification one, and avoiding formal proofs in the retrieval process, that is, providing an approximate retrieval based precisely in the incompleteness of the intermediate models.

Improvements in Model Checking Research. Model checking is inherently vulnerable to the rather practical problem that the number of states may exceed the amount of computer memory available, which is known as the *state-space explosion problem*. Several effective methods have been developed to solve this problem, although the majority of them try to reduce the state-space: (a) by a symbolic representation of state spaces using BBDs (*Binary Decision Diagrams*) [3]; (b) by partial-order reductions [15] which exploits the fact that for checking many properties it is not necessary to consider all possible ways in which a state space can be traversed; (c) by using equivalence and pre-order relations [17], which transforms models into equivalent, but smaller models that satisfy the same properties; and (d) by a compositional verification [5], that is, decomposing properties into sub-properties such that each sub-property can be checked for a part of the state space, and the combination of the sub-properties implies the required global property. Other techniques focus on efficient memory management strategies which try to optimize the use of main memory by using hashing [12], caching techniques [11], and so forth.

Our proposal of reusing results of formal verification supplements the previous ones and try to reduce the great computational charges of model checking. The underlying idea is reusing formal verification results of the same property between *functionally similar* incomplete models.

3   Context

Our reuse environment is included in the software development process based on the SCTL-MUS methodology [18]. This methodology joins: on the one hand, the totally formalization of the process, combining different formal techniques (model-oriented, MUS, and property-oriented, SCTL); and, on the other hand, an incremental point of view. In [18] is included an application example of this methodology, where authors show how to develop all the processes involved in a CSMA/CD protocol.

In this Section, we focus on describing the philosophy of this methodology (Section 3.1) and its mathematical basis (Section 3.2).

3.1   Life-Cycle Description

The first phase of this methodology (*Initial goals*) supports obtaining a complete and consistent functional specification of the system from user's specification (see Fig. 1(a)). At each iteration of this stage: (1) the user identifies and specifies a set of new functional requirements to be added to the functional specification (in box labelled as "*SCTL*"), which lead to a growth in the system functionality; (2) the functional specification is automatically translated into a model or prototype

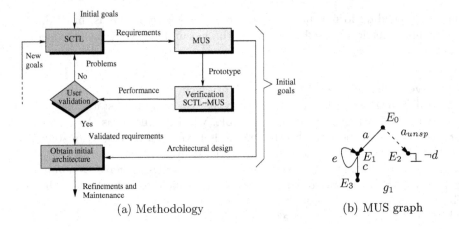

(a) Methodology   (b) MUS graph

Fig. 1. SCTL-MUS Methodology

(in box labelled as *"MUS"*) on which the user may observe the behavior of the system by its animation; (3) the global requirements[1] are verified in the current model or prototype (in box labelled as *"Verification SCTL-MUS"*) to check: if the model already satisfies the requirements; if it is not able to provide these functional requirements nor in the current iteration neither in future ones (inconsistency); or, if the system does not satisfy the requirements, but it is able to do it (incompleteness); and (4) if the user considers the prototype meets all the system goals (in box labelled as *"User validation"*), the initial phase ends, in other case, another iteration is needed.

The second stage of the development process, or *Refinements phase*, starts from the complete and consistent specification of the system requirements obtained in the previous stage, or *Initial goals*, and its main goal is to design the system architecture. This architecture is expressed by a constructive formal technique (LOTOS [13]) which allows a description of the system components, their interactions and interfaces. Finally, *Maintenance stage* is turned into a development phase whose starting point is the MUS model of the current system.

3.2   Formal Basis

MUS formalism [18] (*Model of Unspecified States*) is based on typical labelled-transitions systems and it supports:

(a) Consistency checking by using a model checking algorithm (in box labelled as *"Verification SCTL-MUS"* in Fig. 1(a)). That is, it is possible to do "verification tasks" to analyze if SCTL requirements are consistent with the current model of the system.

---

[1] SCTL requirements which must be satisfied by the specification and which has previously been defined (deadlock-free, for instance, or other system's objectives).

(b) Prototyping and feedback with users (in box labelled as "*MUS*" in Fig. 1(a)).
    That is, it is possible to do "validation tasks" to ensure the incomplete (but
    consistent) model really expresses the functionality desired by the user.

The main difference with traditional labelled-transitions systems is that MUS
allows having *not-yet-specified* elements, which is reflected in both events and
states of the graph. Therefore, an event, a_j, in a state, E_i, of a MUS graph can be
specified to be possible or *true* (1), to be impossible or *false* (0), or in its absence,
to be *unspecified* ($\frac{1}{2}$), which is denoted by $E_i[a_j] \in \{0, \frac{1}{2}, 1\}$. Consequently, a state
where every single event is unspecified, is called an *unspecified state*. A state from
which no evolution is specified is called a *final state*, that is, both unspecified
states and states where only false events have been specified are final states of a
MUS graph.

An example of MUS graphs is shown in Fig. 1(b), where the model g_1 can
evolve from one state into another when an event or an action of $\Lambda = \{a, b, c, d, e\}$
occurs or through the special event a_{unsp}. This special event is used whenever the
user need to specify a transition, but he does not have enough information about
which event is going to enable it. Since a_{unsp} is not a real event, in subsequent
iterations of the requirements capture process, it will evolve to one event of Λ.
In the initial state of the graph in Fig. 1(b), E_0, event a is specified as a possible
one, that is, the system g_1 evolves from this state into state E_1 whenever event a
occurs. The system g_1 evolves from E_0 into state E_2 through an event which has
not been specified yet, which is denoted by a_{unsp}. In subsequent iterations, the
user may specify this transition with a possible event from Λ with the exception
of event a, because MUS graphs are deterministic ones. In state E_2 (a final
state), event d is a impossible one, which is denoted by $\neg d$, and, finally, state E_3
is a totally unspecified state because none event of Λ has been specified in this
state as a possible event or as an impossible one[2].

In SCTL-MUS methodology, functional requirements are specified by using
the many-valued logic SCTL [18] (*Simple Causal Temporal Logic*). The major
motivation behind introducing causal logic into requirements specification is fill-
ing the gap between the natural language, in which users express themselves,
and a formal specification of requirements.

An SCTL requirement follows the pattern: **Premise** $\Rightarrow\otimes$ **Consequence**,
which establishes a causing condition (premise); a temporal operator determining
the applicability of the cause; and a condition which is the effect (consequence).
Syntax of an SCTL requirement $R \in \mathcal{R}_{SCTL}$ is as follows:

$$\langle \mathcal{R}_{SCTL} \rangle ::= R \wedge R \mid R \vee R \mid R \Rightarrow\otimes R \mid \neg R \mid a \in \Lambda \mid \theta \in \Theta$$
$$\langle \Rightarrow\otimes \rangle ::= \Rightarrow \mid \Rightarrow\odot \mid \Rightarrow\bigcirc \tag{1}$$

where $\langle \Rightarrow\otimes \rangle$ is the set of temporal operators; $\theta \in \Theta ::= \{true \mid false \mid \emptyset\}$ are
propositional constants; and $a \in \Lambda$ is the alphabet of events in a model[3]. Tem-

---

[2] Therefore, in this state every event of Λ is unspecified, but for simplicity reasons,
    unspecified events of a state are not represented in Fig. 1(b), only in E_0 because
    a_{unsp} implies an evolution of the model.

[3] $\emptyset$ stands for the empty set or absence of propositional constants.

poral operators $\{\Rightarrow, \Rightarrow\bigodot, \Rightarrow\bigcirc\}$ —referred to as *simultaneously*, *previously* and *next*— define the states in which the consequence of the requirement is caused by its premise. These states are called the applicability states of the requirement and for an SCTL requirement R in a state E_j they are denoted by $\perp (R_{E_j})$. Apart from causation, SCTL adds the concept of *not-yet-specified* which is specially useful to deal with both incomplete and inconsistent information obtained by requirements capture. Although events will be *true* or *false* at the final stage, in intermediate phases of the specification process it is possible that users do not have enough information about them yet, so these events are *unspecified* in these phases. Therefore, it is possible specifying three different values: possible or *true* (1), impossible or *false* (0) and *unspecified* ($\frac{1}{2}$), which is the default value.

Since SCTL-MUS methodology adds the concept of *not-yet-specified*, the level of satisfaction of an SCTL requirement R may not be *false* nor *true*, just as the boolean logic, in fact, it must have a level of satisfaction related to the level of specification of R in the MUS model (totally or partially unspecified on the MUS model). Consequently, this methodology defines six different levels of satisfaction ($\Phi = \{0, \frac{1}{4}, \frac{1}{2}, \widehat{\frac{1}{2}}, \frac{3}{4}, 1\}$). These levels of satisfaction are based on causal propositions: *"an SCTL requirement is satisfied iff its premise is satisfied and its consequence is satisfied according to its temporal operator"*. Therefore, the level of satisfaction of an SCTL requirement R in a state E_i of a MUS graph, denoted by $\vDash (R, E_i)$, depends on the structure of the requirement (equation 1) as follows:

$$
\begin{aligned}
R = a_j \in \Lambda &\Rightarrow \vDash (R, E_i) = E_i[a_j] \\
R = \neg R_1 &\Rightarrow \vDash (R, E_i) = \neg \vDash (R_1, E_i) \\
R = (R_1 \wedge R_2) &\Rightarrow \vDash (R, E_i) = \vDash (R_1, E_i) \wedge \vDash (R_2, E_i) \\
R = (R_1 \vee R_2) &\Rightarrow \vDash (R, E_i) = \vDash (R_1, E_i) \vee \vDash (R_2, E_i) \\
R = (R_1 \Rightarrow R_2) &\Rightarrow \vDash (R, E_i) = \vDash (R_1, E_i) \to \vDash (R_2, E_i) \\
R = (R_1 \Rightarrow\bigcirc R_2) &\Rightarrow \vDash (R, E_i) = \vDash (R_1, E_i) \to \bigwedge_{E_i \in \perp(R_{E_i})} \vDash (R_2, E_i) \\
R = (R_1 \Rightarrow\bigodot R_2) &\Rightarrow \vDash (R, E_i) = \vDash (R_1, E_i) \to \bigwedge_{E_i \in \perp(R_{E_i})} \vDash (R_2, E_i)
\end{aligned}
$$

$$(2)$$

where causal operator, $\to$, is detailed in Fig. 2(b). In short, the level of satisfaction of an SCTL requirement varies according to its closeness to the *true* (or *false*) level of satisfaction. According to this *truth ordering* (Fig. 2(a)), $\Phi = \{0, \frac{1}{4}, \frac{1}{2}, \widehat{\frac{1}{2}}, \frac{3}{4}, 1\}$ is a quasi-boolean lattice with the least upper bound operator $\vee$, the greatest lower bound operator $\wedge$, and the unary operation $\neg$ (defined by horizontal symmetry[4]). The 4-tuple $(\Phi, \vee, \wedge, \neg)$ has the structure of the De Morgan algebra and it is called algebra of MPU [18] (*M*iddle *P*oint *U*ncertainty).

On the other hand, levels of satisfaction can also be partially ordered according to a *knowledge level* ($\leq_k$) (Fig. 3) as follows:

---

[4] That is, according to Fig. 2(a), we have the following values: $(\neg 0) = 1$, $(\neg 1) = 0$, $(\neg\frac{3}{4}) = \frac{1}{4}$, $(\neg\frac{1}{4}) = \frac{3}{4}$, $(\neg\widehat{\frac{1}{2}}) = \widehat{\frac{1}{2}}$, $(\neg\frac{1}{2}) = \frac{1}{2}$

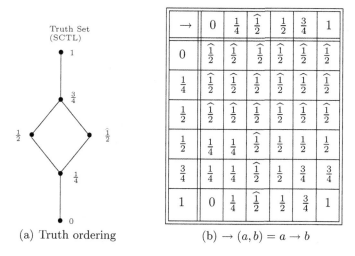

$\rightarrow$	0	$\frac{1}{4}$	$\widehat{\frac{1}{2}}$	$\frac{1}{2}$	$\frac{3}{4}$	1
0	$\widehat{\frac{1}{2}}$	$\widehat{\frac{1}{2}}$	$\widehat{\frac{1}{2}}$	$\widehat{\frac{1}{2}}$	$\widehat{\frac{1}{2}}$	$\widehat{\frac{1}{2}}$
$\frac{1}{4}$	$\widehat{\frac{1}{2}}$	$\widehat{\frac{1}{2}}$	$\widehat{\frac{1}{2}}$	$\widehat{\frac{1}{2}}$	$\widehat{\frac{1}{2}}$	$\widehat{\frac{1}{2}}$
$\frac{1}{2}$	$\widehat{\frac{1}{2}}$	$\widehat{\frac{1}{2}}$	$\widehat{\frac{1}{2}}$	$\widehat{\frac{1}{2}}$	$\widehat{\frac{1}{2}}$	$\widehat{\frac{1}{2}}$
$\frac{1}{2}$	$\frac{1}{4}$	$\frac{1}{4}$	$\widehat{\frac{1}{2}}$	$\frac{1}{2}$	$\frac{1}{2}$	$\frac{1}{2}$
$\frac{3}{4}$	$\frac{1}{4}$	$\frac{1}{4}$	$\widehat{\frac{1}{2}}$	$\frac{1}{2}$	$\frac{3}{4}$	$\frac{3}{4}$
1	0	$\frac{1}{4}$	$\widehat{\frac{1}{2}}$	$\frac{1}{2}$	$\frac{3}{4}$	1

(a) Truth ordering   (b) $\rightarrow (a,b) = a \rightarrow b$

Fig. 2. Causal operator and truth ordering among levels of satisfaction

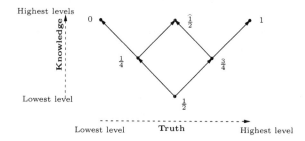

Fig. 3. Knowledge and Truth partial orderings among levels of satisfaction

- $\{1, \widehat{\frac{1}{2}}, 0\}$ are the highest knowledge levels. We know at the current stage of the model the final level of satisfaction of the property: 1 or *true* means the requirement is satisfied; 0 or *false* implies the requirement is not satisfied; and $\widehat{\frac{1}{2}}$ or *contradictory or not applicable* means the requirement cannot become *true* or *false*.

- $\{\frac{1}{4}, \frac{3}{4}\}$ are the middle knowledge levels. Although at the current stage of the model, the property is partially unspecified, we know its satisfaction tendency. That is, for the current value $\frac{1}{4}$, in a subsequent stage of specification, the level of satisfaction ($\phi \in \Phi$) cannot became 1 (*true*), it will be $\frac{1}{4} \leq_k \phi$ ($\phi \in \{\frac{1}{4}, \widehat{\frac{1}{2}}, 0\}$); and for the current value $\frac{3}{4}$, in a subsequent stage of specification, the level of satisfaction ($\phi \in \Phi$) cannot became 0 (*false*), it will be $\frac{3}{4} \leq_k \phi$ ($\phi \in \{\frac{3}{4}, \widehat{\frac{1}{2}}, 1\}$).

- $\{\frac{1}{2}\}$ is the lowest knowledge level. The property is totally unspecified at the current stage of the model and we do not know any information about

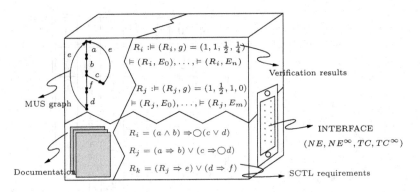

Fig. 4. Reusable component of ARIFS methodology

its future level of satisfaction ($\phi \in \Phi$), that is, it can became $\frac{1}{2} \leq_k \phi$ ($\phi \in \{\frac{1}{2}, \frac{1}{4}, \frac{3}{4}, 0, \widehat{\frac{1}{2}}, 1\}$) in a subsequent stage of specification.

4 What Is a Reusable Component? Retrieval in ARIFS

Generally speaking, ARIFS methodology [10] enables classification, retrieval and adaptation of reusable components at the requirements specification phase of the SCTL-MUS methodology. Each reusable component (Fig. 4) joins: the set of SCTL requirements specified by the developers; the MUS graph modelling the component's functionality; verification information (Section 6) consisting of the set of requirements which had been verified on the MUS graph and their verification results (obtained after running the model checking algorithm); an interface or *functional profile* (Section 5) which is automatically obtained from its functional characteristics and is used to classify and retrieve the component from the repository; and, finally, other documentation about the component (developer, data, etc.).

The information kept in these reusable components is reused in two different ways:

1. Reusing the whole component at the beginning of the requirements capture stage [8, 9]. The underlying idea is reusing already developed MUS prototypes which are functionally close to the functionality specified by the first set of SCTL requirements. Therefore, we are able to avoid synthesis tasks to translate the SCTL requirements into the MUS prototype and we are also able to reuse the verification information linked to the recovered reusable component, saving the very probable future formal proofs.
2. Reusing only the verification information linked to the reusable components (goal of this chapter). The underlying philosophy is reusing the formal verification results linked to those reusable components which are functionally close to the current model of the system. Therefore, we are able to reduce the amount of formal proofs needed to check the consistency of new SCTL requirements on the transient releases of the system in every single iteration of the requirements capture stage.

In both cases, main characteristics of the retrieval process are the following ones:

- We have opted by a formal specification of the reusable components because SCTL-MUS is a totally formalized software process. Although in many of previous approaches (Section 2) these formal representations are only used as a pattern to recover lowly abstract components (like code), in our approach, these formal specifications are just the content of the components, so we have a **content-oriented retrieval**: each component is, simultaneously, index and content of the retrieval.

- As one of our goals is precisely minimizing the amount of verification tasks in the software development process, we have decided not to apply formal proofs in the retrieval process, which entails an exact retrieval. Instead of this, we propose an **approximate components retrieval** which allows an efficient selection of those reusable components which are functionally close to the query. This approximate retrieval is based on the concept of *not-yet-specified* —inherent to incomplete systems obtained from a transient phase of the development process—, that is, not everything is true or false, may not be specified yet.

- We have also defined a two-step retrieval process: firstly a rough search phase, where a little set of components is retrieved; and secondly, a more refined one, where the most suitable components are selected. The main reason of supporting this **layered retrieval process** is basically an efficiency one.

5   Classification of Reusable Components

Having a good classification mechanism which allows an efficient retrieval is essential in any reuse environment. In this Section, we focus on describing how reusable components are classified in ARIFS methodology to recover verification information in an efficient way.

Our main goal is recovering reusable components whose functional characteristics are close to the functional characteristics of the query, because, in this way, the verification information linked to this reusable component may be more useful (Section 7). Therefore, the retrieval criteria must be based on the functional similarities between reusable components and the query. This is the reason why our classification mechanism is also based in functional similarities among reusable components. Generally speaking, the underlying idea behind our classification mechanism is that the closer two reusable components are classified in the repository, the more functional similarities they have.

In order to assess functional similarities between two reusable components, we have defined four functional relationships [10]. Each one is characterized in terms of a function $\mathcal{O}$ that associates with every MUS graph g a set $\mathcal{O}(g)$ which constitutes the observable behavior of g. Basically, these functions distinguish between semantic similarities, which reflects if two reusable component have similar functional features (considering sequences of events), that is, if they act alike [9]; and structural similarities, which reflects if two reusable component have similar representation of their MUS graphs without considering events linked to each transition (only the skeleton of the graph), that is, if they look alike [8].

Although we have defined four different functional relationships, we only focus here on **complete and non finite traces** function, denoted by TC^∞, because the mathematical aspects of sharing verification information exposed in this chapter (Section 7) are only satisfied by components holding a TC^∞-relationship. The remainder functional relationships (NE, NE^∞, TC, see Fig. 4) are used to reuse the whole incomplete specification and they are explained in detail in [10].

TC^∞ associates with every MUS graph $g \in \mathbb{G}$ a set $TC^\infty(g)$ which is based on the traditional complete trace semantics [22] —which obtain sequences of events linked to every single evolution path of the model. However, we also take into account both *true* and *false* events in order to differentiate *false* events from *unspecified* ones, and, besides that, non finite evolution paths of the graph are also reflected in $TC^\infty(g)$.

Example 1.

$$TC^\infty(g) = (b\neg d, ac, a(e)+, aec, a(e) + c)$$

The Figure above shows the result of applying this function to a MUS graph g. In this example, g has five different evolution paths: it can evolve from initial state to a final one where event d is impossible through event b; from initial state to a final one through events a and c; from initial state to a final one through events a, e and c; from initial state to a final one through event a, an undetermined number of events e (a non finite evolution path) and, finally, event c; and from initial state through event a and an infinite number of events e (a non finite evolution path)[5].

For TC^∞, the equivalence relation $=^\infty_{TC} \in \mathbb{G} \times \mathbb{G}$ is given by $g =^\infty_{TC} g' \Leftrightarrow TC^\infty(g) = TC^\infty(g')$, and the pre-order $\sqsubseteq^\infty_{TC} \in \mathbb{G} \times \mathbb{G}$ by $g \sqsubseteq^\infty_{TC} g' \Leftrightarrow TC^\infty(g) \sqsubseteq TC^\infty(g')$, that is, $\sqsubseteq^\infty_{TC}$ provides a partial order between equivalence classes or graph sets indistinguishable using TC^∞-observations, so $(\mathbb{G}, \sqsubseteq^\infty_{TC})$ is a *partially ordered set*, or *poset*. Two graphs g and g' are TC^∞-related iff $g \sqsubseteq^\infty_{TC} g'$ or $g' \sqsubseteq^\infty_{TC} g$. A subset $G_1 \in \mathbb{G}$ is called a *chain* if every two graphs in G_1 are TC^∞-related. Two graphs non TC^∞-related but being in two different chains which share at least one graph are called *potentially TC^∞-related graphs*[6].

$TC^\infty(g)$ is automatically obtained from the MUS graph and it is part of the **profile** or set of characterizing attributes of a reusable component (see "inter-

---

[5] ()+ denotes the set of events inside the parenthesis can be repeated an undetermined number of times.

[6] These relationships among MUS graphs are directly extrapolated to the reusable components which contain them, for instance, two components C and C' are TC^∞-related ($C \sqsubseteq^\infty_{TC} C'$ or $C' \sqsubseteq^\infty_{TC} C$) iff their MUS graphs g and g' are also TC^∞-related.

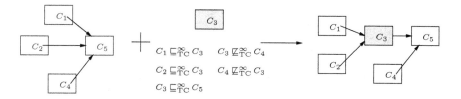

Fig. 5. Example of classification in ARIFS

face" in Fig. 4). This information is used to classify reusable components (C) in the lattice after finding its *correct place*, like Fig. 5 shows. That is, it is necessary looking for those components TC^∞-related to C such as C is TC^∞-included on them, and those components TC^∞-related to C such as they are TC^∞-included on C [7].

6   What Verification Information Is It Reused?

After running the model checking algorithm we achieve a set of levels of satisfaction of an SCTL requirement R in every single state of a MUS graph g (Section 3). We need to store this information because in future iterations it is possible that we need to verify the same requirement —or a subset of it— over the same graph —or over a graph functionally close to it. Depending on the size of the graph, the management of this amount of information may be difficult, so we need to store this information under a more manageable form. Therefore, we have defined four verification results which summarize the available verification information:

- $\exists\, \Diamond R$ expresses that *"some trace of the system satisfies eventually R"* and its level of satisfaction is denoted by $\vDash (\exists\, \Diamond R, g)$.
- $\exists\, \Box R$ expresses that *"some trace of the system satisfies invariantly R"* and its level of satisfaction is denoted by $\vDash (\exists\, \Box R, g)$.
- $\forall\, \Diamond R$ expresses that *"every trace of the system satisfies eventually R"* and its level of satisfaction is denoted by $\vDash (\forall\, \Diamond R, g)$.
- $\forall\, \Box R$ expresses that *"every trace of the system satisfies invariantly R"* and its level of satisfaction is denoted by $\vDash (\forall\, \Box R, g)$.

That is, starting from an SCTL requirement R which has been verified in a MUS graph g, we define four derived properties (above) whose levels of satisfaction make up the level of satisfaction of R in g, denoted by $\vDash (R, g)$:

$$\vDash (R, g) = (\vDash (\exists\, \Diamond R, g), \vDash (\forall\, \Diamond R, g), \vDash (\exists\, \Box R, g), \vDash (\forall\, \Box R, g)) \qquad (3)$$

This quadruple is stored linked to the current reusable component, ready to be recovered whenever it is necessary. In order to obtain this values, we have to

---

[7] In order to eliminate superfluous reusable components connections, anti-symmetric property of TC^∞ is applied.

study the traces of states of the graph, that is, those sequences of states through which the system can evolve in every single evolution path. As consequence, we obtain the following transient information:

$$\vDash (\Diamond R, E(\pi_i)) \;\;=\;\; \vDash (R, E_i^1) \vee \ldots \vee \vDash (R, E_i^n) \tag{4}$$

where $E(\pi_i)$ is one of the traces of states of the system, and $\{E_i^j\}_{j=1}^n$ its set of states. This information expresses if "$E(\pi_i)$ *satisfies eventually* R". The logic connective $\vee$ is the least upper bound operator in the *truth level* partial ordering in Fig. 3.

$$\vDash (\Box R, E(\pi_i)) \;\;=\;\; \vDash (R, E_i^1) \wedge \ldots \wedge \vDash (R, E_i^n) \tag{5}$$

where $E(\pi_i)$ is one of the traces of states of the system, and $\{E_i^j\}_{j=1}^n$ its set of states. In this case, this information expresses if "$E(\pi_i)$ *satisfies invariantly* R". The logic connective $\wedge$ is the greatest lower bound operator in the *truth level* partial ordering in Fig. 3.

Finally, knowing $\vDash (\Box R, E(\pi_i))$ and $\vDash (\Diamond R, E(\pi_i))$ in every trace of states of the graph, we deduce each value of $\vDash (R, g)$ (equation 3):

$$
\begin{aligned}
\vDash (\exists \, \Diamond R, g) &= \vDash (\Diamond R, E(\pi_1)) \vee \ldots \vee \vDash (\Diamond R, E(\pi_m)) \\
\vDash (\forall \, \Diamond R, g) &= \vDash (\Diamond R, E(\pi_1)) \wedge \ldots \wedge \vDash (\Diamond R, E(\pi_m)) \\
\vDash (\exists \, \Box R, g) &= \vDash (\Box R, E(\pi_1)) \vee \ldots \vee \vDash (\Box R, E(\pi_m)) \\
\vDash (\forall \, \Box R, g) &= \vDash (\Box R, E(\pi_1)) \wedge \ldots \wedge \vDash (\Box R, E(\pi_m))
\end{aligned}
\tag{6}
$$

Example 2. In Fig. 6(a), the traces of states of g are the following ones:

$$E(\pi_1) = \{E_0, E_1, E_3\} \qquad E(\pi_2) = \{E_0, E_1, E_4\} \qquad E(\pi_3) = \{E_0, E_2, E_5\}$$

In this case, we obtain the two levels of satisfaction (equations (4) and (5)) of every single trace of the graph as Table 6(c) shows. For instance, in trace $E(\pi_1)$ the results are as follows:

$$
\begin{aligned}
\vDash (\Diamond R, E(\pi_1)) &= \vDash (R, E_0) \vee \vDash (R, E_2) \vee \vDash (R, E_5) = \;\; 1 \vee \tfrac{1}{2} \vee \tfrac{1}{2} = 1 \\
\vDash (\Box R, E(\pi_1)) &= \vDash (R, E_0) \wedge \vDash (R, E_2) \wedge \vDash (R, E_5) = \;\; 1 \wedge \tfrac{1}{2} \wedge \tfrac{1}{2} = \tfrac{1}{4}
\end{aligned}
$$

Finally, the result $\vDash (R, g)$ can be deduced from the results in Table 6(c) and the equations (6), so:

$$\vDash (R, g) = (1, 1, \frac{1}{4}, 0)$$

This verification information entails the following conclusions: because of $\vDash (\forall \, \Diamond R, g) = 1$, every trace of g satisfies eventually R, that is, R is a *liveness property* [1] in g; since $\vDash (\exists \, \Box R, g) = \frac{1}{4}$, R is partially specified in g, but regardless of future iterations, any trace of g does not satisfy invariantly R, that is, R is *not a safety property* [1] in g.

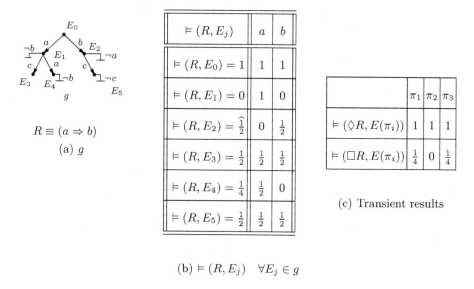

$R \equiv (a \Rightarrow b)$

(a) g

$\vDash (R, E_j)$	a	b
$\vDash (R, E_0) = 1$	1	1
$\vDash (R, E_1) = 0$	1	0
$\vDash (R, E_2) = \widehat{\frac{1}{2}}$	0	$\frac{1}{2}$
$\vDash (R, E_3) = \frac{1}{2}$	$\frac{1}{2}$	$\frac{1}{2}$
$\vDash (R, E_4) = \frac{1}{4}$	$\frac{1}{2}$	0
$\vDash (R, E_5) = \frac{1}{2}$	$\frac{1}{2}$	$\frac{1}{2}$

(b) $\vDash (R, E_j)$ $\forall E_j \in g$

	π_1	π_2	π_3
$\vDash (\Diamond R, E(\pi_i))$	1	1	1
$\vDash (\Box R, E(\pi_i))$	$\frac{1}{4}$	0	$\frac{1}{4}$

(c) Transient results

Fig. 6. Levels of satisfaction of R in every state of g

7 Mathematical Aspects of Sharing Verification Information

The defined classification scheme (Section 5) implies that a component is stored *between* reusable components whose functionalities contain or are contained by it. For instance in Fig. 5, C_1 and C_2 are *functional parts* of C_3, being this one a *functional part* of C_5. In this situation, how can we take advantage of the verification information of one reusable component to obtain verification results of other ones without running the model checking algorithm? That is, for instance, if we know the level of satisfaction of a requirement R in C_1 and/or in C_2 and/or in C_5, what is the level of satisfaction of R in C_3? In this Section, we explain some mathematical aspects directly related to this problem.

As we have explained in Section 3, the six possible levels of satisfaction ($\Phi = \{0, \frac{1}{4}, \frac{1}{2}, \widehat{\frac{1}{2}}, \frac{3}{4}, 1\}$) can be ordered according to a knowledge criterion ($\leq_k$), as Fig. 3 shows. These levels of satisfaction offer information about the current verification results of an SCTL requirement in a model and, if the requirement is partially or totally unspecified in the model, they inform us about the tendency of satisfaction in subsequent iterations of the requirements capture stage.

Property 1. For the poset $(\Phi, \leq_k)$ we have demonstrated [6] that operators $\wedge$, $\vee$, $\neg$ and $\rightarrow$ are monotonic with respect to $\leq_k$, that is:

- $\wedge$ is a monotonic operator with respect to $\leq_k$:

$$\text{if } a \leq_k a' \text{ and } b \leq_k b', \text{ then } (a \wedge b) \leq_k (a' \wedge b')$$

- $\vee$ is a monotonic operator with respect to $\leq_k$:

$$\text{if } a \leq_k a' \text{ and } b \leq_k b', \text{ then } (a \vee b) \leq_k (a' \vee b')$$

- The causal operator $\rightarrow$ is monotonic with respect to $\leq_k$:

$$\text{if } a \leq_k a' \text{ and } b \leq_k b', \text{ then } (a \rightarrow b) \leq_k (a' \rightarrow b')$$

- The operator $\neg$ is monotonic with respect to the ordering $\leq_k$:

$$\text{if } a \leq_k b, \text{ then } \neg a \leq_k \neg b$$

Definition 1. *Let $\sqsubseteq_e$ be a simulation relation between two states E_1 and E_2, denoted by $E_1 \sqsubseteq_e E_2$, satisfying:*

$$\forall E_1' \mid E_1 \overset{\omega}{\rightarrow} E_1' \text{ then } \exists E_2' \mid E_2 \overset{\omega}{\rightarrow} E_2' \text{ and } E_1' \sqsubseteq_e E_2'$$
$$\text{and if } E_1 \overset{\omega}{\nrightarrow} \text{ then } E_2 \overset{\omega}{\nrightarrow}$$

where $E_1 \overset{\omega}{\rightarrow} E_1'$ means the system can evolve from E_1 to E_2 through event ω, that is, ω is a possible event, or true, in this state; and $E_1 \overset{\omega}{\nrightarrow}$ implies the system cannot evolve from E_1 through event ω, that is, ω is impossible, or false, in this state.
Let g and g' be two MUS graphs, g' simulates g, denoted by $g \sqsubseteq_e g'$, iff $E_0 \sqsubseteq_e E_0'$, where E_0 is the initial state of g and E_0' the initial state of g'.

Property 2. Let E and E' be two states satisfying $E \sqsubseteq_e E'$, therefore $\vDash (R, E) \leq_k \vDash (R, E')$. That is, the level of satisfaction of a requirement R in E has a lower knowledge level than its level of satisfaction in E'.

Proof. This property can be demonstrated by induction on the structure of a requirement R (equations 1) and applying the monotonicity of the logic operators $\wedge$, $\vee$ and $\neg$, and the causal operator $\rightarrow$ regarding the ordering $\leq_k$.
BASE. Let $R = a_i \mid a_i \in \Lambda$ be an SCTL requirement where a_i belongs to the alphabet of events. Because of Definition 1, it is satisfied that $\vDash (R, E) \leq_k \vDash (R, E')$. That is, as $E \sqsubseteq_e E'$, therefore every single *true* event and every single *false* event in E keep its specification in E'. Besides that, every single *unspecified* event in E may keep its level of specification in E' or may go to be specified as *true* or *false* in E', that is, may go to a higher knowledge level regarding $\leq_k$. Therefore, $\vDash (R, E) \leq_k \vDash (R, E')$. On the other hand, if $R = \theta \mid \theta \in \Theta = \{true \mid false \mid \emptyset\}$ is an SCTL requirement (equations 1) where θ is a propositional constant, then and because of Definition 1 we know that $\vDash (R, E) = \vDash (R, E')$, therefore $\vDash (R, E) \leq_k \vDash (R, E')$.
INDUCTION. We consider the following cases of an SCTL requirement (see the SCTL requirements' syntax in equations 1):

1. If $R = R_1 \vee R_2$, then

$$\vDash (R, E) \ = \ \vDash (R_1, E) \ \vee \ \vDash (R_2, E) \qquad \text{(equations 2)}$$

By induction hypothesis, $\vDash (R_1, E) \leq_k \vDash (R_1, E')$ and $\vDash (R_2, E) \leq_k \vDash (R_2, E')$. As the logic operator $\vee$ is monotonic with respect to $\leq_k$ (Property 1), then

$$\vDash (R_1, E) \ \vee \ \vDash (R_2, E) \ \leq_k \vDash (R_1, E') \ \vee \ \vDash (R_2, E')$$

2. If $R = R_1 \wedge R_2$, then

$$\vDash (R_1, E) \ \wedge \ \vDash (R_2, E) \ \leq_k \vDash (R_1, E') \ \wedge \ \vDash (R_2, E') \qquad \text{(equations 2)}$$

We prove this property applying the monotonicity of the logic operator $\wedge$ (Property 1) as in item 1.
3. $R = R_1 \Rightarrow R_2$. By induction hypothesis, it is satisfied that $\vDash (R_1, E) \leq_k \vDash (R_1, E')$ and $\vDash (R_2, E) \leq_k \vDash (R_2, E')$. Because causal operator $\rightarrow$ is monotonic with respect to $\leq_k$, then (equations 2)

$$\vDash (R_1 \Rightarrow R_2, E) \ = \ \vDash (R_1, E) \ \rightarrow \ \vDash (R_2, E) \leq_k \vDash (R_1 \Rightarrow R_2, E')$$

4. $R = R_1 \Rightarrow \bigcirc R_2$ (equations 1). The level of satisfaction of an SCTL requirement with this syntax is as follows (equations 2):

$$\vDash (R_1 \Rightarrow \bigcirc R_2, E) \ = \ \vDash (R_1, E) \ \rightarrow \ \bigwedge_{E_i \in \perp (R_E)} \vDash (R_2, E_i)$$

As operators $\rightarrow$ and $\wedge$ are monotonic with respect to $\leq_k$, and because of the induction hypothesis, then $\vDash (R, E) \leq_k \vDash (R, E')$
5. $R = R_1 \Rightarrow \odot R_2$. The level of satisfaction of an SCTL requirement with this syntax is as follows (equations 2):

$$\vDash (R_1 \Rightarrow \odot \ R_2, E) \ = \ \vDash (R_1, E) \ \rightarrow \ \bigwedge_{E_i \in \perp (R_E)} \vDash (R_2, E_i)$$

As operators $\rightarrow$ and $\wedge$ are monotonic with respect to $\leq_k$, and because of the induction hypothesis, then $\vDash (R, E) \leq_k \vDash (R, E')$
6. $R = \neg R_1$. Because of the induction hypothesis, we know that $\vDash (R_1, E) \leq_k \vDash (R_1, E')$ and, as the logic operator $\neg$ is monotonic with respect to $\leq_k$, therefore $\vDash (R, E) \leq_k \vDash (R, E')$.

$\square$

As a result of Property 2, we know a relationship between verification results belonging to two different states which hold a simulation relationship. This is a good starting point to spread out this result from states to evolution paths and, after that, from evolution paths to MUS graphs. Therefore, we firstly need to establish what relationship must hold the evolution paths to extrapolate the results of Property 2:

Table 1. Reusing $\models (R, E(\pi))$ to know $\models (R, E(\pi'))$, where $E(\pi) \sqsubseteq_e E(\pi')$

(a) Results obtained from $\models (\Diamond R, E(\pi))$ **(b)** Results obtained from $\models (\Box R, E(\pi))$

$\models (\Diamond R, E(\pi)) = 1$	$\models (\Diamond R, E(\pi')) = 1$	$\models (\Box R, E(\pi)) = 1$	$\models (\Diamond R, E(\pi')) = 1$
$\models (\Diamond R, E(\pi)) = \widehat{\frac{1}{2}}$	$\models (\Diamond R, E(\pi')) \geq_k \frac{3}{4}$	$\models (\Box R, E(\pi)) = \widehat{\frac{1}{2}}$	$\models (\Diamond R, E(\pi')) \geq_k \frac{3}{4}$
$\models (\Diamond R, E(\pi)) = \frac{3}{4}$		$\models (\Box R, E(\pi)) = \frac{3}{4}$	
$\models (\Diamond R, E(\pi)) = 0$	$\models (\Box R, E(\pi')) = 0$	$\models (\Box R, E(\pi)) = 0$	$\models (\Box R, E(\pi')) = 0$
$\models (\Diamond R, E(\pi)) = \widehat{\frac{1}{2}}$	$\models (\Box R, E(\pi')) \geq_k \frac{1}{4}$	$\models (\Box R, E(\pi)) = \widehat{\frac{1}{2}}$	$\models (\Box R, E(\pi')) \geq_k \frac{1}{4}$
$\models (\Diamond R, E(\pi)) = \frac{1}{4}$		$\models (\Box R, E(\pi)) = \frac{1}{4}$	

Definition 2. *Two evolution paths π and π' are* **corresponding paths**, *denoted by $\pi \sqsubseteq_e \pi'$, if and only if their corresponding traces of states $-E(\pi) = E_0 E_1 \ldots$ and $E(\pi') = E_0' E_1' \ldots -$ are* **corresponding traces of states**, *denoted by $E(\pi) \sqsubseteq_e E(\pi')$, that is, if and only if $\forall i, E_i \sqsubseteq_e E_i'$.*

We have analyzed every single possibility to extract some conclusions about how to reuse the verification results provided by a trace of states — $\models (\Diamond R, E(\pi))$ (equation 4) and $\models (\Box R, E(\pi))$ (equation 5). Our main aim is reusing this information between traces of states corresponding in simulation, that is, $E(\pi) \sqsubseteq_e E(\pi')$ (Tables 1 and 2).

In Table 1.(a), there are summarized the verification results about $\models (R, E(\pi'))$ which can be deduced from $\models (\Diamond R, E(\pi))$, where $E(\pi) \sqsubseteq_e E(\pi')$:

- If $E(\pi)$ satisfies eventually R, that is $\models (\Diamond R, E(\pi)) = 1$, then $E(\pi')$ also satisfies eventually R, that is $\models (\Diamond R, E(\pi')) = 1$.
- If $\models (\Diamond R, E(\pi)) \in \{\widehat{\frac{1}{2}}, \frac{3}{4}\}$ then it is impossible that $E(\pi')$ cannot satisfy $\Diamond R$ in subsequent iterations of the requirements specification phase (Fig. 1(a)), that is, $\models (\Diamond R, E(\pi')) \geq_k \frac{3}{4}$.
- If $E(\pi)$ does not satisfy eventually R, that is $\models (\Diamond R, E(\pi)) = 0$, then $E(\pi')$ does not satisfy invariantly R, $\models (\Box R, E(\pi')) = 0$.
- If $E(\pi)$ cannot satisfy $\Diamond R$ in subsequent iterations of the requirements specification phase, that is, $\models (\Diamond R, E(\pi)) \in \{\widehat{\frac{1}{2}}, \frac{1}{4}\}$, then $E(\pi')$ cannot satisfy $\Box R$ in subsequent iterations, that is, $\models (\Box R, E(\pi')) \geq_k \frac{1}{4}$.

The results obtained after studying $\models (\Box R, E(\pi))$ (Table 1.(b)) offer the same conclusions than the previous ones.

Analyzing the information that the possible verification results of $\models (R, E(\pi'))$ can offer about $\models (R, E(\pi))$, where $E(\pi) \sqsubseteq_e E(\pi')$, we have conclude the following information (Table 2):

Table 2. Reusing $\models (R, E(\pi'))$ to know $\models (R, E(\pi))$, where $E(\pi) \sqsubseteq_e E(\pi')$

(a) Results obtained from $\models (\Diamond R, E(\pi'))$

$\models (\Diamond R, E(\pi')) \leq_k 0$	$\models (\Diamond R, E(\pi)) \leq_k 0$
	$\models (\Box R, E(\pi)) \leq_k 0$
$\models (\Diamond R, E(\pi')) = \widehat{\tfrac{1}{2}}$ or $\models (\Diamond R, E(\pi')) = \tfrac{3}{4}$	$\models (\Diamond R, E(\pi)) \in \Phi - \{1\}$
	$\models (\Box R, E(\pi)) \in \Phi - \{1\}$

(b) Results obtained from $\models (\Box R, E(\pi'))$

$\models (\Box R, E(\pi')) \leq_k 1$	$\models (\Diamond R, E(\pi)) \leq_k 1$
	$\models (\Box R, E(\pi)) \leq_k 1$
$\models (\Box R, E(\pi')) = \widehat{\tfrac{1}{2}}$ or $\models (\Box R, E(\pi')) = \tfrac{1}{4}$	$\models (\Diamond R, E(\pi)) \in \Phi - \{0\}$
	$\models (\Box R, E(\pi)) \in \Phi - \{0\}$

- If $\models (\Diamond R, E(\pi')) \leq_k 0$, then $E(\pi)$ maintains the same level of satisfaction of R as an invariant property and an eventual property, that is, $\models (\Diamond R, E(\pi)) \leq_k 0$ and $\models (\Box R, E(\pi)) \leq_k 0$.
- If $\models (\Diamond R, E(\pi')) \in \{\widehat{\tfrac{1}{2}}, \tfrac{3}{4}\}$, then we only know that $E(\pi)$ does not satisfy eventually R —that is, $\models (\Diamond R, E(\pi)) \neq 1$— and it does not satisfy invariantly R —that is, $\models (\Box R, E(\pi)) \neq 1$.
- If $\models (\Box R, E(\pi')) \leq_k 1$, then $E(\pi)$ maintains the same level of satisfaction of R as an invariant property and an eventual property, that is, $\models (\Diamond R, E(\pi)) \leq_k 1$ and $\models (\Box R, E(\pi)) \leq_k 1$.
- If $\models (\Box R, E(\pi')) \in \{\widehat{\tfrac{1}{2}}, \tfrac{1}{4}\}$, (a) R is partially or totally unspecified in $E(\pi)$, but we cannot know any information about future behavior of R in $E(\pi)$, or (b) R is totally specified in $E(\pi)$ and $\models (\Box R, E(\pi)) = \models (\Diamond R, E(\pi)) \in \{\widehat{\tfrac{1}{2}}, 1\}$.

Property 3. Given two states E and E' such as $E \sqsubseteq_e E'$, then for every evolution path π starting from E there is a corresponding path π' starting from E'.

Proof. Trivial from Definitions 1 and 2.   □

Table 3. Reusing $\models (R, g)$ information to know $\models (R, g')$, where $g \sqsubseteq_e g'$

(a) Results obtained from $\models (\exists \Diamond R, g)$ **(b)** Results obtained from $\models (\forall \Diamond R, g)$

$\models (\exists \Diamond R, g) = 0$	$\models (\forall \Box R, g') = 0$	$\models (\forall \Diamond R, g) = 0$	$\models (\forall \Box R, g') = 0$
$\models (\exists \Diamond R, g) = 1$	$\models (\exists \Diamond R, g') = 1$	$\models (\forall \Diamond R, g) = 1$	$\models (\exists \Diamond R, g') = 1$
$\models (\exists \Diamond R, g) = \widehat{\frac{1}{2}}$	$\models (\forall \Box R, g') \geq_k \frac{1}{4}$	$\models (\forall \Diamond R, g) = \widehat{\frac{1}{2}}$	$\models (\exists \Diamond R, g') \geq_k \frac{3}{4}$
$\models (\exists \Diamond R, g) = \frac{1}{4}$		$\models (\forall \Diamond R, g) = \frac{3}{4}$	

(c) Results obtained from $\models (\exists \Box R, g)$ **(d)** Results obtained from $\models (\forall \Box R, g)$

$\models (\exists \Box R, g) = 0$	$\models (\forall \Box R, g') = 0$	$\models (\forall \Box R, g) = 0$	$\models (\forall \Box R, g') = 0$
$\models (\exists \Box R, g) = 1$	$\models (\exists \Diamond R, g') = 1$	$\models (\forall \Box R, g) = 1$	$\models (\exists \Diamond R, g') = 1$
$\models (\exists \Box R, g) = \widehat{\frac{1}{2}}$	$\models (\forall \Box R, g') \geq_k \frac{1}{4}$	$\models (\forall \Box R, g) = \widehat{\frac{1}{2}}$	$\models (\exists \Diamond R, g') \geq_k \frac{3}{4}$
$\models (\exists \Box R, g) = \frac{1}{4}$		$\models (\forall \Box R, g) = \frac{3}{4}$	

Our main goal is knowing how to predict verification results between graphs holding a simulation relationship, that is, if we know verification results of R in g, what verification information do we have about R in g' if $g \sqsubseteq_e g'$? and viceversa?.

Because of Definition 1 we know that if $g \sqsubseteq_e g'$, then $E_0 \sqsubseteq_e E_0'$, and because of Property 3, then for every single path π starting from E_0, there is a corresponding path starting from E_0'. As we have obtained how to reuse verification information between corresponding paths (Tables 1 and 2), we have also studied how to expand this information throughout the whole MUS graphs. We have concluded that

(a) if we know the level of satisfaction $\models (R, g)$, such as $g \sqsubseteq_e g'$, then we can deduce verification information about $\models (R, g')$ (Table 3); and
(b) if we know the level of satisfaction of an SCTL requirement R in a MUS graph g' ($\models (R, g')$), such as $g \sqsubseteq_e g'$, then we can deduce verification information about $\models (R, g)$ (Table 4).

Apart from the verification results shown in these tables, we can deduce more verification information:

Property 4. Let R be an SCTL requirement which is satisfied in the initial state of a MUS graph g, that is, $\models (R, E_0|_g) = 1$, then we know that $\models (\forall \Diamond R, g') = 1$, $\forall g' \mid g \sqsubseteq_e g'$.

Table 4. Reusing $\models (R, g')$ information to know $\models (R, g)$, where $g \sqsubseteq_e g'$

(a) Results obtained from $\models (\forall \Box R, g')$ (b) Results obtained from $\models (\exists \Diamond R, g')$

$\models (\forall \Box R, g') \leq_k 1$	$\models (\exists \Diamond R, g) \leq_k 1$	$\models (\exists \Diamond R, g') \leq_k 0$	$\models (\exists \Diamond R, g) \leq_k 0$
	$\models (\forall \Diamond R, g) \leq_k 1$		$\models (\forall \Diamond R, g) \leq_k 0$
	$\models (\exists \Box R, g) \leq_k 1$		$\models (\exists \Box R, g) \leq_k 0$
	$\models (\forall \Box R, g) \leq_k 1$		$\models (\forall \Box R, g) \leq_k 0$
$\models (\forall \Box R, g') = \widehat{\tfrac{1}{2}}$ or $\models (\forall \Box R, g') = \tfrac{1}{4}$	$\models (\exists \Diamond R, g) \in \Phi - \{0\}$	$\models (\exists \Diamond R, g') = \widehat{\tfrac{1}{2}}$ or $\models (\exists \Diamond R, g') = \tfrac{3}{4}$	$\models (\exists \Diamond R, g) \in \Phi - \{1\}$
	$\models (\forall \Diamond R, g) \in \Phi - \{0\}$		$\models (\forall \Diamond R, g) \in \Phi - \{1\}$
	$\models (\exists \Box R, g) \in \Phi - \{0\}$		$\models (\exists \Box R, g) \in \Phi - \{1\}$
	$\models (\forall \Box R, g) \in \Phi - \{0\}$		$\models (\forall \Box R, g) \in \Phi - \{1\}$

Proof. Since $\models (R, E_0|_g) = 1$ and since the initial state of a MUS graph is contained in every single trace of states of the graph, then applying equation (4) we know that $\models (\Diamond R, g) = 1$, and applying equation (5), then we know that $\models (\Box R, g) = 1$. According to the information stored in Table 3, therefore $\models (\forall \Diamond R, g') = 1$, $\forall g' \mid g \sqsubseteq_e g'$. $\Box$

Property 5. Given two graphs g and g', the partial ordering defined by $\sqsubseteq_e$ is stronger than the defined by $\sqsubseteq_{TC}^{\infty}$, that is, if $g \sqsubseteq_e g'$ then $g \sqsubseteq_{TC}^{\infty} g'$.

Proof. Trivial by definition of simulation relationship (Definition 1) and by definition of TC^{∞} function (Section 5). $\Box$

Property 6. Given two deterministic graphs g and g', then the partial ordering defined by $\sqsubseteq_e$ is totally equivalent to the partial ordering defined by $\sqsubseteq_{TC}^{\infty}$.

Proof. We try to prove that $g \sqsubseteq_e g' \Leftrightarrow g \sqsubseteq_{TC}^{\infty} g'$. As $\sqsubseteq_e$ is stronger than $\sqsubseteq_{TC}^{\infty}$, then $g \sqsubseteq_e g' \Rightarrow g \sqsubseteq_{TC}^{\infty} g'$ (Property 5). Therefore, we need to prove that $g \sqsubseteq_{TC}^{\infty} g' \Rightarrow g \sqsubseteq_e g'$.

Given g and g' such as $g \sqsubseteq_{TC}^{\infty} g'$, then for every trace $a_0 a_1 \ldots$ in g, there is a trace $a'_0 a'_1 \ldots$ such as the first one is included in the second one.

As g and g' are deterministic graphs, for any trace $a_0 a_1 \ldots$ there is only an evolution path $E(\pi)$ and for any trace $a'_0 a'_1 \ldots$ there is only an evolution path $E(\pi')$.

As $g \sqsubseteq_{TC}^{\infty} g'$, then, applying Definition 2, $E(\pi)$ and $E(\pi')$ are corresponding traces of states. Therefore, if we start in the initial state, $E_0 \sqsubseteq_e E'_0$ and so $g \sqsubseteq_e g'$. $\Box$

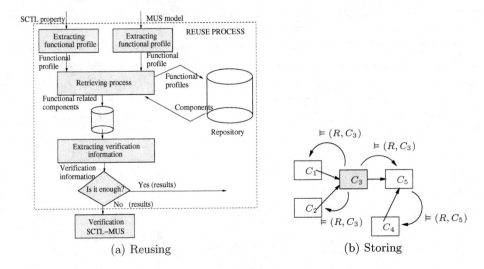

(a) Reusing   (b) Storing

Fig. 7. Managing verification information

Applying Property 6, we know that the information given by Tables 3 and 4, when $g \sqsubseteq_e g'$, are also valid for $g \sqsubseteq_{TC}^\infty g'$. This result is essential because although the information is the same, it is more efficient comparing MUS graphs according to $\sqsubseteq_{TC}^\infty$ criterion than according to $\sqsubseteq_e$ one.

8 How to Manage Verification Information?

The mathematical results of the previous Section allow deducing verification information of an incomplete model from the verification information of other incomplete models. In this Section, we outline how to reuse this verification information and how to store it in the repository.

Whenever we need to verify an SCTL requirement, we proceed as follows (Fig. 7(a)):

1. Obtain the functional profile of the model ($TC^\infty(g)$), needed to locate the reusable components which are TC^∞-related to g.
2. Obtain the functional profile of the requirement or set of requirements ($TC^\infty(R_i)$) to locate those functional requirements which are functionally equivalents to each R_i.
3. Retrieve the closest components to g whose verification information inform about R_i (or equivalent requirements).
4. Extract and analyze verification information about $\vDash (R_i, g)$ from the recovered components.

If the available information is not enough, it is necessary to run the model checking algorithm, but this execution can be reduced depending on the recovered verification information. In fact, it is very probable that we only need to check some states of the graph and so we avoid the exhaustive analysis.

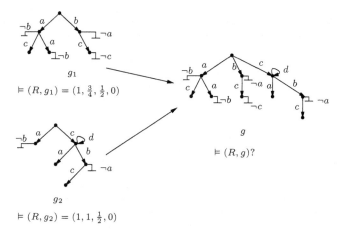

$\models (R, g_1) = (1, \frac{3}{4}, \frac{1}{2}, 0)$

$\models (R, g)?$

$\models (R, g_2) = (1, 1, \frac{1}{2}, 0)$

Fig. 8. Example of TC^∞ lattice

Whenever we have new verification information of an incomplete model, we spread out this data across the lattice to improve the learning process of the repository. This expansion is done off-line, so it does not affect the efficiency of the reuse environment. Fig. 7(b) shows as the verification information linked to C_1, C_2, C_4 and C_5 is updated after C_3 is stored in the repository.

Example 3. We want to know the level of satisfaction of the requirement $R \equiv (c \Rightarrow a)$ in the model g (Fig. 8). Firstly, we need to obtain the functional profiles of the requirement $(TC^\infty(R))$ and the model $(TC^\infty(g))$ to search reusable components that, besides being functionally related to g, they have also verification information about R or an equivalent requirement to R.

Two reusable components (g_1 and g_2) are recovered from the repository and their interesting verification information is shown in Fig. 8. As we want to obtain $\models (R, g)$ from these results, we firstly analyze $\models (R, g_1) = (1, \frac{3}{4}, \frac{1}{2}, 0)$:

- As $\models (\exists \Diamond R, g_1) = 1$, then $\models (\exists \Diamond R, g) = 1$ (Table 3.(a)).
- Neither $\models (\forall \Diamond R, g_1) = \frac{3}{4}$ (Table 3.(b)) nor $\models (\exists \Box R, g_1) = \frac{1}{2}$ (Table 3.(c)) offer useful information about $\models (R, g)$.
- And, finally, $\models (\forall \Box R, g_1) = 0$ implies $\models (\forall \Box R, g) = 0$ (Table 3.(d)).

Secondly, we analyze the information given by the remainder reusable component, $\models (R, g_2) = (1, 1, \frac{1}{2}, 0)$:

- As $\models (R, E_0|_{g_2}) = 1$, then $\models (\forall \Diamond R, g) = 1$ (Property 4).
- And $\models (\exists \Box R, g_2) = \frac{1}{2}$ does not offer more information about $\models (\exists \Box R, g)$ (Table 3.(c)).

To sum up, we have obtained that the level of satisfaction of R in g is

$$\models (R, g) = (1, 1, \phi, 0) \quad \phi \in \Phi$$

where ϕ can be any level of satisfaction of Φ (Section 3). Therefore, R is a *liveness property* in g, that is, every single trace of the model satisfies eventually R —that is, $\models (\forall \Diamond R, g) = 1$—; and R is *not a safety property* in g, that is, there are at least one state which does not satisfy R — $\models (\forall \Box R, g) = 0$. These conclusions have been obtained without running the model checking algorithm, instead of that, we have used the verification information about R in two functional parts of g.

9   Is It Worth Reusing Verification Information?

Reuse benefits whenever we are able to recover the verification information we exactly need are intuitively obvious: firstly, because we are reusing at an early stage (requirements capture) which entails a high quality of the software process; and secondly, because we are avoiding the well-known high computational costs of model checking. Problems start if we want to quantify these benefits, in this case, we propose quantifying the computational cost of reusing and comparing it with the cost of formal verification from scratch, that is, the cost of applying directly the model checking algorithm. The computational cost of reusing verification efforts (C_r) consists of (1) the cost of retrieving and deducing the verification results we exactly need and (2) the cost of retrieving and deducing a sub-set of the verification results we need:

$$C_r = V_r + (1 - p) \cdot (D_f \cdot C_m) \qquad (7)$$

In this equation, V_r stands for the cost of retrieving and deducing the verification results we exactly need, that is, in this case, we do not need to run the model checking algorithm and p is the probability of finding this information in the repository; D_f is the percentage of functional differences between the recovered reusable components and the given one which force us to verify the requirement in a sub-set of the state space of the current model and, finally, C_m is the cost of verifying the incomplete model (MUS graph) from scratch by using the model checking algorithm.

Unfortunately, these parameters are not easy to obtain because they not only depend on the complexity of the retrieving and deducing algorithms and on the amount of reusable components in the repository, but also on both their functional characteristics and the functional characteristics of the verified requirements, which are more difficult to take into account. One of the main problems is obtaining the most adequate minimum functional difference between two reusable components stored in the repository and between two different requirements linked to one reusable component. It is clear that the lower these values are, the more probable finding the verification information we need (p) is. However, we have to come to a compromise solution between the functional closeness among reusable components and the complexity of reuse, because if the minimum functional difference is too low, the repository may become unmanageable because of the massive amount of information stored in it.

If predicting costs of reusing is not easy, estimating reusing benefits is also difficult because we must take into account factors like the possibility of reusing other verification results in subsequent iterations of the capture requirements process, so the comparison between costs and benefits is not so simple as the equation $C_r = V_r + (1 - p) \cdot (D_f \cdot C_m) \leq C_m$ seems. Despite this quantification is not so simple, benefits of reuse are backed up by our experience in applying ARIFS methodology in the field of communication protocols.

10   Summary and Future Work

The work introduced in this chapter focuses on reusing verification information of incomplete models at the requirements specification stage of a totally formalized, incremental and iterative software development process with the aim of improving the efficiency of the consistency checking process. Even though there are other proposal to reuse less formalized results (simulation tests) over code components (algorithms) [14], we really believe that reusing this kind of information at early stages increase the reuse benefits and improve the software process.

We have identified a criteria —based on complete trace semantics— to compare functional specifications. This criteria takes advantage of the possibility of *not-yet-specified* inherent to incomplete models to avoid formal proofs in the retrieval process. We have also identified what verification information can be reused and, besides that, how to apply this information to reduce formal verification necessities.

In order to continue this proposal, we are working on: (a) a *compositional verification*, that is, decomposing properties into sub-properties such that it is possible to reuse verification information about each sub-property, and the combination of the sub-properties implies the required global property; (b) the possibility of reusing verification results of *functionally similar* properties with the given one; (c) studying how to share formal verification results between reusable components holding a structural relationship, given by NE^∞ and NE functions; and (d) obtaining heuristics which enable predicting the values we need to apply equation (7) to quantify the benefits of reusing verification information in this environment.

References

1. Bowen Alpern and Ferd B. Schneider. Recognizing Safety and Liveness. *Distributed Computing Journal*, 2:117–126, 1987.
2. M. Broy. Formal description techniques - how formal and descriptive are they? In Reinhard Gotzhein and Jan Bredereke, editors, *Formal Description Tecniques IX. Theory, application and tools*, pages 95–110. International Federation for Information Processing (IFIP), Chapman & Hill, 1996.
3. R. Bryant. Graph-based Algorithms for Boolean Function Manipulation. *IEEE Transactions on Computers*, 35(8):677–691, 1986.

4. B. H. C. Cheng and J. J. Jeng. Reusing Analogous Components. *IEEE Trans. on Knowledge and Data Engineering*, 9(2), March 1997.

5. E. Clarke, D. Long, and K. McMillan. Compositional model checking. In *Proceedings of the Fourth Annual Symposium on Logic in computer science*, pages 353–362. IEEE Press, 1989.

6. Rebeca P. Díaz Redondo. *Reutilización de Requisitos Funcionales de Sistemas Distribuidos utilizando Técnicas de Descripción Formal*. PhD thesis, Departamento de Enxeería Telemática - Universidade de Vigo, 2002.

7. Rebeca P. Díaz Redondo and José J. Pazos Arias. Reuse of Verification Efforts and Incomplete Specifications in a Formalized, Iterative and Incremental Software Process. In *Proceedings of International Conference on Software Engineering (ICSE) Doctoral Symposium*, Toronto, May 2001.

8. Rebeca P. Díaz Redondo, José J. Pazos Arias, Ana Fernández Vilas, and Belén Barragáns Martínez. Approximate Retrieval of Incomplete and Formal Specifications applied to Horizontal Reuse. In *Proc. of the 28th Euromicro Conf. Component-based Software Engineering*, September 2002.

9. Rebeca P. Díaz Redondo, José J. Pazos Arias, Ana Fernández Vilas, and Belén Barragáns Martínez. Approximate Retrieval of Incomplete and Formal Specifications applied to Vertical Reuse. In *Proc. of International Conference on Software Maintenance*, October 2002.

10. Rebeca P. Díaz Redondo, José J. Pazos Arias, Ana Fernández Vilas, and Belén Barragáns Martínez. ARIFS: an Environment for Incomplete and Formal Specifications Reuse. In *Proc. of Workshop on Formal Methods and Component Interaction.*, volume 66 of *Electronic Notes in Theoretical Computer Science*. Elsevier Science, July 2002.

11. G. J. Holzmann. Tracing Protocols. *ATT Technical Journal*, 64(12):2413–2434, 1985.

12. G. J. Holzmann. An Improved Protocol Reachability Analysis Technique. *Software-Practice and Experience*, 18(2):137–161, 1988.

13. ISO. *Information Processing Systems – Open Systems Interconnection – LOTOS – A Formal Description Technique Based on an Extended State Transition Model*. ISO/IEC/8807, International Standards Organization, 1989.

14. I. Keidar, R. Khazan, N. Lynch, and A. Shvartsman. An Inheritance-Based Technique for Building Simulation Proofs Incrementally. In *22nd International Conference on Software Engineering (ICSE)*, pages 478–487, Limerik, Ireland, June 2000.

15. R. Kurshan, V. Levin, M. Minea, D. Peled, and H. Yenign. Static Partial Order Reduction. *Tools for the Construction and Analysis of Systems, LNCS 1394*, pages 345–357, 1998.

16. W. Lam, J. A. McDermid, and A. J. Vickers. Ten Steps Towards Systematic Requirements Reuse. *Requirements Engineering Journal*, 2:102–113, 1997. Springer Verlag.

17. K. L. McMillan. A Technique of State Space Search based on Unfolding. *Formal Methods in System Design*, 6:45–65, 1995.

18. José J. Pazos-Arias and Jorge García-Duque. SCTL-MUS: A Formal Methodology for Software Development of Distributed Systems. A Case Study. *Formal Aspects of Computing*, 13:50–91, 2001.

19. J. Penix and P. Alexander. Efficient Specification-Based Component Retrieval. *Automated Software Engineering: An International Journal*, 6(2):139–170, April 1999.

20. R. Prieto-Díaz. Software Reuse: Issues and Experiences. *American Programer*, 6(8):10–18, 1993.
21. J. Schumann and Fischer. NORA/HAMMR: Making Deduction-Based Software Component Retrieval Practical. In *Proc. of the 12th International Conference Automated Software Engineering*, pages 246–254, November 1997.
22. R. J. van Glabeek. *Handbook of Process Algebra*, chapter The Linear Time - Branching Time Spectrum I: The Semantics of Concrete, Sequential Processes. Elsevier Science, 2001.
23. A. M. Zaremski and J. M. Wing. Specification Matching of Software Components. *ACM Transactions on Software Engineering and Methodology*, 6(4):333–369, October 1997.

Risk Management
of COTS Based Systems Development

Louis C. Rose

BAE SYSTEMS
11487 Sunset Hills Road
Reston, Virginia 20190
`louis.rose@baesystems.com`

Abstract. The use of commercial off-the-shelf (COTS) components to develop large-scale systems has become increasingly prominent over the past decade. This approach requires more attention to risk management. In addition to the classical risks that exist with developing large systems, the use COTS components requires managers to modify their typical mitigation strategies for some of the classic risks and develop new mitigation strategies for risks that are particular to the use of COTS in system development. This chapter discusses the risks particular to the development of COTS intensive systems and describes some strategies that can be employed to help with risk mitigation.

1   Introduction

The explosion of commercial off-the-shelf (COTS) components in the development of large-scale systems in recent years requires a new look at the methods used to manage the risks during the development of these COTS intensive systems. While most of the familiar principles of project management are applicable to building COTS intensive systems, many risk-relevant issues take on a higher degree of importance than when they are applied to classical, developed-from-scratch systems.

Before proceeding further, it is important to clarify the definition of a COTS component as it is used in the context of this chapter. A COTS component is a software product that is sold or licensed to the general public and is offered by a vendor that is trying to profit from the product. In addition, the vendor retains the intellectual property right to the product and the COTS product is used in the systems development without modification to its internal code. This definition is a summary of that presented in [2] to which has been added the fact that the product has a standalone operational capability (outside of the operating system). This definition includes, but is not limited to, components such as office automation tools, database management systems, financial systems, order processing systems, personnel control systems, web servers and application servers. A consequence of using these types of COTS components is that the internal operations of the components are unknown and the products are a "black boxes" to the system developers. The system developers must

A. Cechich et al. (Eds.): Component-Based Software Quality, LNCS 2693, pp. 352–373, 2003.

rely on documented exposed interfaces and observed operational behavior. The integration of these "black box" components, which are under the "control" of other parties (the vendors), requires a thorough assessment of associated risk. The objective of this chapter is to highlight those risks that are particular to development and maintenance of COTS intensive systems and discuss appropriate risk mitigation techniques that can be applied to help ensure the successful development, deployment, and operation of COTS intensive systems.

2   Background

During the past decade the development of large software intensive systems have undergone some fundamental changes. Gone are the days when the vast majority of the code was uniquely developed from a (hopefully) stable set of requirements. Today's large systems are primarily built with a collection of COTS components that are integrated together generally supporting a fluid set of requirements. There are several key reasons for this evolution of systems development:

- The increased capability of hardware (Moore's Law) [9]
- The slow increase in the efficiency of developing new software
- The increase in commercial software functionality.

The increase in the capability of the hardware over the past decade has followed Moore's law. Moore's Law states that the transistor density on processor chips will double every 18 months or so. Along with this density increase there have been a similar increase in processor speed and a dramatic reduction in the cost per millions of instructions per second and megabytes of random access memory. However, the cost of developing unique software for a system has not matched this dramatic cost reduction in the hardware at all with. In addition, the increased hardware capability enables the software to perform tasks that were previously prohibitive because those solutions would have taken too long to execute or would have been too expensive to host on the platforms that were then available. The use of graphical user interfaces (e.g., Microsoft Windows, X Windows and iMac interfaces) is a prime example of this phenomenon.

The software industry's ability to develop unique solutions in an efficient manner has not kept up with the increase in the capability of the hardware. While the recent industry efforts in system engineering and software development process improvement have had significant and positive impacts on the development of software intensive systems, the results of the improvements have not kept pace with the hardware improvement curve. These improvements in systems development have yielded better estimates in the size, cost and time to develop the systems and produced systems with fewer latent errors, but as the capability of the hardware increases the complexity of the software has increased faster than the ability to build them efficiently. The end result is that it still takes years to build complex systems from scratch while the technology is continuing to follow Moore's Law resulting in systems being obsolete relative to the latest technology by the time they are fielded.

Meanwhile, the vendors developing commercial products have been working diligently to take full advantage of this ever-increasing capability of platform technology. The software vendors are able to focus most of their efforts on particular technology niches and have been able to provide more functionality than ever before. This increase in the functionality of commercially available software along with the increasing domains being addressed by commercial software has made it increasingly attractive for systems developers to consider COTS components in their solution approaches. One key part of this enhanced functionality is the vendor's willingness to include support for the integration of their COTS components with other components or infrastructures. This integration capability can be implemented in one of several ways including compliance with industry standards, supplying application programming interfaces, or strategic relationships made directly with vendors.

In summary, the hardware capability continues to increase at a rate faster than the systems developers' ability to take full advantage of this capability. Add to that the ability of the software vendor's to provide ever increasing functionality in their commercial packages and the resulting conclusion is that the integration of COTS components can deliver a lot of functionality in a short period of time. During the early efforts to deliver systems that contained a lot of COTS components, it was assumed that these efforts would produce better systems cheaper and faster than those developed mostly from scratch. What the industry has come to realize is that integrating a collection of COTS components is not as simple as installing the COTS products and declaring victory. Instead, the development of COTS intensive systems requires unique skill sets, new approaches to the development processes and the consideration of a set of risks that are new to the systems development process and a rethinking of some of the classic risks associated with complex systems development.

3   Lifecycle Development Process

The use of the classic waterfall lifecycle development process results in increase project risk when building COTS intensive systems. The classic waterfall process can be characterized as having requirements determined early in the lifecycle, followed by high-level design (or software architecture design), low-level design, implementation and integration and testing. This linear development process increases the amount of risk associated with the development of COTS intensive systems for several reasons.

Requirements, in a waterfall process, are typically defined from a mission or user perspective with minimal or little regard for COTS component capability or even worse, using misinformation about COTS component capabilities. This inevitably leads to a set of requirements that will have many mismatches with the functionality of the COTS components. These mismatches are generally very difficult or extremely cost prohibitive to address.

In the waterfall process, the high-level design or architecture is developed early on the process and the requirements are allocated to the design elements. When developers have the freedom to design the system elements from scratch,

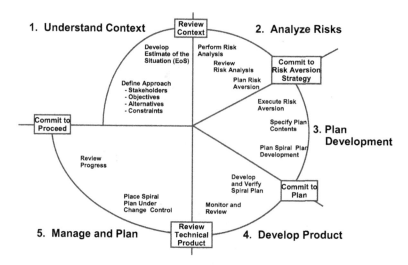

1. Understand Context Review Context **2. Analyze Risks**

Develop Estimate of the Situation (EoS)
Perform Risk Analysis
Review Risk Analysis
Plan Risk Aversion
Commit to Risk Aversion Strategy
Define Approach
- Stakeholders
- Objectives
- Alternatives
- Constraints
Execute Risk Aversion
Commit to Proceed
Specify Plan Contents **3. Plan Development**
Plan Spiral Plan Development
Review Progress
Develop and Verify Spiral Plan **Commit to Plan**
Place Spiral Plan Under Change Control
Monitor and Review
5. Manage and Plan Review Technical Product **4. Develop Product**

Fig. 1. Evolutionary Spiral Process

the requirements can generally be allocated completely because the developer has full control over the system being developed. In order to specify a software (or system) architecture in this upfront manner for a COTS intensive system requires that the developer have an in-depth knowledge of all of the COTS components that are to be integrated into the system solution. Not only is it unlikely that the developer has this in-depth knowledge of all of the COTS components, it is rarely the situation that the developer even knows definitively which COTS components will be included the systems at this early stage.

The waterfall process performs integration and system testing after all of the developed components have been implemented and unit tested. Taking this approach when testing COTS intensive systems is fraught with risk. There are many complexities and unforeseen situations that arise when integrating COTS components and deferring integration and system testing of these components typically results in cost and schedule overruns and performance and quality problems. There will be more detailed discussion of these issues later in the chapter.

Instead of using the traditional waterfall process, a spiral or evolutionary lifecycle process is extremely well suited to help minimize many of the risk associated with the development of COTS intensive systems. The spiral process was developed by Dr. Barry Boehm [5] to specifically incorporate risk analysis into a software development process to help minimize the risk when developing coding systems from scratch. This process has been enhanced by the Software Productivity Consortium with their Evolutionary Spiral Process (ESP) [18]. ESP enhances Dr. Boehm's spiral process by incorporating the risk assessment techniques that are described in [6] and adding an explicit step to explicitly perform risk mitigation within each cycle of the spiral. Fig. 1 identifies the steps in a typical ESP cycle.

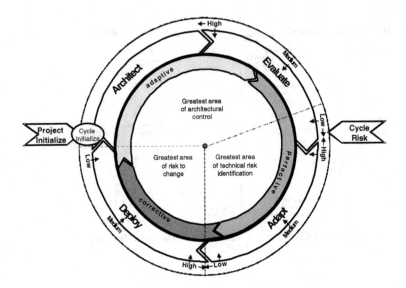

Fig. 2. Phased Integrated COTS Approach

While ESP is generalized development process and can be used to manage the development of COTS intensive systems, the Software Productivity Consortium provided an adaptation of ESP with their Phased-Integrated COTS (PIC) approach that is specifically focused on COTS based development with risk assessment and management as a continuous thread throughout the development. PIC identifies an iterative cycle that consists of steps for 1) architecture, 2) evaluation, 3) adaptation, and 4) deployment. The cycle focuses on developing an evolving architecture that is followed by a set of formal evaluations of the COTS components to be considered for the current cycle with these evaluations being cognizant of the candidate architecture. Next, the adaptation phase performs the integration of the COTS components and the development of any integration code that might be necessary; this is followed by the deployment step that is a deployment for the next PIC cycle and optionally an interim delivery to the customer. Fig. 2 presents the phases within an interaction of the PIC approach.

Also, the Software Engineering Institute has a large ongoing effort to address the development of COTS-Based Systems and they have developed the Evolutionary Process for Integrating COTS-Based Systems (EPIC) [3]. EPIC specifies four major process elements that consist of 1) planning the iteration, 2) gathering information and refining the solution set (this element has its own set of iteration cycles), 3) assembling an executable system, and 4) assessing how closely the iterations objectives were (or were not) achieved. The next cycle then starts with planning for the next iteration. These iterations are worked inside a broader set of phases. Fig. 3 shows these process steps in a typical EPIC iteration cycle.

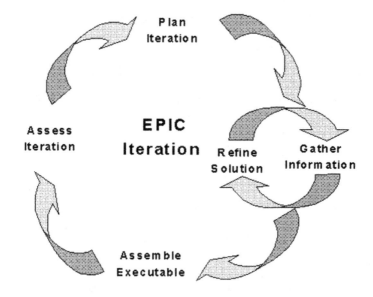

Fig. 3. Evolutionary Process for Integrating COTS-Based Systems

Note the iterative and evolutionary nature inherent in these three approaches to developing systems. When these kinds of approaches are use to develop COTS intensive systems, the developers are allowed to adjust the architecture and system design as more knowledge is gained about the operations of the COTS "black boxes".

Alternatively, the National Aeronautic and Space Administration (NASA) has been developing systems with COTS components for many years. Their experiences have been captured by Moiriso, et al. in [12]. This team of people investigated the various processes that were used across 15 projects at NASA and then they developed a process model that was the most representative of the processes used by the projects. They then worked with the Software Engineering Lab inside NASA to identify the major issued that were found in the process model. Some of the problems that were found included incompatibilities between the vendor product release dates iand the project schedules, unpredictable product learning curves by the development team, promised functionality that was never implemented (i.e., vaporware), and communication problems with the vendors. They then developed a COTS development process that address and other issues that maintain a continuous communication with both the vendor and the customer community with several checkpoints throughout the process.

Regardless of which of these processes one might choose for the development of a COTS intensive system, the basic idea is to plan out the cycles of the integration of COTS packages and let the architecture of the COTS evolve as the system grows in complexity. As each cycle is executed, one or more COTS components are integrated and tested as both the capabilities and limitations of the COTS components are better understood.

4   Risk Management and Assessment Techniques

The development of large complex COTS intensive systems carries with it all
the typical risks that come with this type of activity, for example risks associated with cost, schedule, quality, staffing, and customer acceptance. In addition,
developing COTS intensive systems have some unique risks, many of them non-
technical in nature, that are specific to the development of COTS intensive systems. The brief discussion of risk management techniques that follows provides
a context for the discussion of those risks that are of particular interest during
the development of COTS intensive systems.

4.1   Risk Identification

A typical straightforward technique used to identify the risks in a software development process is to have one or two experienced people think of the project
risks that are then submitted to others in the project for review. While this
may be fairly effective for smaller projects, it is insufficient for large-scale systems, especially complex COTS intensive systems. The more COTS components
that are to be in a system, the more unknowns exist and it becomes difficult,
if not impossible, for a small group to understand all of the risks. It is a rare
case that any one person would have sufficient experience with all of the COTS
components under consideration to be able to identify all of the critical risks.
It is usually the case that a complex COTS intensive system has several, if not
many, components that are new to all personnel on the development team. On
reason for this is that there is generally a strong desire to incorporate the latest
software technologies in the system and these new technologies are most likely
to be unfamiliar to the development team. There are the risks associated with
understanding the operations and functionality of the components; there are
risks associated with the varied integration capabilities of the different COTS
components; risks involved with the impact each COTS component has on the
system resources; and many non-technical risks that vary across the different
COTS vendors.

   A more formal technique for risk identification is most appropriate for complex COTS intensive systems. One such technique is to hold a facilitated risk
identification session (possibly several sessions) lead by an experienced facilitator
that includes representation of all of the critical stakeholders. In such a session,
the facilitator works to get all of the participants relaxed and comfortable stating
their particular risks without reservation. All of the identified risks are recorded
with no value-judgment discussions permitted. This usually produces a fairly
large list of risks, many of them similar and, in fact, many are different facets
of the same risk. The facilitator then leads an analysis of the risks to get the
participants to eliminate duplicates and categorize risks. Once the categories
are created, and the risks categorized, a final review is performed to determine
which risk categories can be stated as a single, high-level risk that covers the
risks in that category, thus consolidating many related risks. Next, the facilitator
queries the participants to identify those risks that are related to others risk. For

example, the occurrence of one risk might trigger the occurrence of another risk, which might not otherwise occur. A final step in this more formal approach is to have the facilitator get the participants to agree to a prioritization of the risks.

The author participated in a team of three facilitators that held risk identification meetings with the program managers of a branch of a military government agency. The agency had mandated that the operational systems were to incorporate as much commercial software as was feasible into the systems under development. To help stimulate discussion, the facilitators developed a problem scenario and provided the program managers with categories of candidate risk areas. The sessions exposed many risks, both technical and non-technical, that included risks associated with the system acquisition process, funding allocations, training, real-time performance and software distribution and licensing. The facilitation process proved to be effective in that it brought to light the need to consider both the technical and non-technical risks associated with the development of COTS intensive systems.

4.2   Risk Assessment

Once the risks have been identified and prioritized an assessment, or analysis, must be performed to determine the criticality of the various risks. The simplest technique to assess the risks is to rate each risk on a High, Medium & Low scale and identify the impact that the risk will have on the project. Typically the risks, their rating and a description of the impact of the risk, should it occur, are placed in a table. As with risk identification, this might be sufficient for smaller projects, but the risks associated with complex COTS intensive systems would be better analyzed with a more formal approach to risk assessment.

The risk assessment approach that is presented in [6] provides a rigorous technique for assessing risks. This technique is based on estimating the probabilities that each risk will occur and a rating of the consequence on the project should the risks actual occur. Each risk is then assigned both a probability (PR) of occurrence and consequence (CR) of occurrence. The PR and CR for each risk can be plotted on a graph that allows all of the risks to be assessed relative to each other. This chart helps understand the nature of the project risks and can be used to track the risks and determine if the project risk exposure is improving or increasing as the project proceeds. For an in depth understanding of this formal assessment methodology, the reader is encouraged to study [6].

4.3   Risk Mitigation

The efforts to identified and assess the risks can be wasted if they are not accompanied by a proactive risk mitigation plan. Each risk should have a mitigation approach identified that determines how the risk is to be addressed. The goal of the risk mitigation is not to try and eliminate all the risks since that would most likely be too expensive, if not impossible. There are several strategies that can be employed to mitigate risks and many ways to implement each strategy. Some of these strategies include:

- Risk Reduction – Take explicit steps to reduce the probability the risk will occur, or the consequences should the risk occur, or both.
- Risk Acceptance – Come to an agreement with the client that the consequence of a risk is within an acceptable tolerance.
- Risk Contingency Fund – Establish resource reserves of both time and money to address risks as they are realized.

Up to this point, the risk management techniques that have been presented are generic and can be applied to most any kind of risk, including those associated with the development of COTS intensive systems. But there are some risk mitigation techniques that are particular to the development of COTS intensive systems. The United States Federal Aviation Administration has developed a comprehensive guide to risk mitigation that provides details into many mitigation techniques [13]. Several of the risk mitigation techniques that are discussed in [13] are:

- Involve COTS-knowledgeable individuals in all analytical processes
- Involve users early and throughout the program lifecycle to identify and resolve COTS-related constraints
- Perform continuous COTS product market research
- Develop and maintain flexible performance requirements suited to the use of COTS products
- Institute and maintain ongoing COTS product testing capability
- Integrate COTS-based technology evolution planning within an Integrated Program Plan
- Emphasize strong and COTS-relevant configuration management practices
- Leverage the commercial infrastructure wherever feasible

Additionally, other mitigation techniques are discussed in [8] where the techniques are categorized into risks involved with operational requirements, risks affecting the technical approach and risks that address business strategy. The reader should be come familiar with these kinds COTS specific risk mitigation techniques and apply those that are appropriate with the context of their particular COTS intensive systems development.

In the subsequent sections of the chapter, some of these mitigation techniques are discussed within the contexts of project planning, requirements engineering, system architecture, system development, and system deployment and maintenance.

4.4   Risk Management Summary

The incorporation of a sound risk management approach will help mitigate one of the initial risks when working on the development of COTS intensive systems. That risk is that management makes the false assumption that the development of a COTS intensive system has fewer risks associated with it than developed-from-scratch software systems. This assumption is based on the false premise that since the development team does not have to develop the code for the functionality present in the COTS components, the system development must be less risky. As we intend to show in the subsequent sections, many usual risks associated with systems develop remain risks with COTS intensive systems, some risks take on a different emphasis and there are new risks particular to COTS intensive systems. A sound risk management and assessment program is essential with the successful development of every large scale COTS intensive system.

5   Project Planning

The initial planning phase of any large software intensive system is difficult unto itself, but the planning of the development of COTS intensive systems adds to the difficulties of project planning. The overriding rationale for this increase in difficulty is the use of COTS components increases the number of unknown factors and many of other factors will prove to be out of your control. There are several particular risks that need to be addressed up front at the start of the planning process that include:

- Lack of skilled personnel
- Insufficient risk management expertise
- Ineffective management of the vendor relationships
- Insufficient time planned for integration code development and integration testing

A discussion on each of these risk areas is presented in the subsequent sections along with the impacts the risks have on the development of COTS intensive systems. In addition, there is a discussion of how the risks should be addressed in the planning phase.

5.1   Lack of Skilled Personnel

The lack of skilled personnel is usually a risk for most large-scale software development projects but this risk takes on more significance with the development of COTS intensive systems [4]. As stated earlier, most COTS intensive systems will contain many COTS components that are new to the development team. Learning new technologies that are represented by these new COTS components is no trivial task. Initially, the COTS component's functional capability must be well understood, which can be a daunting task because there may be a significant amount of functionality to learn and that functionality might be a new technology to the team. Also, there is more to learn than just the functionality. The method (or methods) of integration that the COTS component employs must be understood sufficiently well to ensure that the integration can be properly engineered in to the architecture of the system. Finally, this learning experience must be accomplished at a speed that does not adversely affect the project schedule. When all of these issues are considered, it is clear that this typically requires personnel that are more experienced with previous software and/or have a strong system engineering background [4]. It cannot be assumed that less experienced personnel can do the job.

In order to mitigate this risk, several steps can be taken. It is desirable to find a person that is experienced with each one of the COTS components in the system and has integration experience. However, even if it is possible to arrange for such a skilled team, there is still the chance that not all of the COTS components are known during creation of the system plan. Many of the components won't be identified until after product evaluations are performed. The mitigation of this risk must ensure that there is an appropriate number of senior technical personnel assigned to the project that are adaptable, have demonstrated quick learning curves, and have sound engineering backgrounds. In addition, no matter how intelligent and adaptable the personnel on you team are, it will most likely be necessary to explicitly plan for vendor training for each of the COTS components that are unfamiliar to the team. If this risk mitigation is not implemented, there will most likely be the need for "on-the-job" training, which will almost always increase the schedule risk and may be the cause for false starts when the component integration is begun.

The author has had experiences related to the need for skilled personnel when working COTS components. One project required a series of tasks involving the integration of a sophisticated document processing system with a data repository to provide automatically generated documentation from the information in the repository. The initial individual assigned to the task was able to develop an effective design for the integration but did not have a sound background in working with data repositories. The result was an inefficient operation of the document generation. It turned out that the individual left the company shortly after completing the first task. When the author searched for a replacement, it was clear that an individual with more extension experience database implementations was needed to complete the series of automated document generation tasks. Such an individual was found and was first able to improve the initial document generation performance by 70% and the next set of automated documentation was accomplished in about half the labor effort of the original effort. The original design of the integration was maintained with only minor modifications, but the implementation was greatly improved.

5.2   Insufficient Risk Management

Earlier we discussed the importance of using sound risk management techniques on a COTS intensive development project, but risk identification and assessment is only the beginning of risk management. On too many occasions risk management on projects has stopped once the initial risk assessment has been completed. Since the development of COTS intensive systems is inherently an iterative process (you cannot integrate all COTS components simultaneously) the initially identified risks must be reevaluated throughout the development process and new risks will most likely appear as new COTS components are integrated. To mitigate this risk, ensure that the risk management program is an ongoing activity that maintains a living risk management planning document throughout the duration of the project. In addition, consider explicitly assigning a person to be a risk analyst that is chartered with the responsibility to ensure that the risk management plan is being properly executed and kept up-to-date.

5.3   Insufficient Management of the Vendor Relationships

When it comes to dealing with vendors of COTS components remember the vendors' primary concern is to sell product licenses (i.e., make money). Do not assume that they have that same dedication to the success of the project as the development team. This is not to say that most vendors are going to abandon you once the sale has occurred, most vendors do want to see you succeed in the use of their product, but never forget that their primary driver is profits. To mitigate this risk, it is important to make a concerted effort to enter into a strategic relationship with vendors and have a well-formed vendor management program. There are many aspects of this relationship that need to be considered. Realize that for a COTS intensive system, almost all of the systems executable code will be executed by COTS components [4].

The management of vendors must include an explicit, formal strategic relationship that includes mutual non-disclosure agreements, volume cost discount arrangements, training on the product, clear understanding of data rights issues, understand the licensing arrangements, and the agreements for appropriate technical support. One extremely critical focus of the non-disclosure agreement is ensuring the vendor provides full disclosure of the products future upgrades. Chances are that most of the COTS components will go through at least one upgrade, and most likely more than one upgrade, during the development of the system [4]. It is crucial to know what modifications the upgrades contain as early as possible so you can determine the impact the upgrade will have on the system. The understanding the upgrade cycles is not limited to the development effort; when the system has been fielded, product upgrades inevitable and must be dealt with accordingly. One important final point is that the management of the vendors is primarily a management task and not a technical task. The task involves non-trivial negotiations and should be handled by an individual that is experienced in such matters. The management of the vendors should not be left in the hands of the engineers that generally do not have vendor management expertise. But, the engineer does have the responsibility to work hand in hand with the management and the vendors to handle the technical interchanges that must take place with the vendor to properly understand the integration issues.

The author has had many experiences with vendor management that have resulted in both successful and not so successful engagements. During a project to integrate a set of tools that supported a lifecycle Software Engineering Environment (SEE) there were requirements for tool-to-tool integration and tool-to-repository integration. The author's team was successful in getting three vendors to enhance their product baselines to meet some of the integration requirements. It must me noted, though, that this project had a significant potential of product sales, so the vendors where motivated to understand the integration requirements and provide product upgrades when feasible. Additionally, we were able to obtain vendor supplied consulting services, both at no cost and for fee, to assist the team in using the existing integration capabilities in an efficient and effective manner.

An example of an engagement that was not so successful was a vendor that made a whole scale change of the technology that they used for a portion of the tool's operation. The author's development team had developed an integration module that was based on original technology that had to be completely reworked to handle the new technology. As it turned out, the vendor had purchased a small company with a more capable technology and incorporated it into their product line. Mutual non-disclosure agreements were in place and the development team had been working closely with this vendor for well over a year. There had been several discussions about the pending upgrade, but the development team's concentration was on other areas of the product. The vendor claimed that it had not occurred to them to mention this replacement technology. The development team had chosen to integrate this portion of the tool without having a discussion on the upgrades path about the future of the capability with the vendor. The lesson learned was the need to be as comprehensive as possible when discussing future upgrade with the vendors concerning discussions and nothing should be taken for granted.

5.4   Insufficient Time Planned for Integration Code Development and Integration Testing

In the early days of integrating COTS into a system solution there was a false assumption that the need for integration testing was either minimal or not needed at all. It seems that there was a belief (actually a false hope) that once the COTS components were installed the system would be operational. What made this assumption worse was that it was generally the management (both with the developer and the customer) that had this misconception. Clearly this has proven not to be the case. The integration of COTS components has proven to be an extremely sophisticated task that most of the time requires a significant amount of integration code (also referred to as glue code) and the integration testing of this integration code has also proven to be a substantial effort [4]. Both of these subjects will be discussed further in their technical contexts in subsequent sections in this chapter. With respect to project planning, this risk must be mitigated by management listening to the technical advice of the development experts and ensuring that there is substantial time scheduled for integration coding and testing.

To help further mitigate this risk, the University of Southern California has been developing a cost estimation model call the COnstructive COTS (CO-COTS) cost model [1]. COCOTS explicitly considers the following critical factors that impact the cost and scheduling of COTS intensive systems:

- COTS Assessment – Calculates the effort needed to assess (or evaluate) the different COTS components against a set of context specific criteria
- COTS Tailoring – Calculates the effort needed to configure the COTS components to prepare them for integration and operations within the system

– Glue Code Development – Calculates the effort needed to design and develop the integration software (Or Glue Code) that is needed to integrate the COTS components.

The author had the opportunity to participate in some of the working group meetings during the development of COCOTS and it was clear that the critical issues that have a significant impact on the integration code development and integration testing of COTS intensive systems were being addressed effectively by a solid representation of industry experts.

6   Requirements Engineering

Requirements engineering takes on quite a different role when developing COTS intensive systems. Previously with uniquely developed systems, software require- ments were derived from the customer's systems requirements, the software re- quirements were allocated to system components and the functionality needed to support the software requirements was built into the software components. Initially, it may appear that a similar approach could be used when developing COTS intensive systems. The theory would be that one would "simply" allo- cate the customer's system requirements to the COTS components to be used in the system. Although this appears to be a straightforward solution, it has some problems (risks) associated with it. First, for an approach like this to have any hope of being effective, it would require that the full set of COTS components are known upfront in the development process. As it was stated earlier, this is almost always never the case. Further, even if all of the COTS components were known, the chances that all of the system requirements will map cleanly to the COTS components is not assured and the chances of this occurring will decrease as the system under consideration increases in size and complexity. Finally, those requirements that are not mapped to a COTS component may be very difficult to implement in the solution space outside of the COTS components [12].

The mitigation of the risks associated with taking the approach just pre- sented focuses on engaging in a procedure called requirements negotiation. The basic idea is to negotiate requirements with the customer as the capabilities of the selected COTS components are realized [12]. This method goes hand- in-hand with the spiral development processes described earlier. Requirements negotiation should be an activity that is part of each cycle once the COTS com- ponents being considers for that cycle are selected and integrated. The manner of the negotiation depends on the number and depth of the customer's system requirements. If the customer has specified a large number of requirements then the negotiation must identify which requirements are satisfied by COTS compo- nents. If the customer has specified only a few high level requirements then the negotiation should focus on agreeing to a set of requirements that have been de- rived from the functionality of the COTS components that satisfy some of those high level requirements. Another point that needs to be negotiated is how the unused, but available, features of the COTS software are to be handled. Most all COTS components in a large system will have features that go beyond the requirements of the customer [4] and it is important that this situation be negotiated with the customer. A customer that is experienced with procuring a COTS intensive system should be familiar with this approach to requirements engineering. However, when working with a customer that is inexperienced with COTS intensive systems, there is an additional risk that must be address. Educating the customer in the concept of requirements negotiation will be critical, but this must be accomplished in a manner that is politically viable for the particular customer. Note that this form of requirements negotiation inherently involves the customer throughout the development process, a risk mitigation technique that is applicable to any systems development.

7   System Architecture

The primary goal of COTS intensive systems is that the system is supposed to work as a single unified system after being built from many commercial software packages. However, this goal will most likely not be realized if the COTS components are not organized within a sound system architecture. But the COTS components present a variety of challenges do not make it easy to achieve this goal. The major challenge is that the COTS components have a wide range of methods that are use to support integration of the products into the system. These methods range from the component providing no particular method (leaving it up to the developer to invent a unique method); to providing a data export facility (leaving it up to the developer to built an interpreter of the export file); to providing a fully functional application programming interface.

The heterogeneity in the methods of integration has yielded problems that have come to be known as architectural mismatches [10,14,16]. But the solution to controlling these architectural mismatches does not lie in only addressing the interfaces between each COTS component in the system. This can potentially result in the number of interface solutions approaching N2, where N is equal to the number of COTS components in the system solution [4]; this is clearly a risk that must be avoided. Not only is this a problem during the development and integration testing, this will be a considerable problem during the maintenance of the deployed system. While it is rare that each COTS component must interface with all other components, this situation was presented to emphasize the need to think beyond the component-to-component interface method of integration.

One approach to mitigating this risk is to develop a system architecture of the COTS intensive system under development. There several approaches that are available to help architect the system that contain varying levels of formality. These include the include the use of Architectural Description Languages (ADL) [14], using the Unified Modeling Language (UML) as an architecture design aid, follow the guidance provided in the Department of Defense Architectural Framework [7], or use the Zachman Framework [20], or use a method that focuses on interface analysis within the framework of an architecture [16]. In a situation analogous to the discussion of lifecycle processes earlier in Section 3, one approach is not recommended over another. However, select an architectural design methodology that fits the problem space and the methods for performing systems development that are most familiar to the development team. The ideal is not to approach the development of COTS intensive systems as a component-to-component interface problem. Rather, it should be viewed as an architectural design problem first and then work to select the COTS components that best fit the architecture. Most likely, the architecture that is initially considered will evolve during the development process and architectural evolution should be planned. With each iteration of the spiral or evolutionary development lifecycle, the development team's knowledge and understanding of the COTS components increases and there will be the need to make adjustments to the architecture to take full advantage of some of the features of the components [3,19].

8   System Development

Once a mature development process is established, a project plan have been developed; the customer involvement with the requirements engineering approach has been successfully initiated; and the initial candidate system architecture has been defined; it is time to focus on the development of the COTS intensive system (remember that this development is part of the overall spiral process cycles). The focus during development will be on the evaluation of the COTS components and the development and testing of the integration code.

8.1   COTS Evaluation

In almost every category of commercial software packages, there are usually many vendors that provide many different solutions to a problem. The best way to approach the challenge of selecting the COTS components that best fit into the solution space is to use a well structured, if not formal process to evaluate the commercial products. There are evaluation processes available in the industry [11,15]. One risk that should be avoided when performing these evaluations is not to put a disproportionate weight on evaluating the domain functionality of the COTS software. Of course, domain functionality is important, but most of the COTS packages under evaluation for a particular class of software will deliver very similar functional capability. Basically, the evaluation criteria that are used to judge the domain functionality may not turn out to be the discriminating factor in the selection process. Other criteria, both technical and non-technical should be considered and given an appropriate emphasis [17]. Some of the criteria should focus on how well the integration methods that the COTS components employ fit into the system architecture and what the impact the products have on the system resources. In addition to these technical criteria that extend beyond the product functionality, criteria that focus on non-technical issues are important to consider as well. A sample list of non-technical criteria is show below:

− How long has the vendor been in business?
− What is the financial stability of the vendor?
− What is the market share the product has?

– What are the product upgrade cycles and how will they impact development and maintenance?
– What are the cost implications of the product license arrangements?
– Are the product's data rights compatible with the deployment of the system?

This is by no means an exhaustive list; the point that needs to be emphasized is that some of these non-technical issues are as important as some of the technical criteria. For example, if a vendor has an ideal solution for a critical component of the system, but that vendor is not financially viable and has a chance of going out of business, the impact on the system development or maintenance can be catastrophic.

The author was directly involved with the development of the Component Evaluation Process (CEP) described in [15], which was based primarily on the work in [11]. This process has been used successfully on COTS produces in the areas of change management, decision support, document and record management applications, and knowledge management portals.

In summary, the evaluation of the COTS products needs to be comprehensive and consider applicable technical and non-technical criteria to help minimize the risks that might arise during the development and deployment.

8.2   Integration Code Development

The development of the code that is needed to support the integration of the COTS components is generally quite complex in nature and it takes longer to develop than code developed for a system being built from scratch [1,4]. Not understanding this aspect of developing COTS intensive systems will potentially have significant impacts on costs, schedule and possibly system performance. The most direct way to address this situation is to ensure that the implementation staff contains a sufficient number of experienced development personnel. Realize the situation that is facing the developer of the integration code. They are working with one or more COTS component for which they most likely have only a partial understanding; in addition to needing to understand the syntax of the interfaces they must understand the semantics of the interfaces; and the interfaces were developed by the vendor, not the individuals that have to work with the interfaces. This requires developers that are able to adapt quickly to understand all aspects of the operations of the interfaces, and then they must design and develop methods to implement the integration. One other essential way to help any developer that is involved with COTS integration is to plan for and provide vendor supplied training. Regardless of the amount of documentation that is provided by the vendor, not having vendor provided training leaves the developer to discover how the interfaces operate. It will most likely take much more time for this discovery than the time taken for the training. Also, there is a better chance, that with the training, the integration code will be implemented more effectively with less rework than having to discover how the interface operates.

8.3   Integration Testing

Integration testing for COTS intensive systems brings on some new problems and risks that require specific attention. There are two particular aspects that are worthy of discussion. The first issue is the need to provide an effective configuration of the COTS component. This requirement is sometimes overlooked as being a significant effort, which constitutes a risk. Some COTS components require a concerted configuration effort, not only with the configuration capabilities within the COTS component but also the operating system may require a reasonable amount of configuration to meet the needs of the component [1]. A primary example of this is the tuning of a database management system that usually requires a trained experiences individual playing the role of a Database Administrator. Now multiply this by the number of COTS components in the system and realize that there might very well be some contradictions in the different ways that the components require the operating system to be configured. Treating this situation with an appropriate amount of respect by providing a sufficient time for component and operating system configurations and providing formal documentation of the configurations will server to mitigate this risk.

The second issue is to consider that the COTS components are black boxes to integration test personnel and that this makes the task of investigating problems when they do occur during integration testing an increased challenge. As with the integration code development, this requires personnel with a significant amount of integration testing experience that have strong insight into system thread analysis though these black boxes. Consider a system test thread that requires the services of a substantial number (more than three) of COTS components. When a problem is identified, it may not be very obvious where the root cause of the problem is located. The problem could be in one of the components, it could be in the integration code, it could be a misinterpretation of the semantic operations of a component interface and it could be a problem that manifests itself in one part of the system that actually had a root cause early in the system thread. While these problems also occur with the integration testing of newly developed systems, when the internal operations of the components (the black boxes) are unknown, as is the case with many COTS components, the ability to track down some if these sophisticated problems is greatly hampered. In addition to identifying appropriately experienced personnel to help mitigate these risks, obtaining consulting support directly from the vendor can help resolve some of these problems in a timely manner. But also realize that a vendor's consultant will be knowledge in their product only and if they do not believe the problem lies with their product, they might be quick to point the finger elsewhere.

Another method to help mitigate the risks associated with the integration testing of COTS intensive systems is to initiate testing as early in the life cycle as possible. This should be inherent in the spiral lifecycle processes discussed in Section 3, when they are executed effectively. One approach to this is the creation of a COTS integration test bed. As COTS components are evaluated and selected, they can be integrated into the evolving system in the integration test bed. This can help discover problems early in the lifecycle that may, in fact, influence the selection of COTS components during later cycles of the process. In a related matter, an additional mitigating technique is to do some analysis to determine the order in which the COTS components are to be integrated [19]. Generally, in a large COTS intensive system, there are several COTS components that are critical to the architecture and operation of the system; these critical components should be integrated first to provide a solid foundation for the architecture of the system.

The author successfully utilized both test bed and integration ordering techniques when developing the SEE that was discussed in Section 5.3. The development team had an on going test bed that started with the integration of three critical COTS components that were an automated workflow tool, a system design/code generation tool and a data repository. With this foundation integrated in the test bed, the team proceeded to use the integration test bed as an aid in the selection of the remaining tools that were integrated into the system.

9   System Deployment and Maintenance

Once the COTS intensive system has been developed, tested and ready for deployment, the risks are not over. There are still some significant situations that need to be addressed. First, there are many issues that deal with the COTS component upgrade cycles. These include problems with field installation of these upgrades, the impacts that these upgrades have on system operations, the coordination of the upgrades from the many COTS components in the system and understanding the impacts of the upgrades on the integration code [13]. The creation of strategic relationships with the vendors early in the project is an effective mitigation strategy for this risk, as discussed earlier. These relationships are even more important now that the upgrades are going to have a direct impact on the users that are now using the COTS intensive system. Once again part of the mitigation is the need to have senior analysts directly involve in the analysis of the upgrades and deriving effective field upgrade procedures and schedules. This is a non-trivial systems analyst task that requires appropriate levels of expertise as there is very little in the literature to help guide the analysts to feasible solutions. One way to help further mitigate this problem is to have a fully operational test bed of the system so the impacts of upgrades can be fully analyzed before deployment. Unfortunately, this is cost prohibitive most of the time, but it should be clear that some form of impact analysis is required before the upgrade is released to the field. There is an option of not releasing upgrades to the field, but this carries with it the risk that the vendor will stop the support of older versions, which is a common practice. Typically, vendor stop support versions of products that are more than two or three versions old, so beware of taking the no-upgrade option.

In a related matter, there is the problem of product obsolescence. Obsolescence is when the vendor has stopped the production and sale of the product altogether. This can happen for several reasons. The vendor can conclude that there is an insufficient marketplace for the product and cease its production, the profit margin may be too small and the vendor chooses to apply its resources to the more profitable products, and then there is the case were the vendor is purchased by another vendor for the purpose of eliminating the completion by dropping the purchased vendors product. In any of these situations, the most feasible mitigation of this risk is to develop a backup plan for each of the critical COTS components. An effective way to develop alternatives for COTS components is to maintain a continual watch on the marketplace looking for substitute products as well as new technologies that might replace older technologies [13].

Work on formal techniques to support multiple COTS upgrade cycles and product obsolescence is extremely sparse in the industry and more concentrated efforts in this area would benefit the industry.

10   Future Trends

The future of using COTS components in the development of systems will only continue to expand for the foreseeable future and there will certainly be advancement made in the techniques and standards that will be used to help support the developments of COTS intensive systems. But the methods that are used to develop these systems may very well change dramatically. One particularly interesting and exciting technology that is emerging that may very well help set a new direction for COTS intensive systems focuses on service-centric software. Specifically, the set of standards that support Web Services has the potential to put the development of COTS intensive system in a whole new light. One of the most intriguing aspects of these Web Service standards is that they are all based on the eXtended Markup Language (XML) and most of the leading software vendors are aggressively supporting the Web Services effort. The ideal behind Web Services is to use these XML-based communications standards to expose component interfaces and allow those interfaces to be registered and discovered programmatically and have the invocations of the services dynamically bound. What makes this approach to distributed object processing different that its predecessors like Microsoft's Common Object Model, the Object Management Group's Common Object Request Broker Architecture and Sun Microsystems Enterprise Java Beans is that Web Services provide interface specifications and invocations in a manner that is independent of both the programming language and the underlying infrastructure technology. With Web Services, component services can be discovered and invoked no matter where they reside on a network as long as the Hyper Text Transfer Protocol (HTTP) and the XML are supported, both of which have universal support. One can envision the systems of the future being dynamically composed of registered commercial services that might be driven by a rule-based engine that is interpreting formal system specifications.

11   Conclusion

It should be clear that the there are many risks involved with the development of COTS intensive systems that must be given serious consideration and specifically addressed. It has been shown that some of these risk are classic in nature, some classic risks require new mitigation strategies and some of these risks are rather unique to COTS intensive systems. All of the mitigations of these risks must begin with the understanding that the development of COTS intensive systems is not a shortcut to systems development. COTS development is sophisticated challenge that requires a comprehensive approach to addressing the associated risks. It all starts with selecting a development process that can handle the dynamics and variability that is inherent with the development of COTS intensive systems. A project plan must be developed that is ready to address the realities about developing systems with COTS components that include finding properly skilled personnel, creating a sound risk management approach and planning for strong vendor management. Next there is a need to specifically handle the variability in mapping customer requirements to the capabilities of the COTS components. Taking an architectural view of the COTS intensive system will help control the stability of the systems as the solution evolves as the selection of the COTS components are made. Finally, it is critical that proper analytic expertise be applied to the development, testing and maintenance activities. Although there are many risks when developing COTS intensive systems, there appropriate mitigation techniques that can be applied to ensure a successful development effort.

References

1. Abst, C., Boehm, B., & Clark, E. (2000). COCOTS: A COTS Software Integration Lifecycle Cost Model – Model Overview and Preliminary Data Collection Findings. USC-CSE-2000-501, USC Center for Software Engineering, 2000.
2. Albert, C., Brownsword, L., (2002). Meeting the Challenges of COTS Products: Integrating Technology by a Structured Evolutionary Process (ITSEP). International Conference on COTS Based Software Systems.
3. Albert, C., Brownsword, L., (2002). Evolutionary Process for Integrating COTS-Based Systems (EPIC): An Overview. Technical Report. CMU/SEI-2002-TR-009. Retrieved from
   http://www.sei.cmu.edu/pub/documents/02.reports/pdf/02tr009.pdf.
4. Basili, V., Boehm, B. (2001). COTS-Based Systems Top 10 List. IEEE Computer 34(5), 91-93.
5. Boehm, B. (1988). A Spiral Model of Software Development and Enhancement. IEEE Computer, 21, 61-72.
6. Charette, R. (1989). Software Engineering Risk Analysis and Management. New York, McGraw-Hill.
7. Department of Defense Architectural Framework. (1997). Retrieved from
   http://www.c3i.osd.mil/org/cio/i3/AWG_Digital_Library/pdfdocs/fw.pdf.
8. Engert, P., Clapp, J. (2001). Common Risks and Risk Mitigation Actions for Management of a COTS-Based System. Retrieved from
   http://www.mitre.org/pubs/edge_perspectives/march_01/risks.html.
9. Moore, G. E. (1997). The continuing silicon technology evolution inside the PC platform. Retrieved from
   http://www.intel.com/update/archive/issue2/featrue.htm.

10. Garlan, D., Allen, R., & J. Ockerbloom (1994), "Architectural Mismatch: Why Reuse is So Hard," IEEE Software.
11. Kontio, J. (1996). A Case Study in Applying a Systematic Method for COTS Selection. Proceedings of the International Conference on Software Engineering, Berlin.
12. Morisio, M., Seaman, C., Basili, V., Parra, A., Kraft, S., & Condon, S. (2001). COTS-Based Software Development: Processes and Open Issues. Retrieved from http://www.research.umbc.edu/~cseaman/papers/jss2001.pdf.
13. Shaffer, G., McPerson, G. (2002). FAA COTS Risk Mitigation Guide: Practical Methods For Effective COTS Acquisition and Life Cycle Support. Retrieved from http://www2.faa.gov/aua/resources/cots/Guide/CRMG.htm.
14. Shaw, M. (1997). Software Architecture and Component Integration. Keynote address, 5th Internaitional Symposium on Assessment of Software Tools.
15. Software Productivity Consortium (1999). Component Evaluation Process, SPC-98091-CMC, Version 01.00.02. Retrieved from http://www.software.org/pub/darpa/cep/spc-98091-cmc_pdf.zip.
16. Software Productivity Consortium (2002). COTS Architectural Analysis Method, SPC-2002002-CMC, Version 01.00.00. Retrieved from http://www.software.org/pub/darpa/CAAMPaper.zip.
17. Software Productivity Consortium (2000). COTS Integration Questions and Checklist, SPC-2000018-CMC, Version 01.00.01. Retrieved from http://www.software.org/pub/darpa/cots/spc2000018_cmc.doc.
18. Software Productivity Consortium (1993). Evolutionary Spiral Process Guidebook, SPC-91076-MC, Version 03.00.05.
19. Software Productivity Consortium (2001). Phased-Integrated COTS Approach, SPC-2001006-CMC, Version 01.00.00. Retrieved from http://www.software.org/pub/pic.
20. Zachman, J. (1987) A Framework for Information Systems Architecture. IBM Systems Journal, 26, 3, IBM Publication G321-5298.

A Metrics-Guided Framework for Cost and Quality Management of Component-Based Software

Sahra Sedigh-Ali[1], Arif Ghafoor[1], and Raymond A. Paul[2]

[1] School of Electrical and Computer Engineering, Purdue University
West Lafayette IN 47907, USA
{sedigh,ghafoor}@purdue.edu
[2] Department of Defense, OASD/C3I, Pentagon
Washington DC 20543, USA
ray.paul@oasd.pentagon.mil

Abstract. The growing reliance on commercial-off-the-shelf (COTS) components for large-scale projects has introduced a new paradigm in software engineering, requiring the design of new software development methods and business processes. Large-scale component reuse leads to savings in development resources, but increases the system's vulnerability to risks arising from third-party development, as well as integration difficulties, performance constraints, and incompatibility of components from multiple vendors. The framework discussed in this chapter aims to alleviate quality concerns for COTS-based systems by using software metrics to accurately quantify factors contributing to the overall quality of a component-based system, guiding quality and risk management by identifying and eliminating sources of risk. Tradeoffs between cost and quality in a component-based system are discussed, as well as analytical techniques and formal models for cost and quality decisions.

1 Introduction

The paradigm shift to *commercial off-the-shelf* (COTS) components appears inevitable, necessitating drastic changes to current software development and business practices. Quality and risk concerns currently limit the application of *COTS-based systems* (CBSs) to non-critical applications. New approaches to quality and risk management are needed to handle the growth of CBSs [1, 2]. With software development proceeding at unprecedented speed, in-house development of all system components may prove too costly in terms of both time and money, as witnessed by the outsourcing trend currently present in commercial software development. Large-scale component reuse and COTS component acquisition can generate savings in development resources, which can then be applied to quality improvement, such as enhancements to reliability, availability, and ease of maintenance.

Prudent component deployment can localize the effects of changes made to a particular portion of the application, reducing the ripple effect of system modi-

A. Cechich et al. (Eds.): Component-Based Software Quality, LNCS 2693, pp. 374–402, 2003.

fications. This localization can increase system adaptability by facilitating modifications to system components or integration code, as required for conforming to changes in requirements or system design [1]. COTS component acquisition can reduce time to market by shifting developer resources from component-level development to integration of acquired components. Increased modularity also facilitates rapid incremental delivery, allowing developers to release modules as they integrate them and offer product upgrades as various components evolve.

These advantages bring related disadvantages, including integration difficulties, performance constraints, and incompatibility among products sourced from different vendors. Further, relying on COTS components increases the system's vulnerability to risks arising from third-party development, such as vendor longevity and intellectual-property procurement. Component performance and reliability also vary because component level testing may be limited to black box tests, and inherently biased vendor claims may be the only source of information [3]. Such issues limit COTS component use to non-critical systems that require low to moderate quality. Systems that require high quality cannot afford the risks associated with employing these components [4].

From a historical perspective, software failures in both traditional and component-based systems have had drastic consequences for the organizations employing these systems. Software errors in the automated baggage control system of the Denver International Airport delayed the opening 16 months, dramatically increasing the construction costs [5]. Within the Department of Defense, where software is subject to rigorous testing and debugging, a software error caused severe failure in a mission involving the Clementine satellite. This satellite was launched into lunar orbit in the spring of 1994, and one objective of its launch was the testing of targeting software that may have later been used in missile defense systems [5]. If the failure had gone undetected, and the software system had been used in a missile defense system, such a failure may have had calamitous consequences.

Perhaps the most infamous software failure is that of the Ariane 5 launcher, which exploded 37 seconds after liftoff. An independent inquiry board set up by the French and European Space Agencies analyzed this disaster from the perspectives of software developers, designers, requirements engineers, test engineers, and program managers. The developers attributed the failure to a programming error involving incorrect software exception handling. The designers believed that a poor design was at fault, as it allowed software exceptions to halt hardware units that were functioning correctly. The requirements engineers stated that incorrect analysis of changing requirements was to blame, as the erroneous program module was unnecessary and should not have been reused. The test engineers' blamed the obvious deficiency in testing the system. Finally, the program managers viewed the disaster as the result of ineffective development processes and project management [6].

These perspectives, while differing in the cause attributed to the failure, all lead to the following conclusions:

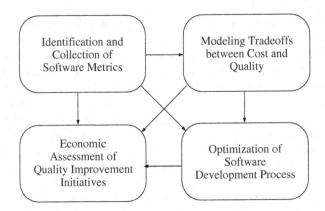

Fig. 1. Components of Software Quality Management Framework

- Risk management should be exercised at every stage of the life cycle.
- Reuse can negatively impact the reliability of a system.
- Rigorous testing is of utmost importance.

Such case studies serve as important stepping-stones on the path to component-based software development, as many of the same problems threaten CBSs.
A rigorous framework for cost and quality management is vital to the development of reliable and safe software systems, whether traditional or component-
based. Quality and performance concerns can be alleviated by using *software
metrics* to guide quality and risk management in a CBS, accurately quantifying
various factors contributing to the overall quality of a CBS, and identifying and
eliminating sources of risk. Metrics can guide decisions throughout the software
life cycle and determine whether software quality improvement initiatives are
financially worthwhile [7, 8, 9].

As in any development or manufacturing process, software quality is achieved
at a cost. This chapter outlines existing challenges in cost and quality management of CBSs and illustrates a metrics-based framework for quantifying the concept of software quality, investigating the tradeoff between cost and quality, and
using the information gained to guide quality management. This framework for
software cost and quality management involves four main components: identification and collection of metrics, modeling of cost-quality tradeoffs, optimization
of the software development process, and economic assessment of quality improvement initiatives. These components are interrelated, as depicted in Fig. 1.

The framework commences cost and quality management by identifying and
collecting appropriate software metrics, as represented by the upper-left component of Fig. 1. The foundation of the framework lies upon this component,
as accurate quantification of quality attributes is critical to successful quality
management. This component influences all three of the remaining components.
The second component, depicted in the upper right of Fig. 1, involves modeling tradeoffs between cost and quality in the software system. The models rely
heavily on the metrics identified and collected by the first component, and in

many cases, the metrics form the parameters of the cost-quality models. These models are in turn utilized by the third component, seen in the lower right of Fig. 1, which involves optimization of the software development process, with the objective of achieving the best quality at the least cost. Once again, quality and cost are quantified using the metrics developed in the first component. The final component of the framework, seen in the lower left of Fig. 1, involves economic assessment of quality improvement initiatives. This component utilizes the results of the first three components to determine whether the quality improvement initiatives taken have been worthwhile. Given adequate time and resources, this framework can be used in an iterative fashion as well, where the results of the economic assessment are used as feedback in refining metrics selection and improving cost-quality models. Given the increasing utilization of component-based development, a pragmatic approach is needed to address CBS quality issues in a comprehensive manner. The framework discussed in this chapter represents an important step towards addressing the growing need for quality management of CBSs.

2   Background

Central to the development of a CBS is the concept of a *software component*, which has various definitions in software engineering literature, including work by Hopkins [10], where a software component is defined as "a physical packaging of executable software with a well-defined and published interface." Szyperski [11] states that a software component is "a unit of composition with contractually specified interfaces and explicit context dependencies only" that "can be deployed independently and is subject to composition by third parties." A third definition [10] identifies a component as "a coherent package of software artifacts that can be independently developed and delivered as a unit and that can be composed, unchanged, with other components to build something larger." These definitions, as well as many others, stress the requirement of well-defined interfaces for a component. The source code of most COTS components is inaccessible to the designers of systems deploying them, making highly structured interfaces essential for the success of the design.

A number of challenging issues hinder the progress of CBSs [10]. *Component granularity* is one of these concerns. Larger components require less inter-component communication, resulting in savings in system resources, but generally employ more complex interfaces. This tradeoff is system-dependent, and deciding on the suitable granularity for components requires careful investigation of the application requirements, in particular complexity and flexibility of design. Deciding on the appropriate level of *specificity*, or the extent to which the component matches the design, is also challenging, as specificity in function facilitates integration, but increases the number of components, while generality in design allows reuse of the component in a broader range of applications, but requires more complex integration. *Platforms* are of importance to component-based design, as some components are limited to the single platform they were designed for, or require extensive modifications before deployment in an alternative platform. Multi-platform, or distributed applications are even more challenging, as they may require multiple versions of a COTS component, one version for each platform that the application is designed for. *Interoperability* is a related challenge, as it may be difficult or impossible to integrate components from different vendors. The *architecture* of the software system is a significant factor in the level of COTS component use, as the lack of an identifiable architecture will render available components less valuable, often complicating the integration of new components. Evolving system architecture may cause problems when the components have been developed for a static architecture. Keeping track of component upgrades is another challenge, as it is necessary to ensure that the appropriate version of a component is being used, these and similar issues fall into the *versioning* category. Finally, *quality* is the concern of most interest to this chapter. COTS components are often acquired as a "black box," hence thorough component level testing is not possible, as the source code of the components is inaccessible. Testing results reported by the component development team may be of limited use, as integration testing is performed at the time of deployment, and discrepancies may arise between the quality perceived at the system and component levels. The concept of quality in component-based systems is further discussed later in this chapter.

In any development process, models depicting the relationship between costs and quality can be used to guide decisions regarding investments in quality improvement. In the case of CBSs, challenges lie in accurately representing the relationship between cost and quality and integration of component level cost-quality models, or system level models defined for an individual quality factor [12]. As in the case of traditional, not component-based, software environments, defining an appropriate set of software metrics can be the first step in developing cost-quality models. Accordingly, an approach is needed that can employ modern high-level analytical techniques, such as statistical decision theory and multiple objective optimization, in conjunction with software metrics to gain knowledge and detailed insight into the CBS development process. The framework discussed in this chapter, and depicted in Fig. 1, aims to provide an assessment of the quality of the product and the risks involved in the completion of the project, and can aid high-level decision-making by the management.

The processes involved in the metrics-guided quality management of Fig. 1 are depicted in Fig. 2. As demonstrated by this figure, these processes encompass all four of the framework components depicted in Fig. 1. Population of the metrics database requires the definition of software metrics, which is the first component of the framework. These metrics are collected from the software system, during the development process, as part of the specification provided by the COTS component vendor, or during testing. The metrics data is then mined and analyzed to facilitate its use in modeling cost and quality relationships in the system. These cost and quality relationships are the knowledge being sought through metrics collection, and relate to the second component of the framework. This knowledge, as well as other information garnered by the data mining and

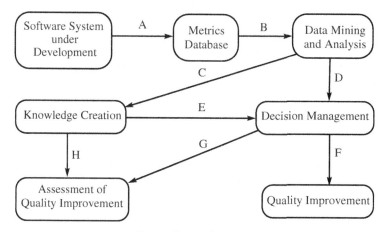

Some Open Questions

A. What metrics data should be collected?
B. How should the metrics data be mined and analyzed?
C. How can usable knowledge be extracted from the metrics data?
D. How can the results of data mining and analysis be used for decision management?
E. How can the extracted knowledge be used for decision management?
F. How can the results of decision management be applied to quality improvement initiatives?
G. How can the use of decision theory be improved?
H. How can the knowledge garnered from the metrics be used to assess quality improvement initiatives?

Fig. 2. Processes of the Metrics-Guided Quality Management Framework

analysis, is applied to decision analysis and quality improvement, corresponding to optimization of the software development process, which is the third component. Finally, assessment of quality improvement is provided through tasks associated with the fourth component, namely, economic assessment of quality improvement initiatives.

Fig. 2 also illustrates a number of open questions associated with the framework, where the arrows between processes are labelled with the letter representing the question addressed. The first question on the list, question A, regards the choice of metrics to be collected. As described in the following section, metrics appropriate for component-based systems differ from metrics for traditional systems. The metrics of interest depend on the particular software system, and the quality attributes most critical to the performance of the system. As metrics are the foundation of the framework, this choice is critical to the success of the quality management. Question B pertains to processing the metrics data, through mining and various analysis techniques, and may involve estimation or aggregation of lower-level metrics. Knowledge creation involves extracting the information required for quality management from the metrics database, in particular information characterizing the relationships between cost and quality, represented by question C. Questions D and E are concerned how to best utilize the metrics data, directly or after knowledge creation, respectively, in making prudent decisions regarding investments in quality initiatives. Question F seeks to determine how the results of decision management and optimization can be applied to quality improvement initiatives, as the application may involve challenges in translating theoretic results to practical initiatives for the system. In question G, we seek to improve the use of decision theory in quality management of the software system. Finally, Question H aims to determine metrics that can be used to assess the financial feasibility and worth of the quality improvement initiatives. The remainder of this chapter seeks ways to answer these questions, in an effort to facilitate the enable the successful utilization of metrics-guided quality management for CBSs.

3   Software Metrics for CBSs

Measurement enables engineers to quantify product quality and performance, to isolate the development process and product attributes that impact quality and performance, and to demonstrate how product and process changes impact these attributes. Furthermore, measurement allows development teams to set achievable goals, demonstrate their potential to meet these goals, track their progress, adjust processes to correct faults, and demonstrate the impact of these adjustments on meeting goals [13]. Projects stand the best chance of success when the goals driving the use of different measures can be stated and mutually pursued. A proper choice of basic metrics combined with a selection of powerful tools and true integration of these metrics and tools forms the foundation of efficient and robust software project management. To this end, a metrics-guided approach to the quality management of CBSs can aim to provide software developers and managers of CBSs with the same benefits attained by metrics in developing in-house software. The first step is identifying a set of metrics tailored to the specific needs of CBSs.

Metrics can guide risk and quality management and help to reduce the risks encountered during the planning and execution of software development, resource and effort allocation, scheduling, and product evaluation [14, 8]. Risks can include performance issues, reliability, adaptability, and return on investment. Risk reduction can take many forms, such as using component wrappers or middleware, replacing components, relaxing system requirements, or even issuing legal disclaimers for certain failure-prone software features. Metrics let developers identify and isolate these risks, then take corrective action. One of the keys to success is selecting appropriate metrics- especially metrics that provide measures applicable over the entire software cycle and address both software processes and products. The identification and collection of appropriate software metrics is an integral component of the quality management framework of Fig. 1. In choosing metrics, the software engineering environment of both the development and maintenance cycles should be considered, as well as the economics of metrics collection and analysis. To reduce the possibility of having a single bottleneck to measurement accuracy, redundant or cross-related metrics can be defined, where each of the related metrics can validate the data provided by the others. The metrics selected should also have a strong basis in industry or government practice for establishing "rule of thumb" thresholds for use by software managers [15, 7].

An important difference between metrics for CBSs and traditional systems is the unavailability of "size" as a metric. Most traditional metrics sets incorporate the size of the source code, measured in *Lines of Code* (LOC), into several metrics. This size is generally not known for COTS components, hence, if a measure of program or component size is required, alternate measures should be used. One such measure is the number of *use cases* - business tasks the application performs-that a given component supports [16]. CBS metrics also approach *time to market* differently. Component acquisition changes the concept of time to market because developers may not know the component development time and cannot incorporate it into time calculations. For CBSs, a simple delivery rate measure can replace the time to market measure. One proposed measure divides the number of use cases by the elapsed time in months. Another research challenge arises from the fact that the thorough component level testing required for metrics collection may not be possible, due to inaccessibility of the component source code. Test results reported by the component development team may be of limited use, as integration testing is performed at the time of deployment, and discrepancies may arise between the metrics collected at system and component levels.

Considerable research has been conducted in software metrics in the past decade, especially on reliability models, cost estimation, and application of software metrics [17, 18, 19, 14, 20]. The bulk of this research is restricted to traditional (not component-based) software systems. A framework for cohesion measurement in object-oriented systems has been proposed in [21] and is later used in [22] to empirically explore relationships between design coupling, cohesion, and inheritance measures for object-oriented (OO) systems. Both studies focus on OO measures, and require at least class-level access to program code. This may limit the applicability of the proposed metrics to COTS components only accessible through interfaces at the component level. In [18] and [23], a formal set of test and evaluation metrics is presented, which similar to the set described here, is comprised of management, requirements, and quality metrics. The metrics proposed in [23] are applied to predicting various software development parameters, such as manpower, reliability, and fault profiles, in [24]. These metrics are defined for traditional software systems, and have not been adapted to CBSs. Both papers also investigate metrics-guided software reuse, which is related to quality management in our proposed research, but the emphasis is on reuse decisions, not quality. Such work can serve as a background for research on metrics-guided quality management.

An initial set of system level metrics for CBSs has been proposed in [8, 9]. These metrics, described in Table 1, are intended to help software developers and managers select appropriate components from a repository of software products

Table 1. System level software engineering metrics for CBSs

Metric	Description
Cost	Total software development expenditure, including costs of component acquisition, integration, and quality improvement
Time to market	Time elapsed between start of development and component acquisition to product delivery
Software engineering environment	Capability and maturity of the development environment
System Resource Utilization	Utilization of target computer resources as a percentage of total capacity
Requirements Conformance	Adherence of integrated product to defined requirements at various levels of software development and integration
Requirements Stability	Level of changes to established software requirements
Adaptability	Integrated system's ability to adapt to requirements changes
Complexity	Component interface and middleware or integration code complexity
Test Coverage	Fraction of the system that has undergone satisfactory integration and/or end-to-end testing
Fault Profiles	Cumulative number of detected faults
Reliability	Probability of failure-free system operation over a specified period of time
Customer Satisfaction	Degree to which the software has met customer expectations

and aid in deciding between using COTS components or developing new components. The primary considerations are cost, time to market, and product quality. The metrics are divided into three categories: management, requirements, and quality.

The *management* metrics include cost, time to market, software engineering environment, and system resource utilization. These management metrics can be used for resource planning or other management tasks or for enterprise resource planning applications. The *cost* metric measures the overall expenses incurred during the course of software development, in terms of software development tools, manpower, licensing fees, and other resources. These expenses include the costs of component acquisition and integration and quality improvements to the system. The *time to market* metric measures the time needed to release the product, from the beginning of development and COTS component acquisition to delivery. The rate of incremental delivery can be measured with a modified version of this metric, assessing the amount of time required to deliver a certain fraction of the overall application functionality. The *software engineering environment* metric measures the capability of producing high-quality software and can be expressed in terms of the Software Acquisition Capability Maturity Model (SA-CMM) [25]. *System resource utilization* determines the percentage of target computer resources the system will consume.

The *requirements* metrics include measures of *requirements conformance* and *requirements stability* of the CBS. These metrics can be used to monitor the specification, translation, and volatility of requirements, as well as the level of adherence of the CBS to the requirements. COTS components are often unstable [26], and component level stability can affect requirements stability if developers adapt requirements to incorporate changes to selected components.

The *quality* metrics include adaptability, complexity of interfaces and integration, integration test coverage, end-to-end test coverage, reliability, and customer satisfaction. *Adaptability* measures a system's flexibility, evaluating its ability to adapt to requirements changes, as a result of system redesign or to accommodate multiple applications. *Complexity* provides an estimate of the complexity of interfaces, middleware, or glue code required for integrating different COTS products. Overly complex interfaces complicate testing, debugging, and maintenance, and degrade the system's quality. This metric can also represent the complexity of the overall system, in terms of the number of components used, as well as the complexity of the interfaces among them. *Integration test coverage* and *end-to-end test coverage* indicate the fraction of the system's functionality that has completed those tests, as well as the effort testing requires. Measures such as statement or path coverage can be used to evaluate coverage, depending on the level of access to system source code. *Reliability* estimates the probability of fault-free system operation over a specified time under specified conditions. Techniques similar to those of traditional systems, including fault injection into the integration code, can be used to collect the data for the reliability metric. *Customer satisfaction* evaluates how well the software meets customer expectations and requirements. Sample predictors of customer satisfaction include schedule requirements, management maturity, customer culture, marketplace trends, and the customer's proficiency. Such estimates can guide development decisions such as release scheduling and can aid in developing a test plan that accurately reflects the product's field use.

Of the twelve metrics defined above, a subset is of particular importance to CBS development and design. This subset, which is italicized in Table 1, includes six metrics: cost, time to market, software engineering environment, complexity, test coverage (integration and/or end-to-end), and reliability. A study of the literature, including industrial case studies [15, 27, 7, 28, 29, 30], underlines the importance of this subset. The emphasis of this chapter is on cost and quality management, leaving cost an obvious choice for the focus group.

Time to market is closely related to cost and directly impacts the market viability of the software product. The software engineering environment metric is of interest due to its potential for predicting quality software. From the quality perspective, the focus is on the test coverage and reliability metrics. Complexity has been chosen, as it impacts the robustness of the software, as well the cost, as detailed later in this chapter. Reliability is currently the bottleneck for CBS development, and is hindering the deployment of CBSs in critical applications [31, 32, 4]. The test coverage metric is of importance, as it is closely related to reliability and provides an automated means for measuring which code has been tested. This subset of metrics satisfies the criteria mentioned above for metrics selection, as the six metrics are relevant to the software engineering environment of CBS development and maintenance, can be collected in a cost-effective manner, are cross-related to each other, and can be used to establish rule-of-thumb guidelines for software management.

The initial set of metrics is defined at the system level. For the majority of these metrics, deriving system level metrics from component level information is not a trivial task, and constitutes a significant research challenge. Similar research has been conducted for the reliability metric, resulting in an expression for system level reliability as a function of component level fault densities [12]. Estimation of COTS integration costs has also been performed in [33]. Both studies can be utilized in developing accurate estimation techniques for the software metrics.

Because the metrics are interdependent, understanding the relationships between them can aid decision-making regarding CBS quality-improvement investments. The most obvious relationship is between cost and the quality metrics, such as reliability [19, 12]. However, more subtle relationships exist, such as those among time to market, test coverage, and reliability. Delayed product release because of testing and debugging can result in reduced revenues or, in extreme cases, loss of the market to a competitor with an earlier release. On the other hand, premature product release can lead to lower reliability. Understanding the relationships among time to market, test coverage, and reliability can help in selecting a suitable release schedule [20]. Another effective strategy involves using the software engineering environment in conjunction with the quality metrics to encourage vendors to improve their software development process and adhere to standards, thus increasing the likelihood that users will select their component.

One possible approach to modeling the relationships among the metrics is an *influence diagram* [34]. An influence diagram is a network for probabilistic and decision analysis modeling. The nodes correspond to variables that can be constants, uncertain quantities, decisions, or objectives. The arcs reveal the probabilistic dependence between the uncertain quantities and the information available at the time of the decisions. Detailed data about the variables is stored within the nodes, so the program graph is compact and focuses attention on the relationships among the variables. The flexibility, tractability, graphic nature, and intuitiveness of influence diagrams make them an attractive choice. To construct the influence diagrams, and to determine the initial metrics values, data from case studies, field tests, and simulation can be used. The main challenge in constructing the influence diagrams is determining the conditional probabilities defining the dependence of one metric upon others. One way of estimating these probability distributions is analyzing metrics data from prior versions of the components. In the absence of prior versions, data from similar components from the same vendor can be used. Estimates of the probability distributions

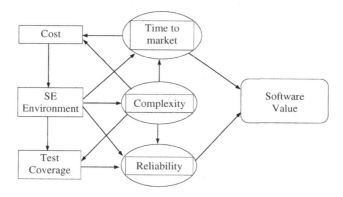

Fig. 3. Sample influence diagram for a subset of the software metrics

can be refined during integration and end-to-end testing of the application being developed. A sample influence diagram is presented in Fig. 3, and depicts the relationships among the focus subset of the metrics. In this figure, the rectangles, ovals, and rounded rectangle represent decisions, uncertain quantities, and the objective value, respectively.

Beginning at the rightmost node of the figure, the objective value being maximized is the software value, which can be expressed in terms of the overall return on investment, the market share, or other common measures of product value. The decisions to be made involve the time to market and reliability of the product. For instance, how long to continue testing and debugging before releasing the product, which in turn determines how quickly the product will be released, and how reliable it will be. These decisions directly impact the software value, as an early product release will lead to a competitive edge, and a possible increase in market share, and higher reliability will make the product more desirable, and hence, more valuable. The uncertain quantities driving the decisions are cost, software engineering environment, and test coverage, as well as the time to market and reliability. The software engineering environment influences all of the other uncertain quantities, as a better software engineering environment will achieve higher test coverage, and hence higher reliability within lower cost and shorter time to market. Test coverage influences reliability, as higher test coverage is more likely to remove a greater number of software faults, leading to a lower failure rate and higher reliability. Time to market influences cost, as the a late release may be costly in terms of increased testing costs, as well as loss of revenue due to losing market share to competitors. Reliability influences time to market, as a more reliable product can be released more quickly. Complexity influences test coverage and reliability, as overly complex software is less likely to be tested thoroughly and will be less reliable as a result. Complexity also influences time to market, as testing will be more time consuming. For reasons described later in this chapter, complexity is also affects the cost of the software. Having a clear picture of these influences and interrelationships facilitates decision-making regarding investments in quality improvement initiatives.

4   Modeling Cost and Quality in CBSs

In deciding between in-house development and COTS component acquisition, the anticipated effect on system quality is an important concern. Software quality can be measured from several different perspectives, including the level of satisfaction of the customer, the key attributes of the software, or freedom from defects in the software's operation. In metrics-guided quality management, software metrics are used to guide the allocation of resources to quality improvement initiatives. The *cost of quality* (CoQ) represents the resources dedicated to improving the quality of the product being developed. For example, increasing or maintaining reliability incurs costs that can be considered the costs of reliability. The overall CoQ is the sum of such costs plus other costs that cannot be directly attributed to factors measured by the quality metrics. Quality costs, then, represent "the difference between the actual cost of a product or service and what the reduced cost would be if there were no possibility of substandard service, failure of products, or defects in their manufacture [35]."

We concern ourselves with the *cost of software quality* (CoSQ)-corresponding to a portion of the cost metric in Table 1 - which can be divided into two major types: cost of conformance and cost of non-conformance.

The cost of conformance derives from the amount the developer spends on attempts to improve quality. We can further divide conformance costs into prevention and appraisal costs. Projects incur prevention costs during activities targeted at preventing defects, such as training costs, software design reviews, and formal quality inspections. Likewise, activities that involve measuring, evaluating, or auditing products to assure conformance to quality standards and performance incur appraisal costs. These activities include code inspections, testing, quality audits, and software measurement activities such as metrics collection and analysis.

The cost of non-conformance includes all expenses the developer incurs when the system does not operate as specified. Internal failure costs stem from non-conformance occurring before the product ships to the customer, such as the costs of rework in programming, defect management, reinspection, and retesting. External failure costs arise from product failure after delivery to the customer. Examples include technical support, maintenance, remedial upgrades, liability damages, and litigation expenses. Table 2 shows the various categories of software quality costs for CBSs.

In any development process, models that depict the relationship between costs and quality can guide decisions regarding investments in quality improvement. Modeling the tradeoff between cost and quality is an important component of the metrics-based quality management framework depicted in Fig. 1. Discussions of such models in the economics and management literature [36, 37, 35] generally depict a nonlinear relationship between CoQ and quality. Accurate cost-quality models can be invaluable to managers and developers, guiding resource and cost management and other aspects of the software development process.

Table 2. Categories of software quality costs

Category	Typical costs of CBS software quality
Appraisal costs	Integration or end-to-end testing, quality audits, component evaluation, metrics collection, and analysis
Prevention costs	Training, software design reviews, process studies, component upgrades
Internal failure costs	Defect management, design and integration rework, component replacement, requirement relaxation
External failure costs	Technical support, maintenance, defect notification, remedial component upgrade or replacement

In [38], the cost of quality and return on quality are evaluated from the perspective of software development. Three metrics are introduced in the software engineering context, CoSQ, *return on software quality* (RoSQ), and *software quality profitability index* (SQPI), which determines whether a particular quality initiative will create value that exceeds its investment. This study also assumes non-CBS software development. Similar composite metrics can be defined for CBSs, and used to model cost-quality tradeoffs in such environments. [39] conducts an assessment of the impact of reuse on quality and productivity in object-oriented systems. The metrics used are size, reusability, effort, productivity, and number of defects. These metrics can be used in CBSs, provided that the notion of size is suitably defined.

Very little, if any, research has been conducted on the economics of quality in CBS development. Cost models for software reuse have been widely studied, but quality is largely ignored in these studies. COCOMO 2.0 [40] takes software reuse into account, and allows the use of logical lines of code (LLOC) as the standard measure. The authors suggest using the checklist developed by Park at the SEI to explicitly define a LLOC. This model has limited applicability to CBS, as COTS software, libraries, and auto-generated code are excluded when counting the LLOCs. Where possible, COCOMO 2.0 can be used to estimate some component level cost factors.

The *Constructive COTS* (COCOTS) model [41, 42], one of the suites of COCOMO models, can be used to estimate effort and schedule for CBS development. This model is an amalgam of four related sub-models: (1) COTS component assessment, (2) COTS component tailoring, (3) COTS glue code development, and (4) COTS volatility. Seventeen attributes, including correctness, availability/robustness, and security, are also defined as most influential during a final selection assessment of COTS software. The assessment sub-model is intended for use in the initial stages of development, and is aimed at selecting the most suitable COTS component from a set of candidates. COCOTS can currently yield effort estimates only; schedule estimation is yet to be incorporated into the model.

Fig. 4(a) depicts the classic model of optimum quality costs. In this model, which shows the relationship between the cost per good unit of product and the

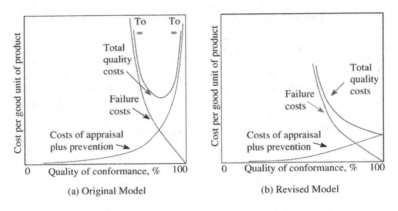

Fig. 4. Optimum quality costs model (adapted from [43])

quality of conformance, expressed as a percentage of total conformance, prevention and appraisal costs rise asymptotically as the product achieves complete conformance. Recent technological developments inspired a revised model that reflects the ability to achieve very high quality, or "perfection," at finite costs. Shown in Fig. 4(b), this model, proposed by Frank Gryna [43], has two key concepts. The first is that moderate investments in quality improvement result in a significant decrease in the cost of non-conformance. The second key concept is that focusing on quality improvement by defect prevention results in an overall decrease in the cost of testing and related appraisal tasks.

These models can be analyzed in terms of the metrics defined for a CBS. The quality of conformance in the original model can represent one quality metric, such as test coverage or reliability. Accordingly, the vertical axis represents a CoSQ component— namely, the portion of quality costs dedicated to improving the particular quality factor. Intuitively, the same nonlinear relationship should hold. Increasing the investment in improving a certain quality factor should increase the value of the corresponding metric, and the amount of this increase should taper off as the product achieves high quality levels. As described in previous sections of this chapter, it is generally difficult to accurately evaluate and quantify the quality and performance of COTS components. Hence, "perfect" quality may be very difficult to claim, and will not be achievable at finite costs. For these reasons, Fig. 4(a) may be a better model for quality costs in CBSs.

In adapting Fig. 4(a) to CBSs, we maintain that conformance costs are lower than those of traditional software systems. For CBSs, only black box testing can generally be assumed feasible, so the costs incurred in white box testing are avoided. These savings may be cancelled by the costs incurred during the selection of appropriate components, leading to the conclusion that appraisal costs for a CBS are comparable to appraisal costs in a traditional software system. Prevention costs may be lower for a CBS, as the black box nature of the components limits the possibility of extensive preventative measures. Comparable appraisal costs and lower prevention costs result in an overall lower cost of conformance.

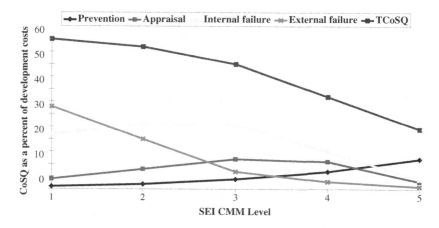

Fig. 5. Knox's model for the cost of software quality

In evaluating the failure costs of a CBS, one should note that the failures occurring later in the software life cycle are costlier than those occurring early in the software life cycle. Generally, internal failure costs incurred due to failures prior to the release of the software, such as defect management, are lower than external failure costs incurred after release, such as defect notification and litigation costs. Due to the limited testing possible for COTS components, in similar software engineering environments, fewer failures will be detected prior to the release of a CBS, as compared to a traditional software system. Fewer detected failures imply lower internal failure costs. If the software being compared is of similar quality (comparable number of failures), this delays the detection of failures to after the release of the software, increasing the cost of such failures, which are now considered external failure costs. Lower internal failure costs and higher external failure costs may lead to comparable overall costs of non-conformance. Considering the lower conformance costs of CBSs, we can generally conclude that the total quality costs of a CBS are lower than a non-component based software system of comparable quality.

Although we may be able to determine the overall CoQ with reasonable accuracy, determining the amount dedicated to improving a particular quality factor is difficult because all factors interrelate. For quality metrics such as customer satisfaction, the relationship between cost and quality may be too complex for such a simple model, as increased investments in quality improvement may be invisible to the customer. For example, users may find 95 percent reliability satisfactory, making further investments in reliability pointless. Further, customer satisfaction may increase in jumps, resulting in a discontinuous cost-quality curve, although empirical studies should verify this behavior.

The return on investments in quality improvement depends on the software engineering environment. In [36], the cost of software quality is discussed based on the Capability Maturity Model for Software (SW-CMM) [44]. SW-CMM is based on the concept that a software development environment has a measur-

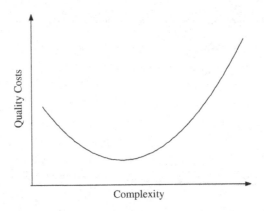

Fig. 6. Relationship between Quality Costs and Complexity of a CBS

able process capability analogous to that of industrial processes. The SW-CMM proposes five levels of capability, ranging from a chaotic, ad hoc development environment to a fully matured and continually optimizing production-line environment. These levels can also be used to express the software engineering environment metric discussed in the previous section. Based on the data presented, Knox makes two assumptions, the first of which is that the total cost of quality at SW-CMM Level 1 equals approximately 60 percent of the total cost of development. The second assumption is that the total cost of quality will decrease by approximately two-thirds as the development process reaches SW-CMM Level 5, or full maturity. Fig. 5 shows the various software cost-of-quality categories, as well as the total cost of software quality, according to Knox, for the five SW-CMM levels.

A combination of Knox's model and traditional models provides a more accurate view of the CoQ in CBSs. A multi-dimensional CoSQ model can be developed based on the cost of quality, quality, and software engineering environment, which can be used to determine financially sound investments in quality, based on the development environment. In the case of CBSs, where different may have widely varying software engineering environments, such a model can be used to guide the vendor selection process. In place of the SW-CMM levels used in traditional development, the software engineering environment can be expressed in terms of SA-CMM levels. SA-CMM [25] evaluates the maturity level of a software acquisition environment. The levels of acquisition maturity range from Initial, at Level 1, to Optimizing, at Level 5. This model defines key process areas for Levels 2 through 5, where a key process area states the goals that must be satisfied to achieve each level of maturity. SA-CMM and SW-CMM are synergistic, and can be used in parallel with each other, by defining a software engineering environment metric with two (weighted) components, one component corresponding to each CMM.

Recent work by Abts [30], examines the relationship between the number of COTS components in a CBS, and tradeoffs between maintaining and retiring the system. Abts postulates that increasing the number of COTS components is economically beneficial only up to a certain point, where the savings resulting from the use of COTS components break even with the maintenance costs arising from the volatility of such components. The study recommends lowering the number of COTS components by increasing the *functional density* of the components used, in other words, using *leaner* components. Although the resulting system will benefit from reduced complexity, the disadvantage to using lean components is the lack of robustness that results. As a component is relied upon for providing a greater number of functions to the system, a failure in the component is more costly to the system due to decreased redundancy in component functionality. Quality costs arising from a lack of robustness can be classified as costs of non-conformance. Conversely, using a greater number of COTS components leads to higher system complexity, increasing not only the maintenance costs mentioned in [30], but also appraisal and prevention costs in general, as testing a complex system is generally lengthy and expensive. A complex system is generally more likely to fail; hence, the costs of non-conformance will also increase in an overly complex system. This leads to a generalization of the results of [30], whereby quality costs are modeled as having a non-linear relationship with complexity, as depicted in Fig. 6. In this view, an optimal value of system complexity will maintain the best balance between leanness and robustness, minimizing quality costs. This figure can be combined with Fig. 4(a) to yield the multi-dimensional model of Fig. 7, which depicts the relationship among quality costs, quality of conformance (as a percentage), and system complexity. In the decision theoretic approach taken by the framework of this chapter, the objective is to find the best tradeoff among the three parameters of Fig. 7, achieving high quality of conformance at low cost and moderate complexity.

In developing the final cost-quality model, the integration of component level cost-quality models, or system level models defined for an individual quality factor, should also be investigated, leading to a hierarchical cost-quality model for the CBS, where component level cost-quality models are combined to determine a system level model for the relationship between cost and quality.

5 Analytical Techniques and Formal Models for Cost and Quality Decisions

A number of challenging issues hinder the development of CBSs, including component granularity, specificity, interoperability, and quality, as discussed in the previous sections of this chapter. Software management decisions can involve any of the aforementioned challenges, and utilizing decision theory in management can lead to financially sound choices. Questions arising about investments in software quality improvement initiatives can be approached from a *return on investment* (ROI) perspective. The ROI can be examined in terms of increased conformance to requirements such as reliability. Metrics can be used to evaluate the quality improvement achieved by a particular investment in software quality improvement initiatives. The assessment of the ROI of quality improvement

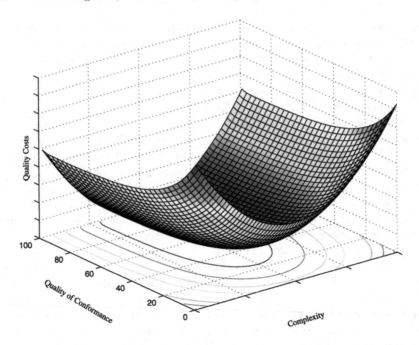

Fig. 7. Relationship among cost, quality of conformance, and system Complexity

initiatives relates to the fourth component of the quality management framework of Fig. 1, as it pertains to economic assessment of the quality improvement initiatives.

Cost-benefit analysis of traditional software systems [38, 35] has concluded that quality improvements yield the greatest returns early in the life cycle. In CBSs, quality improvements are not possible during early stages of the development of the acquired components. To compensate for this problem, quality improvement efforts should be spread throughout various stages of system design and development.

In the design phase, such initiatives include identification of cost factors and cost-benefit analysis involving the unique risks associated with CBSs, determination of the level of architectural match between the application and the COTS components, and evaluation of the complexity and cost associated with integration, interoperability and middleware development. The metrics and models discussed can guide these evaluations, with the objective of deciding between in-house development and COTS acquisition, and if the latter is chosen, selecting the most suitable component from a set of available alternatives.

In the development phase, metrics-based cost-quality models can be applied to estimate the costs associated with the development process. During the entire life cycle, the models can guide quality decisions by estimating the costs associated with the unique testing requirements of COTS-based systems, such as integration, end-to-end and thread testing. After delivery, the cost metrics and models can be used for trend analysis of the COTS market.

Metrics-guided quality management can involve formulating software development decisions as optimization problems, and solving the resulting problem. For instance, for the parameters of Fig. 7, namely, quality costs, quality, and complexity, a tradeoff can be achieved where a high quality CBS can be developed at low cost, without becoming overly complex. Stochastic decision processes can also be used to select suitable policies for decision making in the presence of uncertainty.

In related work, the tradeoff between cost and reliability has been widely studied, and several formulations for optimizing software reliability have been proposed. In [12], system level reliability has been evaluated as a function of component level failure intensities, and the optimization problem seeks to minimize the total cost of achieving the desired reliability, by allocating specific failure intensities to the components. This approach may be applicable to the development of similar formulations for other software metrics. [19] proposes a method for estimating the development costs of a software module, taking into account the target reliability. A decomposition technique is used to estimate the cost of development, based on an estimate of the number of faults that need to be found and fixed in order to achieve the desired reliability. This model only considers costs of coding and testing, and hence does not provide a comprehensive method for allocating effort to quality initiatives. Other studies [17, 45] determine optimal release strategies based on reliability and cost criteria, but do not provide a unified approach to optimizing more than one component of quality.

Off-the-Shelf Option (OTSO) [46] is a method supporting the search, evaluation and selection of reusable software. This method relies on the use of multi-level programming in its optimization. This technique is not useful for situations where several of the criteria are of comparable importance. In addition, the OTSO method does not provide a metrics set that can be used in the evaluation criteria, and does not explicitly determine the factors contributing to the quality of the CBS.

An optimization model for developing a modular software system is presented in [47]. The system is assumed to be comprised of a set of serially executed modules, where each module is configured with only one COTS product. The objective function of the model minimizes the system development cost. The model presented in [47] is severely limited by the assumption of a single COTS product in each module, as well as the serial execution of the modules. Furthermore, it does not consider quality factors other than failure rate in the analysis.

5.1 Multiple Objective Optimization for Software Development Decisions

In developing quality software within a limited budget, compromises may be required in order to meet the cost restrictions set forth by budget guidelines. As seen in Fig. 4, optimum quality costs are achieved by striking a balance between increasing appraisal and prevention costs, and decreasing failure costs. Careful selection of target values for quality attributes is necessary. One method involves selecting metric values by using *multiple objective optimization* (MOO) techniques [48, 49], which optimize a number of criteria simultaneously. In most cases, it is unlikely that different objectives would be optimized by the same alternative parameter choices. Hence, a tradeoff among the target quality attributes may be needed. Formally, a MOO problem (MOP) aims to optimize $F(x)$, which is a vector of objective functions, $f_i(x)$, subject to a set of constraints denoted by C. In the context of CBSs, $f_i(x)$ can be the cost associated with an individual quality metric, such as reliability, and the constraints in C can stem from system level or component level constraints such as the overall budget or time to market derived from the system specifications.

$$\min_{x \in C} F(x) = \begin{bmatrix} f_1(x) \\ f_2(x) \\ \vdots \\ f_n(x) \end{bmatrix} \quad \text{where } n \geq 2, \quad \text{and} \tag{1}$$

$$C = \{x : h(x) = 0, g(x) \leq 0, a \leq x \leq b\}$$

Any quality attribute can be represented as an objective function of the MOP, $f_i(x)$, using the cost-quality models developed for the CBS. In terms of Fig. 7, $F(x)$ could be composed of representing the complexity and quality costs of the CBS, constrained by C, the quality specifications of the system. Alternatively, $F(x)$ could be composed of representing the complexity and other quality attributes of the CBS, and the budget for quality costs could be represented by C.

As the scalar concept of "optimality" does not directly apply to the multiple objective setting, *Pareto-optimal* [50] solutions can be developed. A Pareto-optimal solution is one that cannot be improved with respect to any one objective without worsening some other objective; hence, a compromise is reached between the various objectives. Fig. 7 represents a typical surface for which Pareto-optimal solutions can be found.

In a common solution technique, the MOP is solved by combining the multiple objectives into one scalar objective whose solution is a Pareto-optimal point for the original MOP. This is an intuitive technique in the case of cost management, as resulting scalar objective can then be used to represent the overall quality of the system. The scalar objective function can be computed by minimizing the weighted sums of functions, or alternatively, by multilevel programming, as both techniques are applicable to both linear and nonlinear problems. In *minimizing the weighted sums of functions*, a positively weighted convex sum of the objectives, $\sum_{i=1}^{n} \alpha_i f_i(x)$, $\alpha_i > 0, i \in \{1, 2, \ldots, n\}$, is minimized. For CBS quality management, the weights can be chosen to represent the relative importance of the metrics. This approach gives an idea of the shape of the Pareto surface and provides insight into the trade-off among the various quality attributes.

The second technique, *multilevel programming*, is a one-shot optimization technique and is intended to find just one "optimal" point as opposed to the entire Pareto surface. In this method, the objectives are ordered according to the relative importance of the corresponding quality metrics. The optimization then begins by finding the optimizers of the first objective function and recursively proceeds to find the optimizers of all of the objective functions, using the optimizers of the previous step as the feasible set for the current step. This approach is useful when the hierarchical order among the quality metrics is of prime importance and the continuous trade-off among them is not of interest. However, problems lower in the hierarchy become very tightly constrained and often become numerically infeasible, so that the less important software metrics wield no influence on the final quality. Hence, multilevel programming should be avoided in cases where a sensible compromise among the metrics is sought. Other commonly used techniques, such as homotopy techniques and goal programming, are not effective in MOPs with more than two objectives [51, 52], whereas software quality management generally requires consideration of more than two metrics.

Simulation and case studies can be used to evaluate and fine-tune the MOP solutions. Depending on the nature of the MOP, and the parameter values determined by the solution, a combination of discrete and continuous optimization may be necessary. A further challenge lies in applying the solution to the system. The parameter values determined by the solution are in terms of the software metrics, and will need to be translated to the actual resources available for software development. For instance, applying the value obtained for the software engineering environment requires interpreting this value in terms of manpower, tools, and developer skill levels. This may require approximating the solution value by a value in its neighborhood, leading to a change in other related metrics. Such subtleties are extremely system-dependent.

5.2   Decision Management in the Presence of Uncertainty

Due to the unpredictable nature of the economy, uncertainty is inherent to any software development process. For CBSs, this uncertainty is much greater, as detailed information about the individual components is usually lacking. COTS components are often delivered as a black box, with no access to the source code. This may prevent developers from testing the component thoroughly, which leaves vendor claims as the only source of information about the internal workings of the component. These vendor claims may be vague or imprecise, leading to uncertainty regarding the performance of the component. Vendor delivery schedules are another source of uncertainty. A vendor may not meet a certain release deadline for a component, unpredictably delaying the release of any applications employing the component. Component upgrades can also lead to uncertainty. Vendors may fail to upgrade components to comply with operating system upgrades, limiting the feasibility of upgrading systems employing the component. In the worst case, a vendor may go out of business, rendering component upgrades and maintenance impossible.

When uncertainty cannot be neglected in cost and quality management, *statistical decision theory models* can be applied to cost and quality management. Such models use probability distributions to yield decisions based on the expected values of alternate acts. They can be used for decision making under conditions of *risk*, where the set of future events and their probabilities are known, as well as conditions of *total uncertainty*, where only the set of future events is known [53].

Due to the sequential nature of decision making in software development, *decision trees* are a suitable approach. In this approach, the decisions, results, and future states of nature span a time horizon broken down into sequenced periods. For each time period, the probability distributions of the states of nature are known, as well as the rewards they generate for each alternative. Thus, for every period, the reward for an alternative can be calculated based on the occurrence of a particular state of nature and the specified preceding states of nature. Provided that the transition probabilities have the Markov property, which can be assumed for many CBSs, the decision tree will have an underlying *Markov Decision Process* (MDP), which can be characterized by a finite set of states S, a finite set of actions A, a transition function $T(s, a, s')$, which for all $s \in S$, $a \in A$, defines $\Pr(s'|s, a)$, and a reward function $R(s, a)$ for all $s \in S$, $a \in A$ [54].

The main challenge of metrics-based decision management lies in formulating quality management decision sequences as MDPs. The uncertainty in such decisions arises not only from economic uncertainty, but also from the adaptive nature of the software development process. Changes to the of a CBS environment may have many different sources, including modifications to the testing process, changes in system configuration, requirements instability or change, modification of customer specifications, and availability or lack of third-party components. Each of these changes affects the state of the system, and can be represented by an element of S. The states most specific to CBS environments represent alternative system configurations resulting from the acquisition of competing components. The states can be characterized in terms of software metrics, with the objective of determining a one-to-one mapping between a combination metrics data, and an element of S. In terms of Fig. 7, a state of the system could be determined by the complexity, cost, and quality of conformance at a point in time. These states could be considered to be akin to various values of $f(x)$ for the MOP of the previous subsection.

The set A can be populated with actions representing any software development initiatives, with the focus on quality improvement initiatives, such as investments aimed at increasing reliability or adaptability or decreasing the cost of quality. Due to the component-based nature of the systems, investigating the acquisition of alternative components is also a major research challenge. Other examples of actions investigated include managerial decisions regarding the continuation or termination of testing, determining a suitable release time for the product, deploying increased manpower, budget allocation, and requirements specification. These actions can be characterized in terms of the software metrics, with each action corresponding to a set of changes to the metrics. The actions are what change the state of the system, and can be thought of as moving the system from one point on the surface of Fig. 7 to another, or changing the value of $F(x)$ in the MOP of the previous subsection.

The rewards, $R(s,a)$, can be determined in terms of reductions in cost or increases in quality. Similar to the other components of the MDP, the rewards can be characterized in terms of the software metrics, developing the reward functions from a composite of the software metrics in the corresponding system state. Using Fig. 7 as an example, the reward function could be the ROI achieved for each combination of quality, cost, and complexity. In This reward could be considered the analog of $F(x)$ for the MOP, as it is the value being optimized. Another important component of the formulation are the transition probabilities, $Pr(s'|s,a)$, which can be determined by estimation, empirical observation, and theoretical modeling. The influence diagrams developed to study the relationships between the metrics can also be used to determine transition probabilities.

MDPs have been studied extensively [55, 56], and are typically solved by value iteration or policy space iteration [57]. Linear programming formulations are well-suited to MDPs [58], due to their ease of automation and low complexity.

5.3 Economic Assessment of Quality Improvement Initiatives

The previous section of this chapter discusses two formulations for optimizing the development of a CBS. In both formulations, a measure of the "value" of the software can guide the optimization. In formulating software development as a MOP, the "value" of the software can be used as the objective function we are seeking to optimize, namely, $F(x)$. If uncertainty of economic conditions, engineering environment, or other factors discussed in the previous subsection prompt the formulation of software development as an MDP, the most obvious analogy would be using the "value" of the software product as the reward function of the MDP. In either case, this "value" should be quantification, in terms of the software metrics, of quality attributes desirable for the product, taking into consideration cost and time to market.

In software development, as in any other production activity, valuable resources are invested under uncertainty with the objective of maximizing the value of the product [59]. The traditional approach to valuing an asset in business and software engineering uses the static *net present value* (NPV) concept. The NPV of an asset is taken as the value that it adds to the enterprise. This leads to a natural interpretation of NPV for components comprising, or being considered candidates for a CBS, whereby the NPV of each component can be interpreted as the value added to the overall system as a consequence of employing the component. The computation of NPV applies the principle of discounting, which assumes that a dollar spent or earned today is worth $(1 + d)^T$ dollars at time T in the future. The discount rate, d, is a positive value representing the risk inherent to the project. The actual value of product risk is difficult to quantify, especially for a CBS, for reasons discussed earlier in this chapter.

[60] divides a software project into *development* and *operation* phases, as depicted in Fig. 6. The paper then proceeds to define the NPV of a software

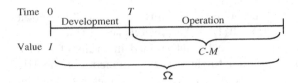

Fig. 8. Software Development Timeline (adapted from [60])

development project as a function of six economic value determinants. This function is given in Equation 2.

$$NPV = (C - M)/(1 + d)^T - I + \Omega \ . \tag{2}$$

In the equation above:

I is the present value of initial development cost. This cost includes acquisition costs and initial quality costs

T is the time to market, previously discussed as one of the software metrics.

C is the remaining asset value of the project calculated at time T. This amount includes the expected revenues, but excludes direct costs such as licensing fees paid to component vendors.

M is the total operation cost, including cost of maintenance, calculated at time T.

Ω is the flexibility premium. It quantifies the benefit of the flexibility of the product under conditions of uncertainty. Ω is related to the software metric quantifying adaptability of the system.

d is the product risk, which is used to discount all cash flows of the project.

Fig. 8 displays the software development timeline discussed in [60], and illustrates how the economic value determinants used in calculating the NPV relate to this timeline. In the development phase, in today's dollars, an initial investment of I is made at time 0. This initial investment is a portion of the cost metric previously discussed, more specifically, it is the initial development cost. The duration of the development phase, in other words, the time to market is T. At time T, the product is released and the operation phase begins. At any time after T, the value of the product is $C - M$, which represents revenues minus operation costs. The NPV is calculated by discounting this value at rate d, subtracting the initial development costs, and adding the flexibility premium, which represents the value added to the product as a result of its inherent flexibility.

In the timeline of Fig. 8, the initial investment decision is made at time 0. This decision is irreversible, and cannot be revised to adapt to changing product requirements or market conditions. This fails to capture the dynamic optimization needed for investments in quality or component acquisitions made after development has commenced. *Real options theory* can be a more suitable approach for rapidly changing environments. In this approach, flexibility is treated as an *option* and is valued using techniques related to financial option pricing [60, 59]. A financial option confers, the right, but not the obligation, to buy or sell an asset. The option expires after a predetermined time. An option to purchase is denoted a *call option*, and an option to sell a *put option*. [60] classifies the flexibility to replace COTS components as a call option, the option to delay or skip upgrades as a *put* option, and the option to abandon the project as a put option.

Combined with the MOP and MDP formulations previously discussed in this chapter, real options analysis can be used to determine the best investments in quality improvement initiatives for the software system. The determination of the financial worth of quality improvement initiatives can refine the cost-quality model of the software and guide the optimization of software development processes.

6 Conclusions

Quality and risk concerns currently limit the application of COTS-based system design to non-critical applications. New approaches to quality and risk management will be needed to handle the growth of CBSs. The metrics-based framework for cost and quality management discussed in this chapter can aid developers and managers in deciding on optimal quality improvement initiatives for CBSs, as well as analyzing the return on investment in quality improvement initiatives. The metrics discussed in this chapter also facilitate the modeling of cost and quality, although more complex models may be needed to capture the intricate relationships between cost and quality metrics in a CBS. Research on metrics-guided quality management can enable extensive economic and engineering analysis for CBSs, including identification of cost factors and cost-benefit analysis involving the unique risks associated with CBSs, determination of the complexity and cost associated with integration, interoperability, and middleware development, and estimation of the costs associated with the unique testing requirements of CBSs. The findings can alleviate concerns about the risks associated with deploying COTS components in critical applications, facilitating the use of components in a broader range of applications.

References

1. Boehm, B., Abts, C.: COTS integration: Plug and pray? IEEE Computer **32** (1999) 135–138
2. Brereton, P., Budgen, D.: Component-based systems: A classification of issues. IEEE Computer **33** (2000) 54–62
3. McDermid, J.: The cost of COTS. IEEE Computer **31** (1998) 46–52
4. Voas, J.M.: The challenges of using COTS software in component-based development. IEEE Computer **31** (1998) 44–45
5. Gibbs, W.W.: Software's chronic crisis. Scientific American **271** (1994) 72–81
6. Nuseibeh, B.: Ariane 5: Who dunnit? IEEE Software **14** (1997) 15–16
7. Weller, E.: Using metrics to manage software products. IEEE Software **11** (1994) 27–33
8. Sedigh-Ali, S., Ghafoor, A., Paul, R.A.: Software engineering metrics for COTS-based systems. IEEE Computer **34** (2001) 44–50
9. Sedigh-Ali, S., Ghafoor, A., Paul, R.A.: Metrics-guided quality management for component-based software systems. In: Proc. of the 2001 Int'l Conf. on Computer Software and Applications (COMPSAC 2001). (2001) 303–308

10. Hopkins, J.: Component primer. Comm. of the ACM **43** (2000) 27–30
11. Szyperski, C.: Component Software: Beyond Object-Oriented Programming. Addison Wesley Longman Ltd (1998)
12. Helander, M.E., Zhao, M., Ohlsson, N.: Planning models for software reliability and cost. IEEE Trans. on Software Eng. **24** (1998) 420–434
13. Khoshgoftaar, T.M., Oman, P.: Software metrics: Charting the course. IEEE Software **11** (1994) 13–15
14. Schneidwind, N.F.: Software metrics for quality control. In: Proc. 4th Int'l Software Metrics Symposium (METRICS '97), Los Alamitos, Calif., IEEE CS Press (1997) 127–136
15. Grady, R.B.: Successfully applying software metrics. IEEE Software **11** (1994) 18–25
16. Tsagias, M., Kitchenham, B.: An evaluation of the business object approach to software development. J. Systems and Software **52** (2000) 149–156
17. Ashrafi, N., Zahedi, F.: Software reliability allocation based on structure, utility, price and cost. IEEE Tran. on Software Eng. **17** (1991) 345–356
18. Paul, R., Shinagawa, Y., Day, Y.F., Khan, M.F., Ghafoor, A.: Object-oriented framework for metrics-guided risk management. In: Proc. of the 1996 Int'l Conf. on Computer Software and Applications (COMPSAC '96). (110-115) 1996
19. Burnett, R.: A trade-off method between cost and reliability. In: Proc. 17th Int'l Conf. Chilean Computer Science Society (SCCC '97). (1997)
20. Chàvez, T.: A decision-analytic stopping rule for validation of commercial software systems. IEEE Tran. on Software Eng. **26** (2000) 907–918
21. Briand, L.C., Daly, J.W., Wüst, J.: A unified framework for cohesion measurement in object-oriented systems. Empirical Software Engineering: An International Journal **3** (1998) 65–117
22. Briand, L.C., Wüst, J., Ikonomovski, S.V., Lounis, H.: Investigating quality factors in object-oriented designs: An industrial case study. In: ICSE99. (1999) 345–354
23. Paul, R.A., Kunii, T., Shinagawa, Y., Khan, M.F.: Software metrics knowledge and databases for project management. IEEE Trans. on Knowledge and Data Eng. **11** (1999) 255–264
24. Paul, R.A.: Software Metrics. PhD thesis, School of Electrical Eng., Tokyo University, Tokyo, Japan (1999)
25. Cooper, J., Fisher, M., Sherer, S.W.: Software Acquisition Capability Maturity Model (SA-CMM) version 1.02. Technical Report CMU/SEI-99-TR-002, Carnegie Mellon Software Eng. Inst., Philadelphia (1999)
26. Basili, V.R., Boehm, B.: COTS-Based systems top 10 list. IEEE Computer **34** (2001) 91–93
27. Horga, J.R., London, S., Lyu, M.R.: Achieving software quality with testing coverage measures. IEEE Software **11** (1994) 60–69
28. Stark, G., Durst, R.C., Vowell, C.W.: Using metrics in management decision making. IEEE Software **11** (1994) 42–48
29. Sledge, C., Carney, D.: Case study: Evaluating COTS products for DoD information systems. SEI Monographs on the Use of Commercial Software in Govt. Systems (1998)
30. Abts, C.: COTS-Based Systems (CBS) functional density – a heuristic for better CBS design. In Dean, J., Gravel, A., eds.: Proc. of the 2002 Int'l Conf. on COTS-Based Software Systems (ICCBSS 2002). Volume 2255 of Lecture Notes in Computer Science., Springer (2002) 1–9

31. Schneidwind, N.F.: Methods for assessing COTS reliability, maintainability, and availability. In: Proc. of the Int'l Conf. on Software Maintenance (ICSM '98). (1998)
32. Rodriguez-Dapena, P.: Software safety certification: A multidomain problem. IEEE Software **16** (1999) 31–38
33. Jilani, L.L., Mili, A.: Estimating COTS integration: An analytical approach. In: Proc. 5th Maghrebian Conf. on Software Eng. and Artificial Intelligence. (1998)
34. Shachter, R.D.: Evaluating influence diagrams. Operations Research **34** (1986) 871–882
35. Campanella, J.: Principles of Quality Costs: Principles, Implementation, and Use. 3rd edn. ASQ Quality Press, Milwaukee, Wis. (1999)
36. Knox, S.T.: Modeling the cost of software quality. Digital Technical Journal **5** (1993) 9–16
37. Haley, T.J.: Software process improvement at raytheon. IEEE Software **13** (1996) 33–41
38. Slaughter, S.A., Harter, D.E., Krishnan, M.S.: Evaluating the cost of software quality. Comm. of the ACM **41** (1998) 67–73
39. Melo, W.L., Briand, L.C., Basili, V.R.: Measuring the impact of reuse on software quality and productivity. Technical Report CS-TR-3395, Univ. of Maryland, College Park, MD (1995)
40. Boehm, B., Clark, B., Horowitz, E., Westland, C., Madachy, R., Selby, R.: Cost models for future lifecycle processes: COCOMO 2.0. Annals of Software Engineering **1** (1995) 57–94
41. Abts, C.: COTS software integration cost modeling study. Technical Report USC-CSE-98-520, University of Southern California, Los Angeles (1998)
42. Baik, J., Eickelmann, N., Abts, C.: Empirical software simulation for COTS glue code development and integration. In: Proc. of the 2001 Int'l Conf. on Computer Software and Applications (COMPSAC 2001). (2001) 297–302
43. Juran, J.M., Gryna, F.M.: Juran's Quality Control Handbook. 4th edn. McGraw-Hill, New York (1988)
44. Paulk, M.C., Curtis, B., Chrissis, M.B., Weber, C.V.: Capability maturity model, version 1.1. IEEE Software **10** (1993) 18–27
45. Xie, M.: On the determination of optimum software release time. In: Proc. Int'l Symposium on Software Reliability Eng. (1991) 218–224
46. Kontio, J.: A case study in applying a systematic method for COTS selection. In: Proc. 18th Int'l Conf. on Software Engineering (ICSE'96). (1996) 201–209
47. Jung, H.W., Chung, C.S., Lee, K.O.: Selecting optimal COTS products considering cost and failure rate. In: Proc. of the 10th Int'l Symposium on Software Reliability Eng. (ISSRE'99). (1999)
48. Sawaragi, Y., Nakayama, H., Tanino, T.: Theory of Multiobjective Optimization. edn. Academic Press, Inc, Orlando, FL (1985)
49. Statnikov, R.B., Matusov, J.B.: Multicriteria Optimization and Engineering. edn. Chapman and Hall, New York (1995)
50. Rakowska, J., Haftka, R.T., Watson, L.T.: Tracing the efficient curve for multi-objective control-structure optimization. Computing Systems in Engineering **2** (1991) 461–471
51. Rao, J.R., Papalambros, P.Y.: A non-linear programming continuation strategy for one parameter design optimization problems. In: Proc. of the ASME Design Automation Conf. (1989) 77–89
52. J.Schniederjans, M.: Goal programming: Methodology and Applications. edn. Kluwer Academic Publishers, Boston (1995)

53. Brodley, C.E., Utgoff, P.E.: Multivariate versus univariate decision trees. Technical Report COINS-CR-92-8, University of Massachusetts, Amherst, MA (1992)
54. Puterman, M.L.: Markov Decision Processes: Discrete Stochastic Dynamic Programming. John Wiley and Sons (1994)
55. Lin, S., Dean, T.: Generating optimal policies for markov decision processes formulated as plans with conditional branches and loops. In: Proc. 2nd European Planning Workshop. (1995)
56. Lusena, C., Goldsmith, J., Mundhenk, M.: Nonapproximability results for markov decision processes. Technical Report 274-98, University of Kentucky (1998)
57. White, D.J.: Markov Decision Processes. John Wiley and Sons (1993)
58. Schultz, T.: Linear programming approaches for solving markov decision processes. The Institute of Management Sciences, Southeastern Chapter (1989) 149–151
59. Sullivan, K.J., Chalasani, P., Jha, S., Sazawal, V.: Software design as an investment activity: A real options perspective. In Trigeorgis, L., ed.: Real Options and Business Strategy: Applications to Decision Making. Risk Books (1999)
60. Erdogmus, H.: Comparative evaluation of software development strategies based on net present value. In: Proc. ICSE'99 Workshop on Economics Driven Software Engineering Research (EDSER1). (1999)

Author Index

Lecture Notes in Computer Science

For information about Vols. 1–2632
please contact your bookseller or Springer-Verlag

Vol. 2673: N. Ayache, H. Delingette (Eds.), Surgery Simulation and Soft Tissue Modeling. Proceedings, 2003. XII, 386 pages. 2003.

Vol. 2674: I.E. Magnin, J. Montagnat, P. Clarysse, J. Nenonen, T. Katila (Eds.), Functional Imaging and Modeling of the Heart. Proceedings, 2003. XI, 308 pages. 2003.

Vol. 2675: M. Marchesi, G. Succi (Eds.), Extreme Programming and Agile Processes in Software Engineering. Proceedings, 2003. XV, 464 pages. 2003.

Vol. 2676: R. Baeza-Yates, E. Chávez, M. Crochemore (Eds.), Combinatorial Pattern Matching. Proceedings, 2003. XI, 403 pages. 2003.

Vol. 2678: W. van der Aalst, A. ter Hofstede, M. Weske (Eds.), Business Process Management. Proceedings, 2003. XI, 391 pages. 2003.

Vol. 2679: W. van der Aalst, E. Best (Eds.), Applications and Theory of Petri Nets 2003. Proceedings, 2003. XI, 508 pages. 2003.

Vol. 2680: P. Blackburn, C. Ghidini, R.M. Turner, F. Giunchiglia (Eds.), Modeling and Using Context. Proceedings, 2003. XII, 525 pages. 2003. (Subseries LNAI).

Vol. 2681: J. Eder, M. Missikoff (Eds.), Advanced Information Systems Engineering. Proceedings, 2003. XV, 740 pages. 2003.

Vol. 2685: C. Freksa, W. Brauer, C. Habel, K.F. Wender (Eds.), Spatial Cognition III. X, 415 pages. 2003. (Subseries LNAI).

Vol. 2686: J. Mira, J.R. Álvarez (Eds.), Computational Methods in Neural Modeling. Proceedings, Part I. 2003. XXVII, 764 pages. 2003.

Vol. 2687: J. Mira, J.R. Álvarez (Eds.), Artificial Neural Nets Problem Solving Methods. Proceedings, Part II. 2003. XXVII, 820 pages. 2003.

Vol. 2688: J. Kittler, M.S. Nixon (Eds.), Audio- and Video-Based Biometric Person Authentication. Proceedings, 2003. XVII, 978 pages. 2003.

Vol. 2689: K.D. Ashley, D.G. Bridge (Eds.), Case-Based Reasoning Research and Development. Proceedings, 2003. XV, 734 pages. 2003. (Subseries LNAI).

Vol. 2691: V. Mařík, J. Müller, M. Pěchouček (Eds.), Multi-Agent Systems and Applications III. Proceedings, 2003. XIV, 660 pages. 2003. (Subseries LNAI).

Vol. 2692: P. Nixon, S. Terzis (Eds.), Trust Management. Proceedings, 2003. X, 349 pages. 2003.

Vol. 2693: A. Cechich, M. Piattini, A. Vallecillo (Eds.), Component-Based Software Quality. X, 403 pages. 2003.

Vol. 2694: R. Cousot (Ed.), Static Analysis. Proceedings, 2003. XIV, 505 pages. 2003.

Vol. 2695: L.D. Griffin, M. Lillholm (Eds.), Scale Space Methods in Computer Vision. Proceedings, 2003. XII, 816 pages. 2003.

Vol. 2697: T. Warnow, B. Zhu (Eds.), Computing and Combinatorics. Proceedings, 2003. XIII, 560 pages. 2003.

Vol. 2698: W. Burakowski, B. Koch, A. Bęben (Eds.), Architectures for Quality of Service in the Internet. Proceedings, 2003. XI, 305 pages. 2003.

Vol. 2701: M. Hofmann (Ed.), Typed Lambda Calculi and Applications. Proceedings, 2003. VIII, 317 pages. 2003.

Vol. 2702: P. Brusilovsky, A. Corbett, F. de Rosis (Eds.), User Modeling 2003. Proceedings, 2003. XIV, 436 pages. 2003. (Subseries LNAI).

Vol. 2704: S.-T. Huang, T. Herman (Eds.), Self-Stabilizing Systems. Proceedings, 2003. X, 215 pages. 2003.

Vol. 2706: R. Nieuwenhuis (Ed.), Rewriting Techniques and Applications. Proceedings, 2003. XI, 515 pages. 2003.

Vol. 2707: K. Jeffay, I. Stoica, K. Wehrle (Eds.), Quality of Service – IWQoS 2003. Proceedings, 2003. XI, 517 pages. 2003.

Vol. 2709: T. Windeatt, F. Roli (Eds.), Multiple Classifier Systems. Proceedings, 2003. X, 406 pages. 2003.

Vol. 2710: Z. Ésik, Z, Fülöp (Eds.), Developments in Language Theory. Proceedings, 2003. XI, 437 pages. 2003.

Vol. 2711: T.D. Nielsen, N.L. Zhang (Eds.), Symbolic and Quantitative Approaches to Reasoning with Uncertainty. Proceedings, 2003. XII, 608 pages. 2003. (Subseries LNAI).

Vol. 2712: A. James, B. Lings, M. Younas (Eds.), New Horizons in Information Management. Proceedings, 2003. XII, 281 pages. 2003.

Vol. 2713: C.-W. Chung, C.-K. Kim, W. Kim, T.-W. Ling, K.-H. Song (Eds.), Web and Communication Technologies and Internet-Related Social Issues – HSI 2003. Proceedings, 2003. XXII, 773 pages. 2003.

Vol. 2714: O. Kaynak, E. Alpaydin, E. Oja, L. Xu (Eds.), Artificial Neural Networks and Neural Information Processing – ICANN/ICONIP 2003. Proceedings, 2003. XXII, 1188 pages. 2003.

Vol. 2715: T. Bilgiç, B. De Baets, O. Kaynak (Eds.), Fuzzy Sets and Systems – IFSA 2003. Proceedings, 2003. XV, 735 pages. 2003. (Subseries LNAI).

Vol. 2716: M.J. Voss (Ed.), OpenMP Shared Memory Parallel Programming. Proceedings, 2003. VIII, 271 pages. 2003.

Vol. 2718: P. W. H. Chung, C. Hinde, M. Ali (Eds.), Developments in Applied Artificial Intelligence. Proceedings, 2003. XIV, 817 pages. 2003. (Subseries LNAI).

Vol. 2719: J.C.M. Baeten, J.K. Lenstra, J. Parrow, G.J. Woeginger (Eds.), Automata, Languages and Programming. Proceedings, 2003. XVIII, 1199 pages. 2003.

Vol. 2721: N.J. Mamede, J. Baptista, I. Trancoso, M. das Graças Volpe Nunes (Eds.), Computational Processing of the Portuguese Language. Proceedings, 2003. XIV, 268 pages. 2003. (Subseries LNAI).

Vol. 2725: W.A. Hunt, Jr., F. Somenzi (Eds.), Computer Aided Verification. Proceedings, 2003. XII, 462 pages. 2003.

Vol. 2726: E. Hancock, M. Vento (Eds.), Graph Based Representations in Pattern Recognition. Proceedings, 2003. VIII, 271 pages. 2003.

Vol. 2727: R. Safavi-Naini, J. Seberry (Eds.), Information Security and Privacy. Proceedings, 2003. XII, 534 pages. 2003.

Vol. 2731: C.S. Calude, M.J. Dinneen, V. Vajnovszki (Eds.), Discrete Mathematics and Theoretical Computer Science. Proceedings, 2003. VIII, 301 pages. 2003.

Vol. 2734: P. Perner, A. Rosenfeld (Eds.), Machine Learning and Data Mining in Pattern Recognition. Proceedings, 2003. XII, 440 pages. 2003. (Subseries LNAI).

Vol. 2745: M. Guo, L.T. Yang (Eds.), Parallel and Distributed Processing and Applications. Proceedings, 2003. XII, 450 pages. 2003.